ASPEN COMICS PRESENTS:

In Association with
BLOCKADE ENTERTAINMENT

Executive Assistant: Iris
[VOLUME ONE]

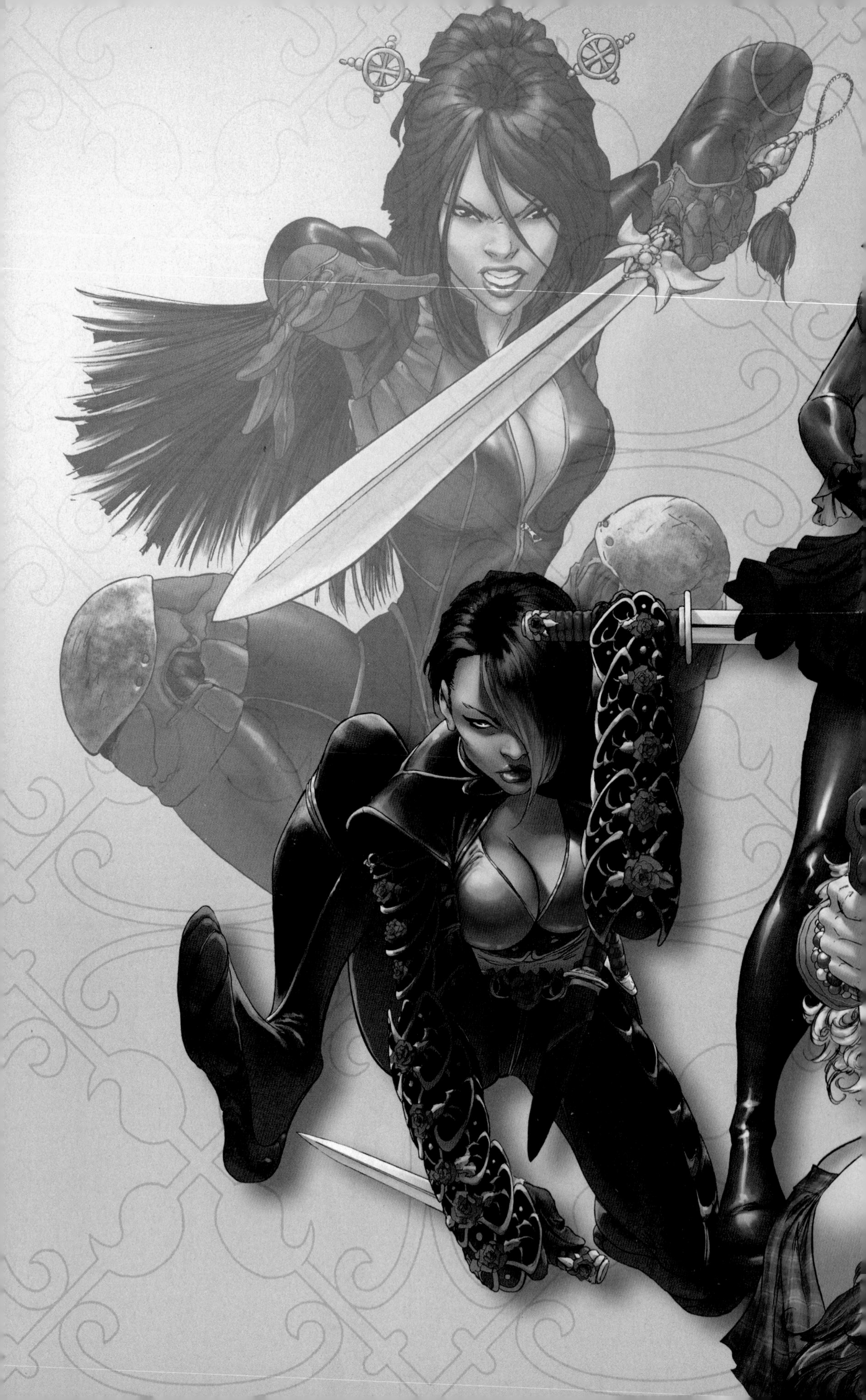

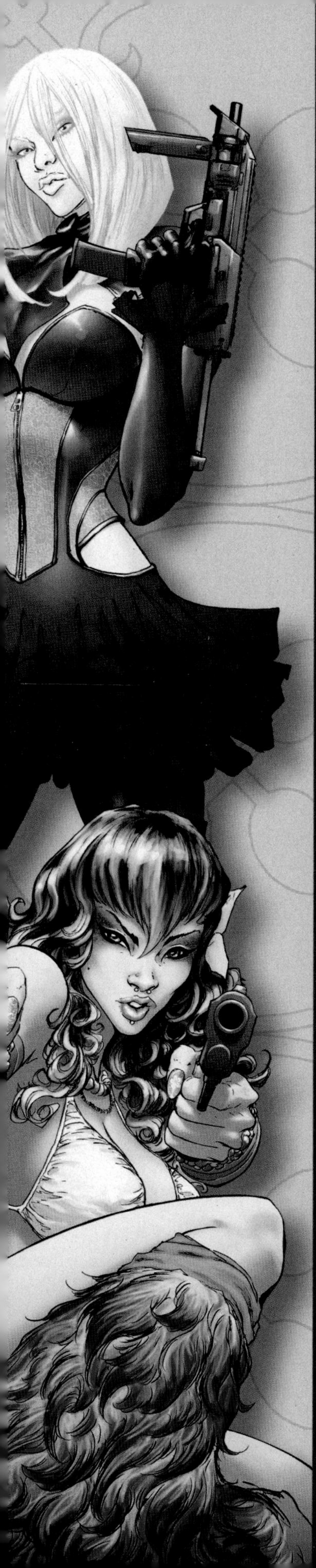

Created & Story by: *David Wohl, Brad Foxhoven & Michael Turner*

Script:
David Wohl

Illustrations:
Eduardo Francisco

Colors:
John Starr

Letters:
Josh Reed

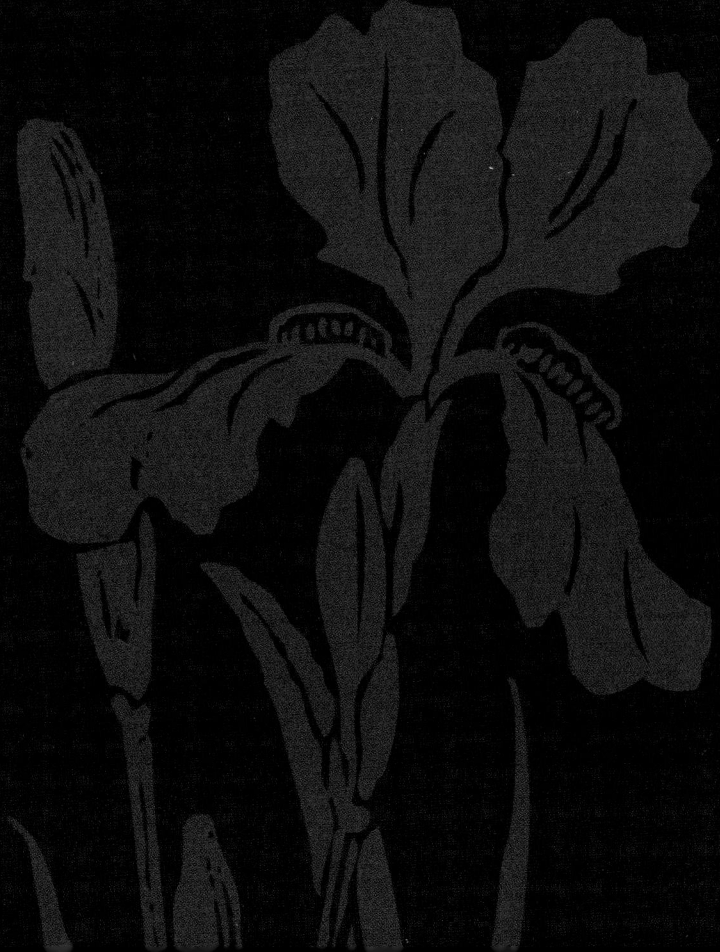

Executive Assistant: Iris created by: David Wohl, Brad Foxhoven & Michael Turner

EXECUTIVE ASSISTANT: IRIS™ VOLUME 1
ISBN: 978-1-941511-68-8 SECOND PRINTING, 2019. *Collects material originally published as Executive Assistant: Iris Volume One, Issues 0.1-6.*

PUBLISHED BY ASPEN MLT, LLC.
Office of Publication: 5701 W. Slauson Ave. Suite. 120, Culver City, CA 90230.

Address correspondence to:
EA: IRIS c/o Aspen MLT, LLC.
5701 W. Slauson Ave. Suite. 120
Culver City, CA. 90230-6946
or fanmail@aspencomics.com

Visit us on the web at:
aspencomics.com
aspenstore.com
facebook.com/aspencomics
twitter.com/aspencomics

Original Series Editors:
VINCE HERNANDEZ and JOSH REED

For this Edition:
Supervising Editor: FRANK MASTROMAURO
Editor: GABE CARRASCO
Cover, Book Design and Production: MARK ROSLAN
Logo Design: PETER STEIGERWALD and MARK ROSLAN
Cover Illustration: JOE BENITEZ and PETER STEIGERWALD

For Aspen:
FOUNDER: MICHAEL TURNER
CO-OWNER: PETER STEIGERWALD
CO-OWNER/PRESIDENT: FRANK MASTROMAURO
VICE PRESIDENT/EDITOR IN CHIEF: VINCE HERNANDEZ
VICE PRESIDENT/DESIGN AND PRODUCTION: MARK ROSLAN
MANAGING EDITOR: GABE CARRASCO
MARKETING ASSISTANT: CORINNE CHUAH
PRODUCTION ASSISTANT: JUSTIN VANCHO
OFFICE COORDINATOR: MEGAN MADRIGAL
AspenStore.com: CHRIS RUPP

TO FIND THE
COMIC SHOP
NEAREST YOU...

COMIC SHOP LOCATOR SERVICE
888-COMIC-BOOK
csls.diamondcomics.com
1-888-266-4226

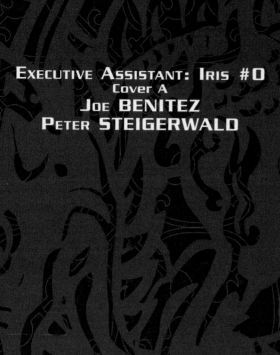

EXECUTIVE ASSISTANT: IRIS #0
Cover A
JOE BENITEZ
PETER STEIGERWALD

EXECUTIVE ASSISTANT: IRIS #0
Retailer Incentive Exclusive Cover B
TALENT CALDWELL
PETER STEIGERWALD

EXECUTIVE ASSISTANT: IRIS #0
Convention Exclusive Cover C
JOE BENITEZ
PETER STEIGERWALD

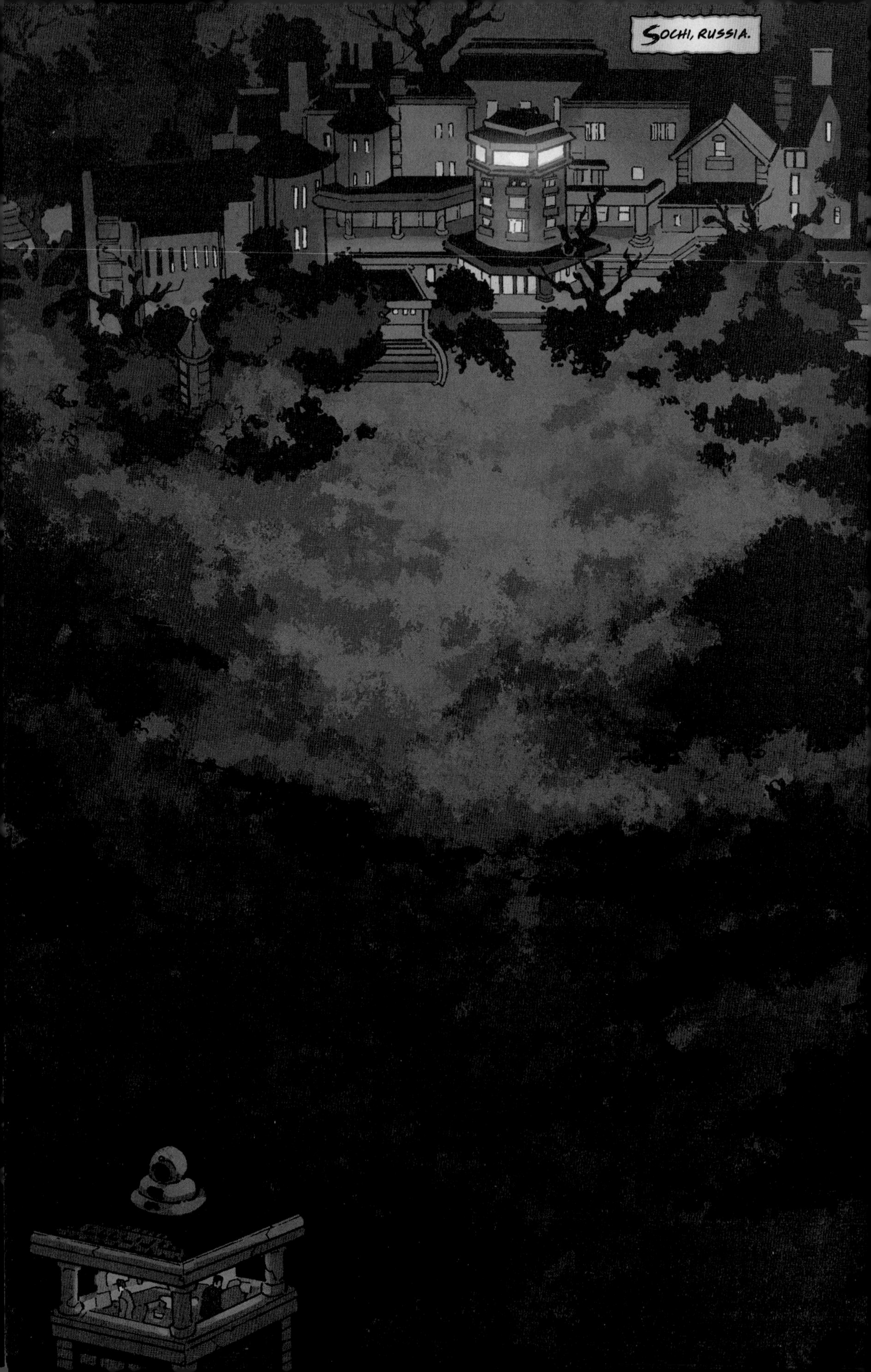

SOCHI, RUSSIA.

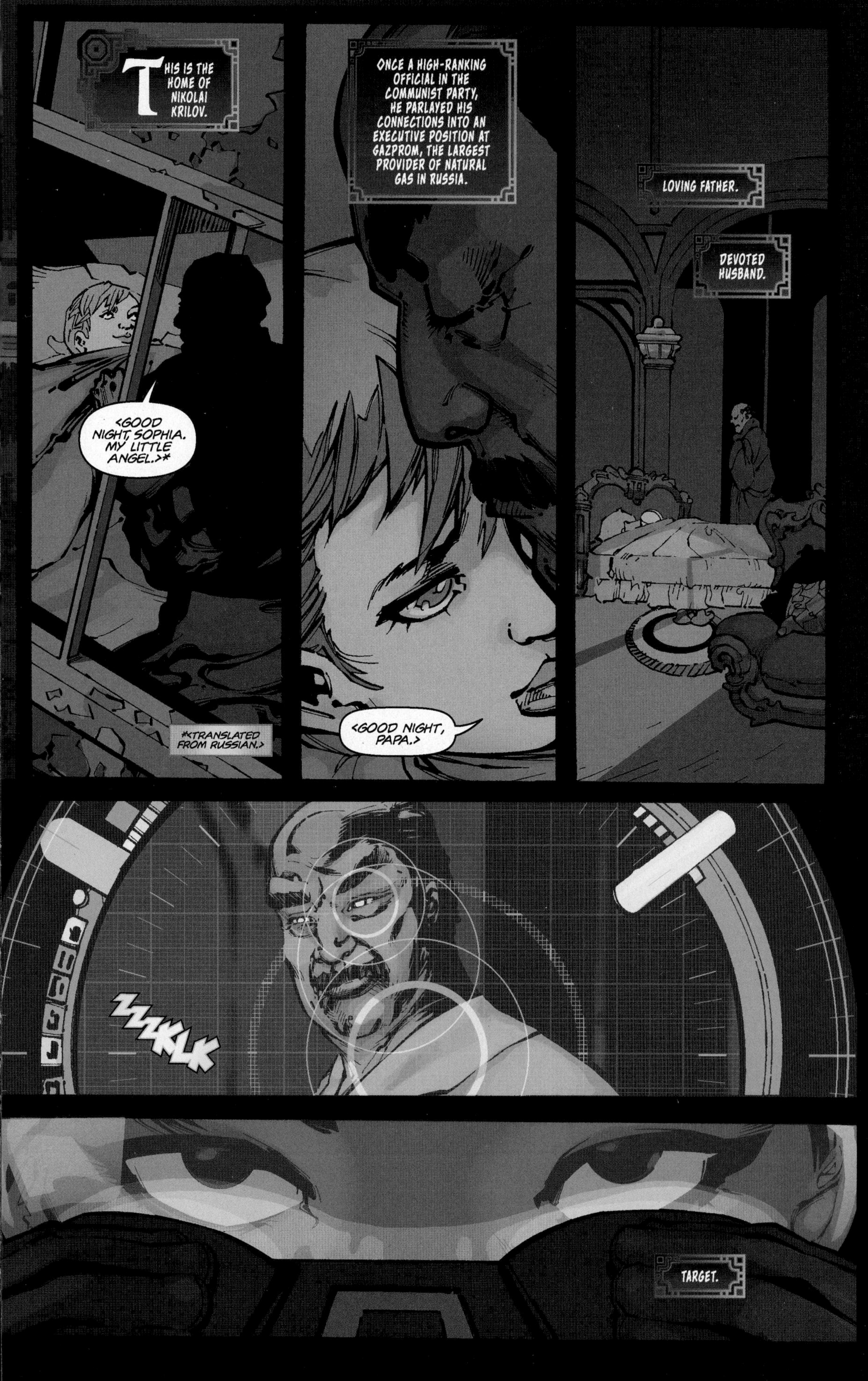
This is the home of Nikolai Krilov.
<Good night, Sophia. My little angel.>*
*Translated from Russian.>
Once a high-ranking official in the Communist Party, he parlayed his connections into an executive position at Gazprom, the largest provider of natural gas in Russia.
<Good night, Papa.>
Loving father.
Devoted husband.
ZZZKLK
Target.

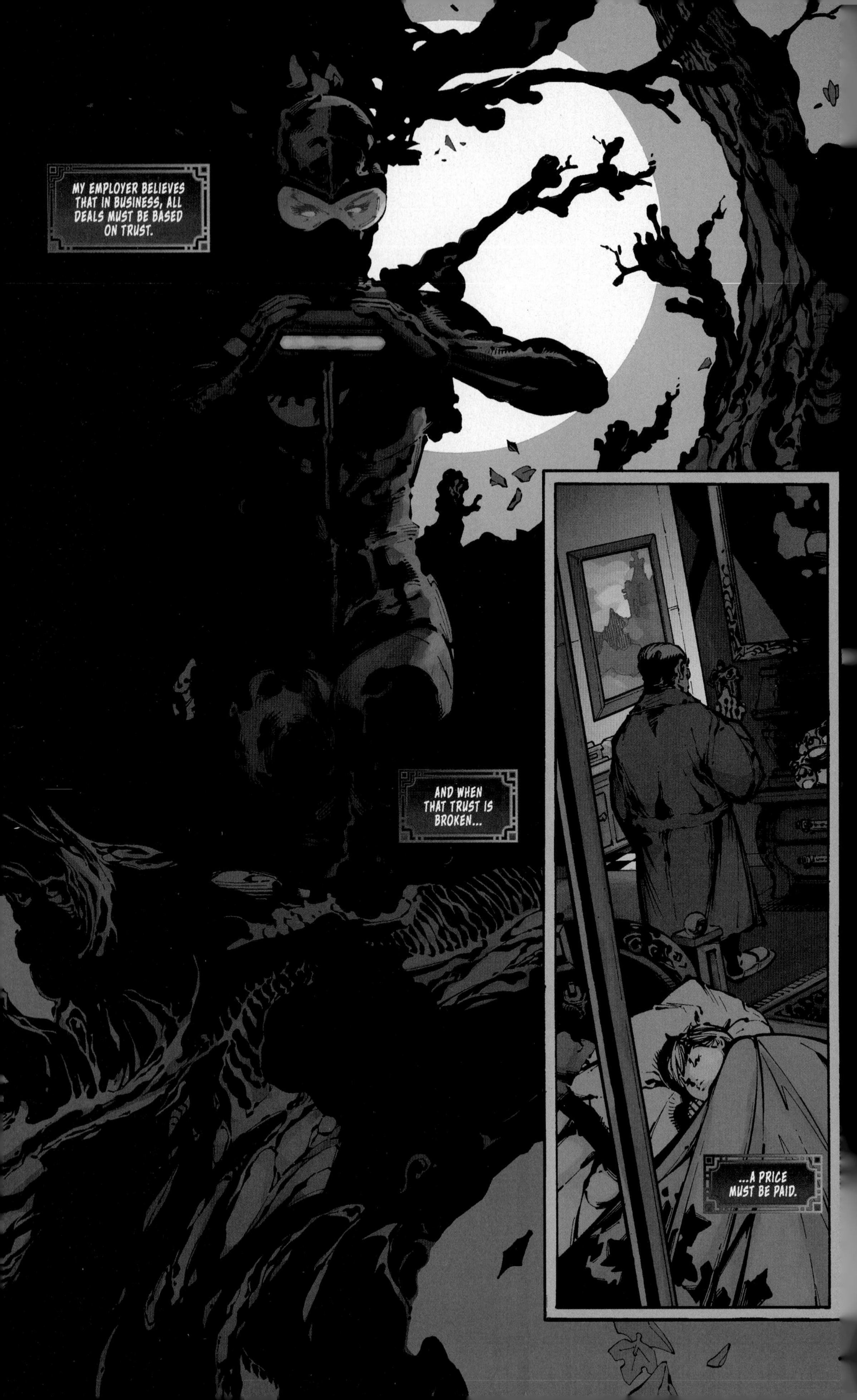
MY EMPLOYER BELIEVES THAT IN BUSINESS, ALL DEALS MUST BE BASED ON TRUST.
AND WHEN THAT TRUST IS BROKEN...
...A PRICE MUST BE PAID.

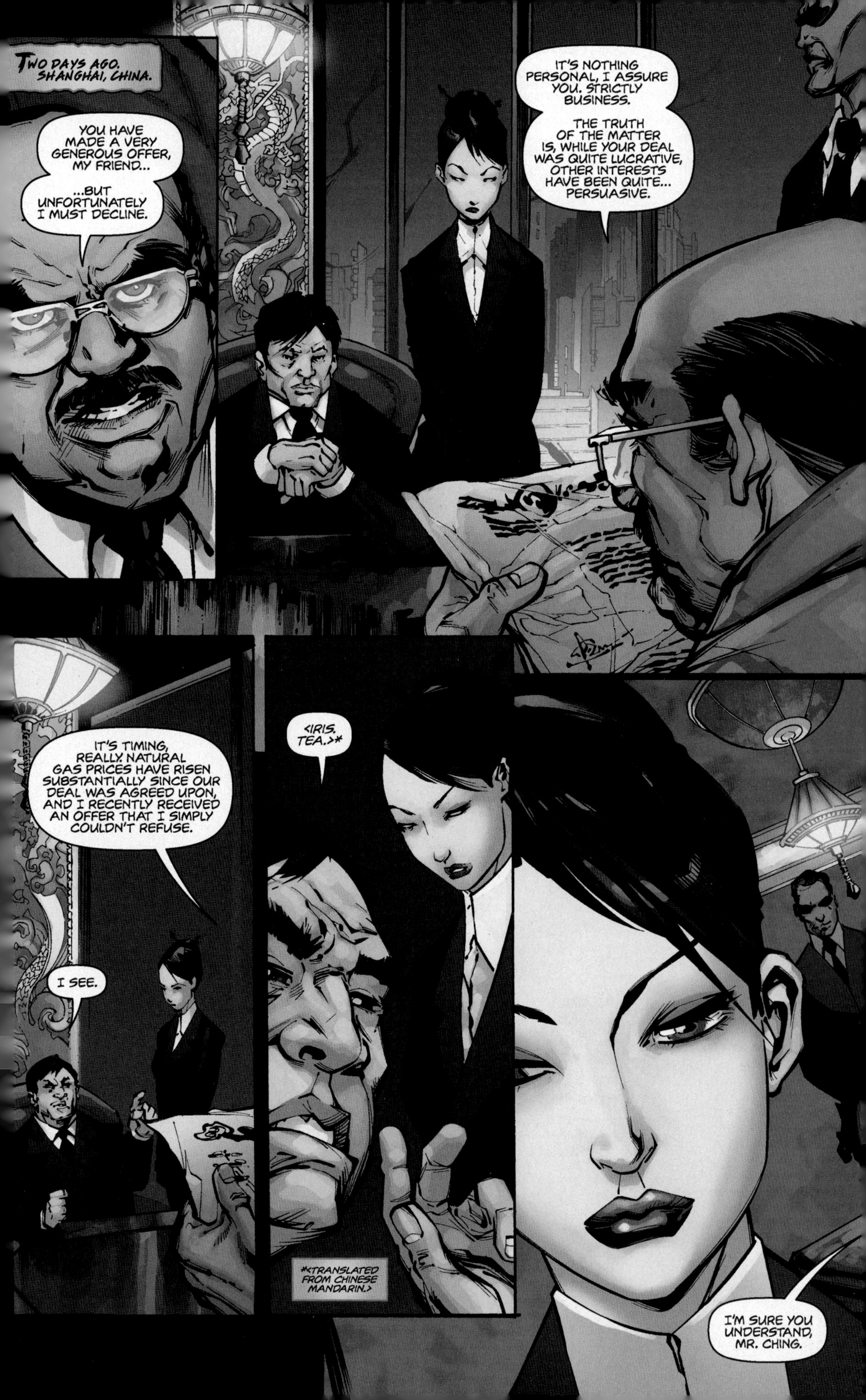

TWO DAYS AGO. SHANGHAI, CHINA.
YOU HAVE MADE A VERY GENEROUS OFFER, MY FRIEND...
...BUT UNFORTUNATELY I MUST DECLINE.
IT'S NOTHING PERSONAL, I ASSURE YOU. STRICTLY BUSINESS.
THE TRUTH OF THE MATTER IS, WHILE YOUR DEAL WAS QUITE LUCRATIVE, OTHER INTERESTS HAVE BEEN QUITE... PERSUASIVE.
IT'S TIMING, REALLY. NATURAL GAS PRICES HAVE RISEN SUBSTANTIALLY SINCE OUR DEAL WAS AGREED UPON, AND I RECENTLY RECEIVED AN OFFER THAT I SIMPLY COULDN'T REFUSE.
I SEE.
<IRIS. TEA.>*
*<TRANSLATED FROM CHINESE MANDARIN.>
I'M SURE YOU UNDERSTAND, MR. CHING.

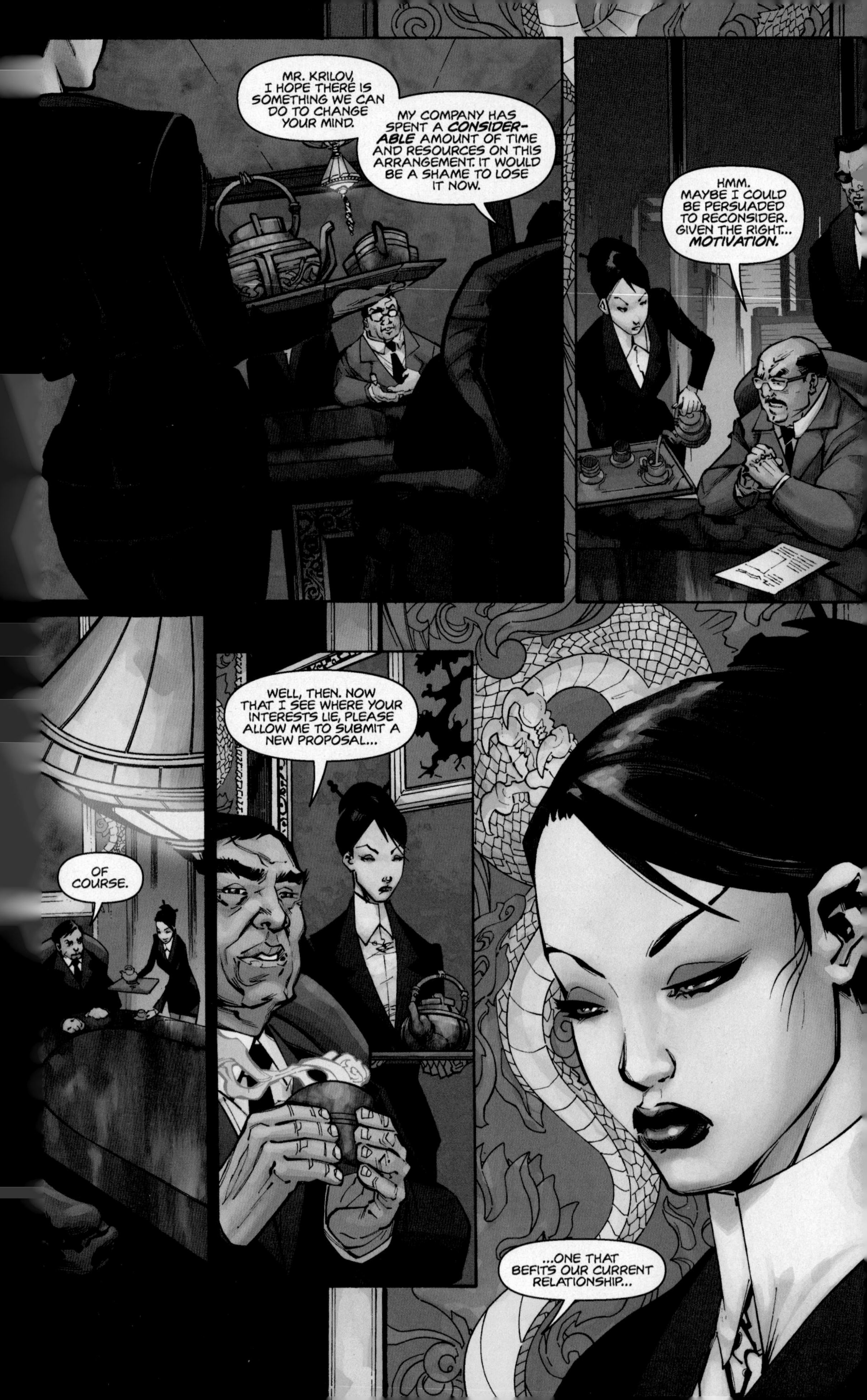
MR. KRILOV, I HOPE THERE IS SOMETHING WE CAN DO TO CHANGE YOUR MIND.
MY COMPANY HAS SPENT A CONSIDERABLE AMOUNT OF TIME AND RESOURCES ON THIS ARRANGEMENT. IT WOULD BE A SHAME TO LOSE IT NOW.
HMM. MAYBE I COULD BE PERSUADED TO RECONSIDER. GIVEN THE RIGHT... MOTIVATION.
OF COURSE.
WELL, THEN. NOW THAT I SEE WHERE YOUR INTERESTS LIE, PLEASE ALLOW ME TO SUBMIT A NEW PROPOSAL...
...ONE THAT BEFITS OUR CURRENT RELATIONSHIP...

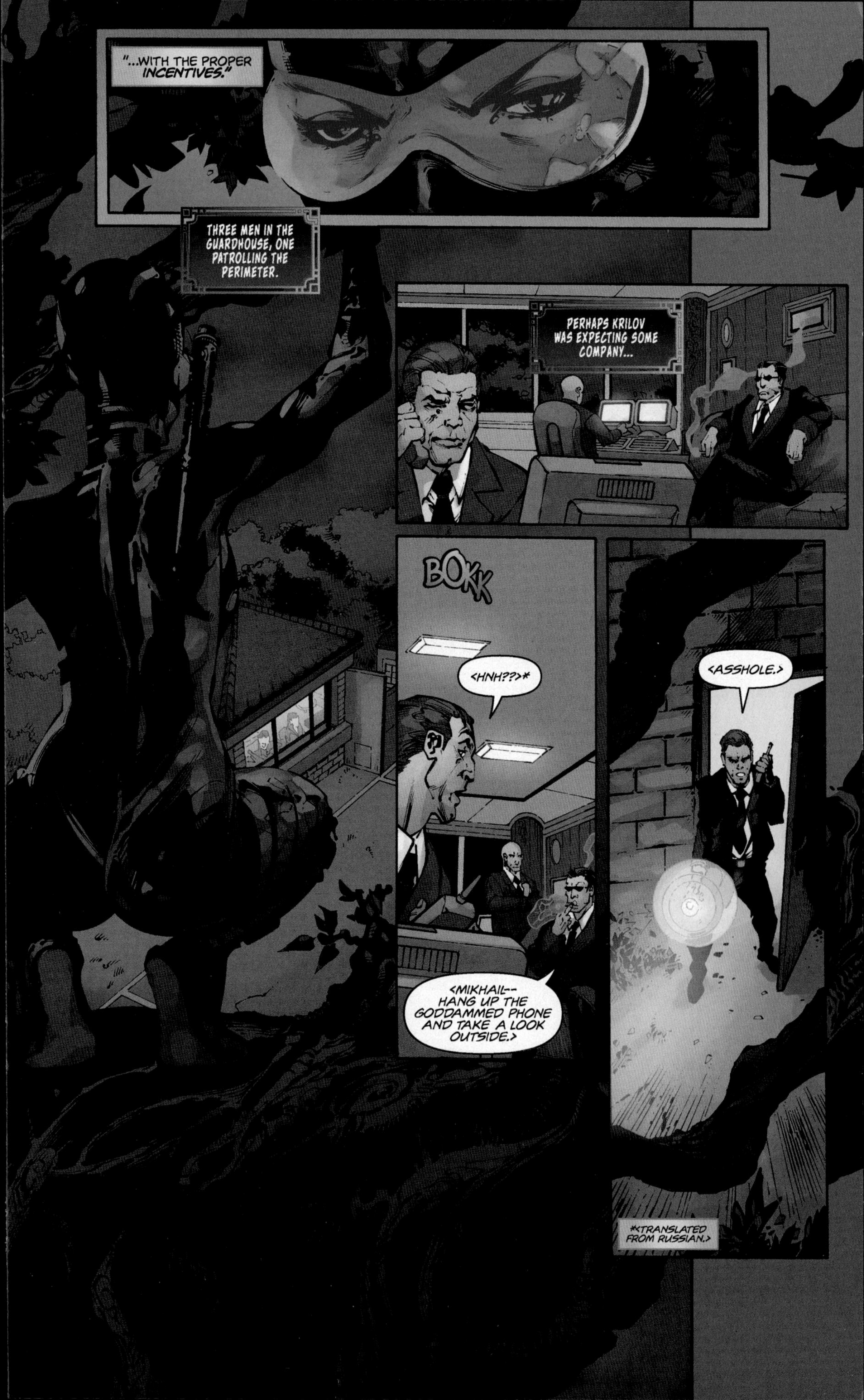
"...WITH THE PROPER INCENTIVES."
THREE MEN IN THE GUARDHOUSE, ONE PATROLLING THE PERIMETER.
PERHAPS KRILOV WAS EXPECTING SOME COMPANY...
BOKK
<HNH??>*
<MIKHAIL-- HANG UP THE GODDAMMED PHONE AND TAKE A LOOK OUTSIDE.>
<ASSHOLE.>
*TRANSLATED FROM RUSSIAN.>

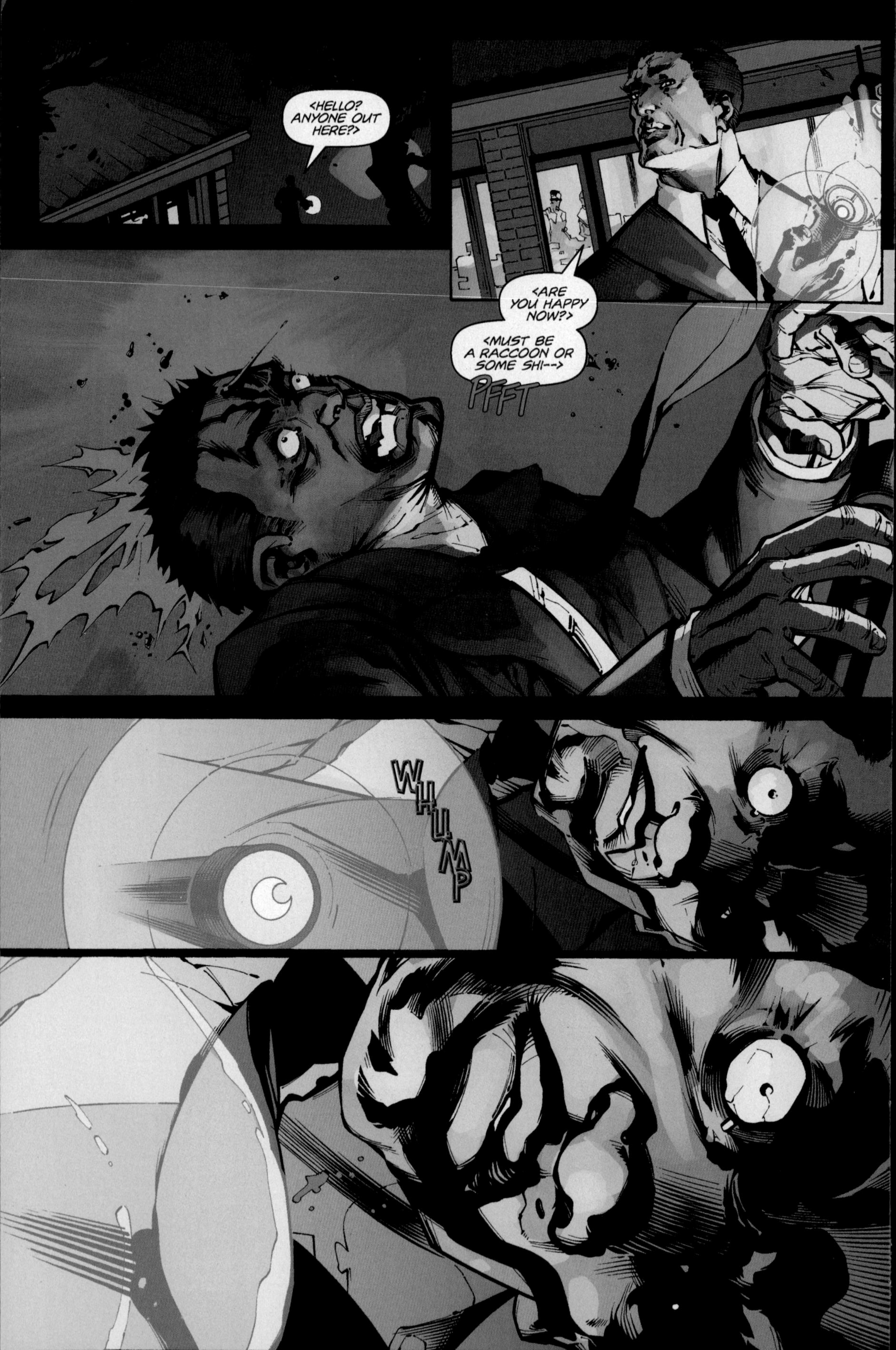

<HELLO? ANYONE OUT HERE?>
<ARE YOU HAPPY NOW?>
<MUST BE A RACCOON OR SOME SHI-->
PFFT
WHUMP

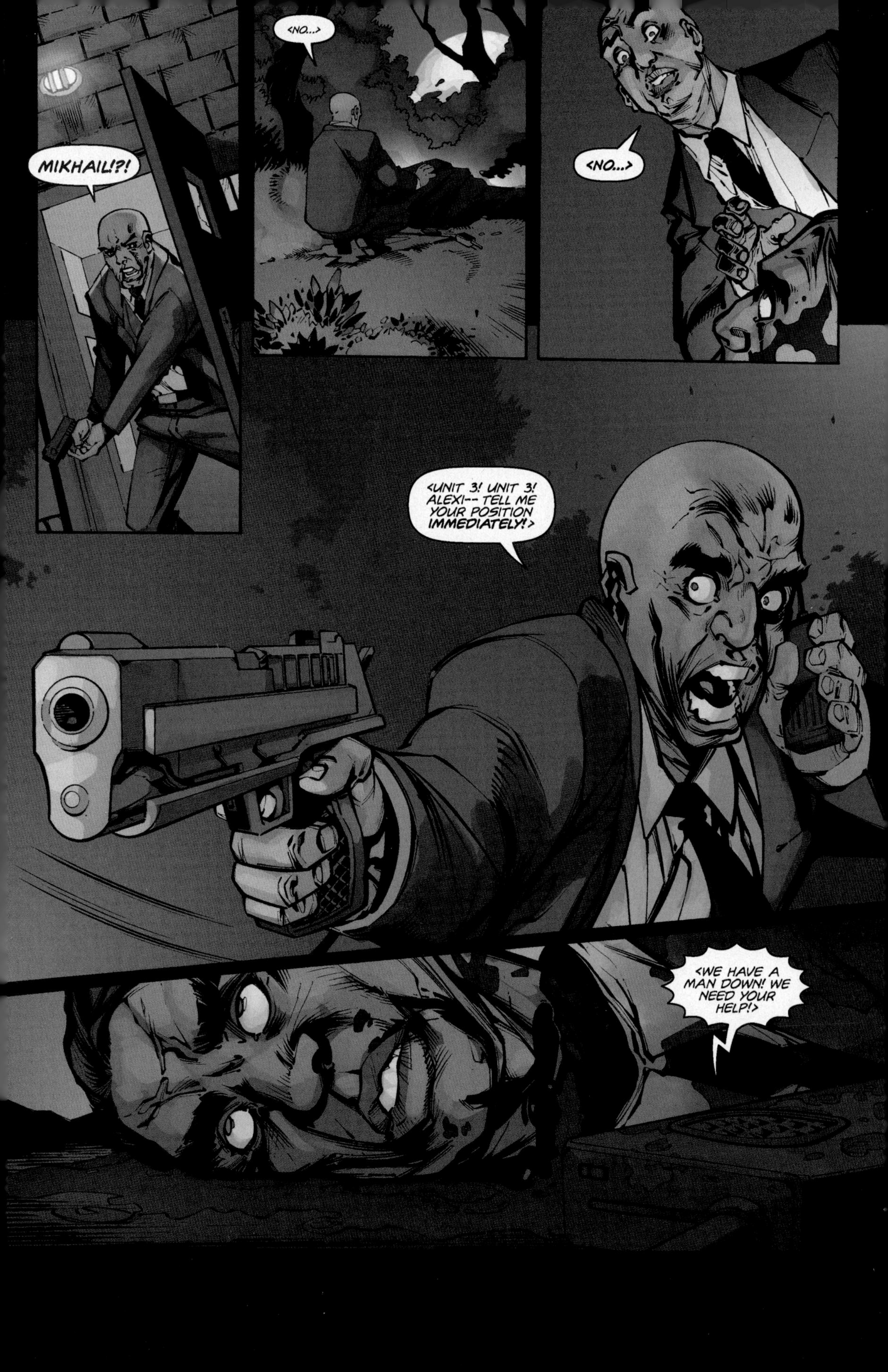

MIKHAIL!?!
<NO...>
<NO...>
<UNIT 3! UNIT 3! ALEXI-- TELL ME YOUR POSITION IMMEDIATELY!>
<WE HAVE A MAN DOWN! WE NEED YOUR HELP!>

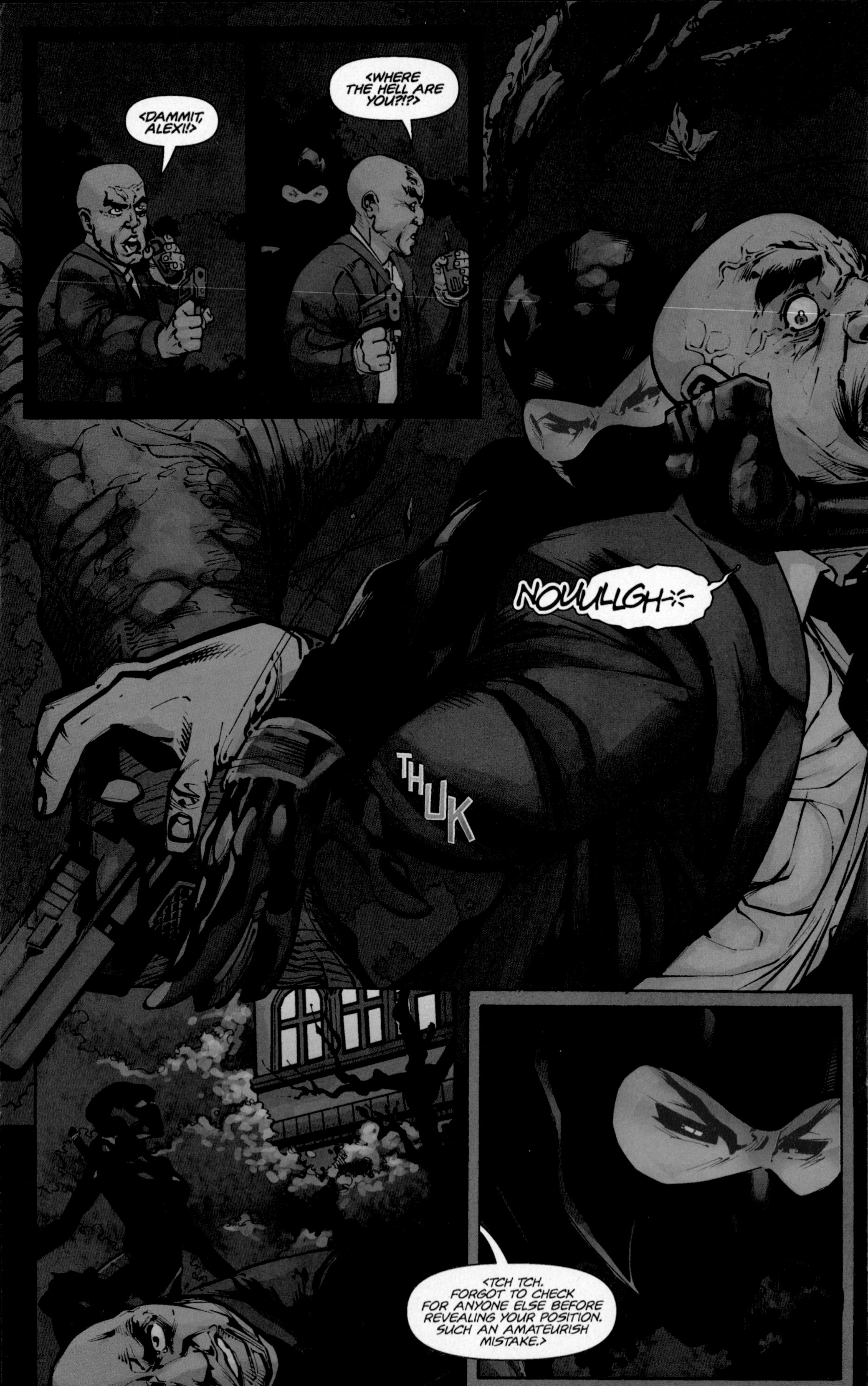
<DAMMIT, ALEXI!>
<WHERE THE HELL ARE YOU?!?>
NOUUUGH
THUK
<TCH TCH. FORGOT TO CHECK FOR ANYONE ELSE BEFORE REVEALING YOUR POSITION. SUCH AN AMATEURISH MISTAKE.>

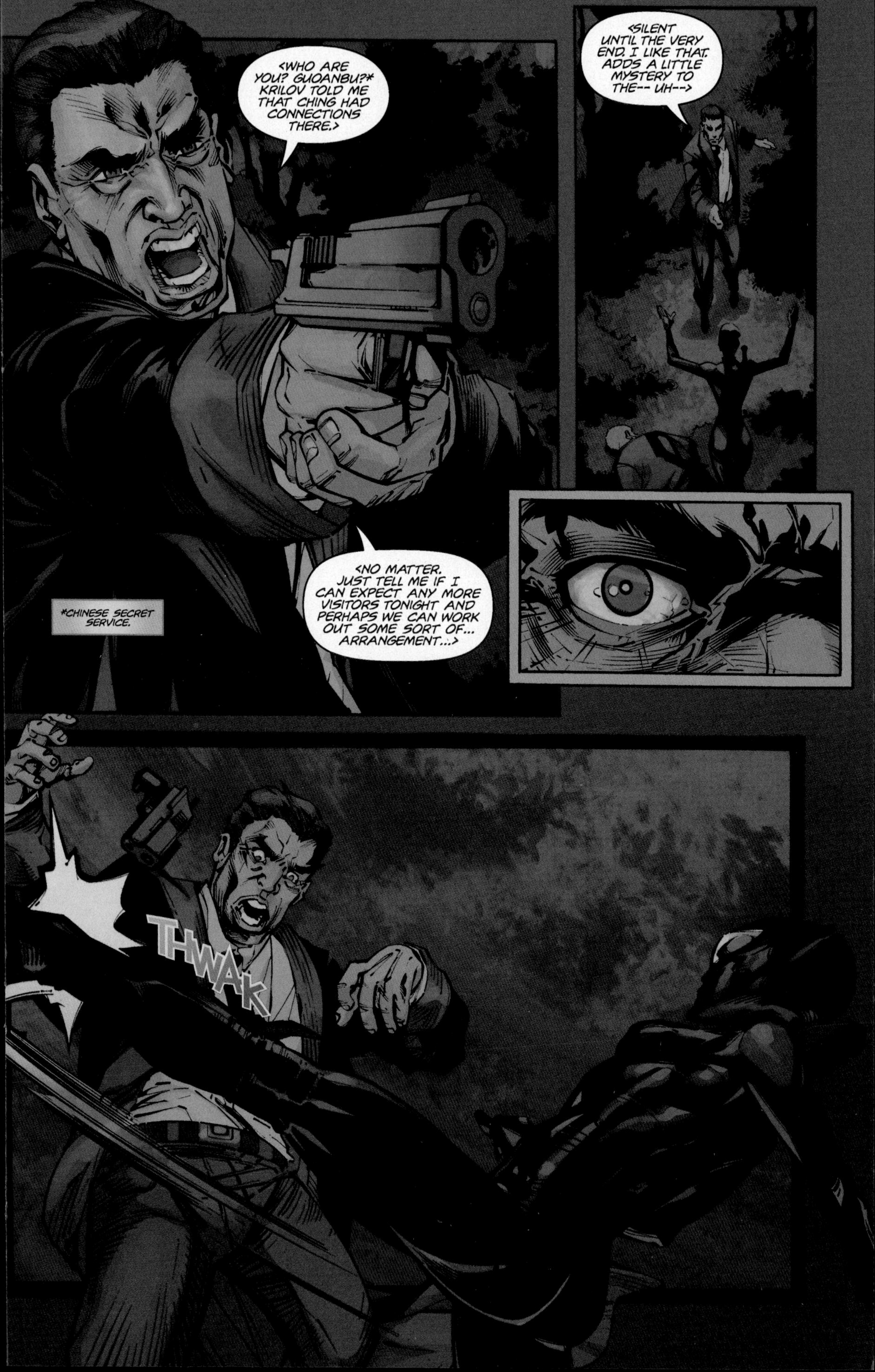
<WHO ARE YOU? GUOANBU?* KRILOV TOLD ME THAT CHING HAD CONNECTIONS THERE.>
<SILENT UNTIL THE VERY END. I LIKE THAT. ADDS A LITTLE MYSTERY TO THE-- UH-->
<NO MATTER. JUST TELL ME IF I CAN EXPECT ANY MORE VISITORS TONIGHT AND PERHAPS WE CAN WORK OUT SOME SORT OF... ARRANGEMENT...>
*CHINESE SECRET SERVICE.
THWAK

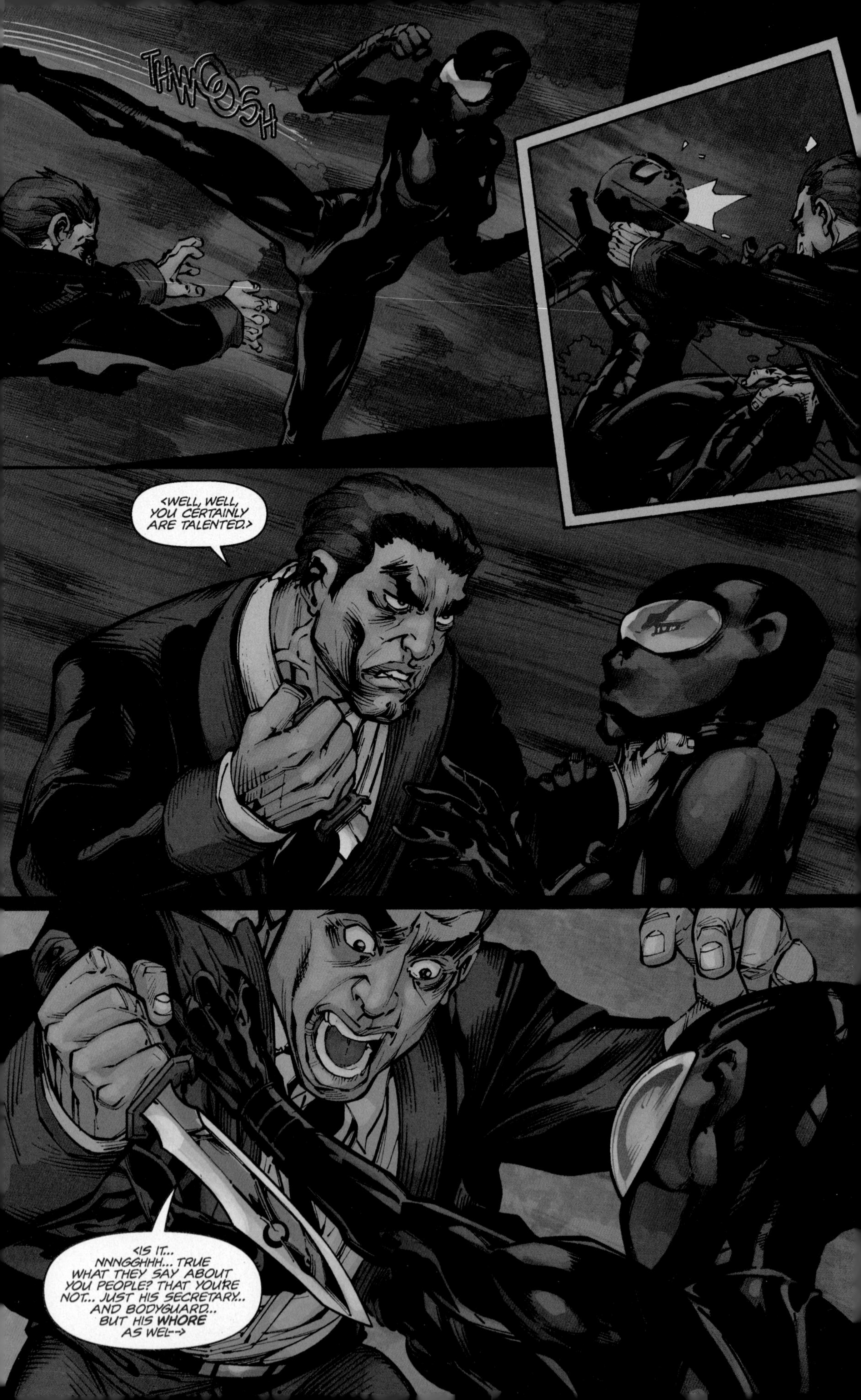
THWOOSH
<WELL, WELL, YOU CERTAINLY ARE TALENTED.>
<IS IT... NNNGGHHH... TRUE WHAT THEY SAY ABOUT YOU PEOPLE? THAT YOU'RE NOT... JUST HIS SECRETARY... AND BODYGUARD... BUT HIS WHORE AS WEL-->

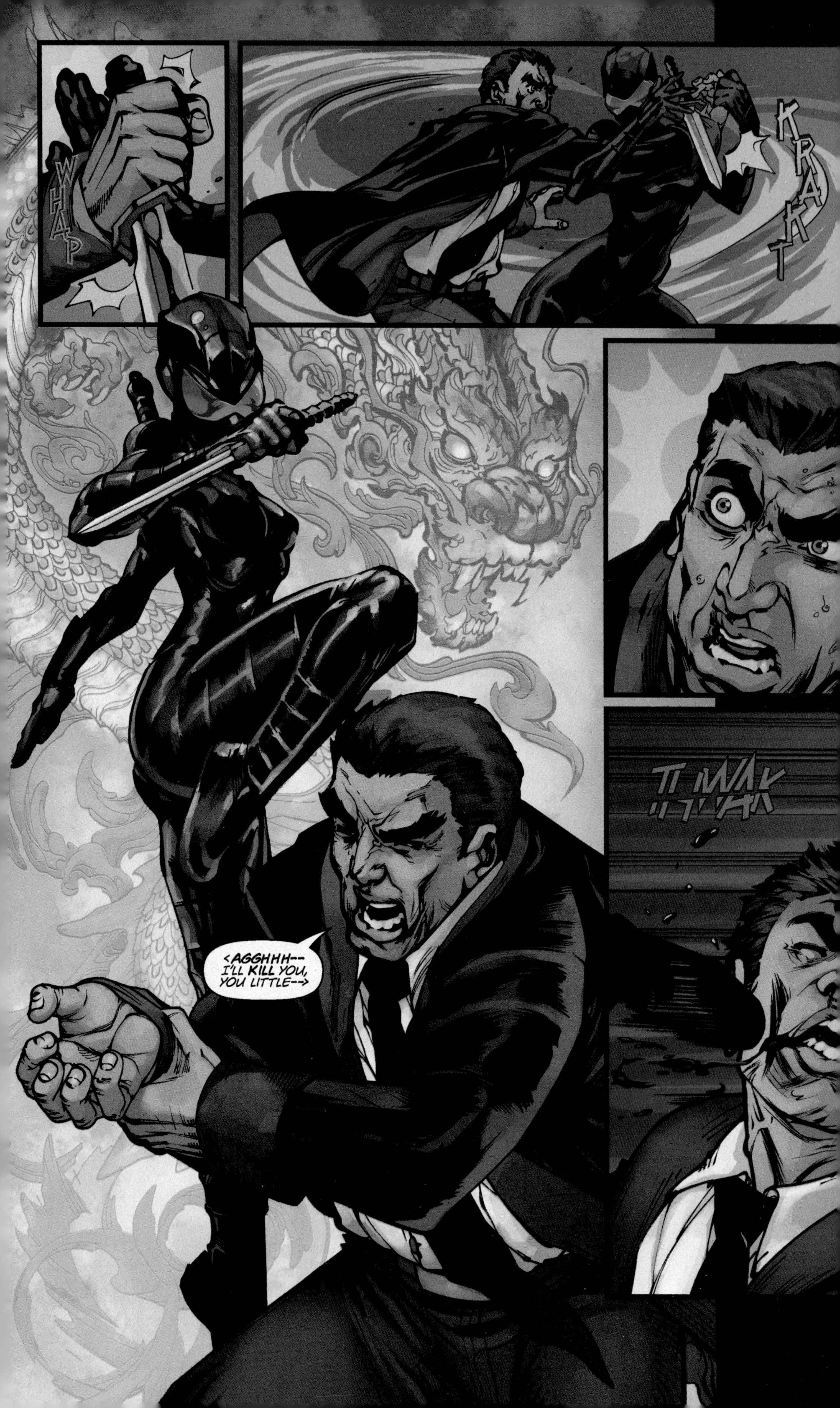
WHAP
KRAKT
<AGGHHH--
I'LL KILL YOU,
YOU LITTLE-->
THWAK

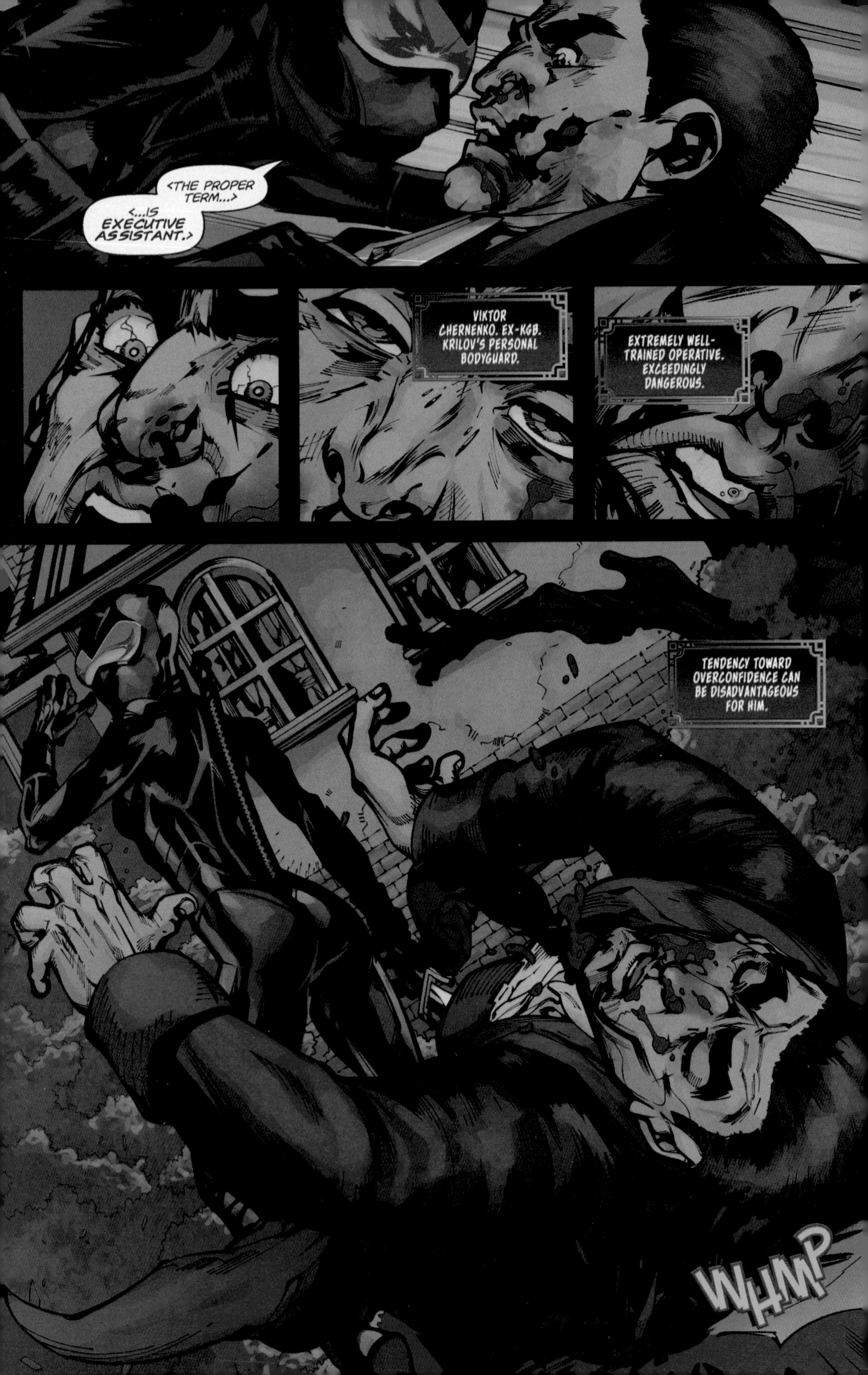
<THE PROPER TERM...>
<...IS EXECUTIVE ASSISTANT.>
VIKTOR CHERNENKO. EX-KGB. KRILOV'S PERSONAL BODYGUARD.
EXTREMELY WELL-TRAINED OPERATIVE. EXCEEDINGLY DANGEROUS.
TENDENCY TOWARD OVERCONFIDENCE CAN BE DISADVANTAGEOUS FOR HIM.
WHMP

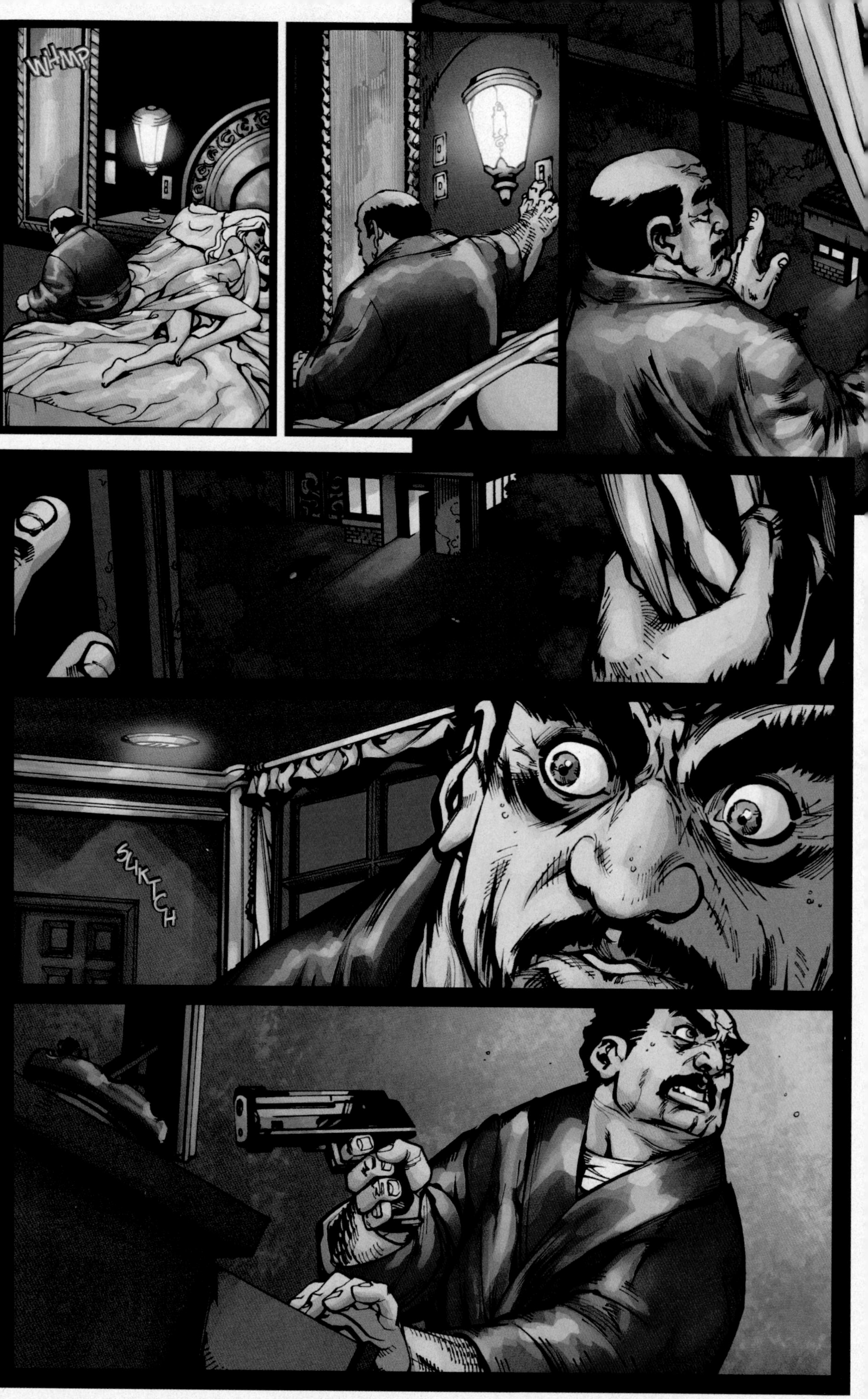
WHMP
SLKTCH

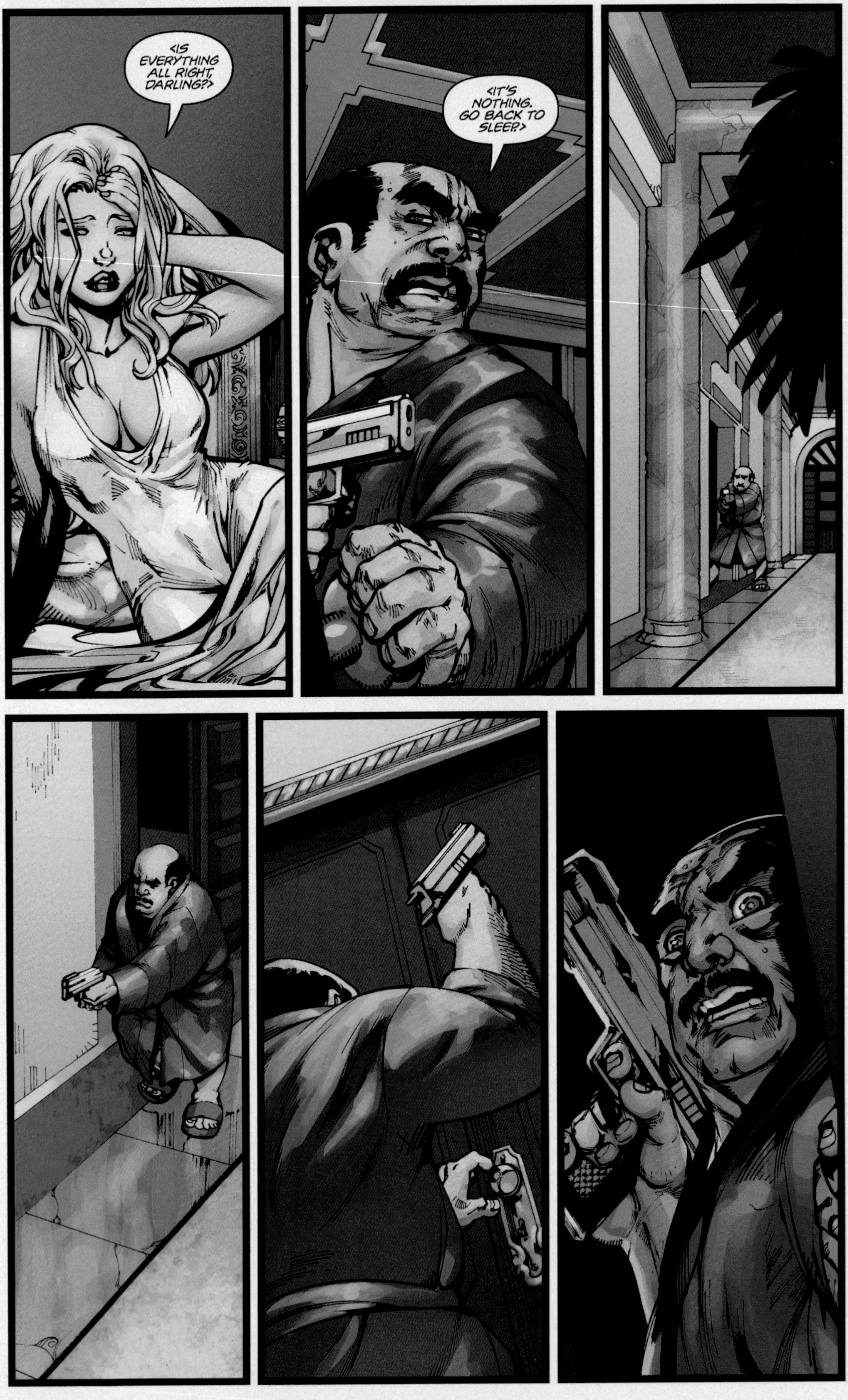
<IS EVERYTHING ALL RIGHT, DARLING?>
<IT'S NOTHING. GO BACK TO SLEEP.>

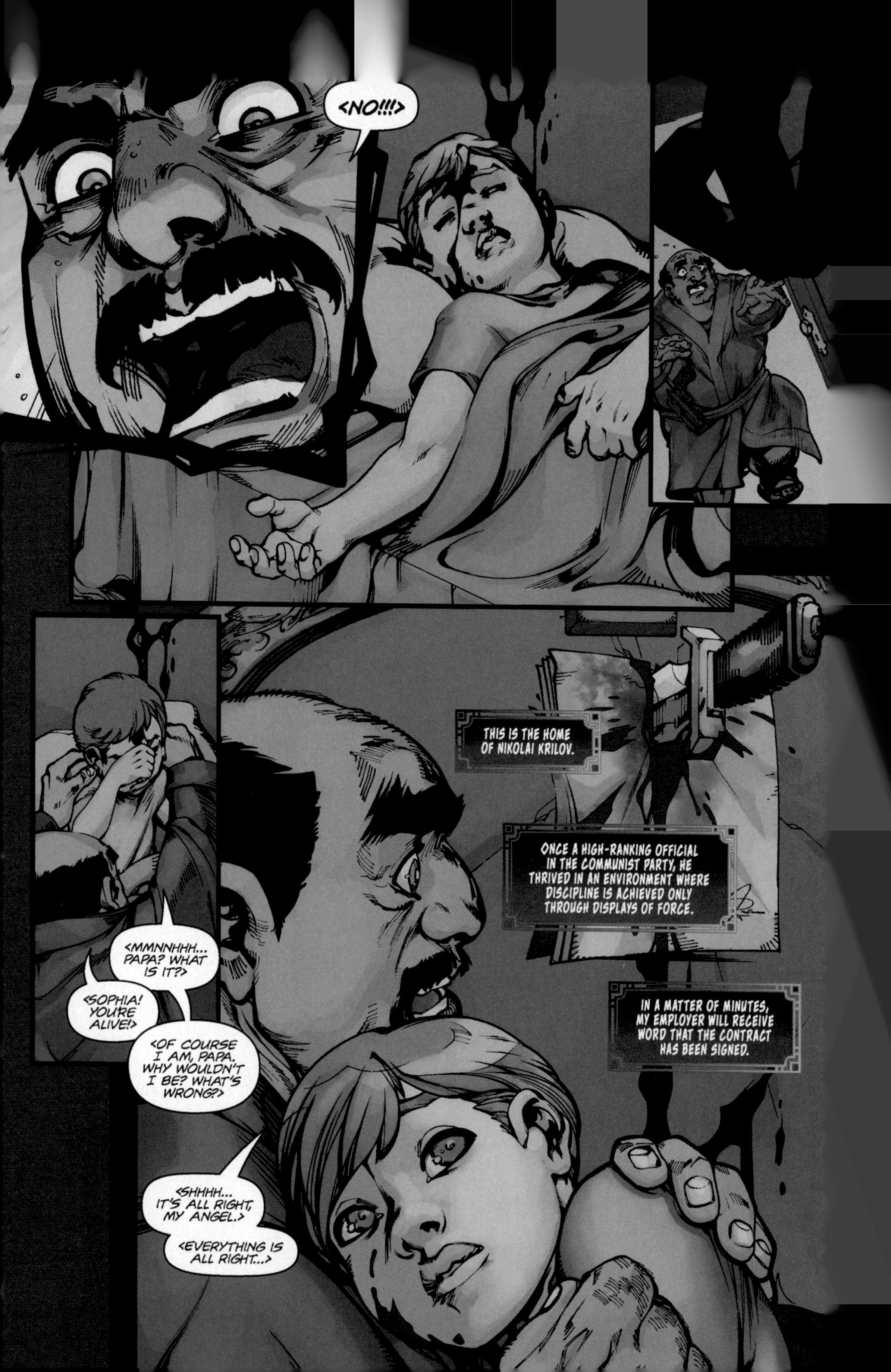

<NO!!!>
THIS IS THE HOME OF NIKOLAI KRILOV.
ONCE A HIGH-RANKING OFFICIAL IN THE COMMUNIST PARTY, HE THRIVED IN AN ENVIRONMENT WHERE DISCIPLINE IS ACHIEVED ONLY THROUGH DISPLAYS OF FORCE.
IN A MATTER OF MINUTES, MY EMPLOYER WILL RECEIVE WORD THAT THE CONTRACT HAS BEEN SIGNED.
<MMNNHHH... PAPA? WHAT IS IT?>
<SOPHIA! YOU'RE ALIVE!>
<OF COURSE I AM, PAPA. WHY WOULDN'T I BE? WHAT'S WRONG?>
<SHHHH... IT'S ALL RIGHT, MY ANGEL.>
<EVERYTHING IS ALL RIGHT...>

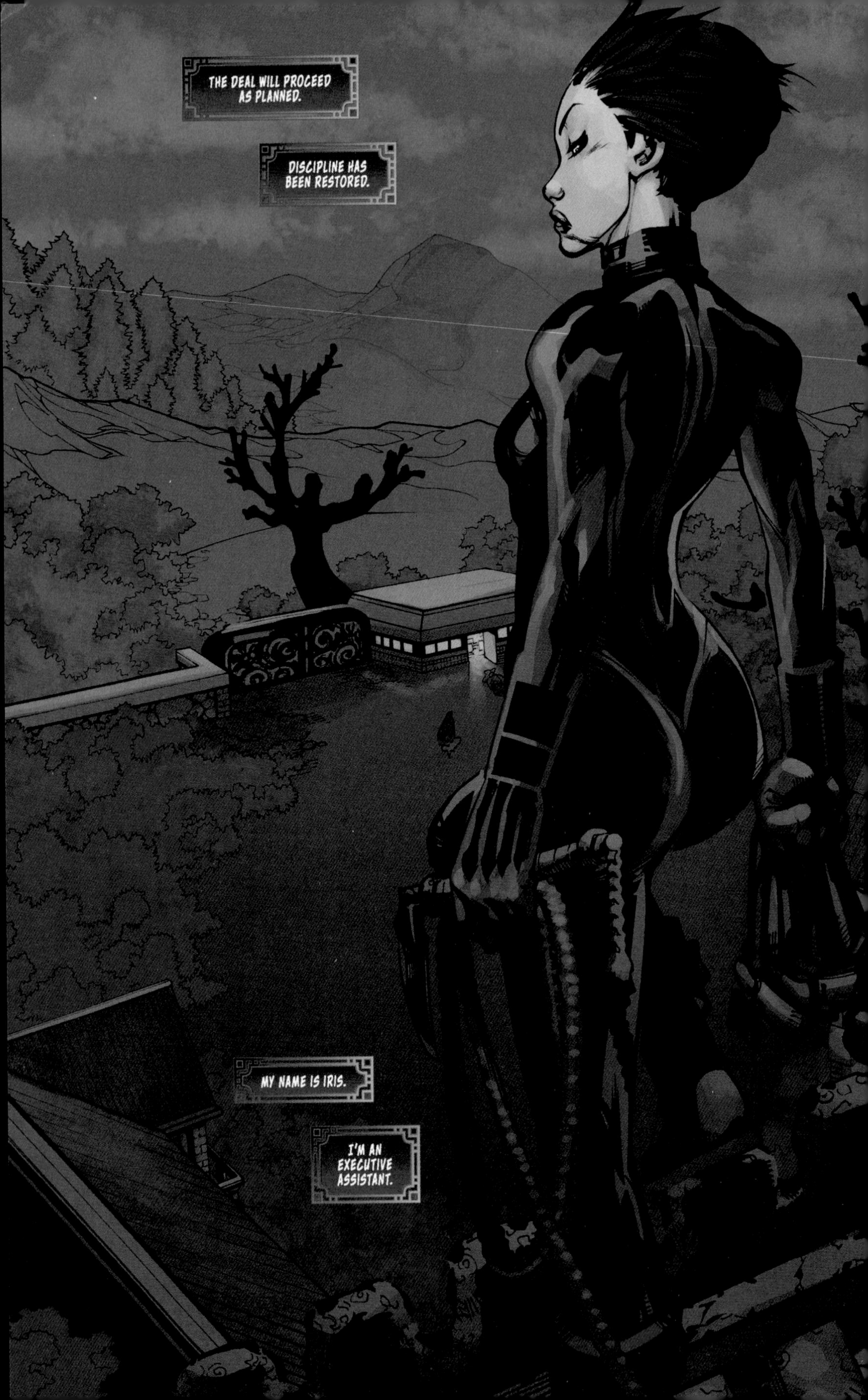
THE DEAL WILL PROCEED AS PLANNED.
DISCIPLINE HAS BEEN RESTORED.
MY NAME IS IRIS.
I'M AN EXECUTIVE ASSISTANT.

EXECUTIVE ASSISTANT: IRIS #1
Cover A
EDUARDO FRANCISCO
JOHN STARR

EXECUTIVE ASSISTANT: IRIS #1
Cover B
JOE BENITEZ
PETER STEIGERWALD

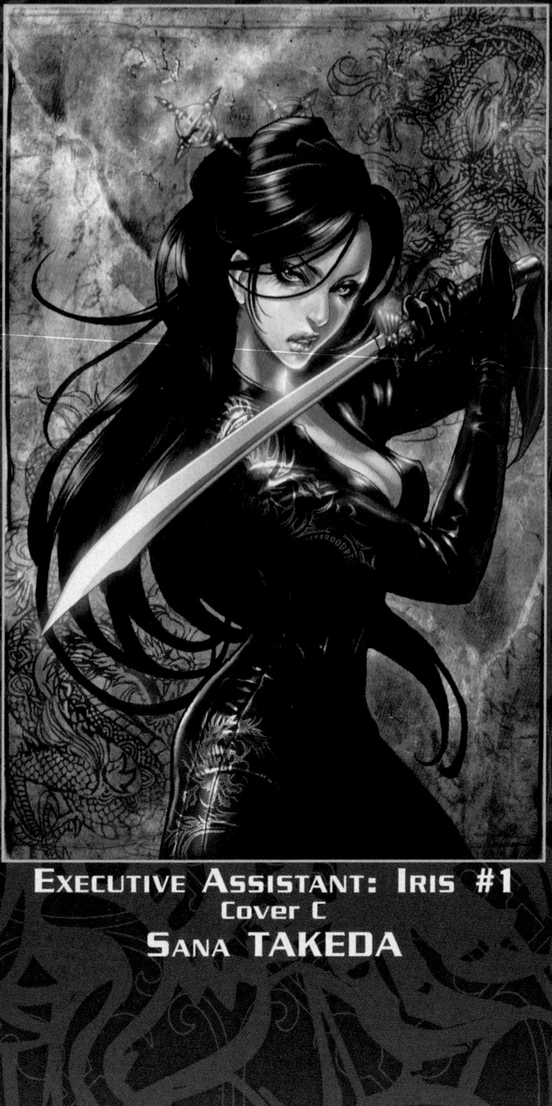

Executive Assistant: Iris #1
Cover C
Sana TAKEDA

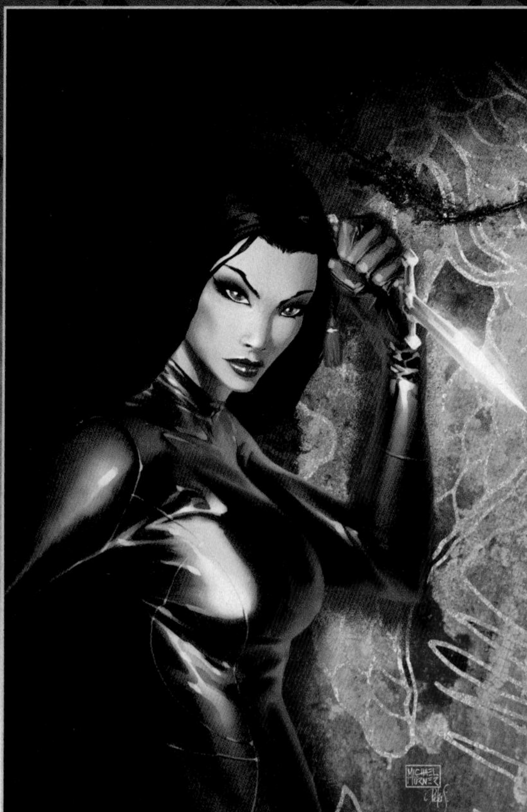
MICHAEL TURNER

Executive Assistant: Iris #1
Retailer Incentive Exclusive Cover D
Michael TURNER
Peter STEIGERWALD

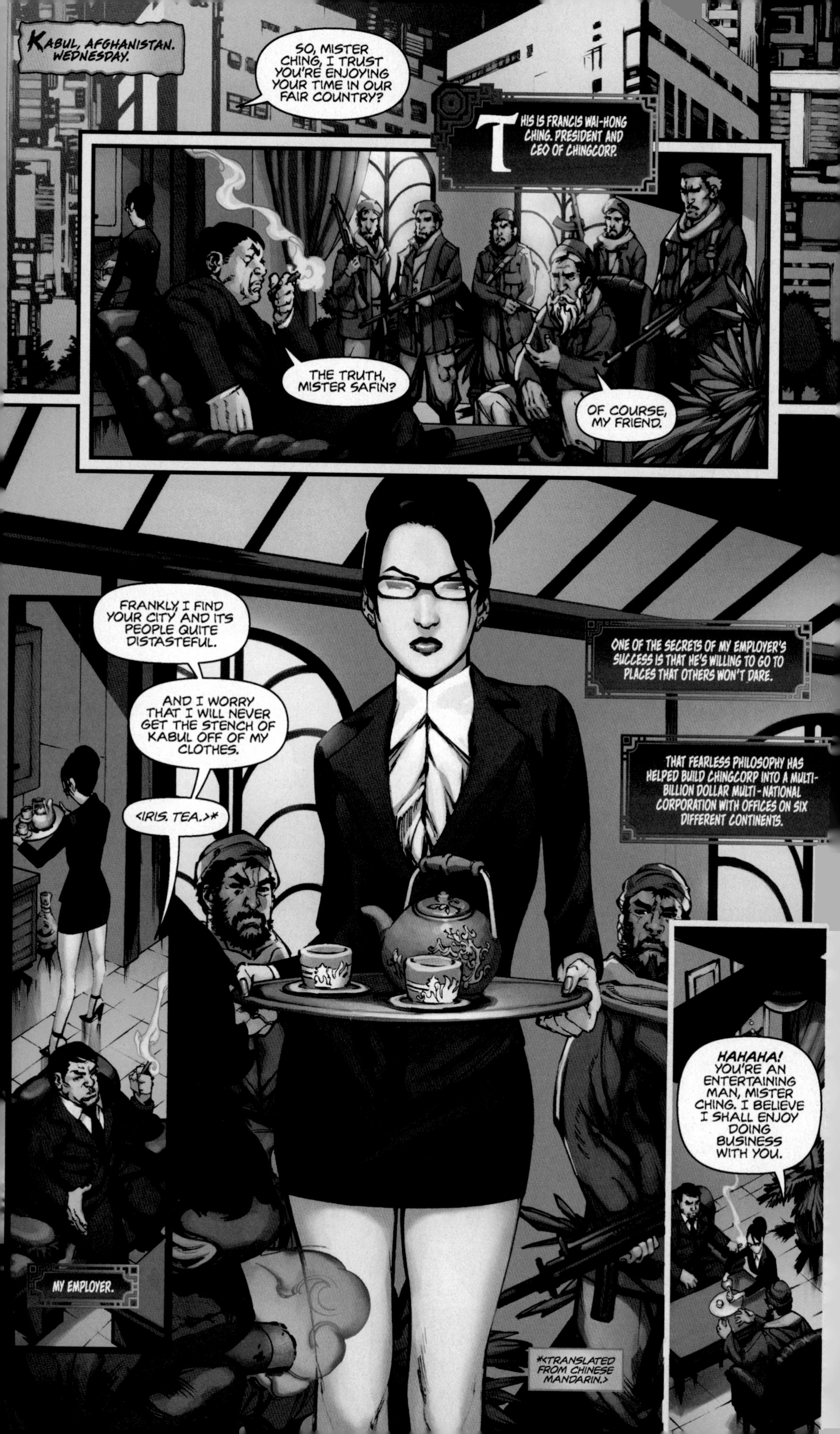
KABUL, AFGHANISTAN. WEDNESDAY.
SO, MISTER CHING, I TRUST YOU'RE ENJOYING YOUR TIME IN OUR FAIR COUNTRY?
THIS IS FRANCIS WAI-HONG CHING. PRESIDENT AND CEO OF CHINGCORP.
THE TRUTH, MISTER SAFIN?
OF COURSE, MY FRIEND.
FRANKLY, I FIND YOUR CITY AND ITS PEOPLE QUITE DISTASTEFUL.
AND I WORRY THAT I WILL NEVER GET THE STENCH OF KABUL OFF OF MY CLOTHES.
<IRIS. TEA.>*
MY EMPLOYER.
ONE OF THE SECRETS OF MY EMPLOYER'S SUCCESS IS THAT HE'S WILLING TO GO TO PLACES THAT OTHERS WON'T DARE.
THAT FEARLESS PHILOSOPHY HAS HELPED BUILD CHINGCORP INTO A MULTI-BILLION DOLLAR MULTI-NATIONAL CORPORATION WITH OFFICES ON SIX DIFFERENT CONTINENTS.
HAHAHA! YOU'RE AN ENTERTAINING MAN, MISTER CHING. I BELIEVE I SHALL ENJOY DOING BUSINESS WITH YOU.
*<TRANSLATED FROM CHINESE MANDARIN.>

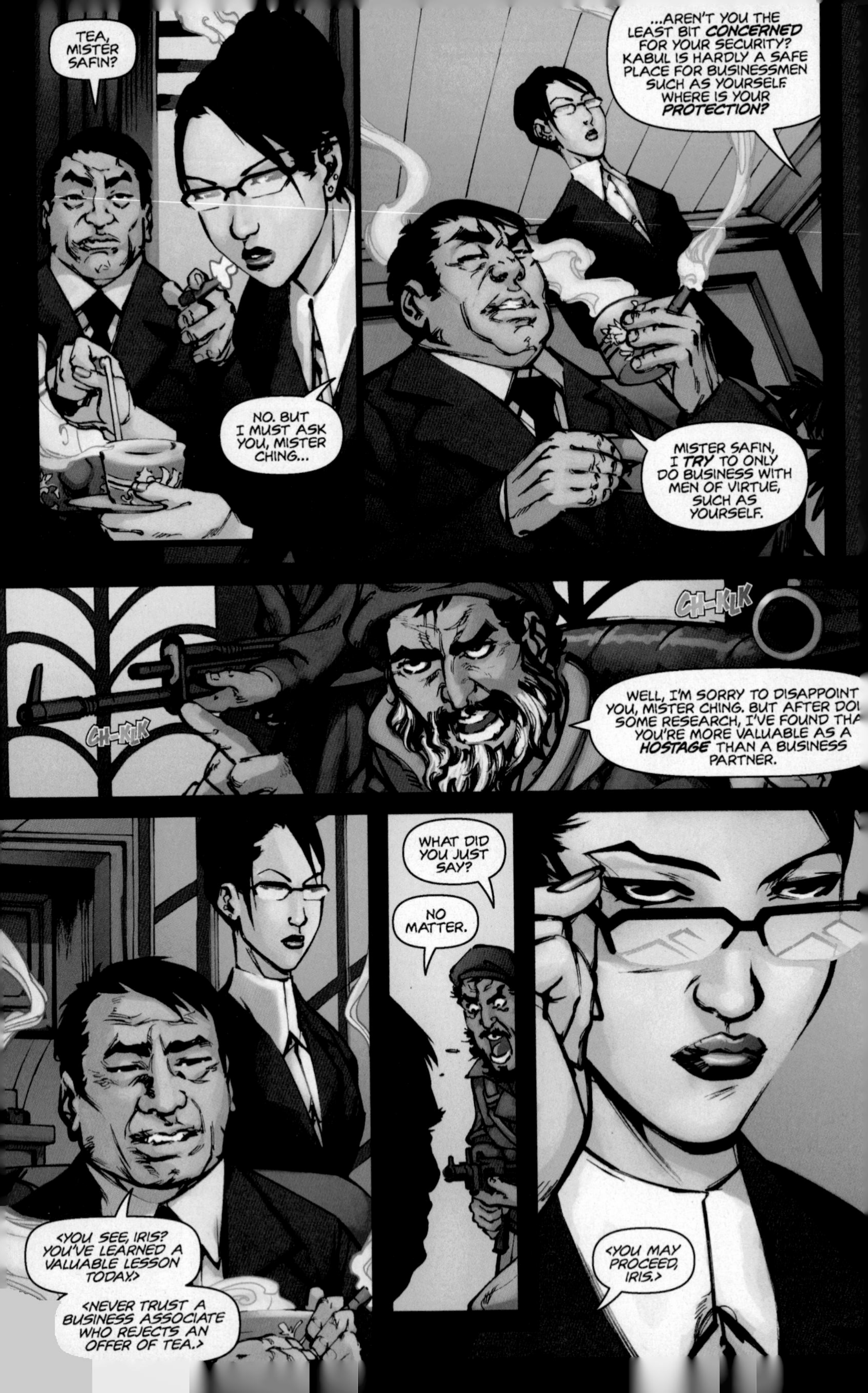
TEA, MISTER SAFIN?
NO. BUT I MUST ASK YOU, MISTER CHING...
...AREN'T YOU THE LEAST BIT CONCERNED FOR YOUR SECURITY? KABUL IS HARDLY A SAFE PLACE FOR BUSINESSMEN SUCH AS YOURSELF. WHERE IS YOUR PROTECTION?
MISTER SAFIN, I TRY TO ONLY DO BUSINESS WITH MEN OF VIRTUE, SUCH AS YOURSELF.
CH-KLK
CH-KLK
WELL, I'M SORRY TO DISAPPOINT YOU, MISTER CHING. BUT AFTER DOI SOME RESEARCH, I'VE FOUND THA YOU'RE MORE VALUABLE AS A HOSTAGE THAN A BUSINESS PARTNER.
<YOU SEE, IRIS? YOU'VE LEARNED A VALUABLE LESSON TODAY>
<NEVER TRUST A BUSINESS ASSOCIATE WHO REJECTS AN OFFER OF TEA.>
WHAT DID YOU JUST SAY?
NO MATTER.
<YOU MAY PROCEED, IRIS.>

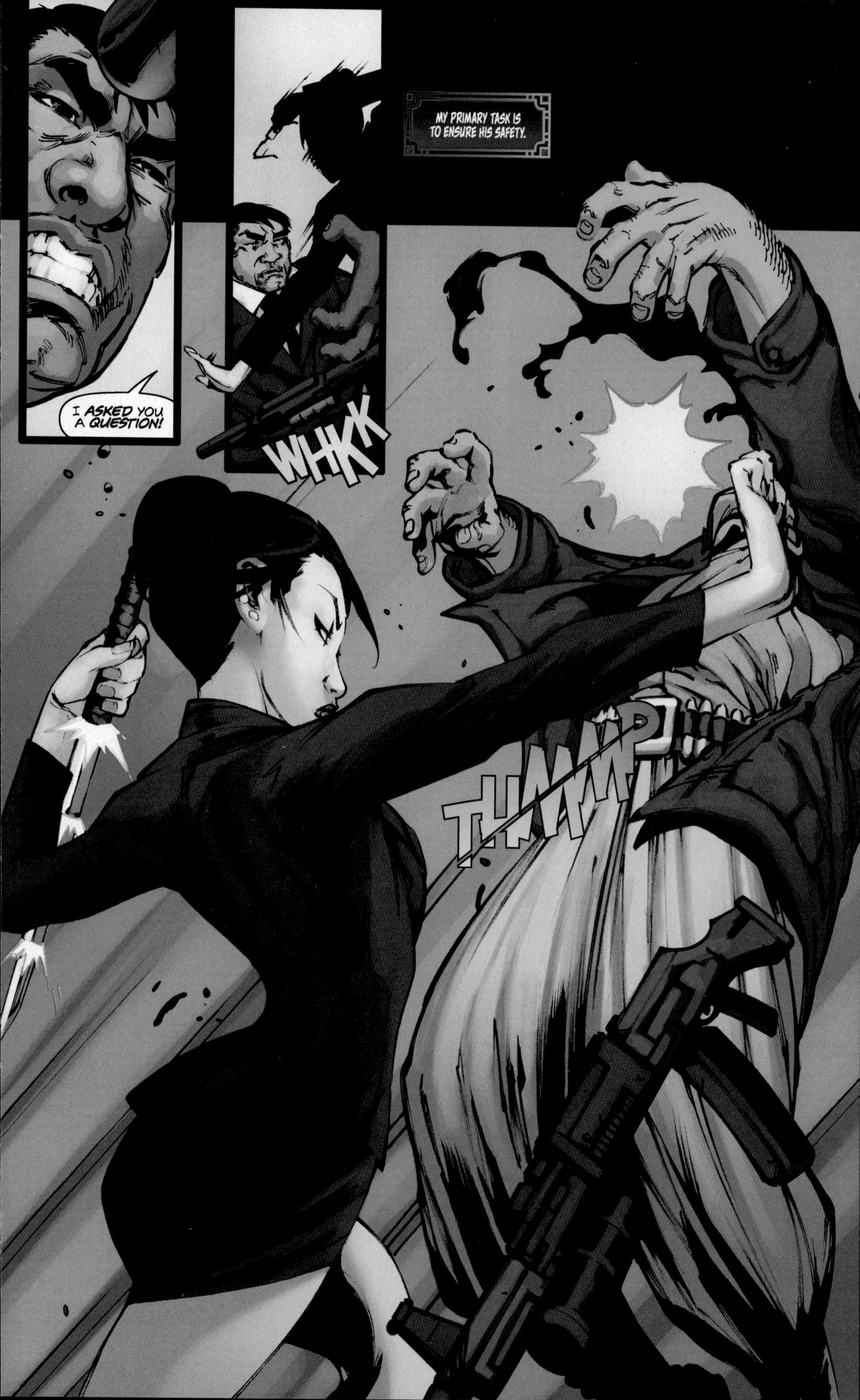
I ASKED YOU A QUESTION!
MY PRIMARY TASK IS TO ENSURE HIS SAFETY.
WHKK
THWMP

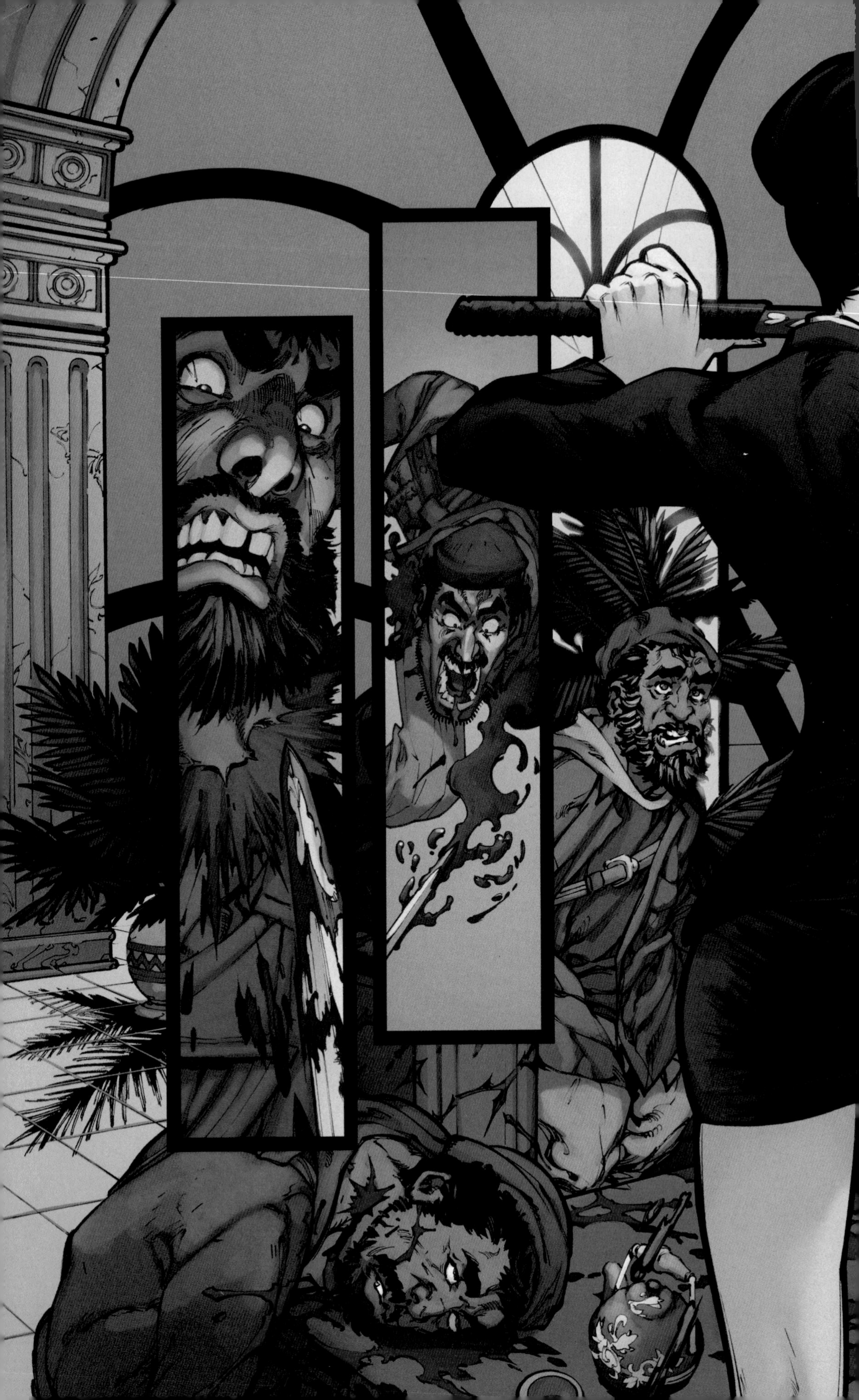

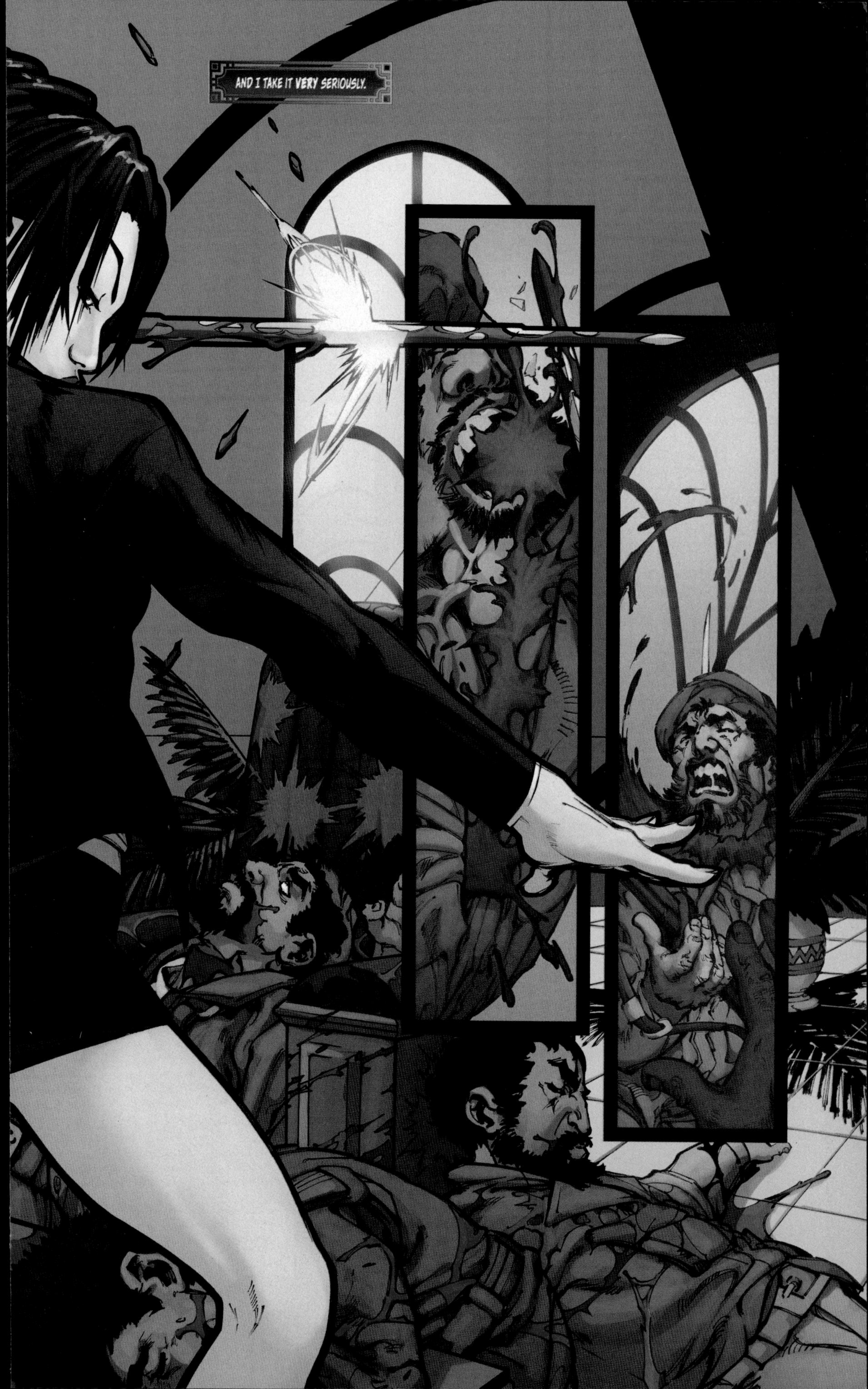
AND I TAKE IT VERY SERIOUSLY.

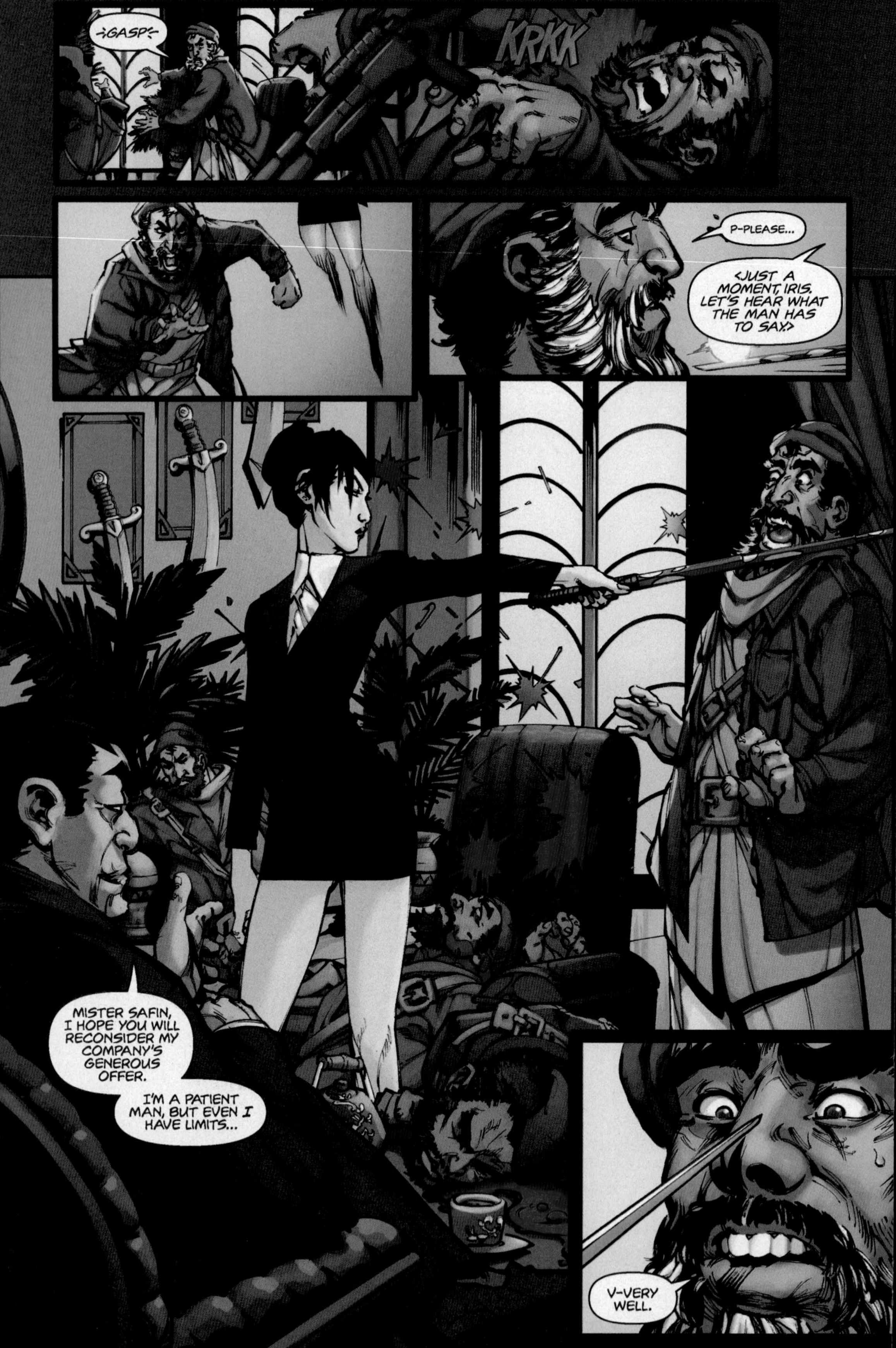

¡GASP¡
KRKK
P-PLEASE...
<JUST A MOMENT, IRIS. LET'S HEAR WHAT THE MAN HAS TO SAY.>
MISTER SAFIN, I HOPE YOU WILL RECONSIDER MY COMPANY'S GENEROUS OFFER.
I'M A PATIENT MAN, BUT EVEN I HAVE LIMITS...
V-VERY WELL.

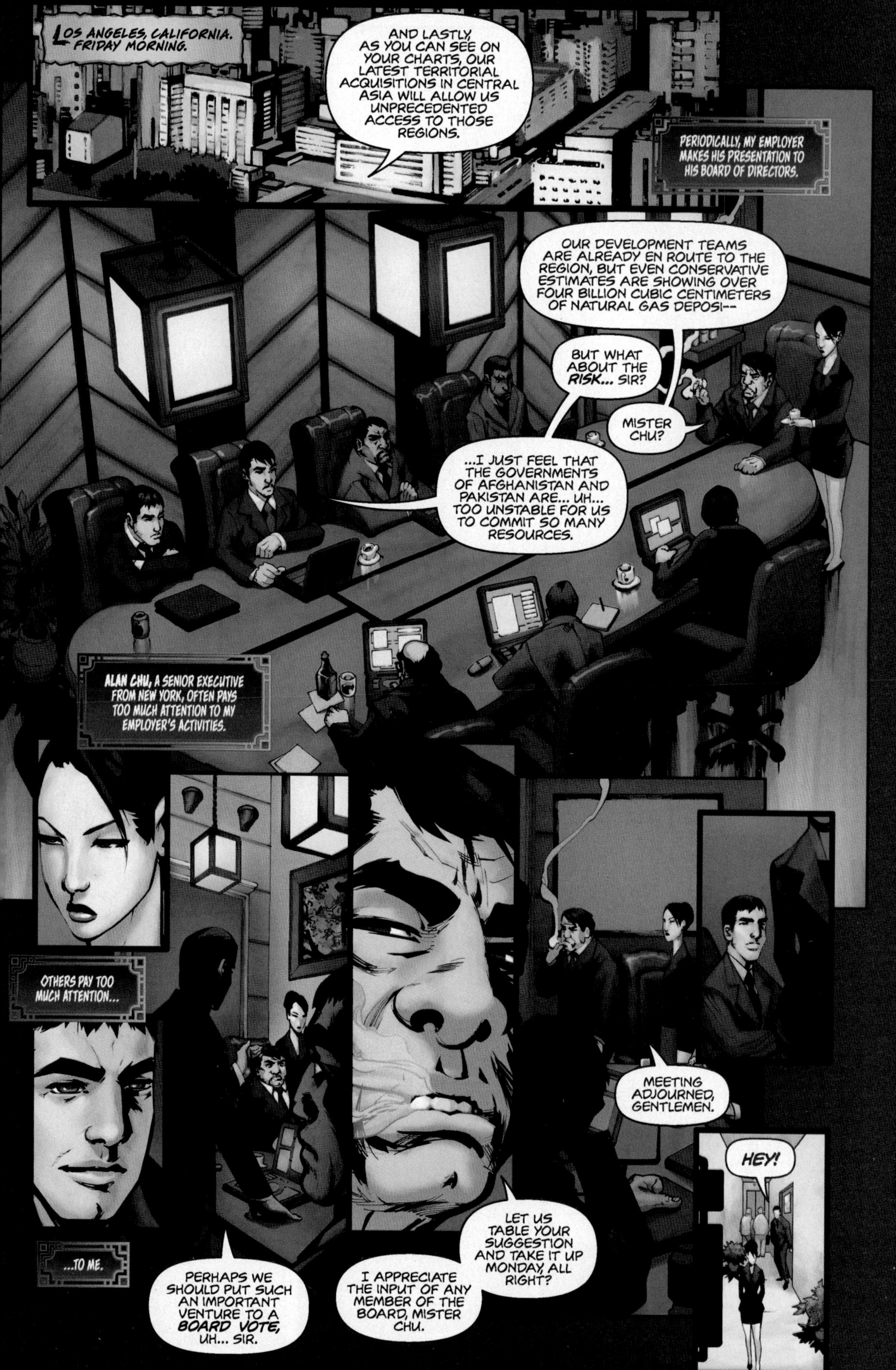

LOS ANGELES, CALIFORNIA. FRIDAY MORNING.
AND LASTLY, AS YOU CAN SEE ON YOUR CHARTS, OUR LATEST TERRITORIAL ACQUISITIONS IN CENTRAL ASIA WILL ALLOW US UNPRECEDENTED ACCESS TO THOSE REGIONS.
PERIODICALLY, MY EMPLOYER MAKES HIS PRESENTATION TO HIS BOARD OF DIRECTORS.
OUR DEVELOPMENT TEAMS ARE ALREADY EN ROUTE TO THE REGION, BUT EVEN CONSERVATIVE ESTIMATES ARE SHOWING OVER FOUR BILLION CUBIC CENTIMETERS OF NATURAL GAS DEPOSI--
BUT WHAT ABOUT THE RISK... SIR?
MISTER CHU?
...I JUST FEEL THAT THE GOVERNMENTS OF AFGHANISTAN AND PAKISTAN ARE... UH... TOO UNSTABLE FOR US TO COMMIT SO MANY RESOURCES.
ALAN CHU, A SENIOR EXECUTIVE FROM NEW YORK, OFTEN PAYS TOO MUCH ATTENTION TO MY EMPLOYER'S ACTIVITIES.
OTHERS PAY TOO MUCH ATTENTION...
...TO ME.
PERHAPS WE SHOULD PUT SUCH AN IMPORTANT VENTURE TO A BOARD VOTE, UH... SIR.
I APPRECIATE THE INPUT OF ANY MEMBER OF THE BOARD, MISTER CHU.
LET US TABLE YOUR SUGGESTION AND TAKE IT UP MONDAY, ALL RIGHT?
MEETING ADJOURNED, GENTLEMEN.
HEY!

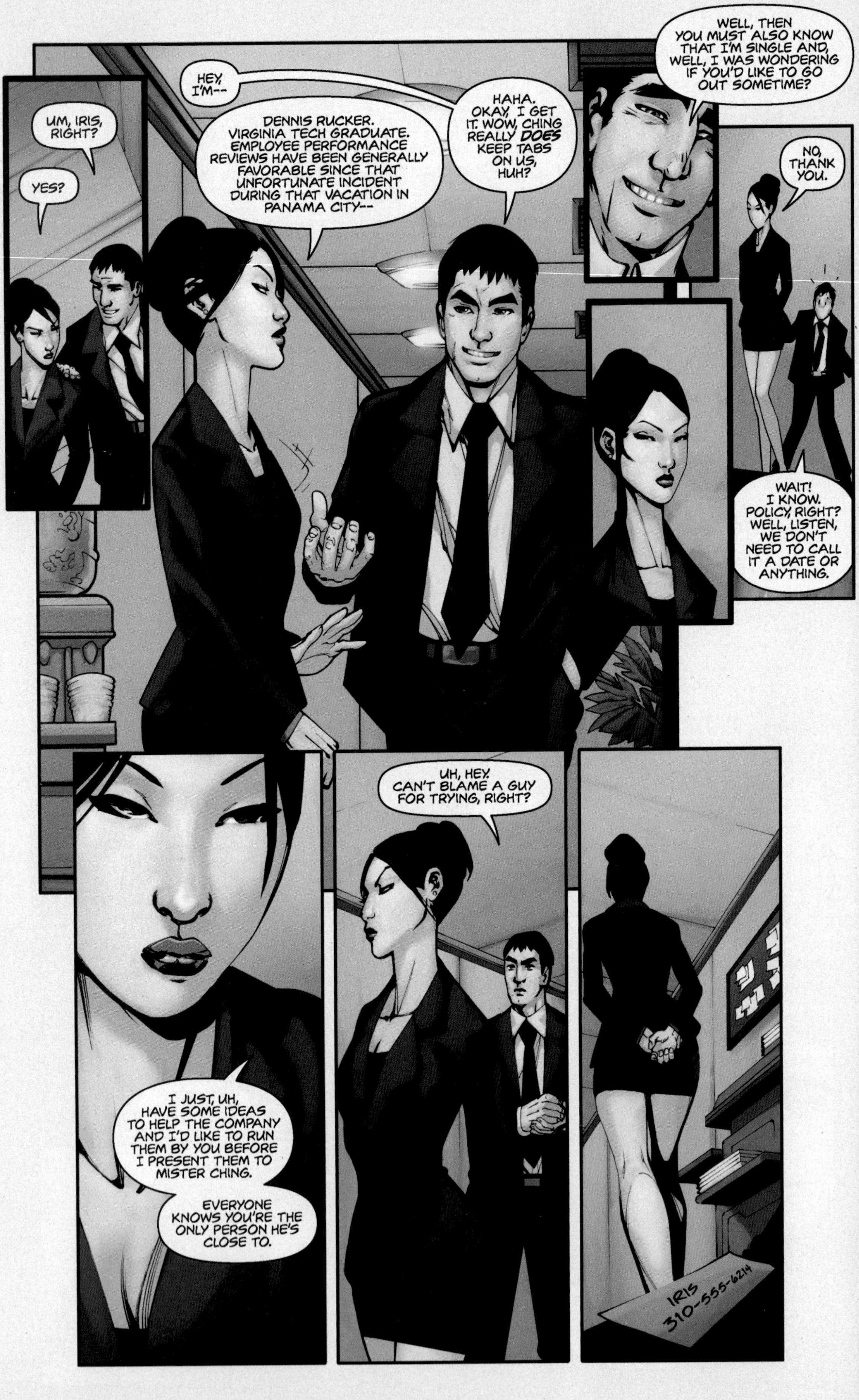
UM, IRIS, RIGHT?
YES?
HEY, I'M--
DENNIS RUCKER. VIRGINIA TECH GRADUATE. EMPLOYEE PERFORMANCE REVIEWS HAVE BEEN GENERALLY FAVORABLE SINCE THAT UNFORTUNATE INCIDENT DURING THAT VACATION IN PANAMA CITY--
HAHA. OKAY, I GET IT. WOW, CHING REALLY DOES KEEP TABS ON US, HUH?
WELL, THEN YOU MUST ALSO KNOW THAT I'M SINGLE AND, WELL, I WAS WONDERING IF YOU'D LIKE TO GO OUT SOMETIME?
NO, THANK YOU.
WAIT! I KNOW. POLICY, RIGHT? WELL, LISTEN, WE DON'T NEED TO CALL IT A DATE OR ANYTHING.
I JUST, UH, HAVE SOME IDEAS TO HELP THE COMPANY AND I'D LIKE TO RUN THEM BY YOU BEFORE I PRESENT THEM TO MISTER CHING.
EVERYONE KNOWS YOU'RE THE ONLY PERSON HE'S CLOSE TO.
UH, HEY. CAN'T BLAME A GUY FOR TRYING, RIGHT?
IRIS
310-555-6214

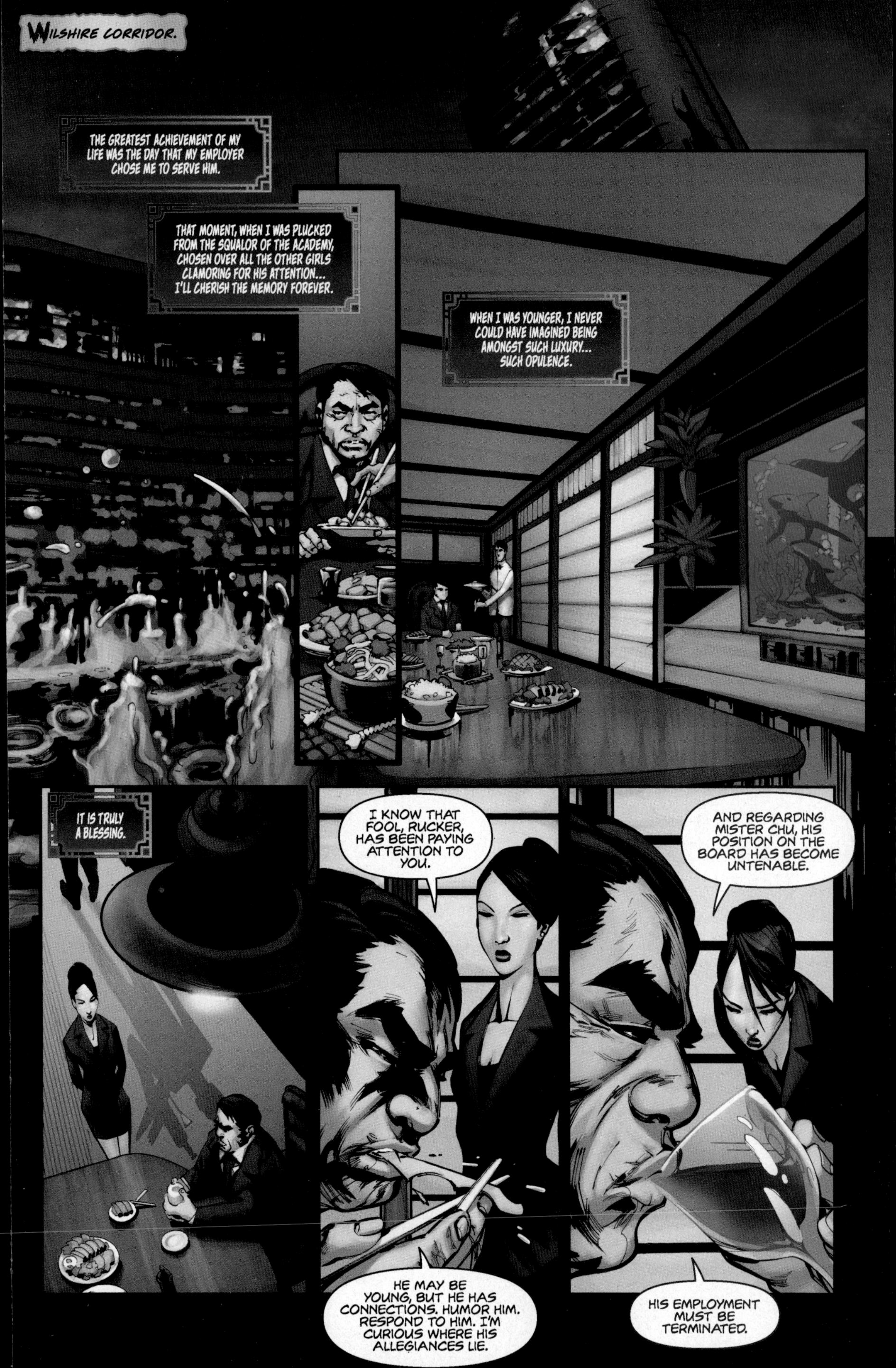
WILSHIRE CORRIDOR.
THE GREATEST ACHIEVEMENT OF MY LIFE WAS THE DAY THAT MY EMPLOYER CHOSE ME TO SERVE HIM.
THAT MOMENT, WHEN I WAS PLUCKED FROM THE SQUALOR OF THE ACADEMY, CHOSEN OVER ALL THE OTHER GIRLS CLAMORING FOR HIS ATTENTION... I'LL CHERISH THE MEMORY FOREVER.
WHEN I WAS YOUNGER, I NEVER COULD HAVE IMAGINED BEING AMONGST SUCH LUXURY... SUCH OPULENCE.
IT IS TRULY A BLESSING.
I KNOW THAT FOOL, RUCKER, HAS BEEN PAYING ATTENTION TO YOU.
HE MAY BE YOUNG, BUT HE HAS CONNECTIONS. HUMOR HIM. RESPOND TO HIM. I'M CURIOUS WHERE HIS ALLEGIANCES LIE.
AND REGARDING MISTER CHU, HIS POSITION ON THE BOARD HAS BECOME UNTENABLE.
HIS EMPLOYMENT MUST BE TERMINATED.

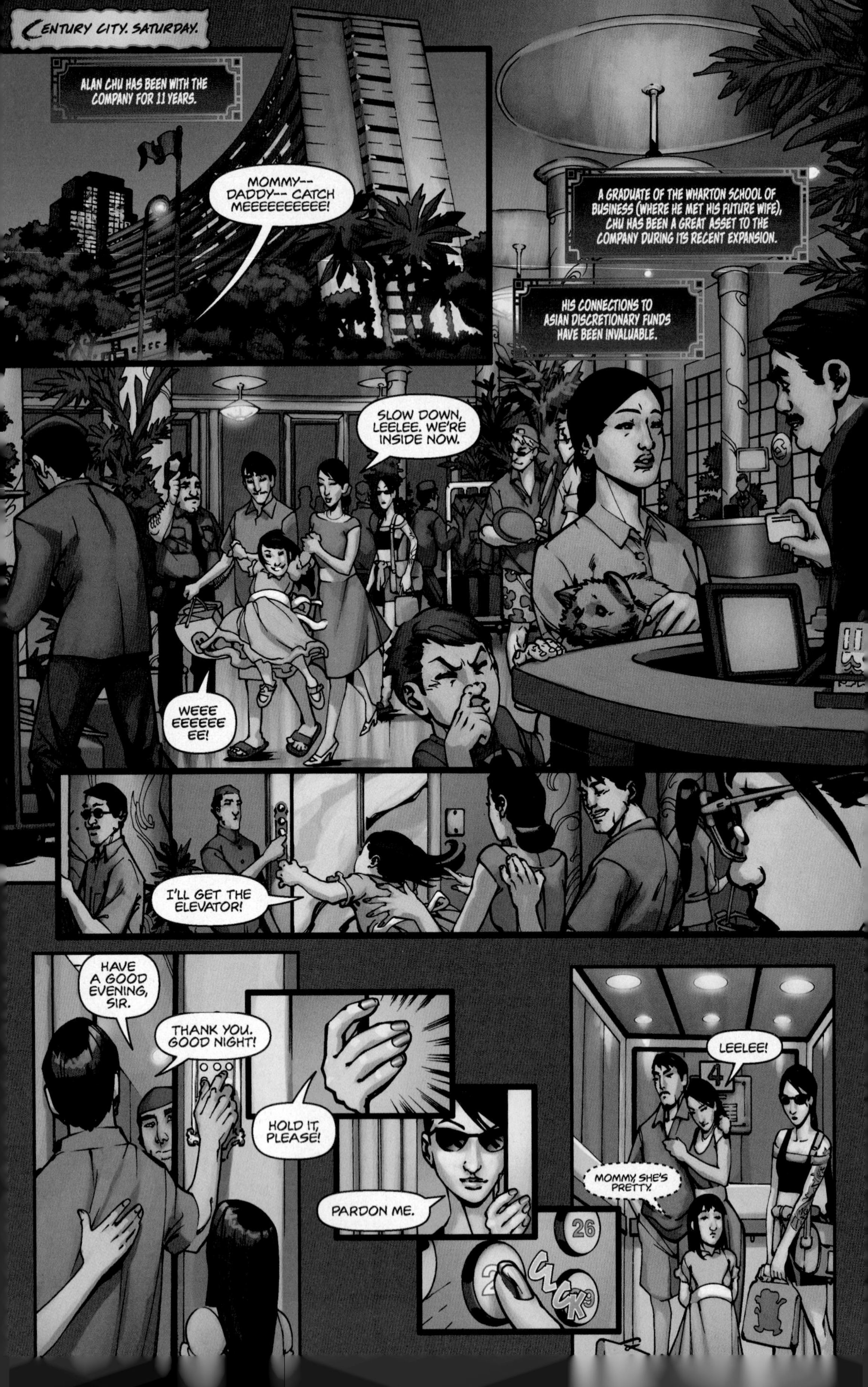
CENTURY CITY. SATURDAY.
ALAN CHU HAS BEEN WITH THE COMPANY FOR 11 YEARS.
MOMMY-- DADDY-- CATCH MEEEEEEEEEE!
A GRADUATE OF THE WHARTON SCHOOL OF BUSINESS (WHERE HE MET HIS FUTURE WIFE), CHU HAS BEEN A GREAT ASSET TO THE COMPANY DURING ITS RECENT EXPANSION.
HIS CONNECTIONS TO ASIAN DISCRETIONARY FUNDS HAVE BEEN INVALUABLE.
SLOW DOWN, LEELEE. WE'RE INSIDE NOW.
WEEE EEEEEE EE!
I'LL GET THE ELEVATOR!
HAVE A GOOD EVENING, SIR.
THANK YOU. GOOD NIGHT!
HOLD IT, PLEASE!
PARDON ME.
CLICK
LEELEE!
MOMMY, SHE'S PRETTY.

HERE WE ARE. COME ON, LEELEE!

LEELEE...

...WHAT DID I TELL YOU ABOUT STARING?

SORRY, MOMMY.

HE APPEARS TO HAVE A GOOD RELATIONSHIP WITH HIS WIFE AND CHILD, AS WELL.

INFLUENTIAL FRIENDS. CLOSE FAMILY.

UNFORTUNATE.

WHEN PEOPLE CARE ABOUT YOU, IT'S MORE DIFFICULT TO MAKE YOUR DEATH SEEM LIKE "NATURAL CAUSES" BECAUSE THEY TEND TO MAKE INQUIRIES AND REQUEST INVESTIGATIONS.

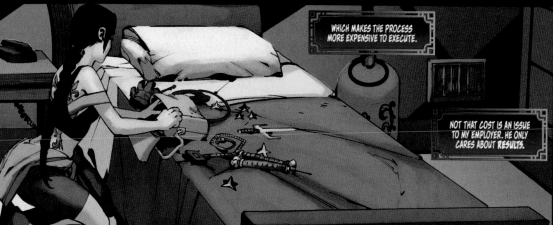

WHICH MAKES THE PROCESS MORE EXPENSIVE TO EXECUTE.

NOT THAT COST IS AN ISSUE TO MY EMPLOYER. HE ONLY CARES ABOUT RESULTS.

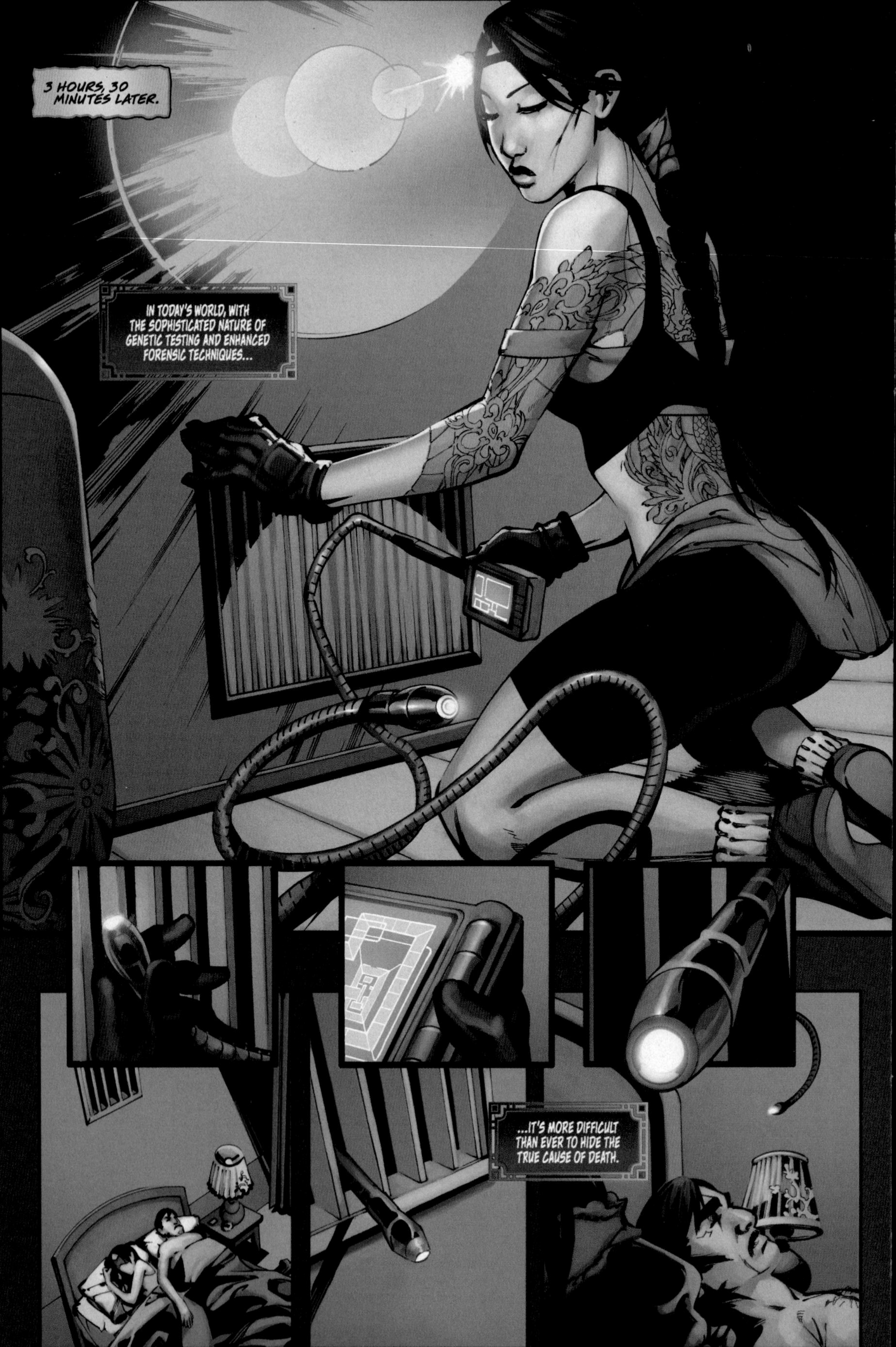
3 HOURS, 30 MINUTES LATER.
IN TODAY'S WORLD, WITH THE SOPHISTICATED NATURE OF GENETIC TESTING AND ENHANCED FORENSIC TECHNIQUES...
...IT'S MORE DIFFICULT THAN EVER TO HIDE THE TRUE CAUSE OF DEATH.

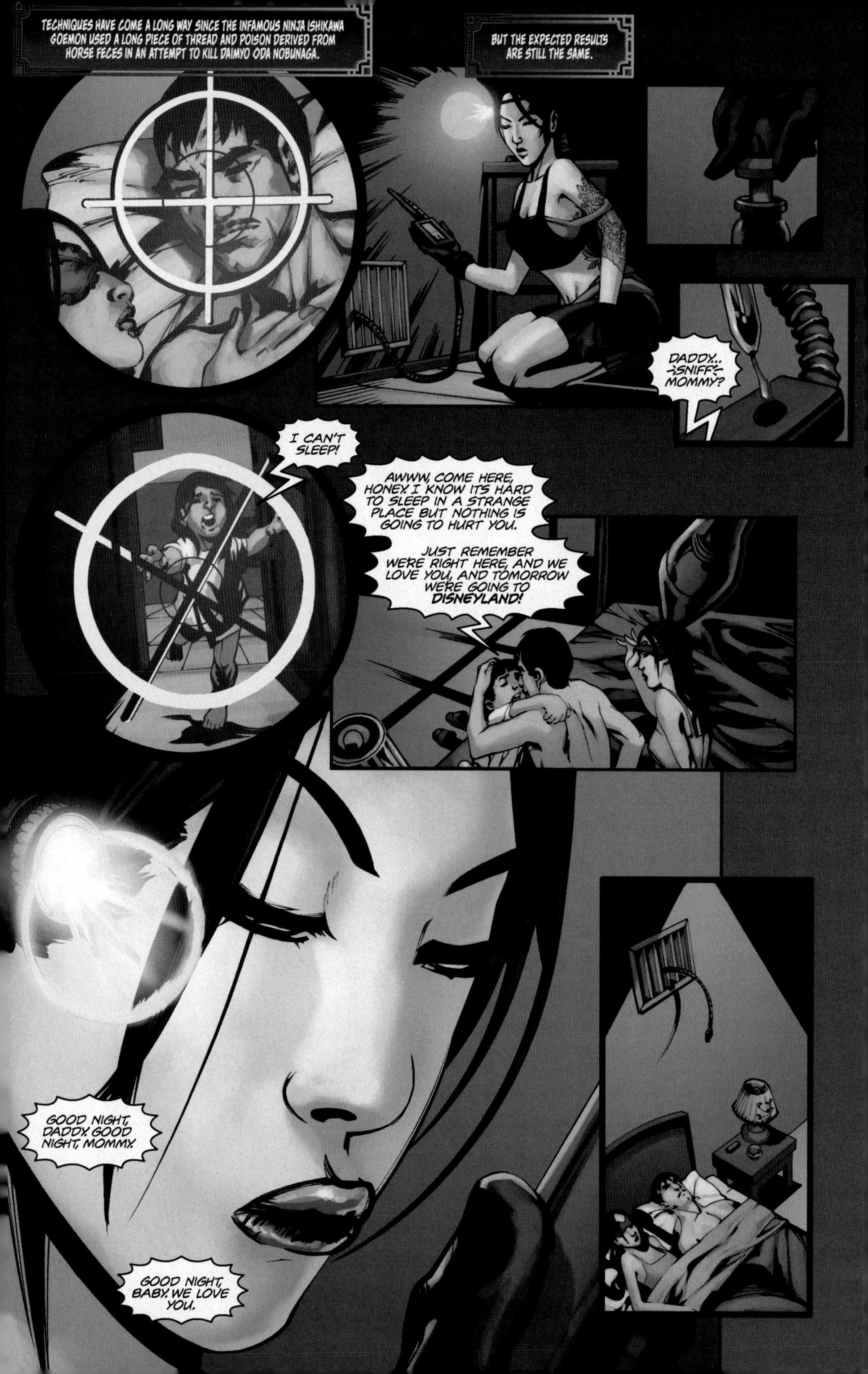
TECHNIQUES HAVE COME A LONG WAY SINCE THE INFAMOUS NINJA ISHIKAWA GOEMON USED A LONG PIECE OF THREAD AND POISON DERIVED FROM HORSE FECES IN AN ATTEMPT TO KILL DAIMYO ODA NOBUNAGA.
BUT THE EXPECTED RESULTS ARE STILL THE SAME.
DADDY... SNIFF MOMMY?
I CAN'T SLEEP!
AWWW, COME HERE, HONEY. I KNOW ITS HARD TO SLEEP IN A STRANGE PLACE BUT NOTHING IS GOING TO HURT YOU.
JUST REMEMBER WE'RE RIGHT HERE, AND WE LOVE YOU, AND TOMORROW WE'RE GOING TO DISNEYLAND!
GOOD NIGHT, DADDY. GOOD NIGHT, MOMMY.
GOOD NIGHT, BABY. WE LOVE YOU.

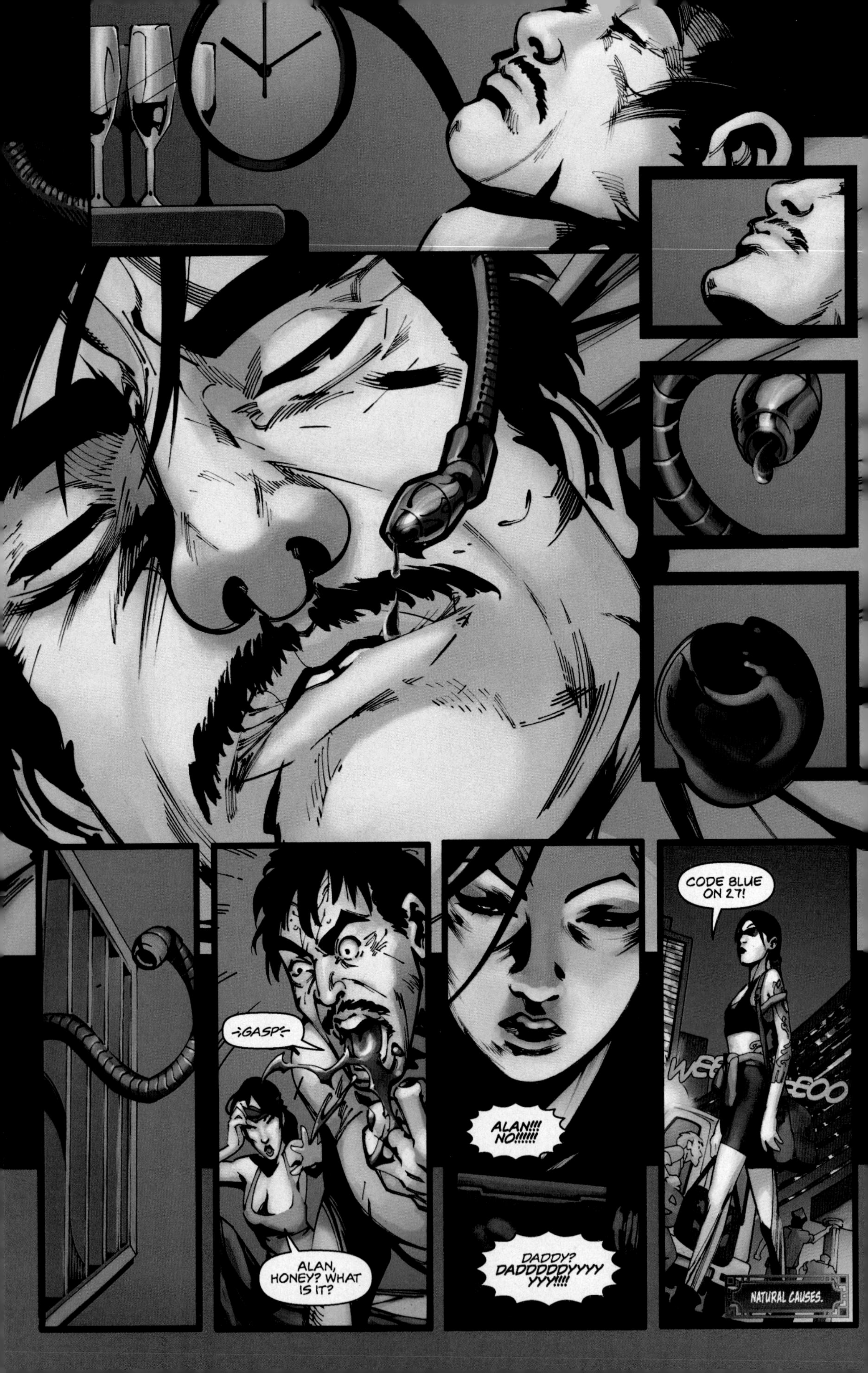

-GASP-
ALAN, HONEY? WHAT IS IT?
ALAN!!! NO!!!!!!
DADDY? DADDDDDYYYY YYY!!!!
CODE BLUE ON 27!
NATURAL CAUSES.

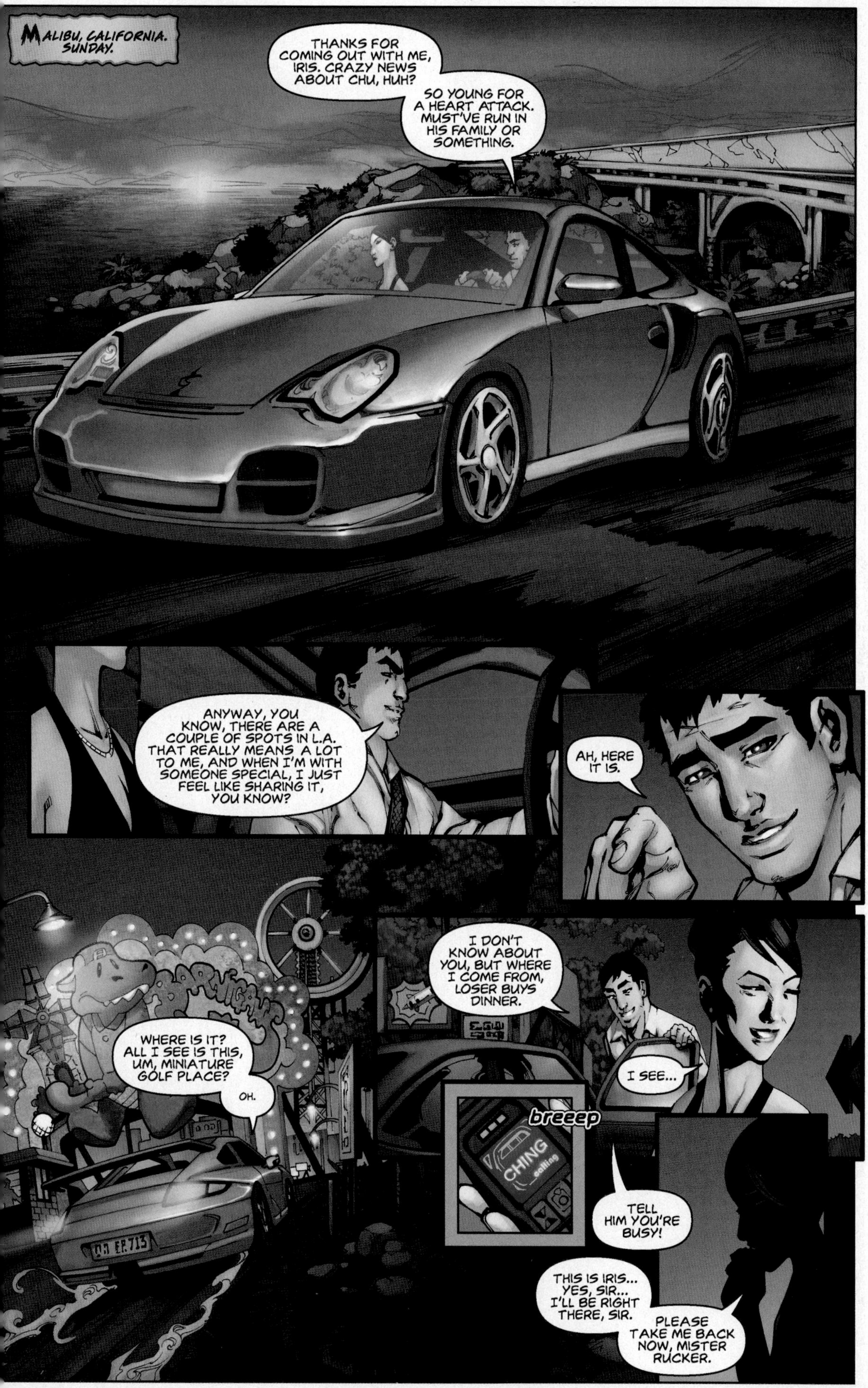
MALIBU, CALIFORNIA. SUNDAY.
THANKS FOR COMING OUT WITH ME, IRIS. CRAZY NEWS ABOUT CHU, HUH?
SO YOUNG FOR A HEART ATTACK. MUST'VE RUN IN HIS FAMILY OR SOMETHING.
ANYWAY, YOU KNOW, THERE ARE A COUPLE OF SPOTS IN L.A. THAT REALLY MEANS A LOT TO ME, AND WHEN I'M WITH SOMEONE SPECIAL, I JUST FEEL LIKE SHARING IT, YOU KNOW?
AH, HERE IT IS.
WHERE IS IT? ALL I SEE IS THIS, UM, MINIATURE GOLF PLACE?
OH.
I DON'T KNOW ABOUT YOU, BUT WHERE I COME FROM, LOSER BUYS DINNER.
I SEE...
breeep
CHING
TELL HIM YOU'RE BUSY!
THIS IS IRIS... YES, SIR... I'LL BE RIGHT THERE, SIR.
PLEASE TAKE ME BACK NOW, MISTER RUCKER.

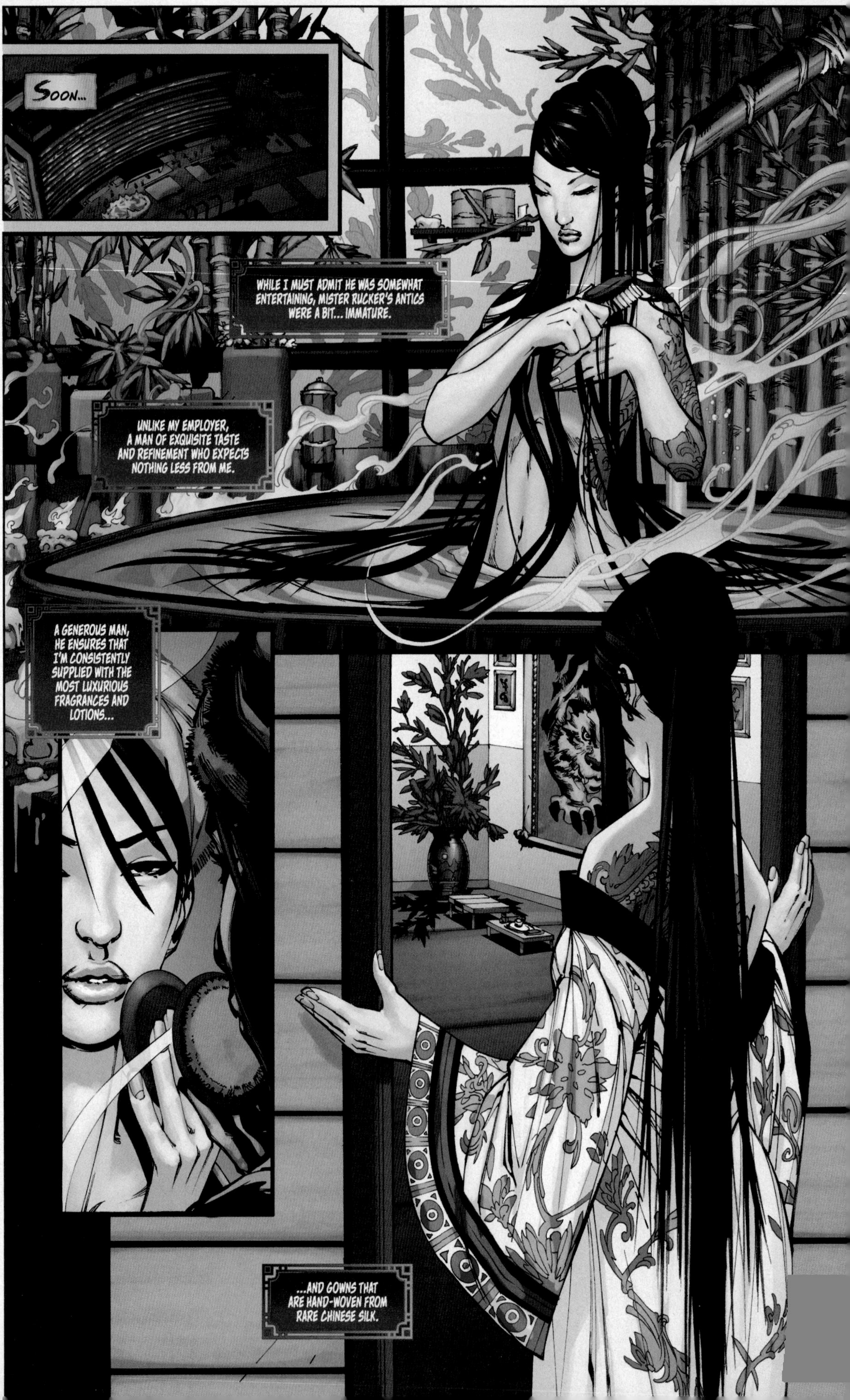
Soon...
While I must admit he was somewhat entertaining, Mister Rucker's antics were a bit... immature.
Unlike my employer, a man of exquisite taste and refinement who expects nothing less from me.
A generous man, he ensures that I'm consistently supplied with the most luxurious fragrances and lotions...
...and gowns that are hand-woven from rare Chinese silk.

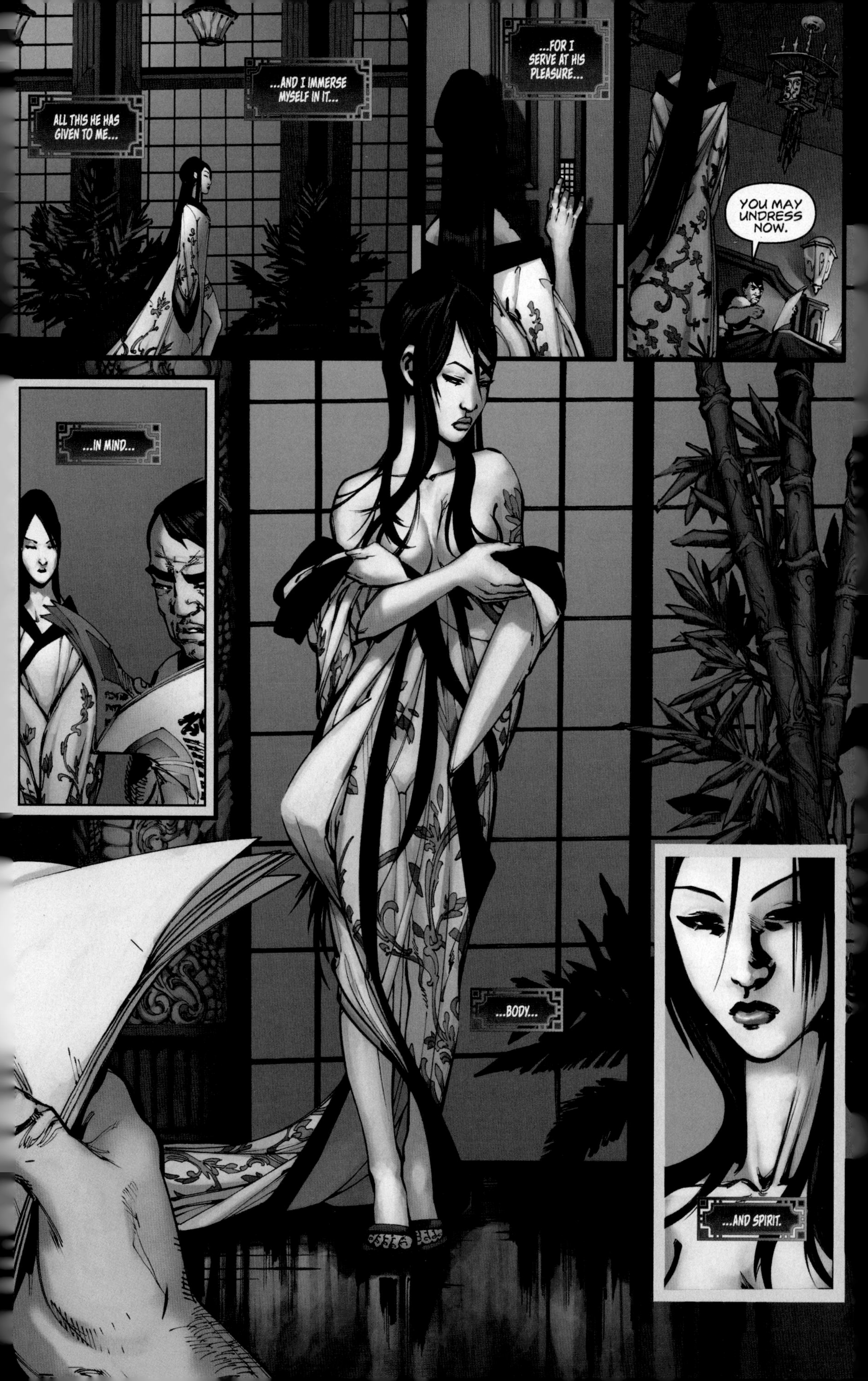
ALL THIS HE HAS GIVEN TO ME...
...AND I IMMERSE MYSELF IN IT...
...FOR I SERVE AT HIS PLEASURE...
YOU MAY UNDRESS NOW.
...IN MIND...
...BODY...
...AND SPIRIT.

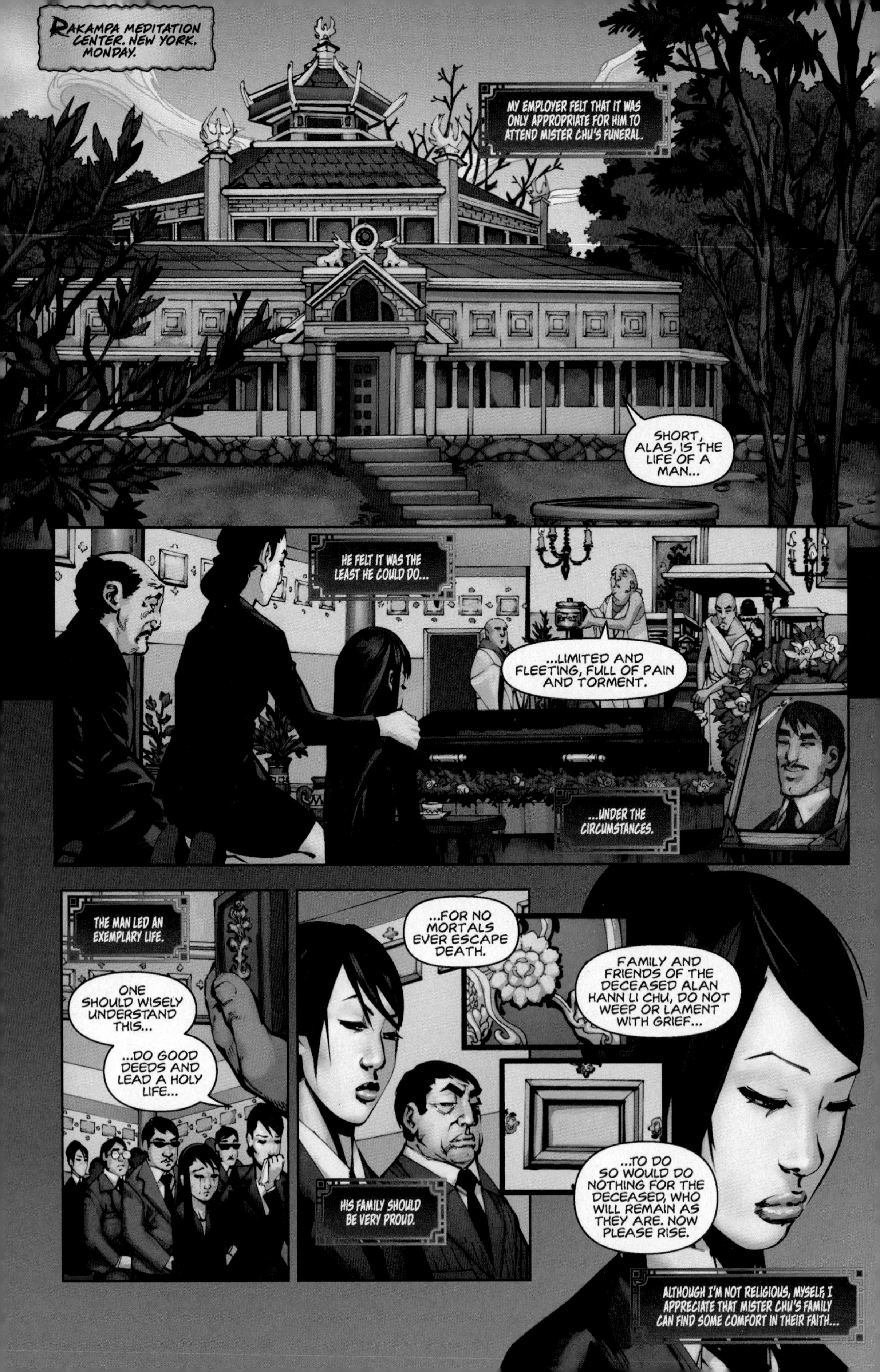
RAKAMPA MEDITATION CENTER. NEW YORK. MONDAY.
MY EMPLOYER FELT THAT IT WAS ONLY APPROPRIATE FOR HIM TO ATTEND MISTER CHU'S FUNERAL.
SHORT, ALAS, IS THE LIFE OF A MAN...
HE FELT IT WAS THE LEAST HE COULD DO...
...LIMITED AND FLEETING, FULL OF PAIN AND TORMENT.
...UNDER THE CIRCUMSTANCES.
THE MAN LED AN EXEMPLARY LIFE.
ONE SHOULD WISELY UNDERSTAND THIS...
...DO GOOD DEEDS AND LEAD A HOLY LIFE...
...FOR NO MORTALS EVER ESCAPE DEATH.
HIS FAMILY SHOULD BE VERY PROUD.
FAMILY AND FRIENDS OF THE DECEASED ALAN HANN LI CHU, DO NOT WEEP OR LAMENT WITH GRIEF...
...TO DO SO WOULD DO NOTHING FOR THE DECEASED, WHO WILL REMAIN AS THEY ARE. NOW PLEASE RISE.
ALTHOUGH I'M NOT RELIGIOUS, MYSELF, I APPRECIATE THAT MISTER CHU'S FAMILY CAN FIND SOME COMFORT IN THEIR FAITH...

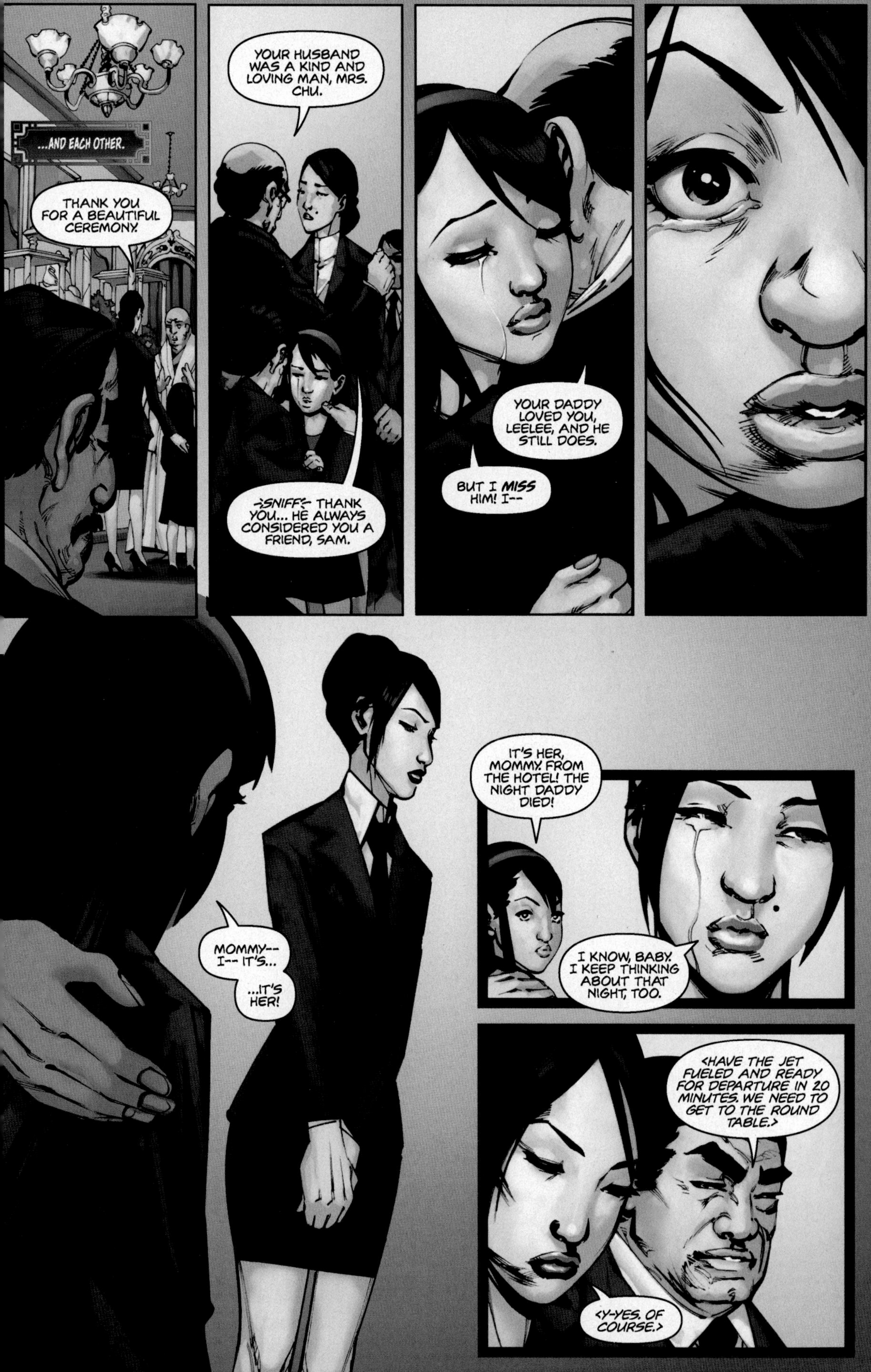
...AND EACH OTHER.
THANK YOU FOR A BEAUTIFUL CEREMONY.
YOUR HUSBAND WAS A KIND AND LOVING MAN, MRS. CHU.
-SNIFF- THANK YOU... HE ALWAYS CONSIDERED YOU A FRIEND, SAM.
YOUR DADDY LOVED YOU, LEELEE, AND HE STILL DOES.
BUT I MISS HIM! I--
MOMMY-- I-- IT'S...
...IT'S HER!
IT'S HER, MOMMY. FROM THE HOTEL! THE NIGHT DADDY DIED!
I KNOW, BABY. I KEEP THINKING ABOUT THAT NIGHT, TOO.
<HAVE THE JET FUELED AND READY FOR DEPARTURE IN 20 MINUTES. WE NEED TO GET TO THE ROUND TABLE.>
<Y-YES. OF COURSE.>

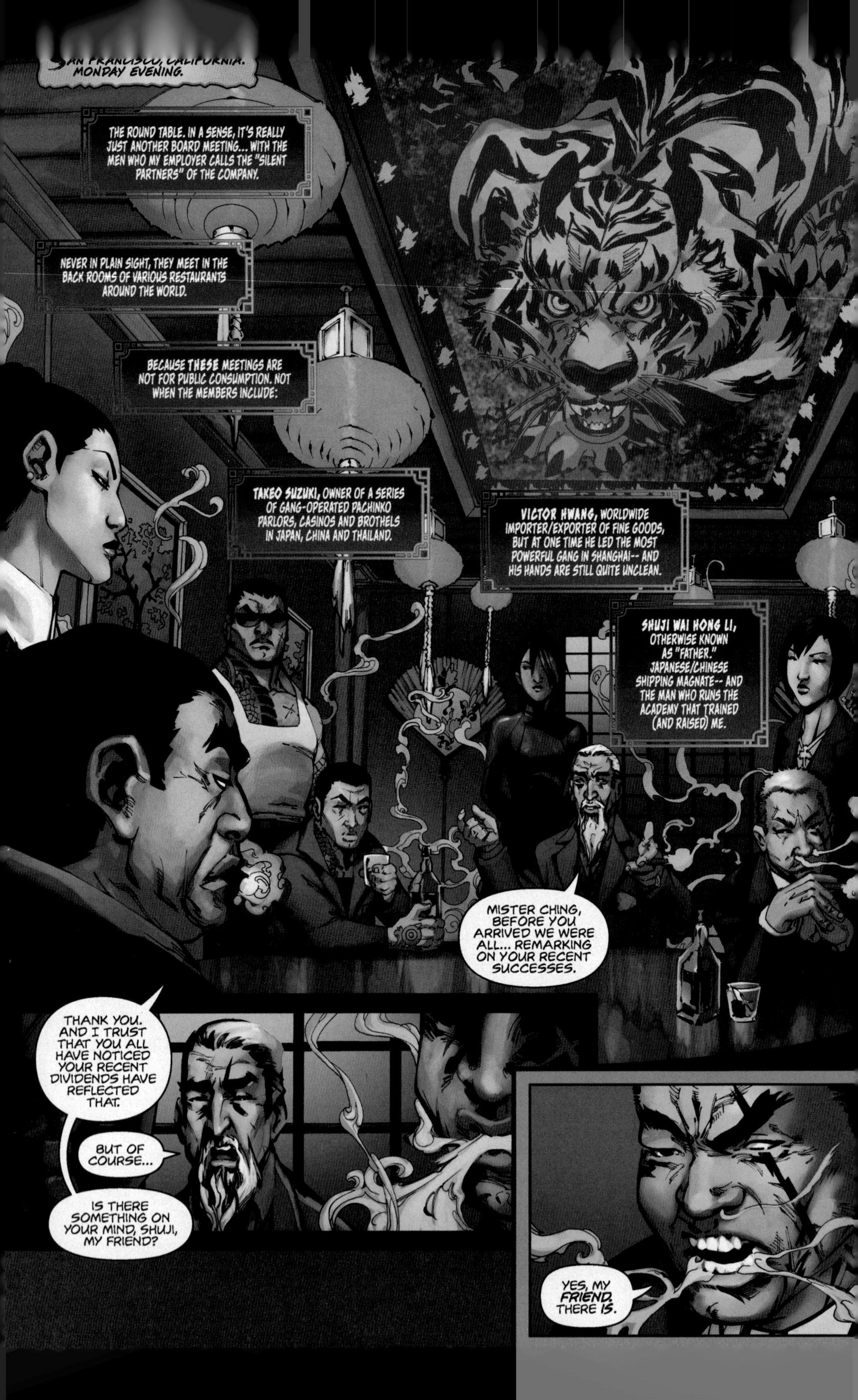
SAN FRANCISCO, CALIFORNIA. MONDAY EVENING.
THE ROUND TABLE. IN A SENSE, IT'S REALLY JUST ANOTHER BOARD MEETING... WITH THE MEN WHO MY EMPLOYER CALLS THE "SILENT PARTNERS" OF THE COMPANY.
NEVER IN PLAIN SIGHT, THEY MEET IN THE BACK ROOMS OF VARIOUS RESTAURANTS AROUND THE WORLD.
BECAUSE THESE MEETINGS ARE NOT FOR PUBLIC CONSUMPTION. NOT WHEN THE MEMBERS INCLUDE:
TAKEO SUZUKI, OWNER OF A SERIES OF GANG-OPERATED PACHINKO PARLORS, CASINOS AND BROTHELS IN JAPAN, CHINA AND THAILAND.
VICTOR HWANG, WORLDWIDE IMPORTER/EXPORTER OF FINE GOODS, BUT AT ONE TIME HE LED THE MOST POWERFUL GANG IN SHANGHAI-- AND HIS HANDS ARE STILL QUITE UNCLEAN.
SHUJI WAI HONG LI, OTHERWISE KNOWN AS "FATHER." JAPANESE/CHINESE SHIPPING MAGNATE-- AND THE MAN WHO RUNS THE ACADEMY THAT TRAINED (AND RAISED) ME.
MISTER CHING, BEFORE YOU ARRIVED WE WERE ALL... REMARKING ON YOUR RECENT SUCCESSES.
THANK YOU. AND I TRUST THAT YOU ALL HAVE NOTICED YOUR RECENT DIVIDENDS HAVE REFLECTED THAT.
BUT OF COURSE...
IS THERE SOMETHING ON YOUR MIND, SHUJI, MY FRIEND?
YES, MY FRIEND. THERE IS.

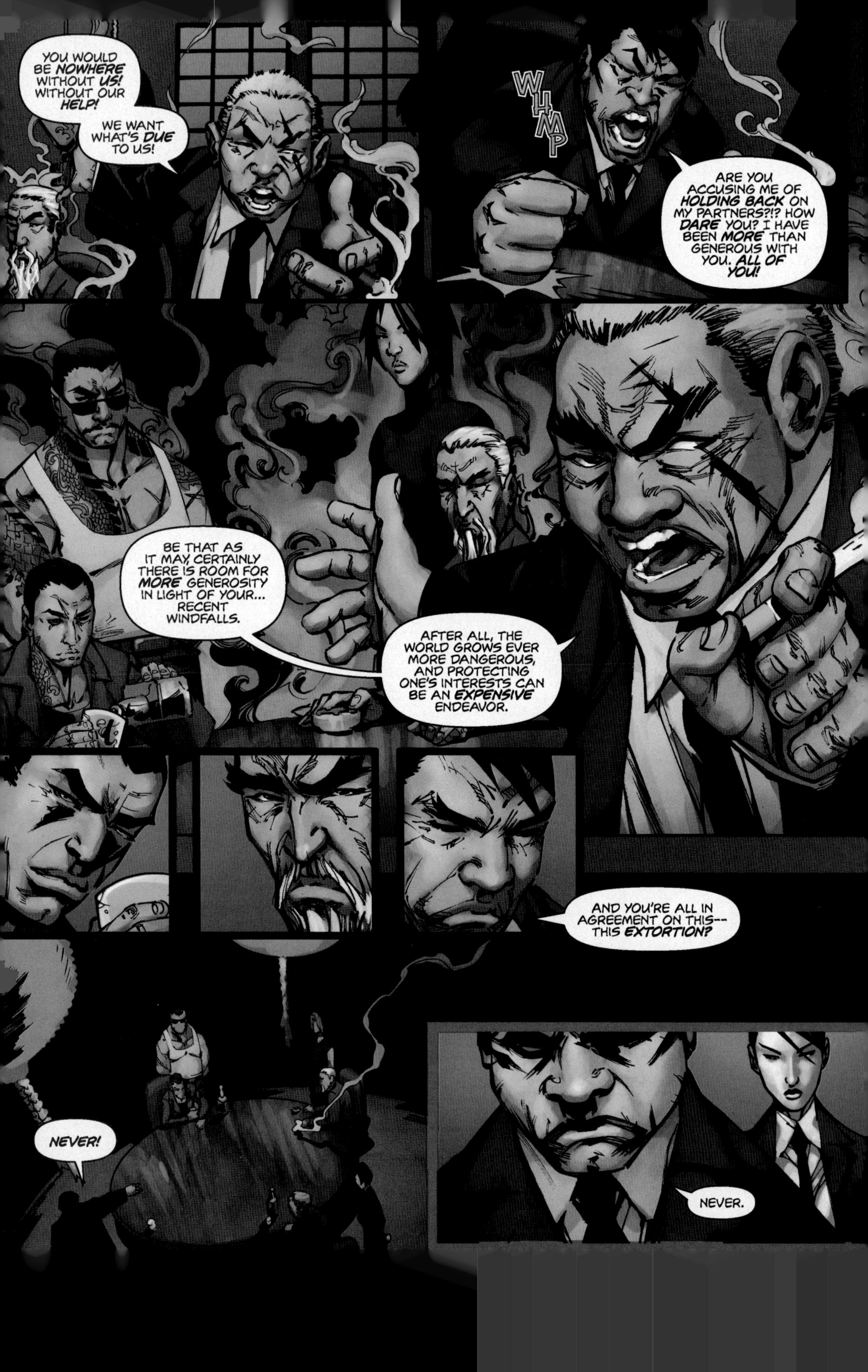

YOU WOULD BE NOWHERE WITHOUT US! WITHOUT OUR HELP!
WE WANT WHAT'S DUE TO US!
WHAP
ARE YOU ACCUSING ME OF HOLDING BACK ON MY PARTNERS?!? HOW DARE YOU? I HAVE BEEN MORE THAN GENEROUS WITH YOU. ALL OF YOU!
BE THAT AS IT MAY, CERTAINLY THERE IS ROOM FOR MORE GENEROSITY IN LIGHT OF YOUR... RECENT WINDFALLS.
AFTER ALL, THE WORLD GROWS EVER MORE DANGEROUS, AND PROTECTING ONE'S INTERESTS CAN BE AN EXPENSIVE ENDEAVOR.
AND YOU'RE ALL IN AGREEMENT ON THIS-- THIS EXTORTION?
NEVER!
NEVER.

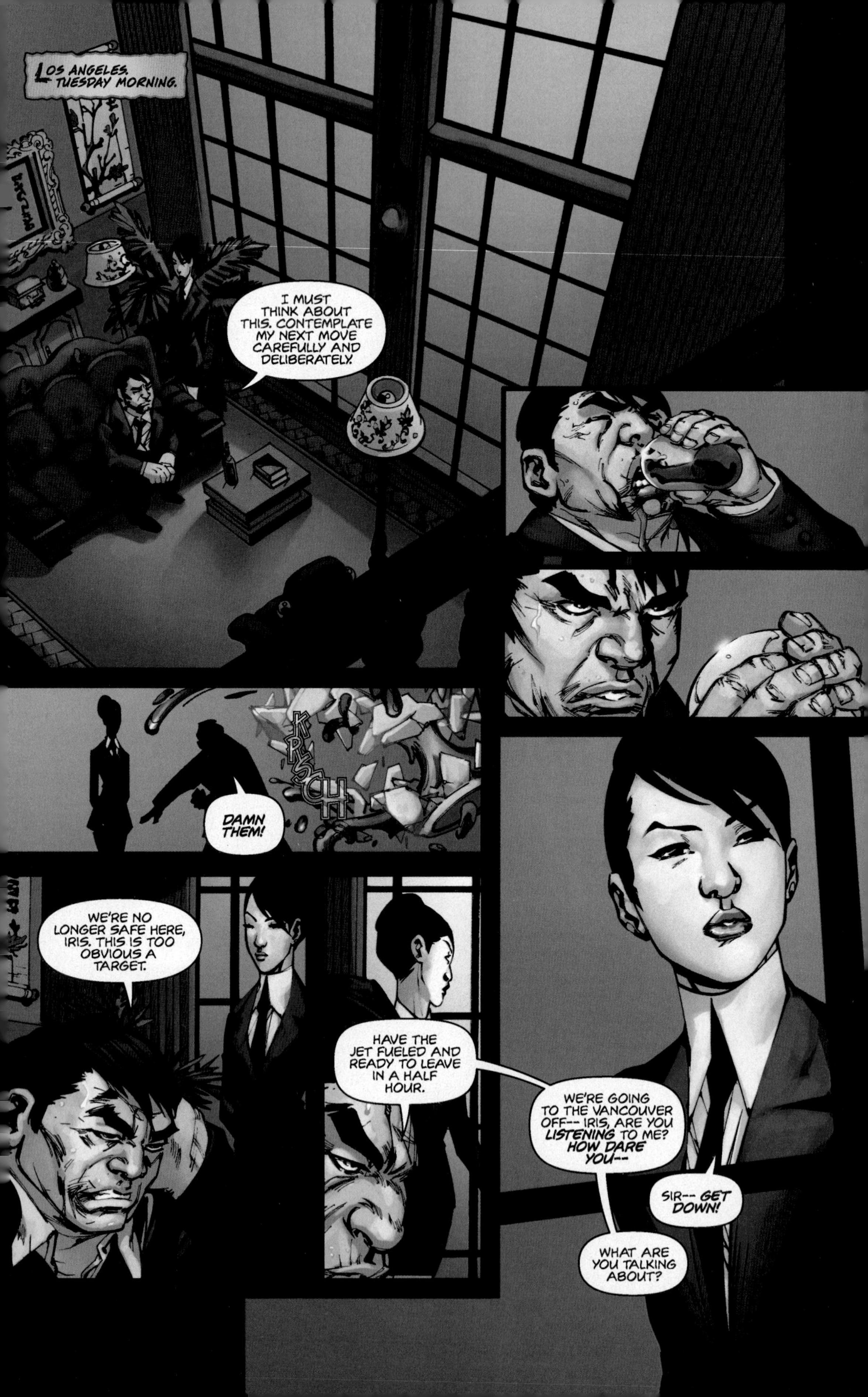
LOS ANGELES. TUESDAY MORNING.
I MUST THINK ABOUT THIS. CONTEMPLATE MY NEXT MOVE CAREFULLY AND DELIBERATELY.
DAMN THEM!
KRSCH
WE'RE NO LONGER SAFE HERE, IRIS. THIS IS TOO OBVIOUS A TARGET.
HAVE THE JET FUELED AND READY TO LEAVE IN A HALF HOUR.
WE'RE GOING TO THE VANCOUVER OFF-- IRIS, ARE YOU LISTENING TO ME? HOW DARE YOU--
SIR-- GET DOWN!
WHAT ARE YOU TALKING ABOUT?

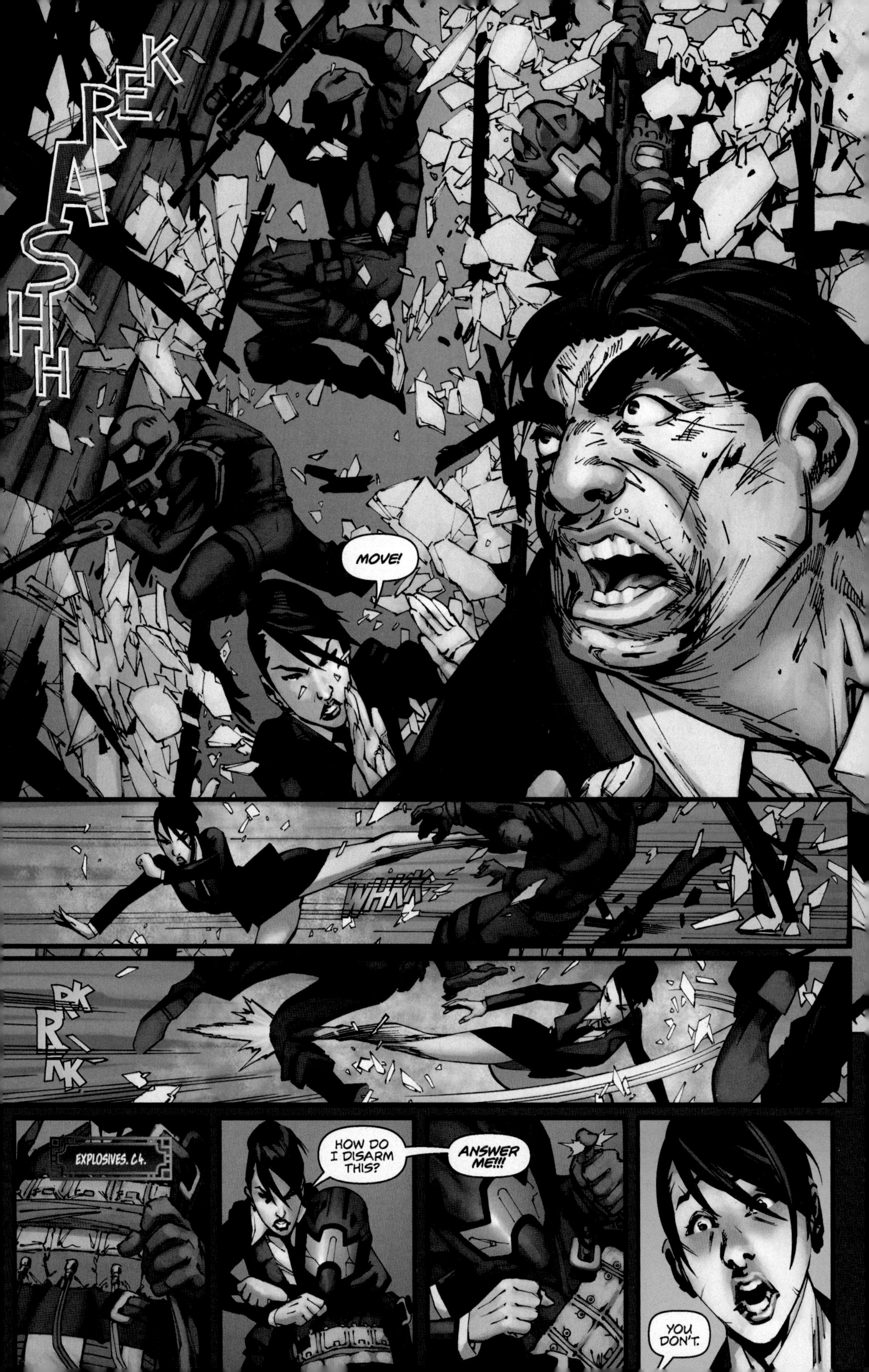

KRASH
REK
MOVE!
WHAK
KRAK
EXPLOSIVES. C4.
HOW DO I DISARM THIS?
ANSWER ME!!!
YOU DON'T.

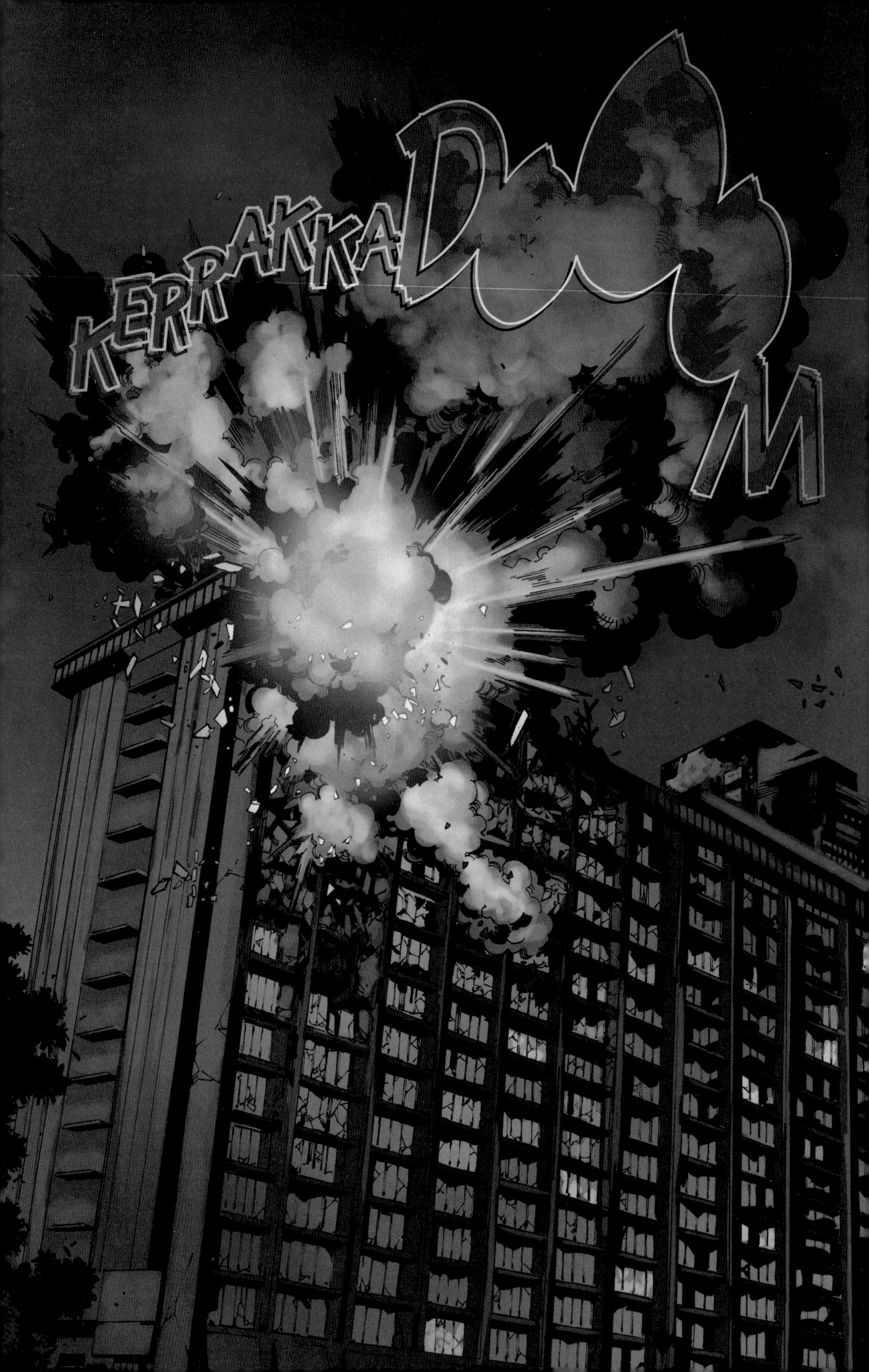
KERRAKKADOOM

EXECUTIVE ASSISTANT: IRIS #2
Cover A
EDUARDO FRANCISCO
JOHN STARR

EXECUTIVE ASSISTANT: IRIS #2
Cover B
JOE BENITEZ
PETER STEIGERWALD

EXECUTIVE ASSISTANT: IRIS #2
Cover C
FRANCIS MANAPUL
PETER STEIGERWALD

EXECUTIVE ASSISTANT: IRIS #2
Retailer Incentive Exclusive Cover E
JOE BENITEZ
MARK ROSLAN

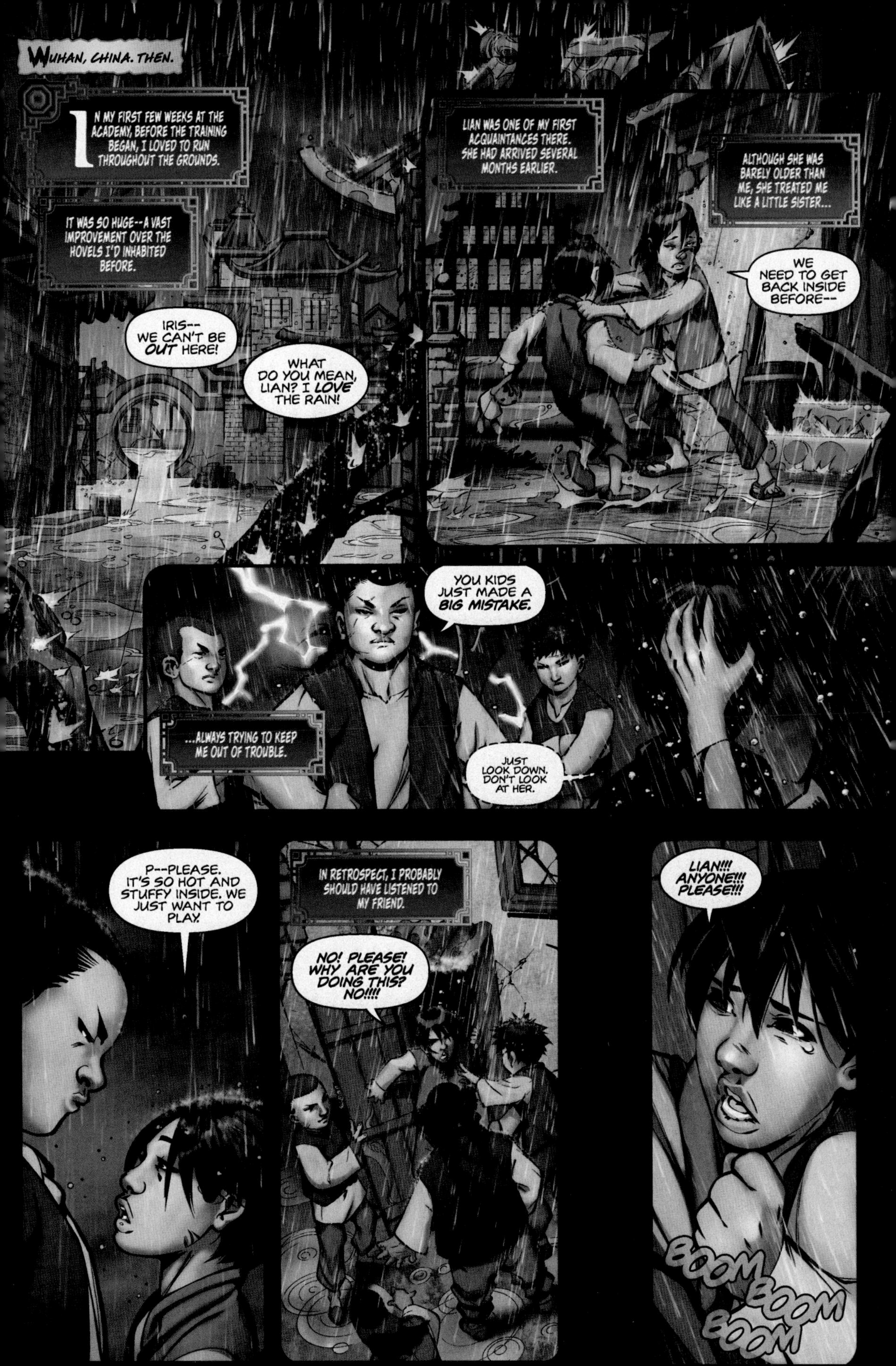
WUHAN, CHINA. THEN.
IN MY FIRST FEW WEEKS AT THE ACADEMY, BEFORE THE TRAINING BEGAN, I LOVED TO RUN THROUGHOUT THE GROUNDS.
IT WAS SO HUGE--A VAST IMPROVEMENT OVER THE HOVELS I'D INHABITED BEFORE.
IRIS-- WE CAN'T BE OUT HERE!
WHAT DO YOU MEAN, LIAN? I LOVE THE RAIN!
LIAN WAS ONE OF MY FIRST ACQUAINTANCES THERE. SHE HAD ARRIVED SEVERAL MONTHS EARLIER.
ALTHOUGH SHE WAS BARELY OLDER THAN ME, SHE TREATED ME LIKE A LITTLE SISTER...
WE NEED TO GET BACK INSIDE BEFORE--
...ALWAYS TRYING TO KEEP ME OUT OF TROUBLE.
YOU KIDS JUST MADE A BIG MISTAKE.
JUST LOOK DOWN. DON'T LOOK AT HER.
P--PLEASE. IT'S SO HOT AND STUFFY INSIDE. WE JUST WANT TO PLAY.
IN RETROSPECT, I PROBABLY SHOULD HAVE LISTENED TO MY FRIEND.
NO! PLEASE! WHY ARE YOU DOING THIS? NO!!!!
LIAN!!! ANYONE!!!! PLEASE!!!
BOOM BOOM BOOM

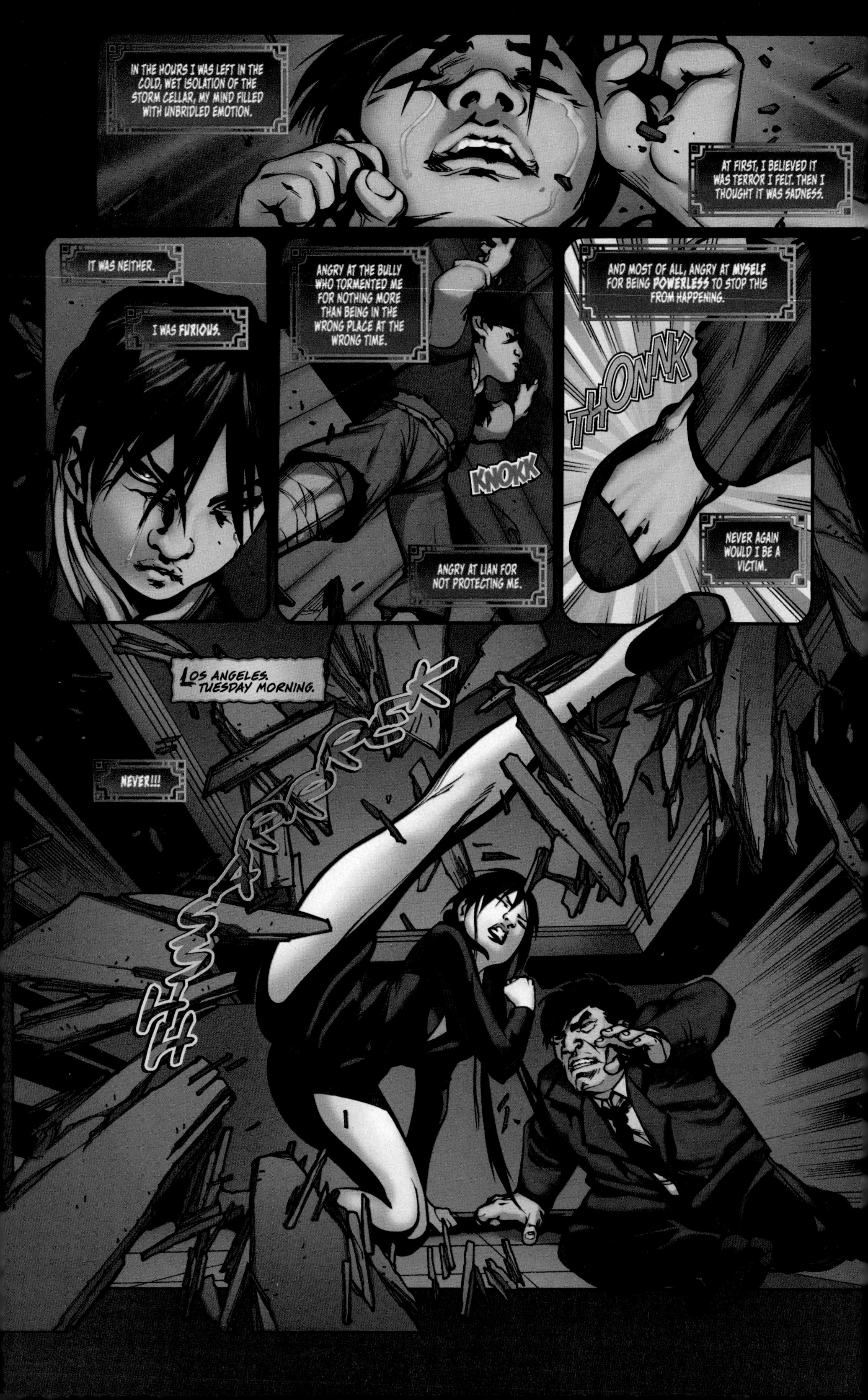

IN THE HOURS I WAS LEFT IN THE COLD, WET ISOLATION OF THE STORM CELLAR, MY MIND FILLED WITH UNBRIDLED EMOTION.
AT FIRST, I BELIEVED IT WAS TERROR I FELT. THEN I THOUGHT IT WAS SADNESS.
IT WAS NEITHER.
I WAS FURIOUS.
ANGRY AT THE BULLY WHO TORMENTED ME FOR NOTHING MORE THAN BEING IN THE WRONG PLACE AT THE WRONG TIME.
KNOKK
ANGRY AT LIAN FOR NOT PROTECTING ME.
AND MOST OF ALL, ANGRY AT MYSELF FOR BEING POWERLESS TO STOP THIS FROM HAPPENING.
THONNK
NEVER AGAIN WOULD I BE A VICTIM.
LOS ANGELES. TUESDAY MORNING.
NEVER!!!

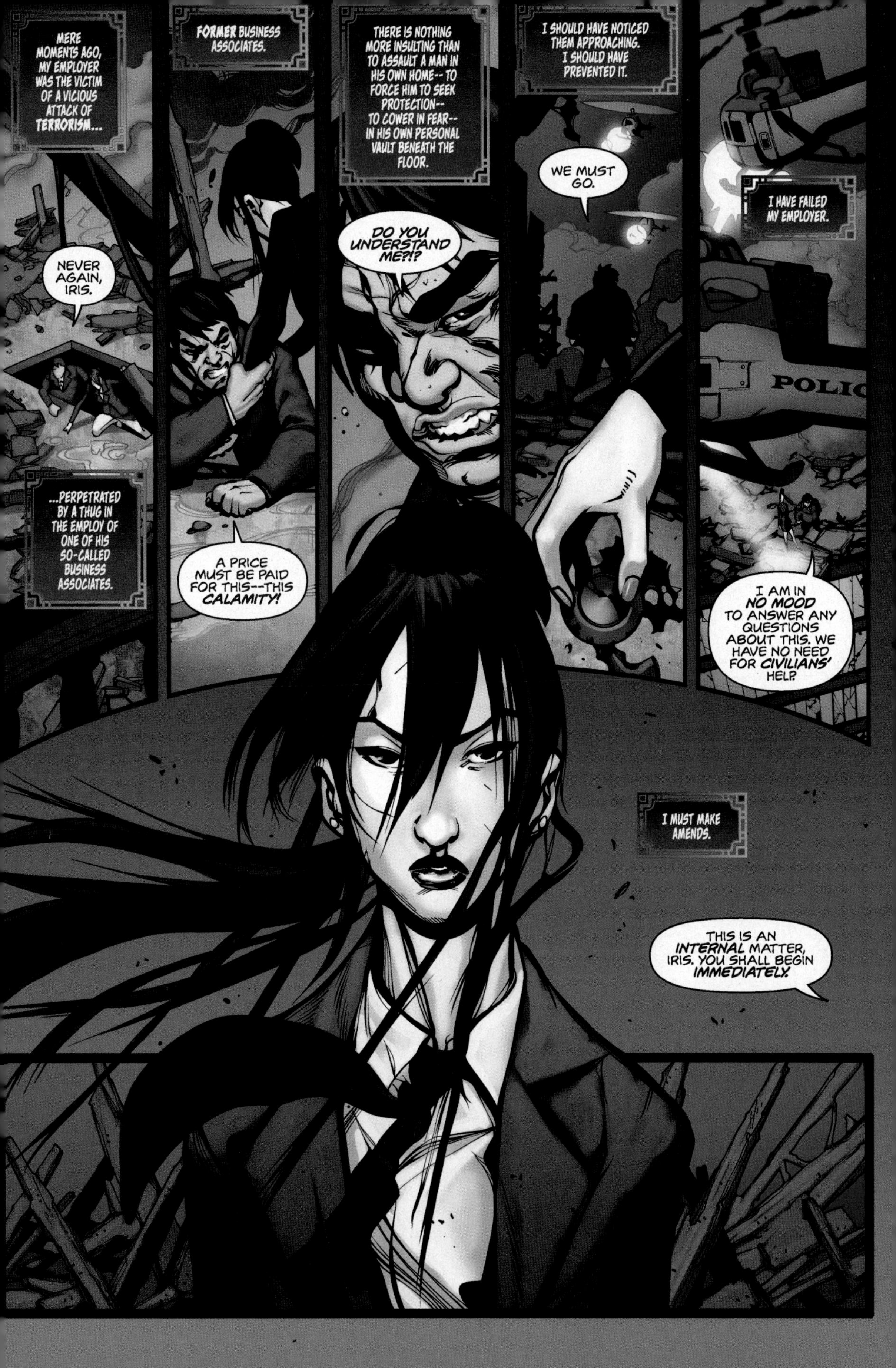
MERE MOMENTS AGO, MY EMPLOYER WAS THE VICTIM OF A VICIOUS ATTACK OF TERRORISM...
NEVER AGAIN, IRIS.
...PERPETRATED BY A THUG IN THE EMPLOY OF ONE OF HIS SO-CALLED BUSINESS ASSOCIATES.
FORMER BUSINESS ASSOCIATES.
A PRICE MUST BE PAID FOR THIS--THIS CALAMITY!
THERE IS NOTHING MORE INSULTING THAN TO ASSAULT A MAN IN HIS OWN HOME-- TO FORCE HIM TO SEEK PROTECTION-- TO COWER IN FEAR-- IN HIS OWN PERSONAL VAULT BENEATH THE FLOOR.
DO YOU UNDERSTAND ME?!?
I SHOULD HAVE NOTICED THEM APPROACHING. I SHOULD HAVE PREVENTED IT.
WE MUST GO.
I HAVE FAILED MY EMPLOYER.
POLIC
I AM IN NO MOOD TO ANSWER ANY QUESTIONS ABOUT THIS. WE HAVE NO NEED FOR CIVILIANS' HELP.
I MUST MAKE AMENDS.
THIS IS AN INTERNAL MATTER, IRIS. YOU SHALL BEGIN IMMEDIATELY.

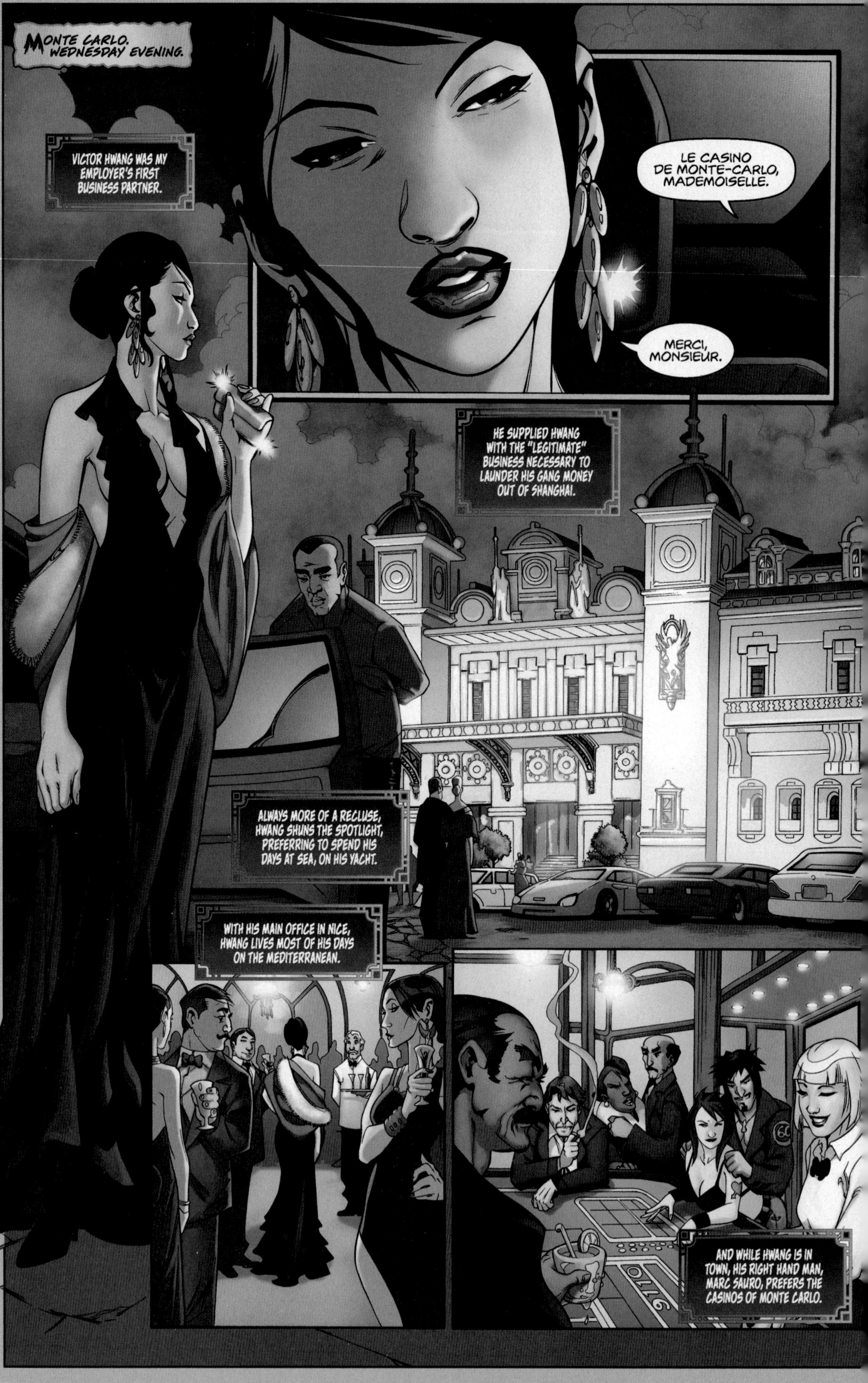
MONTE CARLO. WEDNESDAY EVENING.
VICTOR HWANG WAS MY EMPLOYER'S FIRST BUSINESS PARTNER.
LE CASINO DE MONTE-CARLO, MADEMOISELLE.
MERCI, MONSIEUR.
HE SUPPLIED HWANG WITH THE "LEGITIMATE" BUSINESS NECESSARY TO LAUNDER HIS GANG MONEY OUT OF SHANGHAI.
ALWAYS MORE OF A RECLUSE, HWANG SHUNS THE SPOTLIGHT, PREFERRING TO SPEND HIS DAYS AT SEA, ON HIS YACHT.
WITH HIS MAIN OFFICE IN NICE, HWANG LIVES MOST OF HIS DAYS ON THE MEDITERRANEAN.
AND WHILE HWANG IS IN TOWN, HIS RIGHT HAND MAN, MARC SAURO, PREFERS THE CASINOS OF MONTE CARLO.

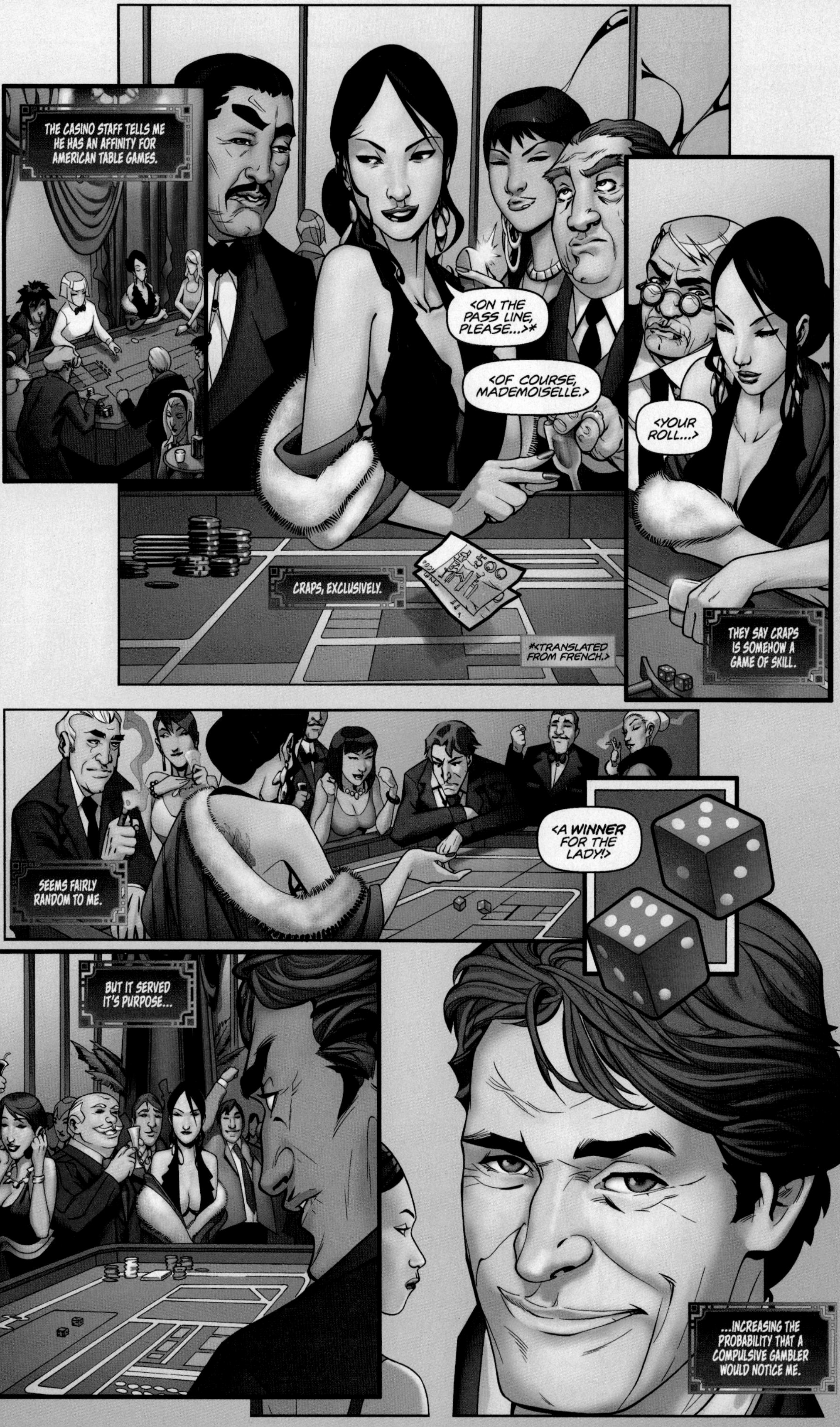
THE CASINO STAFF TELLS ME HE HAS AN AFFINITY FOR AMERICAN TABLE GAMES.
<ON THE PASS LINE, PLEASE...>*
<OF COURSE, MADEMOISELLE.>
CRAPS, EXCLUSIVELY.
*<TRANSLATED FROM FRENCH.>
<YOUR ROLL...>
THEY SAY CRAPS IS SOMEHOW A GAME OF SKILL.
SEEMS FAIRLY RANDOM TO ME.
<A WINNER FOR THE LADY!>
BUT IT SERVED IT'S PURPOSE...
...INCREASING THE PROBABILITY THAT A COMPULSIVE GAMBLER WOULD NOTICE ME.

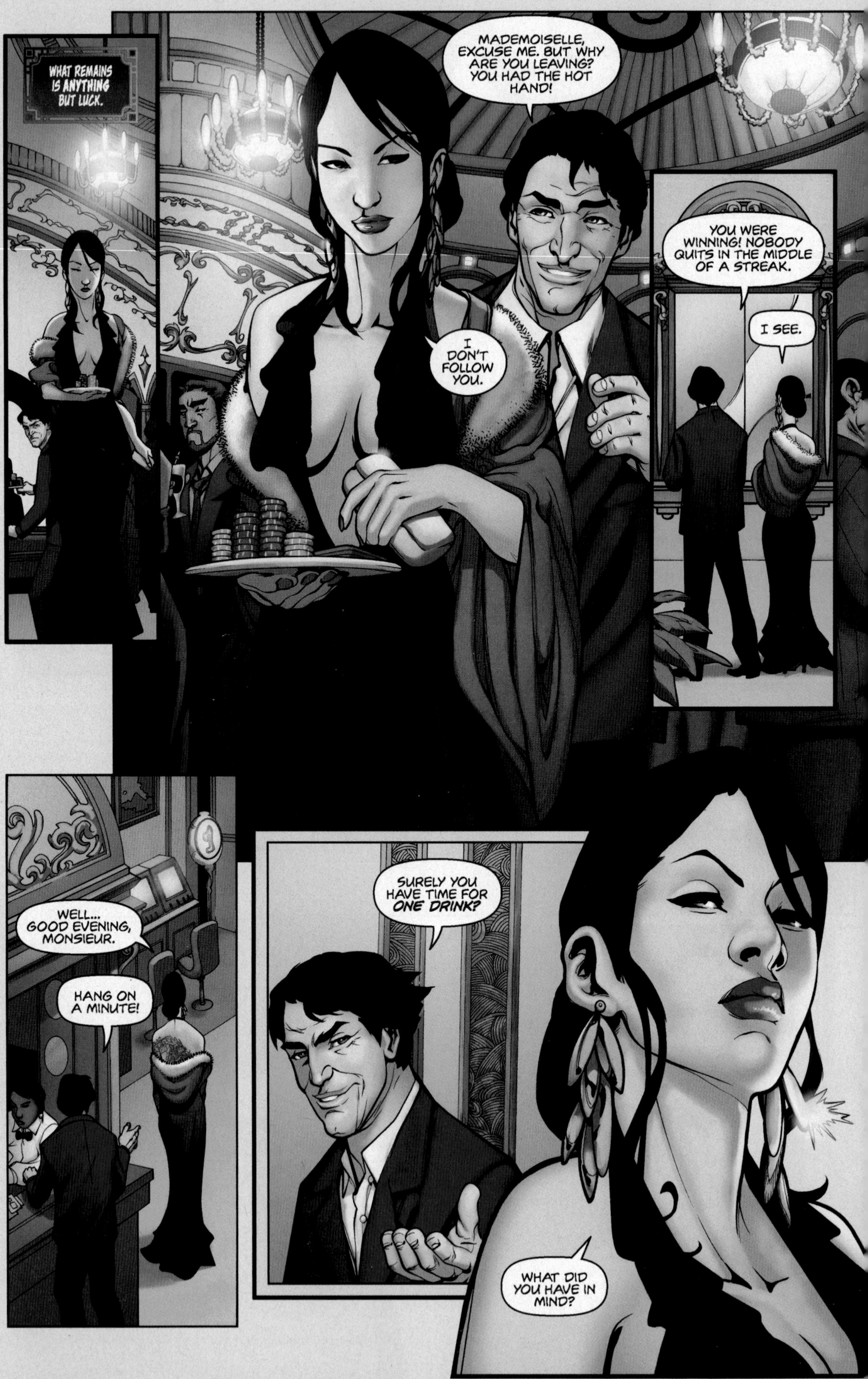
WHAT REMAINS IS ANYTHING BUT LUCK.
MADEMOISELLE, EXCUSE ME. BUT WHY ARE YOU LEAVING? YOU HAD THE HOT HAND!
I DON'T FOLLOW YOU.
YOU WERE WINNING! NOBODY QUITS IN THE MIDDLE OF A STREAK.
I SEE.
WELL... GOOD EVENING, MONSIEUR.
HANG ON A MINUTE!
SURELY YOU HAVE TIME FOR ONE DRINK?
WHAT DID YOU HAVE IN MIND?

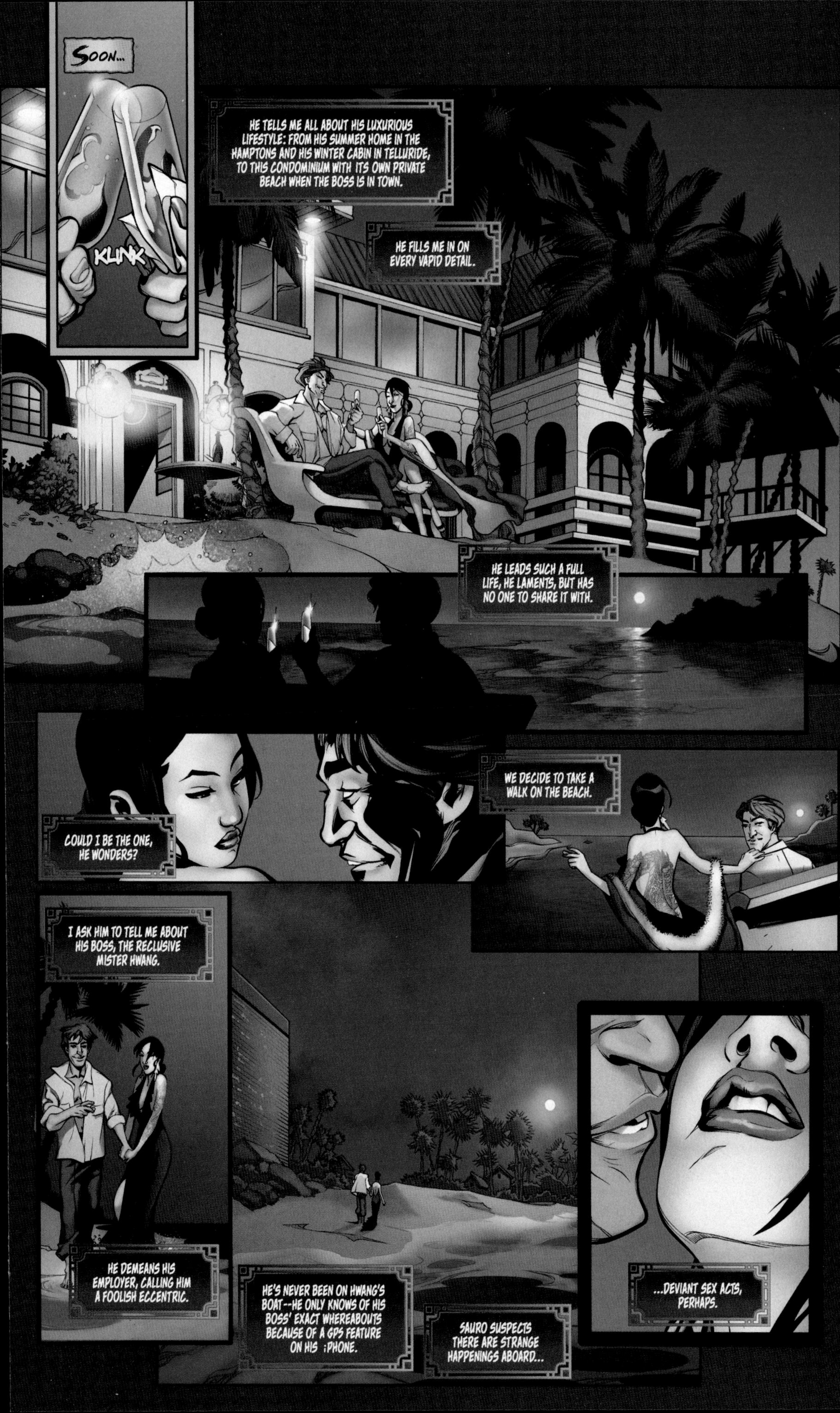
SOON...
KLINK
HE TELLS ME ALL ABOUT HIS LUXURIOUS LIFESTYLE: FROM HIS SUMMER HOME IN THE HAMPTONS AND HIS WINTER CABIN IN TELLURIDE, TO THIS CONDOMINIUM WITH ITS OWN PRIVATE BEACH WHEN THE BOSS IS IN TOWN.
HE FILLS ME IN ON EVERY VAPID DETAIL.
HE LEADS SUCH A FULL LIFE, HE LAMENTS, BUT HAS NO ONE TO SHARE IT WITH.
COULD I BE THE ONE, HE WONDERS?
WE DECIDE TO TAKE A WALK ON THE BEACH.
I ASK HIM TO TELL ME ABOUT HIS BOSS, THE RECLUSIVE MISTER HWANG.
HE DEMEANS HIS EMPLOYER, CALLING HIM A FOOLISH ECCENTRIC.
HE'S NEVER BEEN ON HWANG'S BOAT--HE ONLY KNOWS OF HIS BOSS' EXACT WHEREABOUTS BECAUSE OF A GPS FEATURE ON HIS iPHONE.
SAURO SUSPECTS THERE ARE STRANGE HAPPENINGS ABOARD...
...DEVIANT SEX ACTS, PERHAPS.

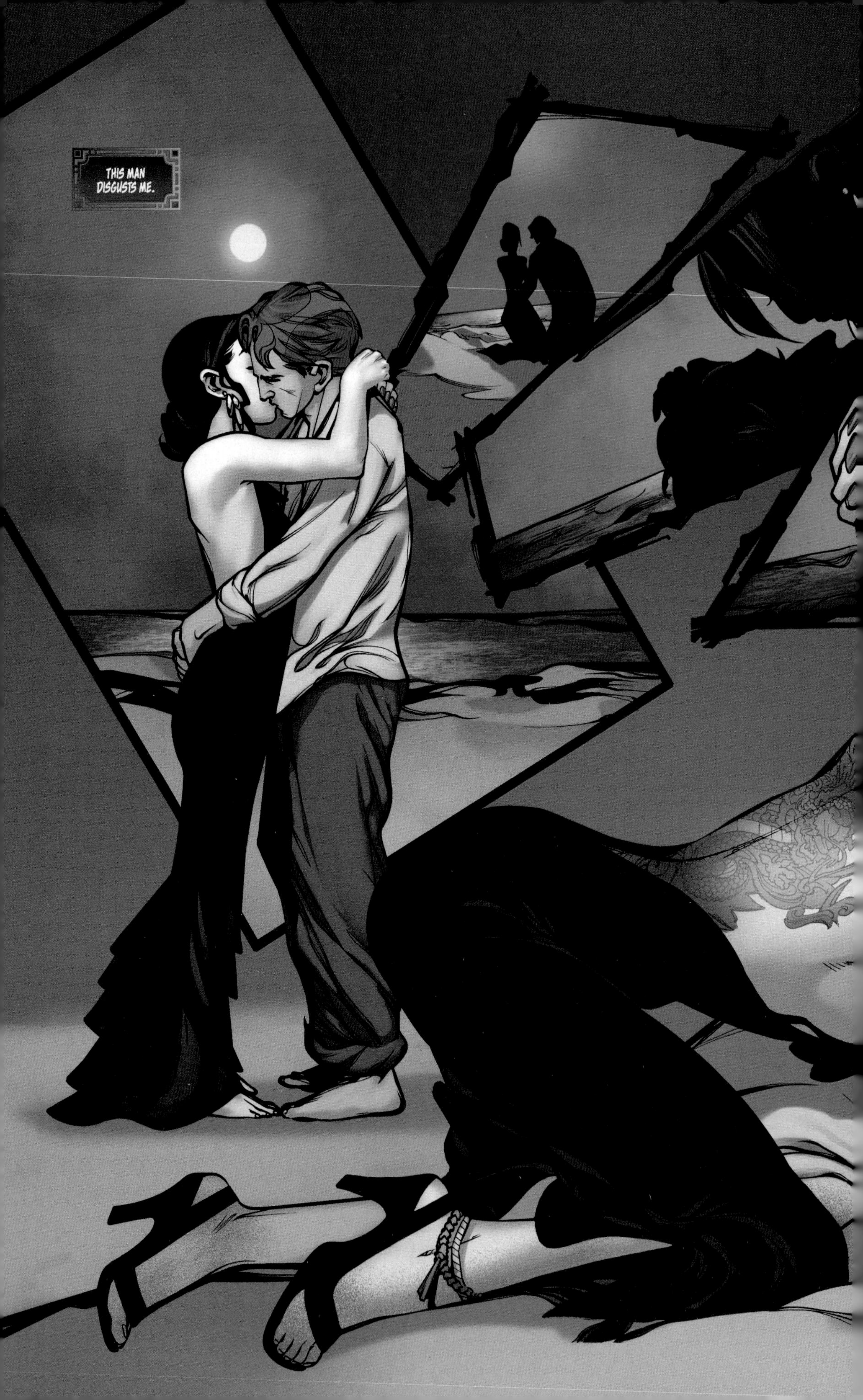
THIS MAN
DISGUSTS ME.

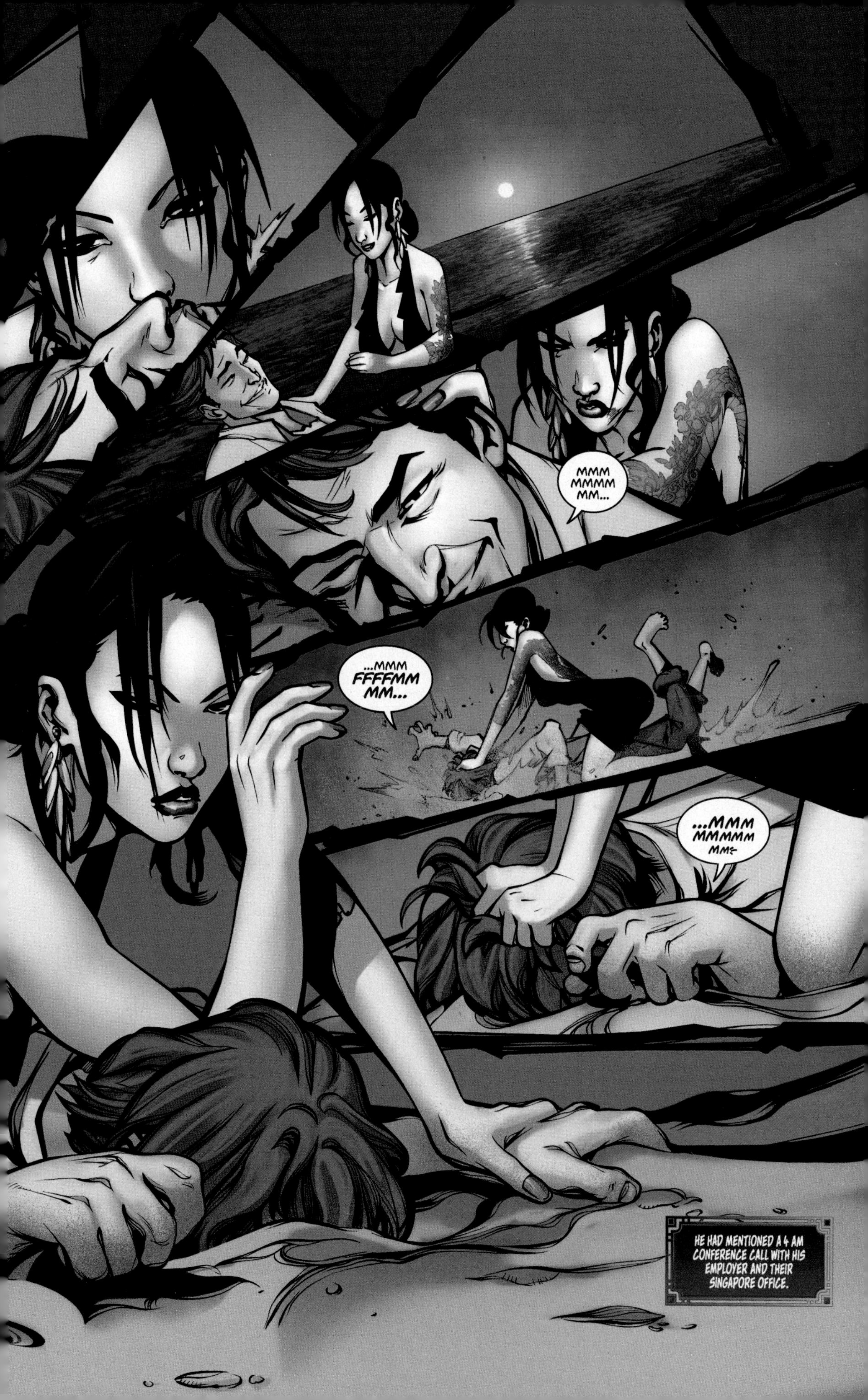
MMM MMMM MM...
...MMM FFFFMM MM...
...MMM MMMMM MM-
HE HAD MENTIONED A 4 AM CONFERENCE CALL WITH HIS EMPLOYER AND THEIR SINGAPORE OFFICE.

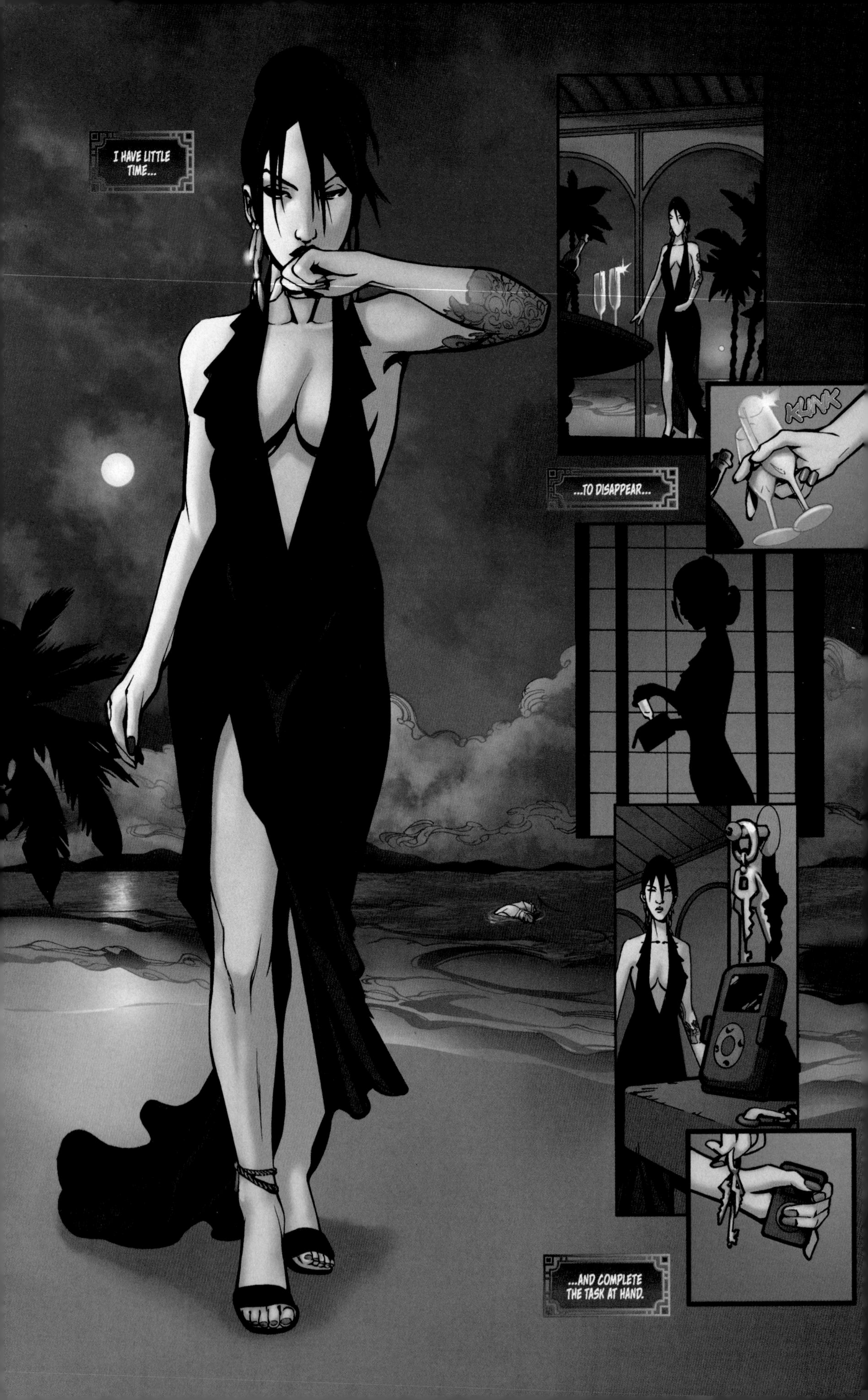
I HAVE LITTLE TIME...
...TO DISAPPEAR...
KLINK
...AND COMPLETE THE TASK AT HAND.

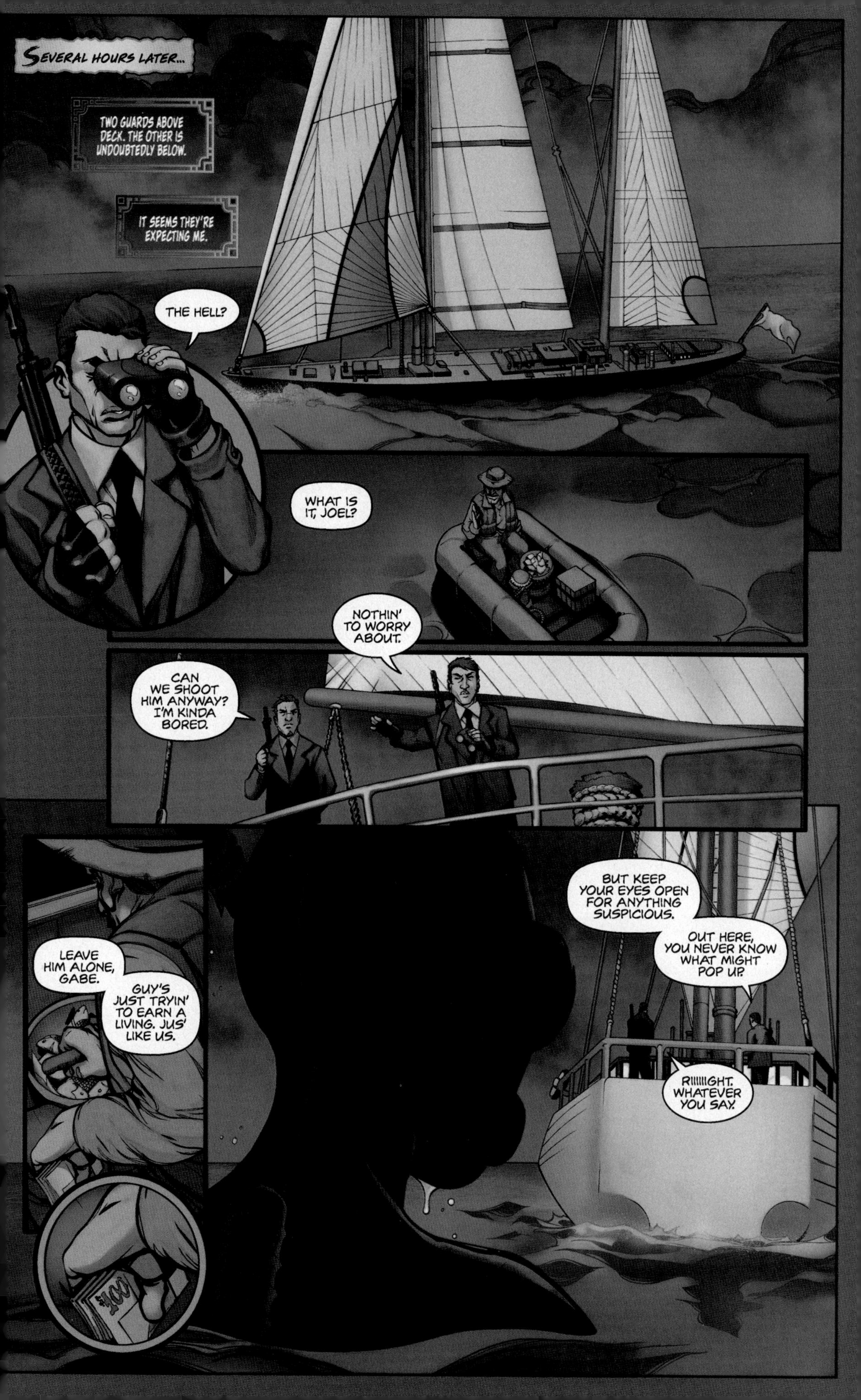
SEVERAL HOURS LATER...
TWO GUARDS ABOVE DECK. THE OTHER IS UNDOUBTEDLY BELOW.
IT SEEMS THEY'RE EXPECTING ME.
THE HELL?
WHAT IS IT, JOEL?
NOTHIN' TO WORRY ABOUT.
CAN WE SHOOT HIM ANYWAY? I'M KINDA BORED.
LEAVE HIM ALONE, GABE.
GUY'S JUST TRYIN' TO EARN A LIVING. JUS' LIKE US.
BUT KEEP YOUR EYES OPEN FOR ANYTHING SUSPICIOUS.
OUT HERE, YOU NEVER KNOW WHAT MIGHT POP UP.
RIIIIIGHT. WHATEVER YOU SAY.
$100

WELL, COULD WE AT LEAST ASK THE GUY FOR ONE OF HIS FISH? I'M STARVIN'.
HEY, YOU THINK THE GALLEY IS STILL OPEN? I COULD USE A CREPE.
HOW THE HELL SHOULD I KNOW? GO SEE FOR YOURSELF.
ALL RIGHT. JEEZ-- A GUY CAN'T ASK A FREAKIN' QUESTION WITHOUT--HNH?
THWSHH
HRK? HRKLLLKK KK--
HKKKLL LLLAAK K--
JESUS, GABE! I GET IT. YOU'RE HUNGRY! JUST GO DOWNSTAIRS AND--
GABE?!?
THWSSHK
SPLOOSH

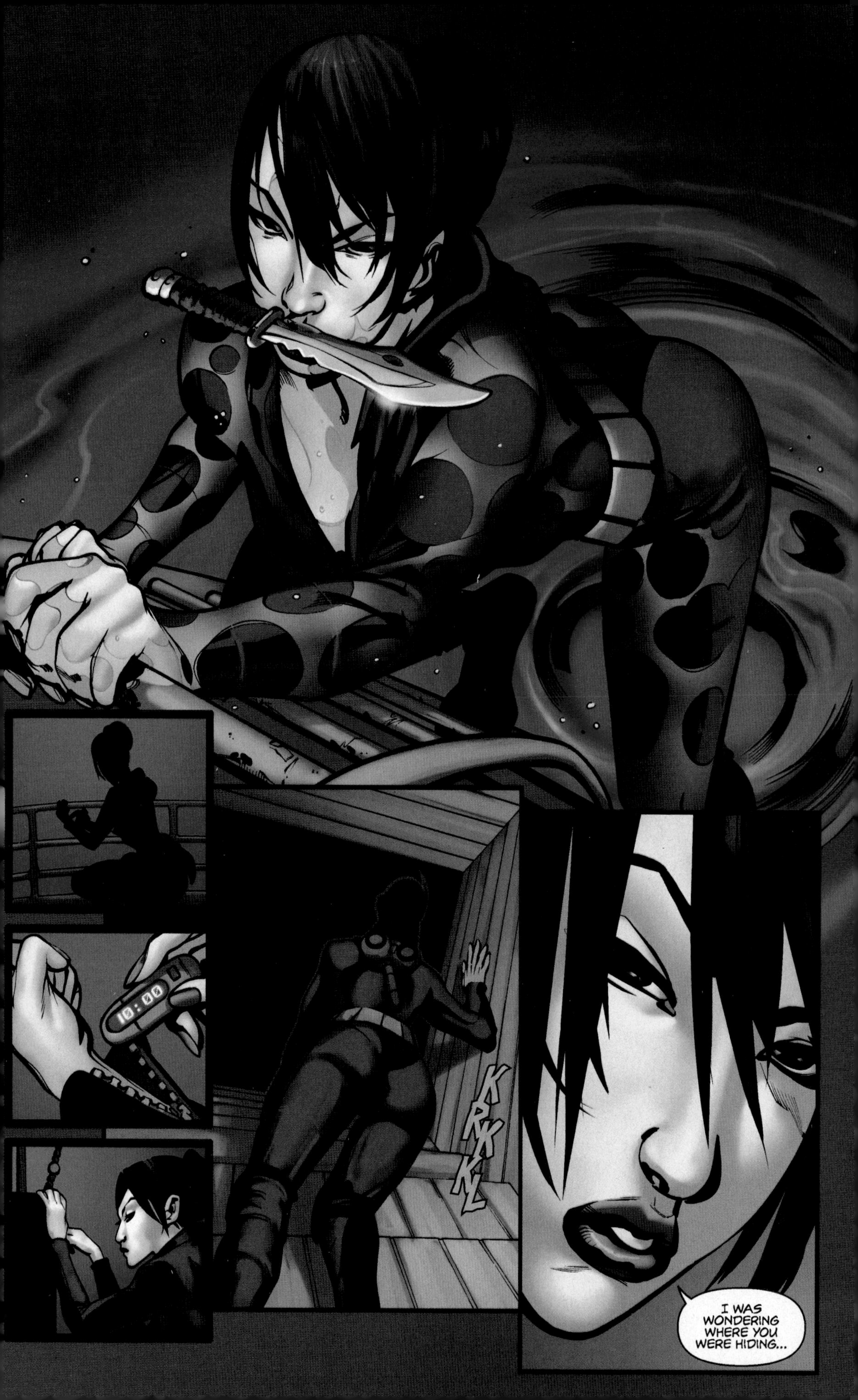
10:00
KRKKL
I WAS WONDERING WHERE YOU WERE HIDING...

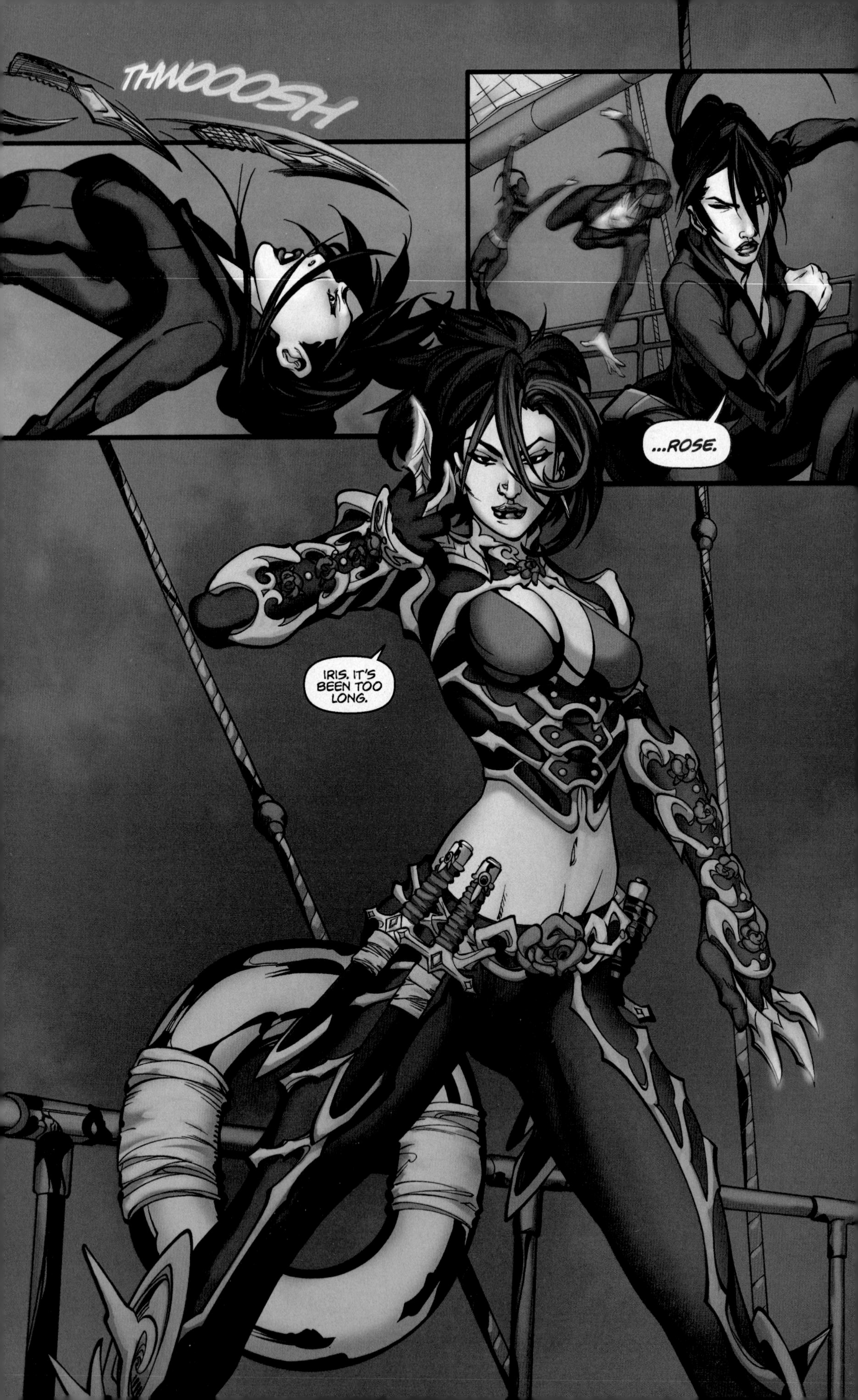
THWOOOSH
...ROSE.
IRIS. IT'S BEEN TOO LONG.

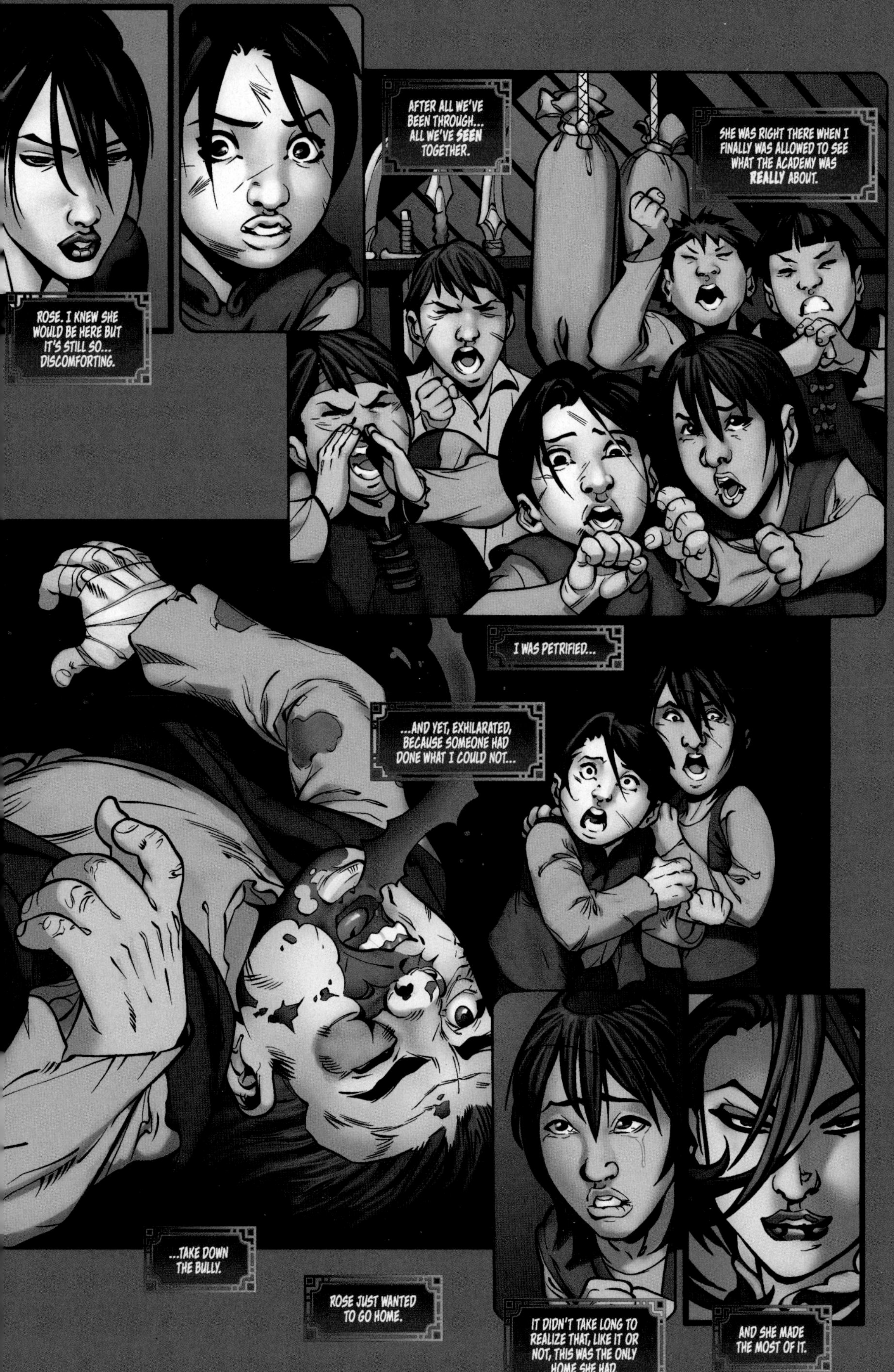
ROSE. I KNEW SHE WOULD BE HERE BUT IT'S STILL SO... DISCOMFORTING.
AFTER ALL WE'VE BEEN THROUGH... ALL WE'VE SEEN TOGETHER.
SHE WAS RIGHT THERE WHEN I FINALLY WAS ALLOWED TO SEE WHAT THE ACADEMY WAS REALLY ABOUT.
I WAS PETRIFIED...
...AND YET, EXHILARATED, BECAUSE SOMEONE HAD DONE WHAT I COULD NOT...
...TAKE DOWN THE BULLY.
ROSE JUST WANTED TO GO HOME.
IT DIDN'T TAKE LONG TO REALIZE THAT, LIKE IT OR NOT, THIS WAS THE ONLY HOME SHE HAD.
AND SHE MADE THE MOST OF IT.

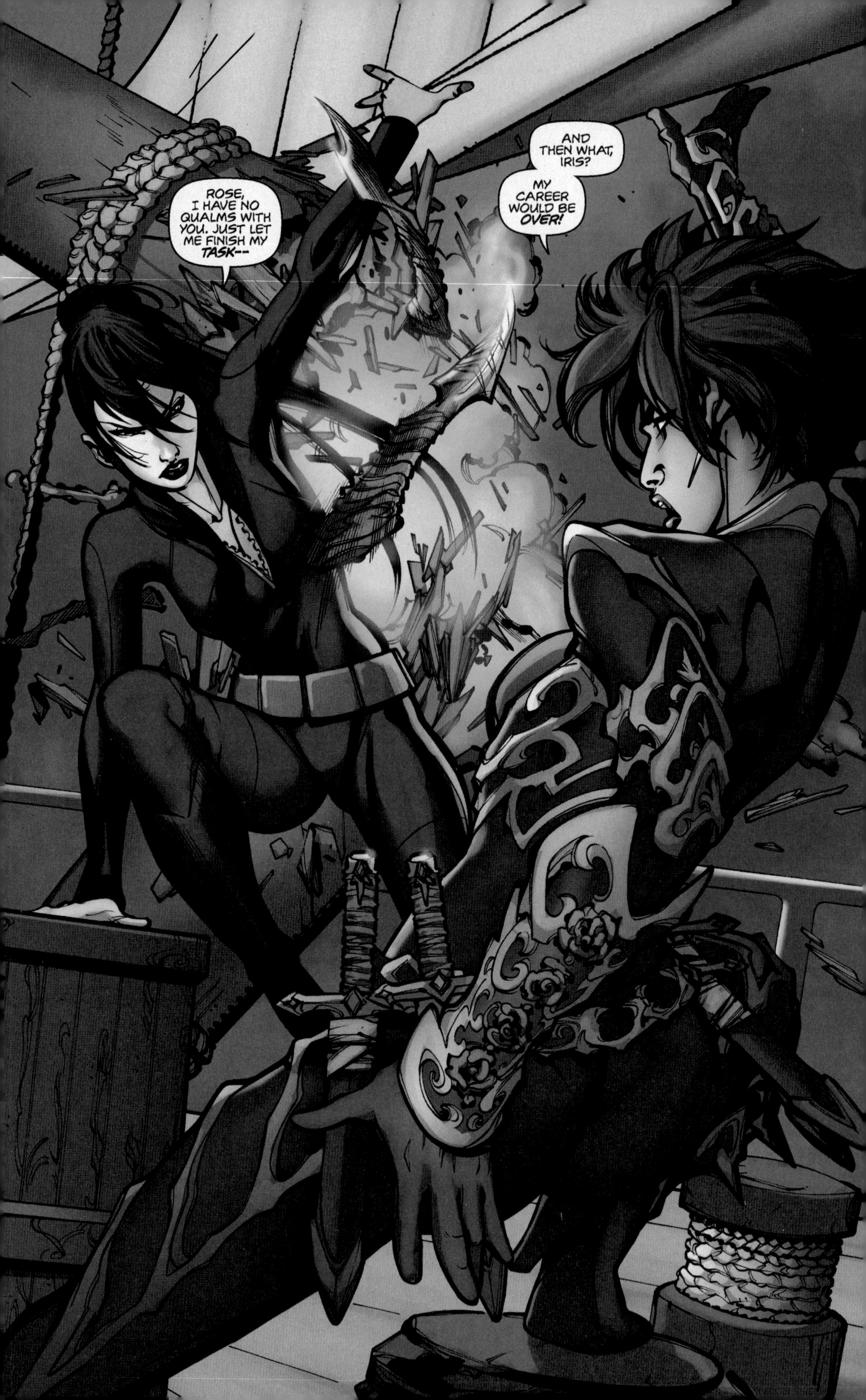
ROSE, I HAVE NO QUALMS WITH YOU. JUST LET ME FINISH MY *TASK*--
AND THEN WHAT, IRIS?
MY CAREER WOULD BE *OVER!*

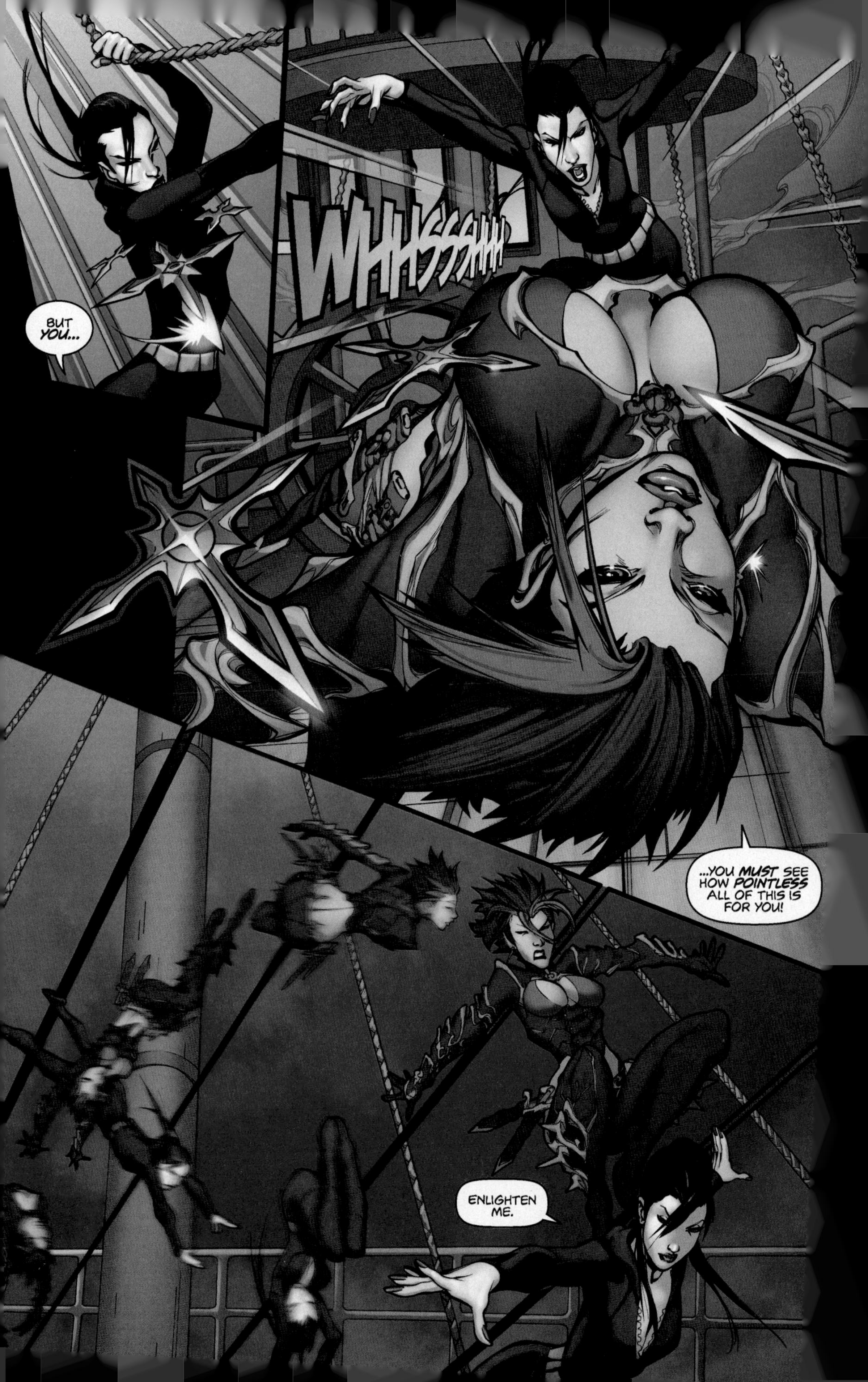
WHHSSHHH
BUT YOU...
...YOU MUST SEE HOW POINTLESS ALL OF THIS IS FOR YOU!
ENLIGHTEN ME.

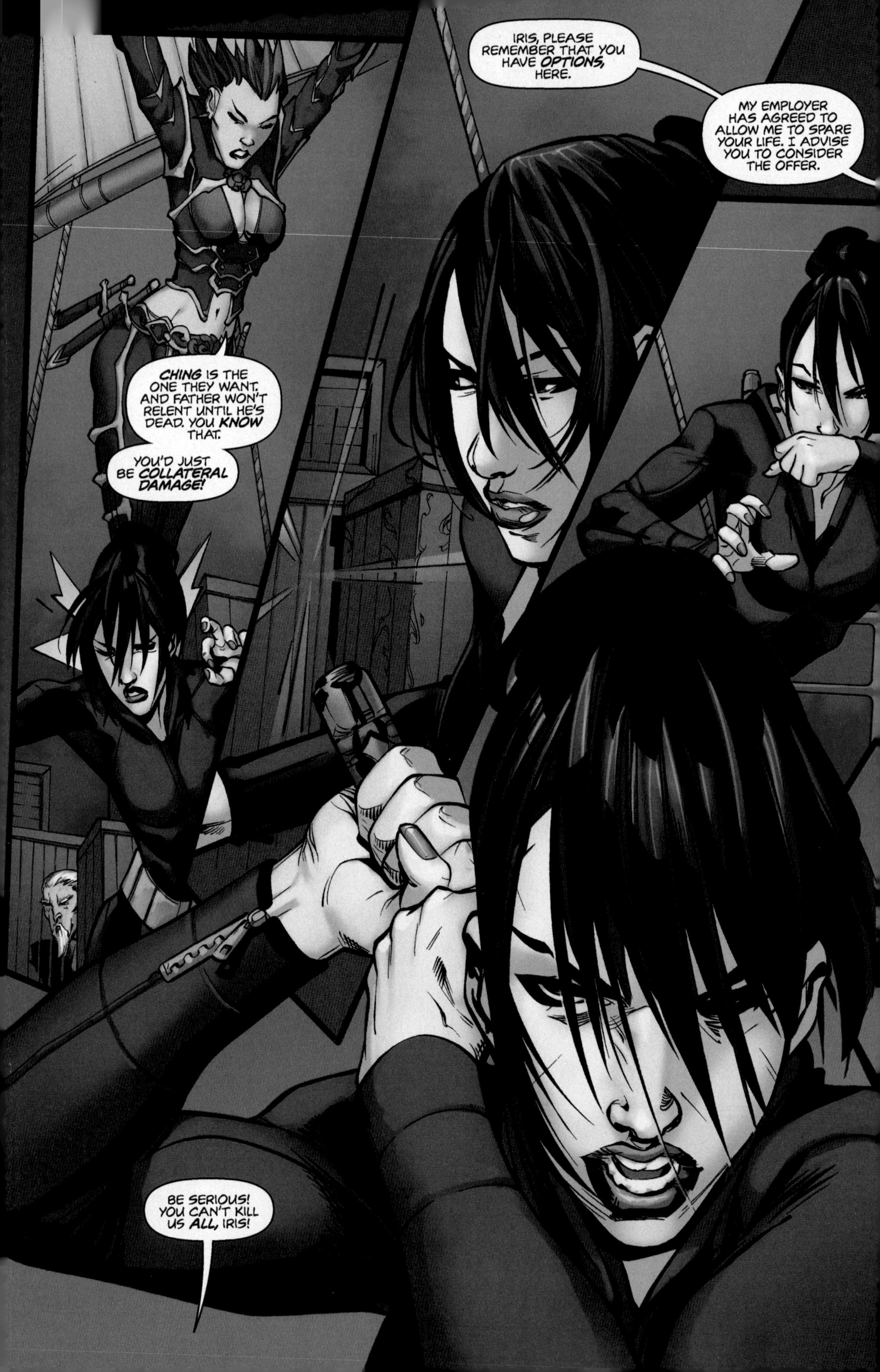
IRIS, PLEASE REMEMBER THAT YOU HAVE OPTIONS, HERE.
MY EMPLOYER HAS AGREED TO ALLOW ME TO SPARE YOUR LIFE. I ADVISE YOU TO CONSIDER THE OFFER.
CHING IS THE ONE THEY WANT. AND FATHER WON'T RELENT UNTIL HE'S DEAD. YOU KNOW THAT.
YOU'D JUST BE COLLATERAL DAMAGE!
BE SERIOUS! YOU CAN'T KILL US ALL, IRIS!

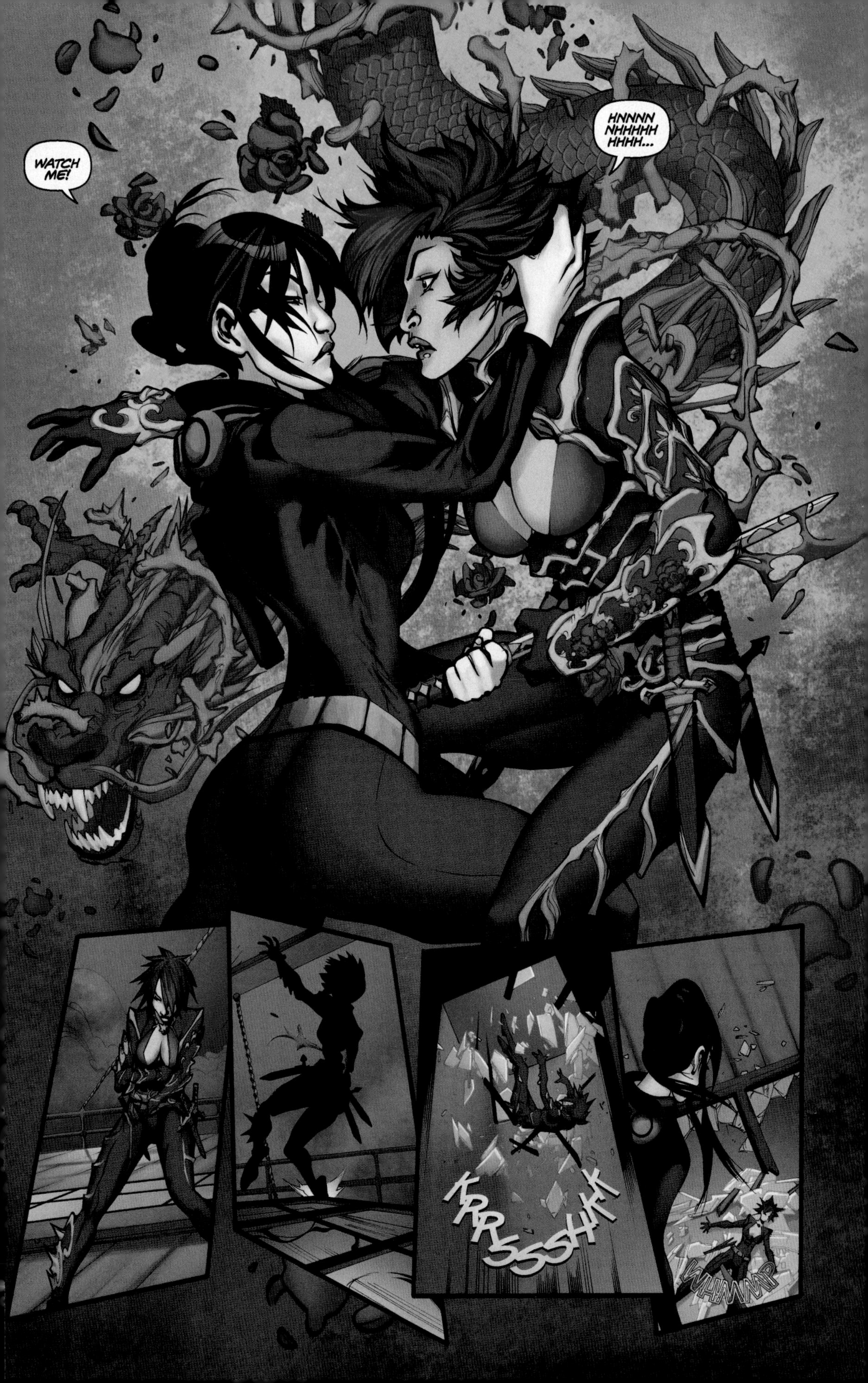
WATCH ME!
HNNNN NHHHHH HHHH...
KRRSSSHKK
WHMMP

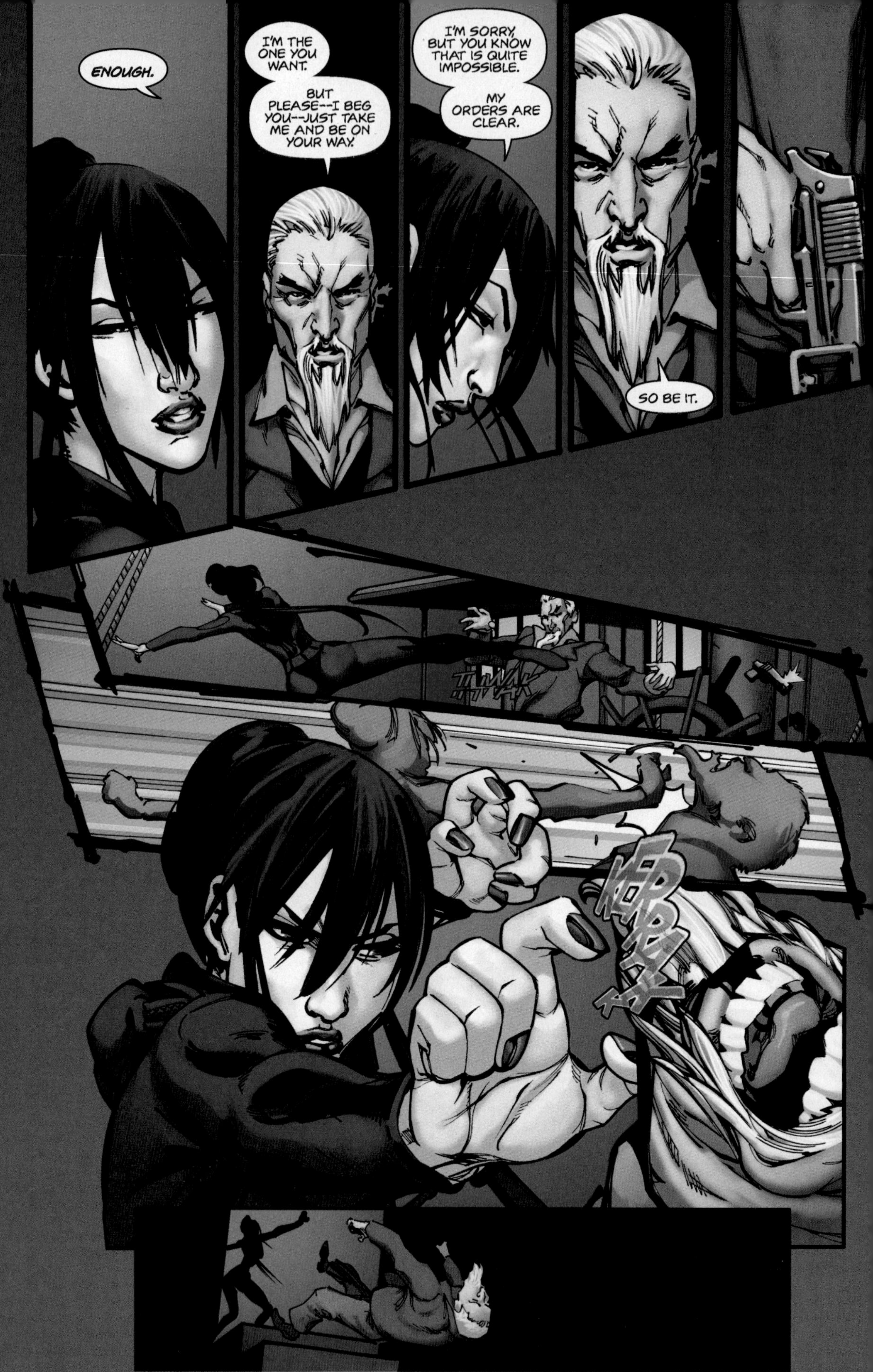
ENOUGH.
I'M THE ONE YOU WANT.
BUT PLEASE--I BEG YOU--JUST TAKE ME AND BE ON YOUR WAY.
I'M SORRY, BUT YOU KNOW THAT IS QUITE IMPOSSIBLE.
MY ORDERS ARE CLEAR.
SO BE IT.

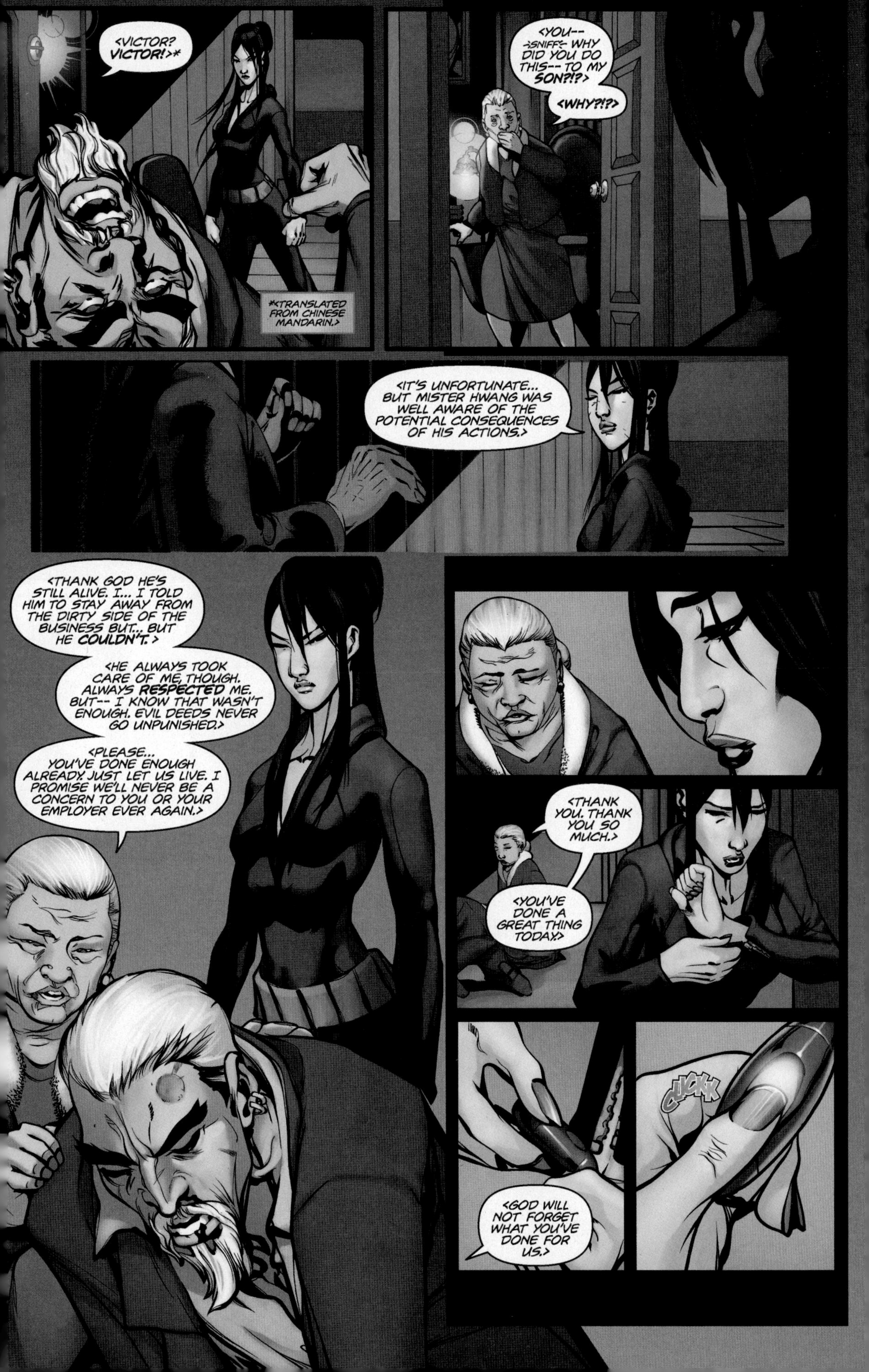
<VICTOR? VICTOR!>*
*TRANSLATED FROM CHINESE MANDARIN.>
<YOU-- -SNIFF- WHY DID YOU DO THIS-- TO MY SON?!?>
<WHY?!?>
<IT'S UNFORTUNATE... BUT MISTER HWANG WAS WELL AWARE OF THE POTENTIAL CONSEQUENCES OF HIS ACTIONS.>
<THANK GOD HE'S STILL ALIVE. I... I TOLD HIM TO STAY AWAY FROM THE DIRTY SIDE OF THE BUSINESS BUT... BUT HE COULDN'T.>
<HE ALWAYS TOOK CARE OF ME, THOUGH. ALWAYS RESPECTED ME. BUT-- I KNOW THAT WASN'T ENOUGH. EVIL DEEDS NEVER GO UNPUNISHED.>
<PLEASE... YOU'VE DONE ENOUGH ALREADY. JUST LET US LIVE. I PROMISE WE'LL NEVER BE A CONCERN TO YOU OR YOUR EMPLOYER EVER AGAIN.>
<THANK YOU. THANK YOU SO MUCH.>
<YOU'VE DONE A GREAT THING TODAY.>
CLICKK
<GOD WILL NOT FORGET WHAT YOU'VE DONE FOR US.>

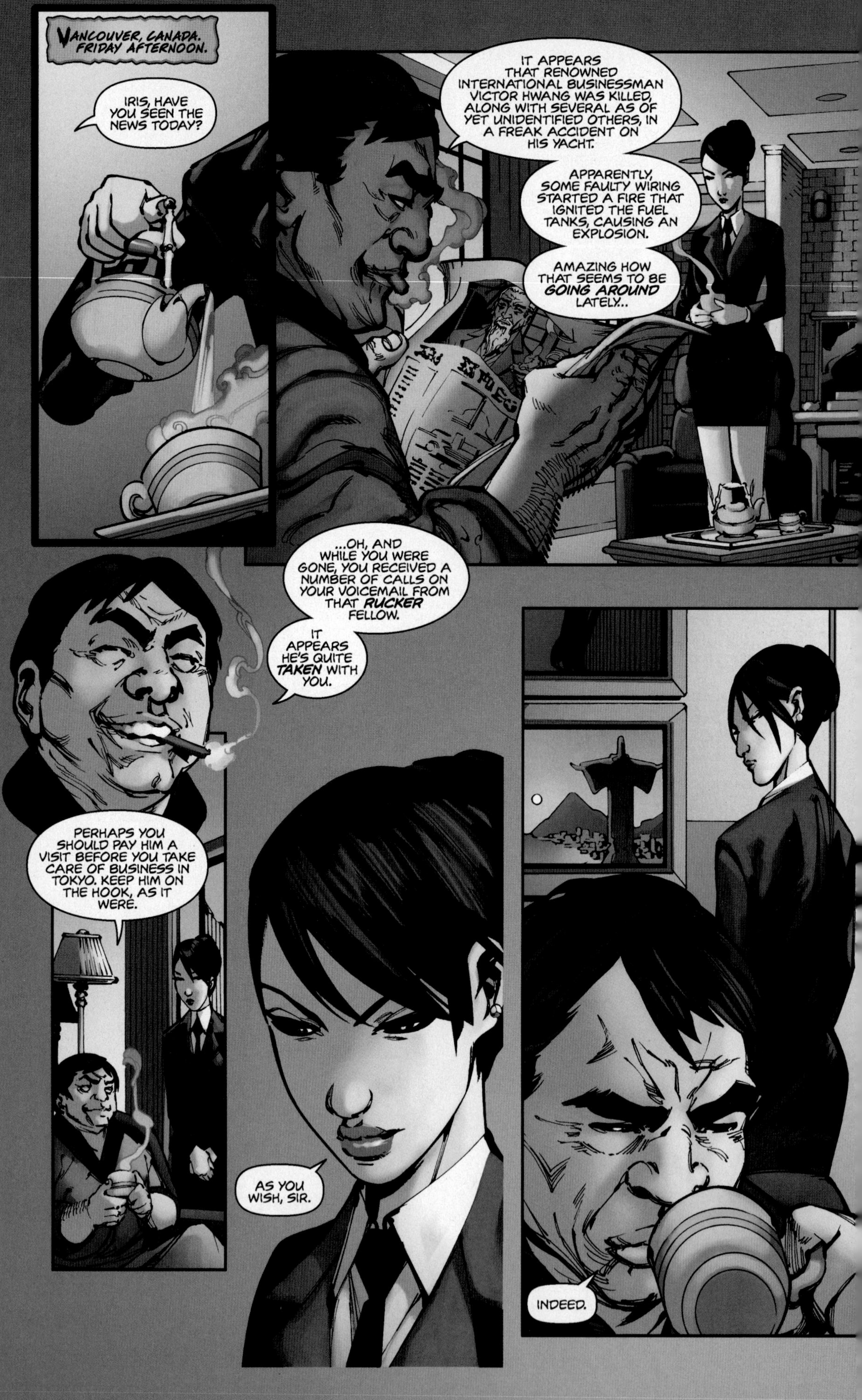
VANCOUVER, CANADA. FRIDAY AFTERNOON.
IRIS, HAVE YOU SEEN THE NEWS TODAY?
IT APPEARS THAT RENOWNED INTERNATIONAL BUSINESSMAN VICTOR HWANG WAS KILLED, ALONG WITH SEVERAL AS OF YET UNIDENTIFIED OTHERS, IN A FREAK ACCIDENT ON HIS YACHT.
APPARENTLY, SOME FAULTY WIRING STARTED A FIRE THAT IGNITED THE FUEL TANKS, CAUSING AN EXPLOSION.
AMAZING HOW THAT SEEMS TO BE GOING AROUND LATELY...
...OH, AND WHILE YOU WERE GONE, YOU RECEIVED A NUMBER OF CALLS ON YOUR VOICEMAIL FROM THAT RUCKER FELLOW.
IT APPEARS HE'S QUITE TAKEN WITH YOU.
PERHAPS YOU SHOULD PAY HIM A VISIT BEFORE YOU TAKE CARE OF BUSINESS IN TOKYO. KEEP HIM ON THE HOOK, AS IT WERE.
AS YOU WISH, SIR.
INDEED.

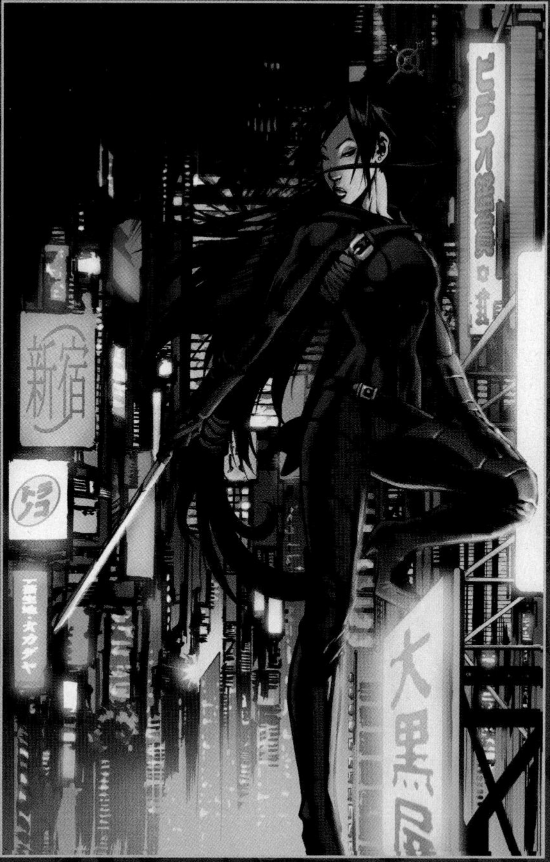
新宿

Executive Assistant: Iris #3
Cover A
Eduardo FRANCISCO
John STARR

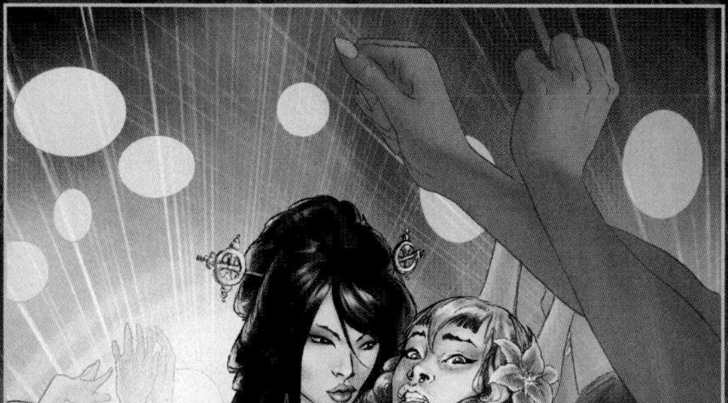

Executive Assistant: Iris #3
Cover B
Joe BENITEZ
Peter STEIGERWALD

EXECUTIVE ASSISTANT: IRIS #3
Cover C
MARCUS TO
PETER STEIGERWALD

EXECUTIVE ASSISTANT: IRIS #3
Long Beach Comic Con Exclusive Cover D
EDUARDO FRANCISCO
PETER STEIGERWALD

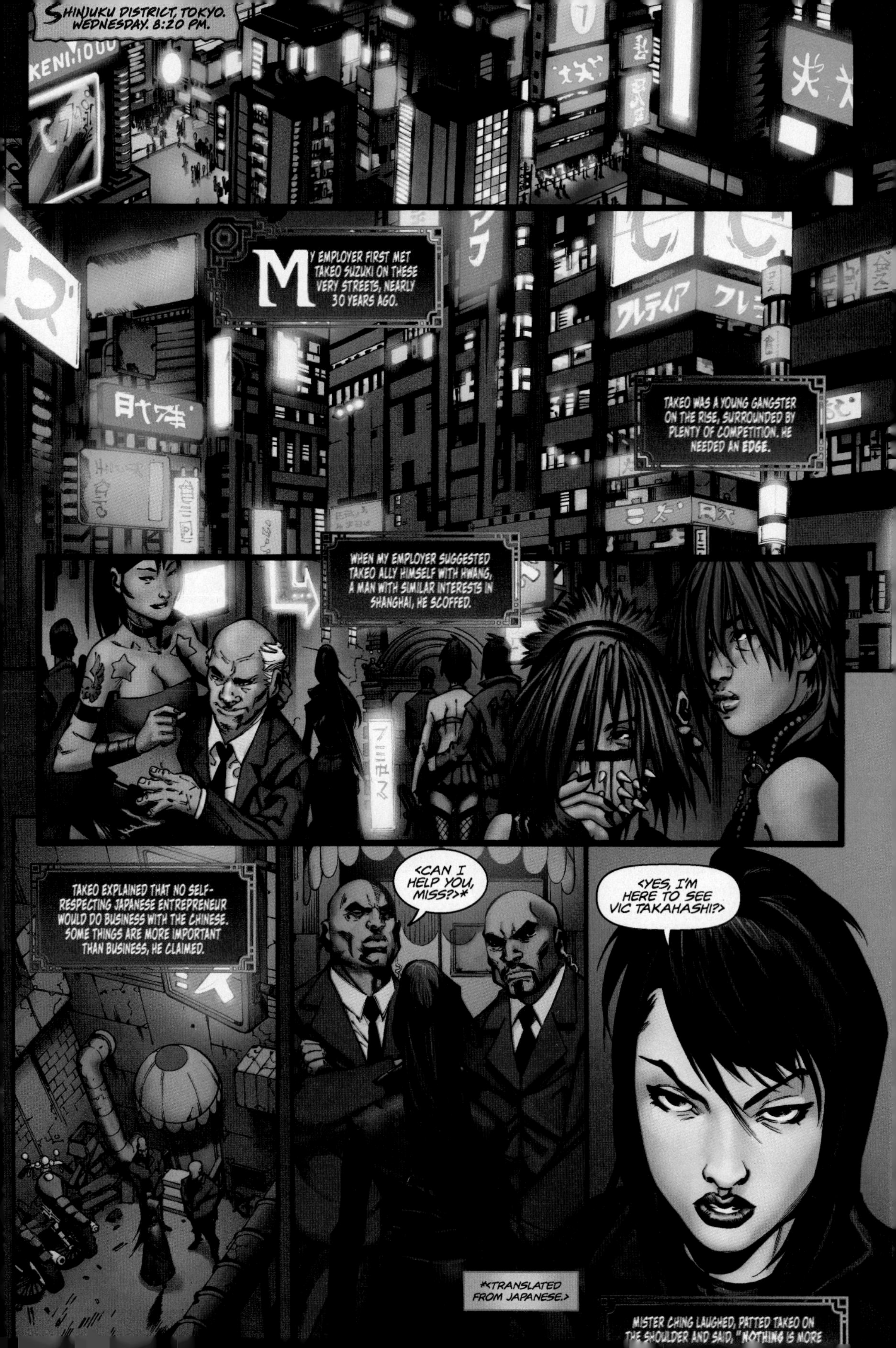

SHINJUKU DISTRICT, TOKYO. WEDNESDAY. 8:20 PM.
MY EMPLOYER FIRST MET TAKEO SUZUKI ON THESE VERY STREETS, NEARLY 30 YEARS AGO.
TAKEO WAS A YOUNG GANGSTER ON THE RISE, SURROUNDED BY PLENTY OF COMPETITION. HE NEEDED AN EDGE.
WHEN MY EMPLOYER SUGGESTED TAKEO ALLY HIMSELF WITH HWANG, A MAN WITH SIMILAR INTERESTS IN SHANGHAI, HE SCOFFED.
TAKEO EXPLAINED THAT NO SELF-RESPECTING JAPANESE ENTREPRENEUR WOULD DO BUSINESS WITH THE CHINESE. SOME THINGS ARE MORE IMPORTANT THAN BUSINESS, HE CLAIMED.
<CAN I HELP YOU, MISS?>*
<YES, I'M HERE TO SEE VIC TAKAHASHI?>
*<TRANSLATED FROM JAPANESE.>
MISTER CHING LAUGHED, PATTED TAKEO ON THE SHOULDER AND SAID, "NOTHING IS MORE

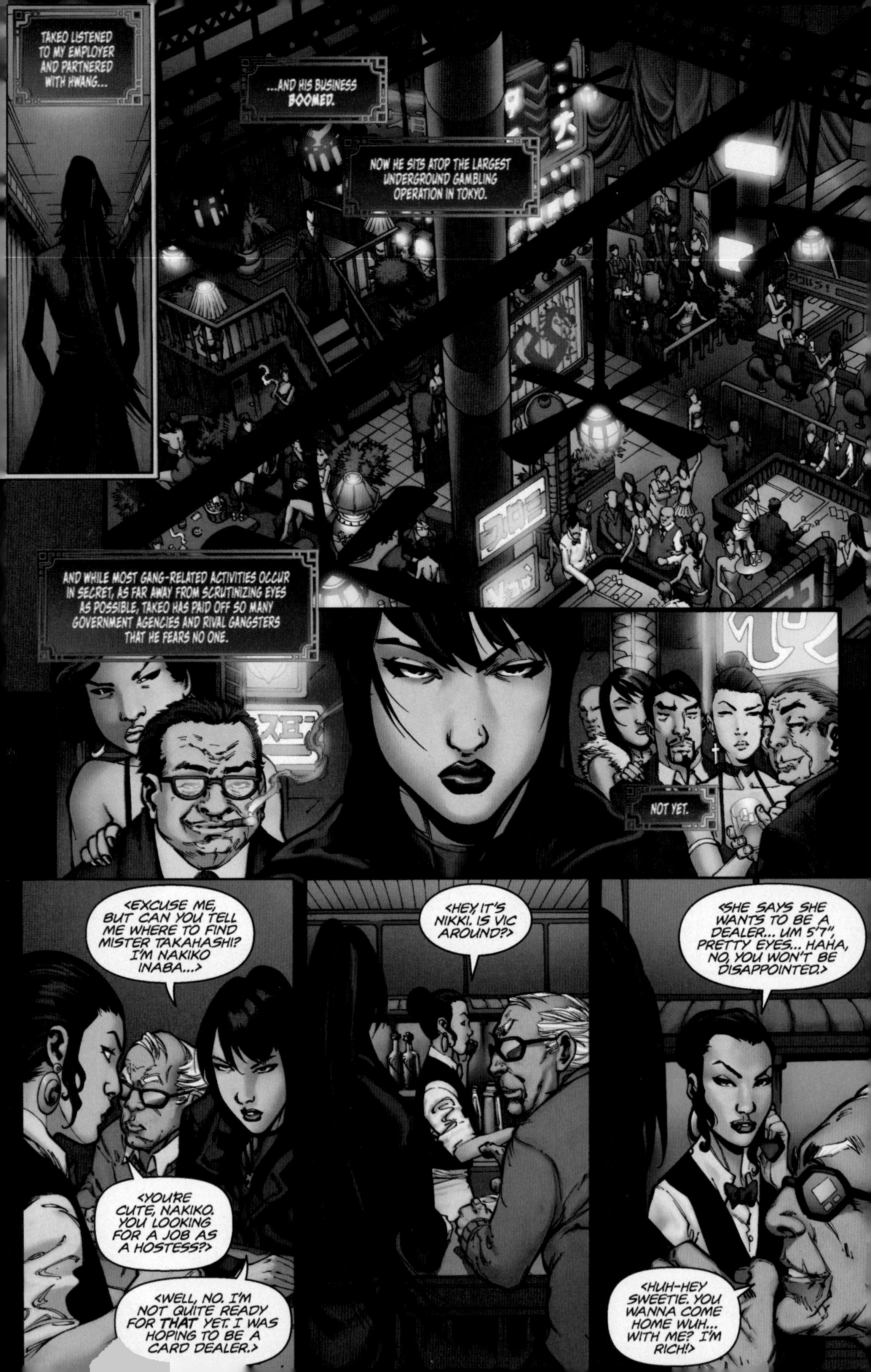
TAKEO LISTENED TO MY EMPLOYER AND PARTNERED WITH HWANG...
...AND HIS BUSINESS BOOMED.
NOW HE SITS ATOP THE LARGEST UNDERGROUND GAMBLING OPERATION IN TOKYO.
AND WHILE MOST GANG-RELATED ACTIVITIES OCCUR IN SECRET, AS FAR AWAY FROM SCRUTINIZING EYES AS POSSIBLE, TAKEO HAS PAID OFF SO MANY GOVERNMENT AGENCIES AND RIVAL GANGSTERS THAT HE FEARS NO ONE.
NOT YET.
<EXCUSE ME, BUT CAN YOU TELL ME WHERE TO FIND MISTER TAKAHASHI? I'M NAKIKO INABA...>
<YOU'RE CUTE, NAKIKO. YOU LOOKING FOR A JOB AS A HOSTESS?>
<WELL, NO. I'M NOT QUITE READY FOR THAT YET. I WAS HOPING TO BE A CARD DEALER.>
<HEY, IT'S NIKKI. IS VIC AROUND?>
<SHE SAYS SHE WANTS TO BE A DEALER... UM 5'7", PRETTY EYES... HAHA, NO, YOU WON'T BE DISAPPOINTED.>
<HUH-HEY SWEETIE. YOU WANNA COME HOME WUH... WITH ME? I'M RICH!>

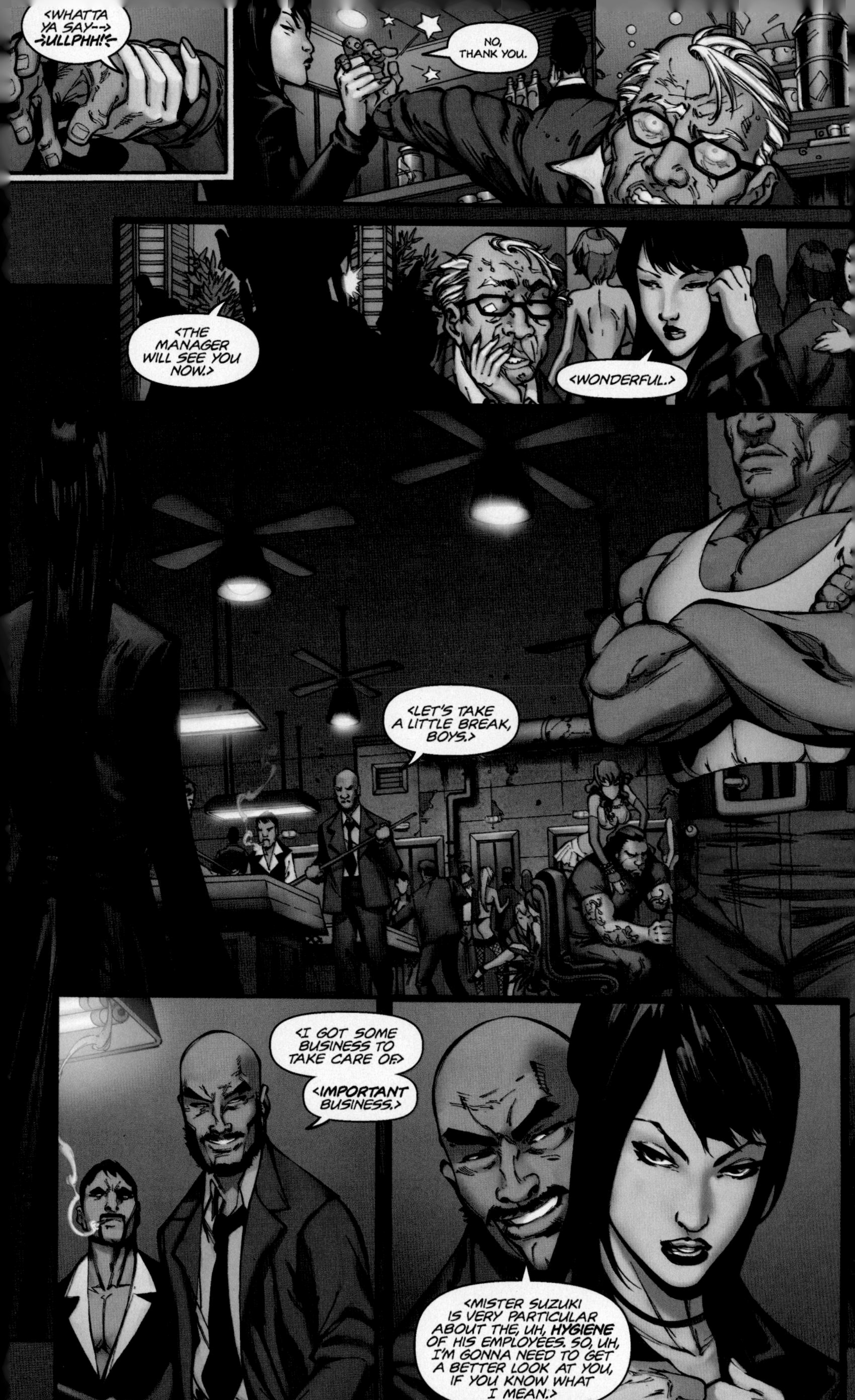
<WHATTA YA SAY-->
-ULLPHH!-
NO, THANK YOU.
<THE MANAGER WILL SEE YOU NOW.>
<WONDERFUL.>
<LET'S TAKE A LITTLE BREAK, BOYS.>
<I GOT SOME BUSINESS TO TAKE CARE OF.>
<IMPORTANT BUSINESS.>
<MISTER SUZUKI IS VERY PARTICULAR ABOUT THE, UH, **HYGIENE** OF HIS EMPLOYEES. SO, UH, I'M GONNA NEED TO GET A BETTER LOOK AT YOU, IF YOU KNOW WHAT I MEAN.>

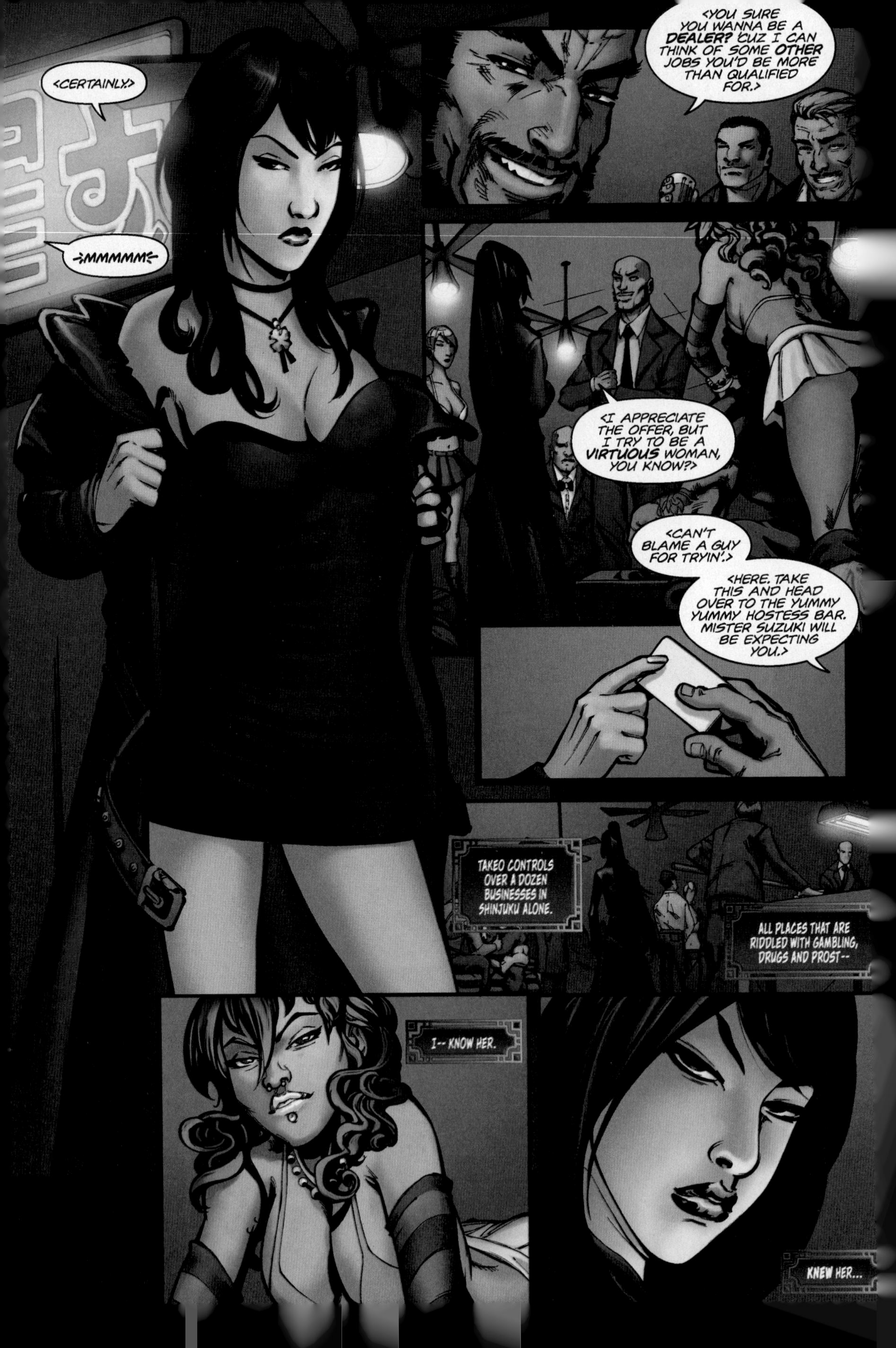
<CERTAINLY.>
-:MMMMM:-
<YOU SURE YOU WANNA BE A DEALER? 'CUZ I CAN THINK OF SOME OTHER JOBS YOU'D BE MORE THAN QUALIFIED FOR.>
<I APPRECIATE THE OFFER, BUT I TRY TO BE A VIRTUOUS WOMAN, YOU KNOW?>
<CAN'T BLAME A GUY FOR TRYIN'.>
<HERE. TAKE THIS AND HEAD OVER TO THE YUMMY YUMMY HOSTESS BAR. MISTER SUZUKI WILL BE EXPECTING YOU.>
TAKEO CONTROLS OVER A DOZEN BUSINESSES IN SHINJUKU ALONE.
ALL PLACES THAT ARE RIDDLED WITH GAMBLING, DRUGS AND PROST--
I-- KNOW HER.
KNEW HER...

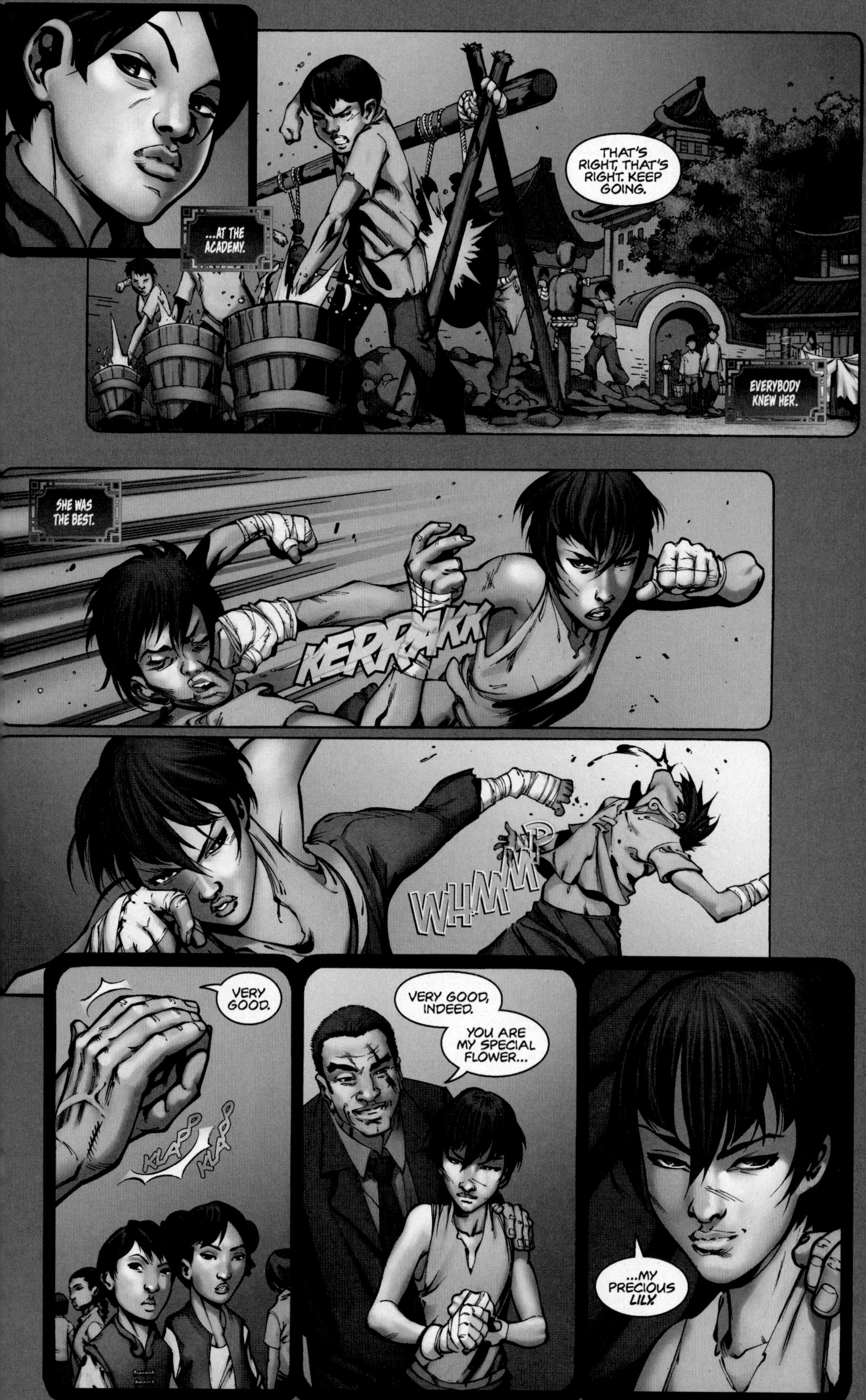
...AT THE ACADEMY.
THAT'S RIGHT, THAT'S RIGHT. KEEP GOING.
EVERYBODY KNEW HER.
SHE WAS THE BEST.
KERRAKK
WHMMP
VERY GOOD.
KLAPP KLAPP
VERY GOOD, INDEED.
YOU ARE MY SPECIAL FLOWER...
...MY PRECIOUS LILY.

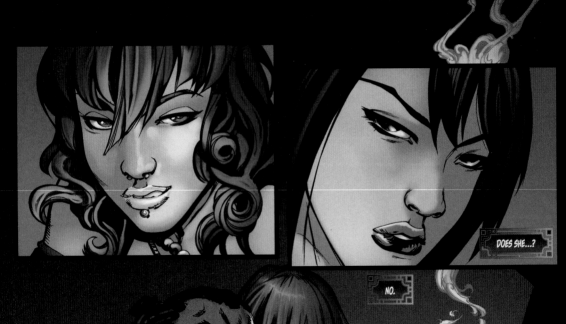

DOES SHE...?

NO.

HEY--

HNH?

--WHAT'S THE RUSH, BABY? YOU UP FOR A LITTLE *FUN* WITH MY GIRL AND I? I THINK SHE *LIKES* YOU...

OH. THANK YOU. BUT I'M LATE FOR A JOB INTERVIEW.

THAT WAS TOO CLOSE.

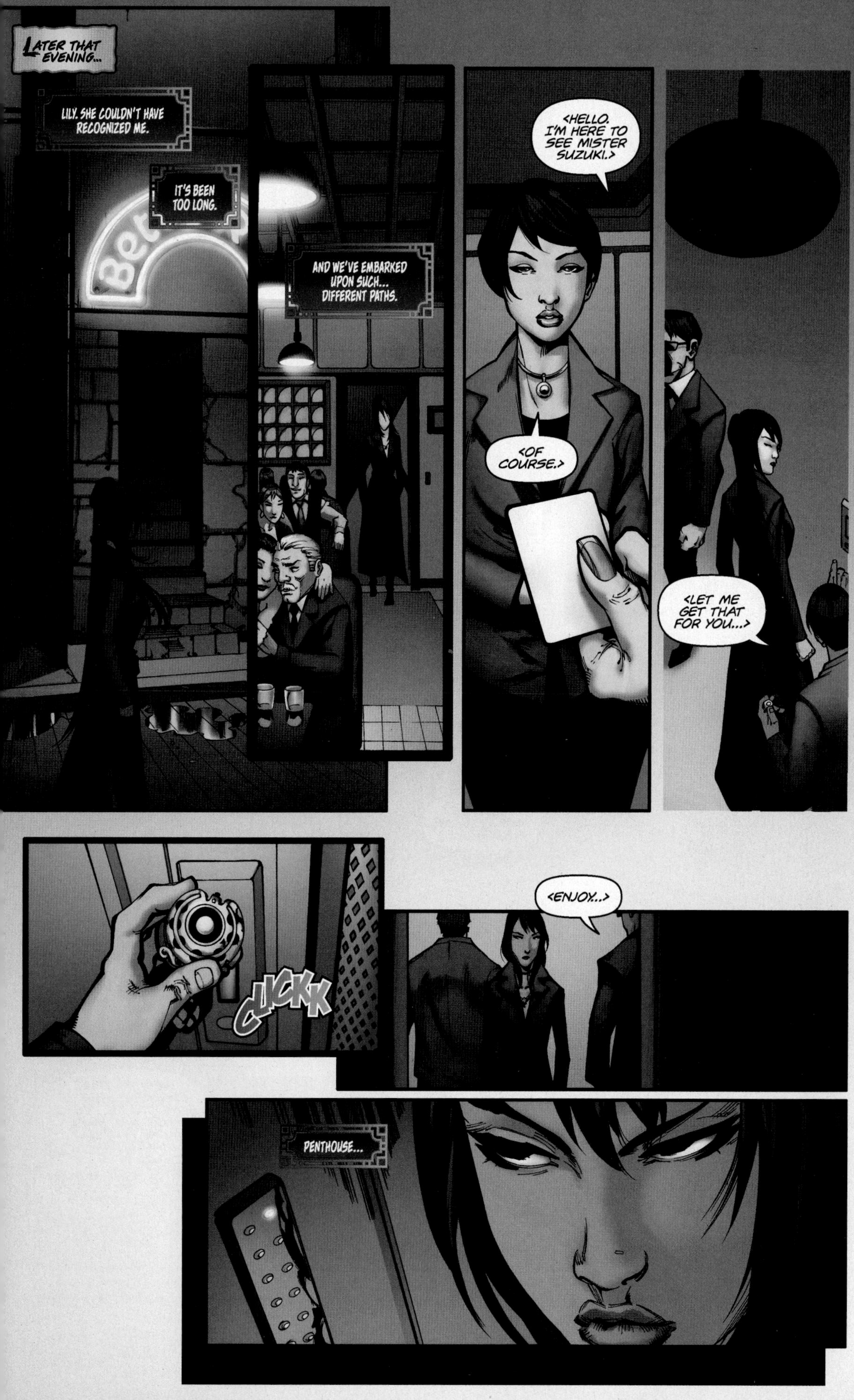
LATER THAT EVENING...
LILY. SHE COULDN'T HAVE RECOGNIZED ME.
IT'S BEEN TOO LONG.
AND WE'VE EMBARKED UPON SUCH... DIFFERENT PATHS.
<HELLO. I'M HERE TO SEE MISTER SUZUKI.>
<OF COURSE.>
<LET ME GET THAT FOR YOU...>
CLICKK
<ENJOY...>
PENTHOUSE...

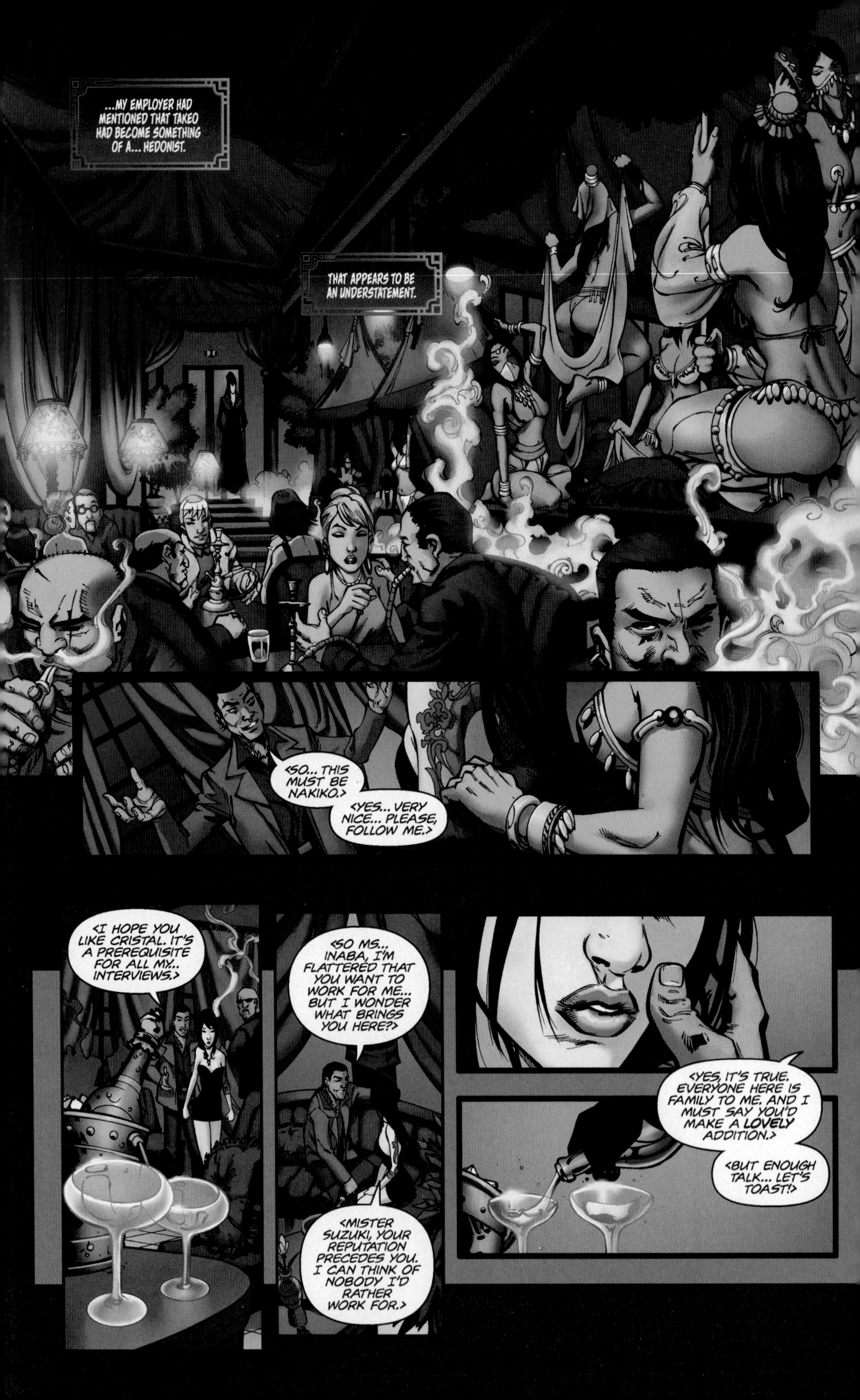
...MY EMPLOYER HAD MENTIONED THAT TAKEO HAD BECOME SOMETHING OF A... HEDONIST.
THAT APPEARS TO BE AN UNDERSTATEMENT.
<SO... THIS MUST BE NAKIKO.>
<YES... VERY NICE... PLEASE, FOLLOW ME.>
<I HOPE YOU LIKE CRISTAL. IT'S A PREREQUISITE FOR ALL MY.. INTERVIEWS.>
<SO MS... INABA, I'M FLATTERED THAT YOU WANT TO WORK FOR ME... BUT I WONDER WHAT BRINGS YOU HERE?>
<MISTER SUZUKI, YOUR REPUTATION PRECEDES YOU. I CAN THINK OF NOBODY I'D RATHER WORK FOR.>
<YES, IT'S TRUE. EVERYONE HERE IS FAMILY TO ME. AND I MUST SAY YOU'D MAKE A LOVELY ADDITION.>
<BUT ENOUGH TALK... LET'S TOAST!>

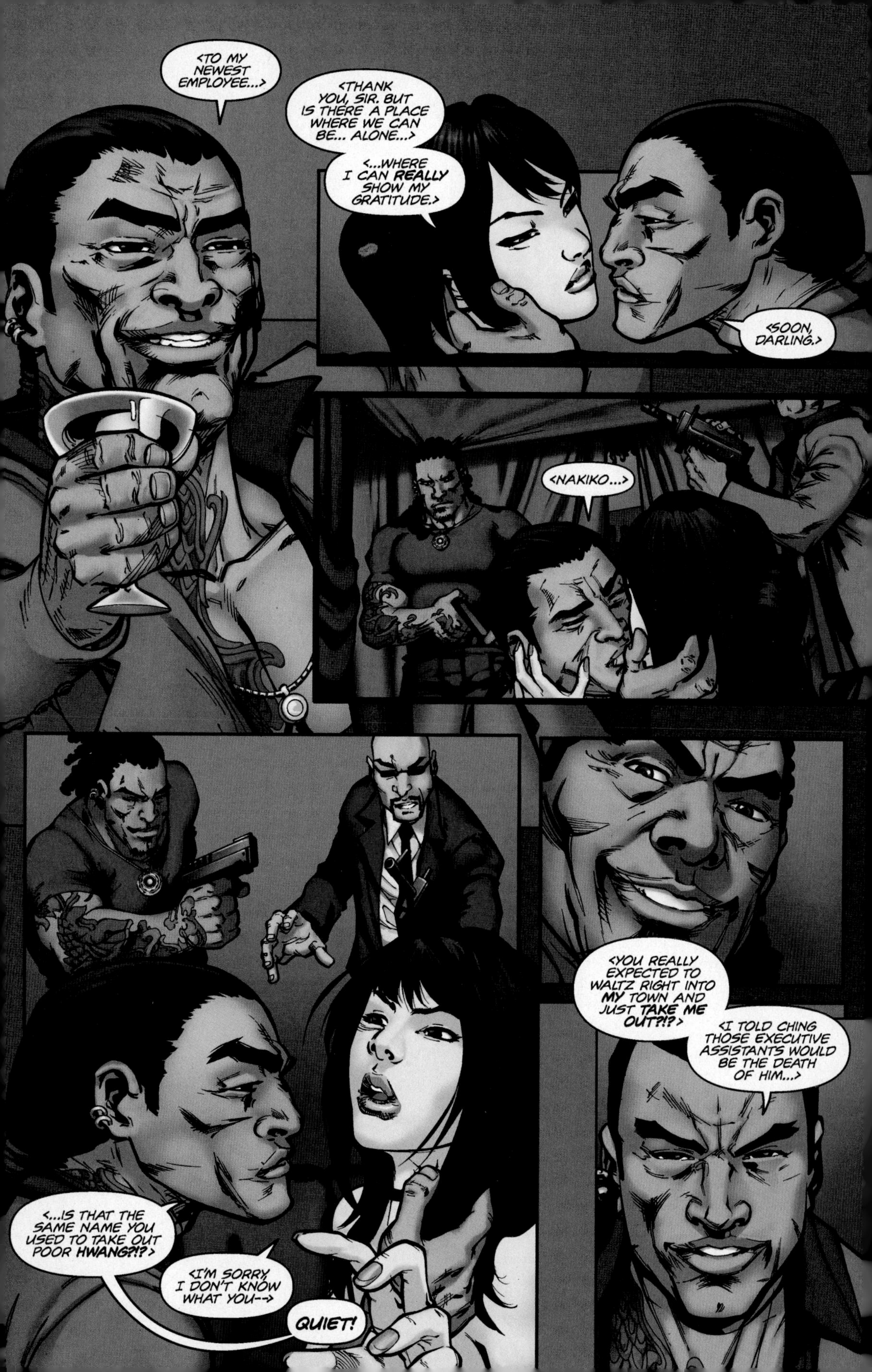
<TO MY NEWEST EMPLOYEE...>
<THANK YOU, SIR. BUT IS THERE A PLACE WHERE WE CAN BE... ALONE...>
<...WHERE I CAN **REALLY** SHOW MY GRATITUDE.>
<SOON, DARLING.>
<NAKIKO...>
<...IS THAT THE SAME NAME YOU USED TO TAKE OUT POOR **HWANG?!?**>
<I'M SORRY, I DON'T KNOW WHAT YOU-->
QUIET!
<YOU REALLY EXPECTED TO WALTZ RIGHT INTO **MY** TOWN AND JUST **TAKE ME OUT?!?**>
<I TOLD CHING THOSE EXECUTIVE ASSISTANTS WOULD BE THE DEATH OF HIM...>

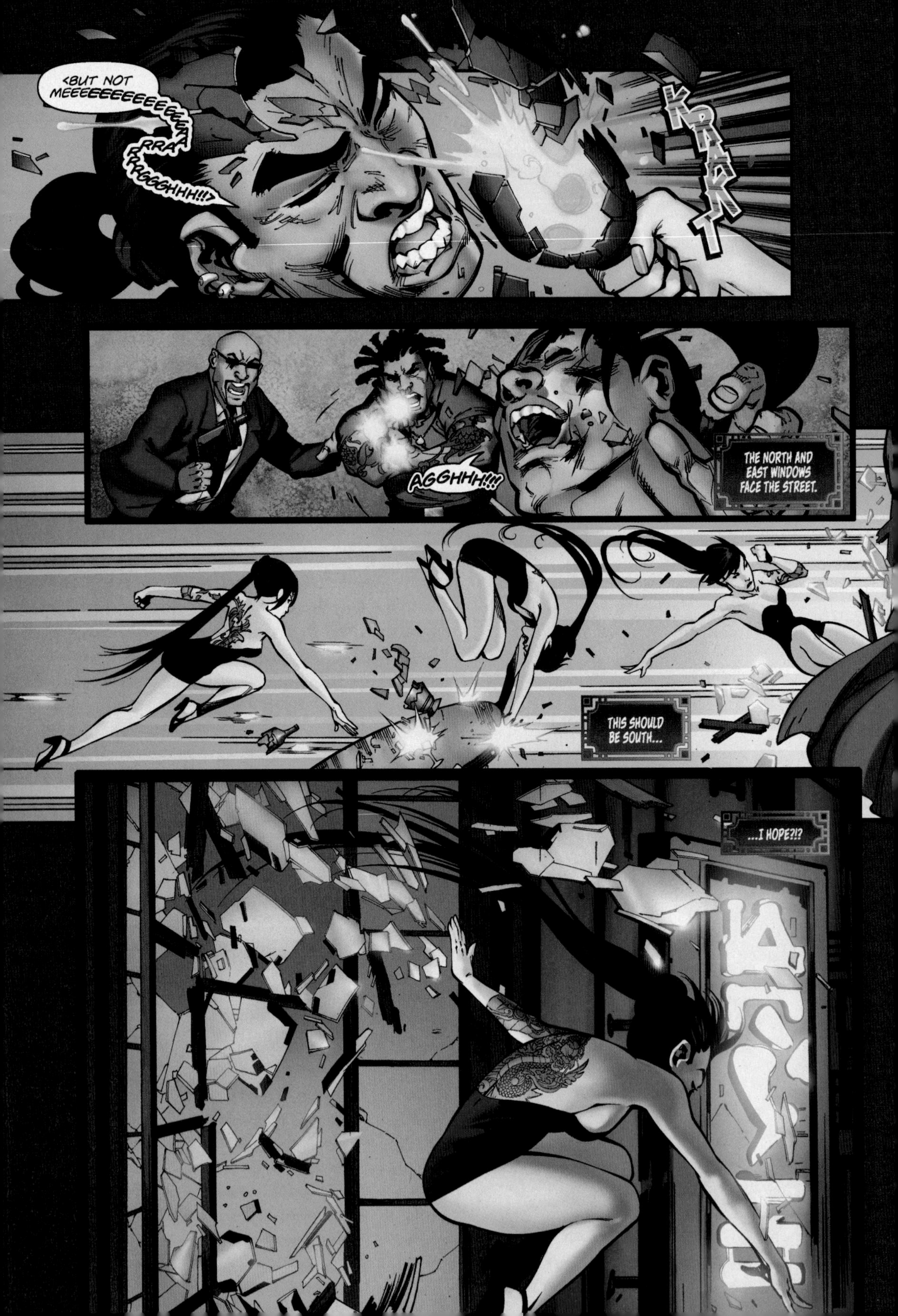
<BUT NOT MEEEEEEEEEEEEEEEARRRARRRGGGHHH!!!>
KRAKT
AGGHHH!!!
THE NORTH AND EAST WINDOWS FACE THE STREET.
THIS SHOULD BE SOUTH...
...I HOPE?!?

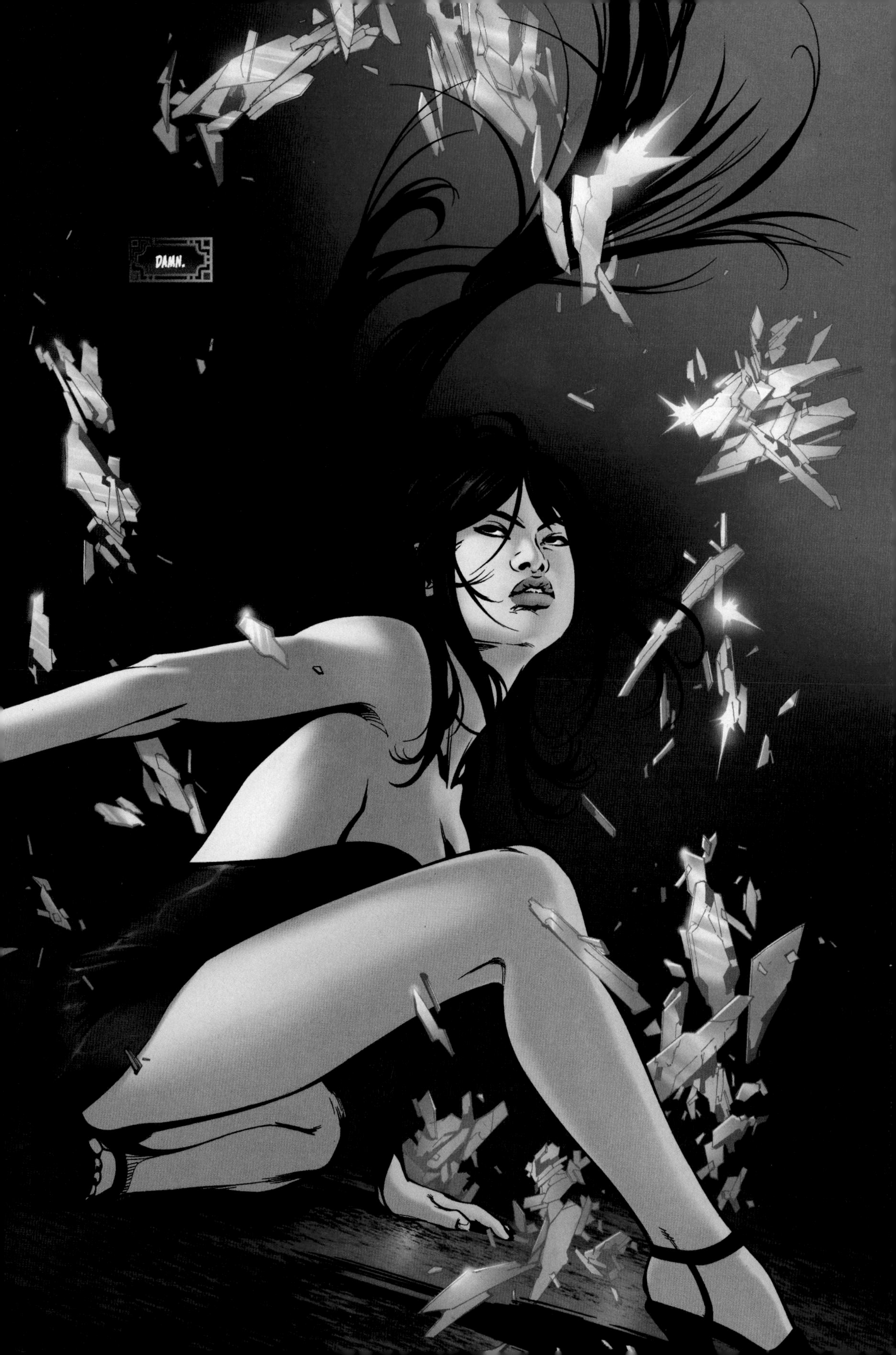
DAMN.

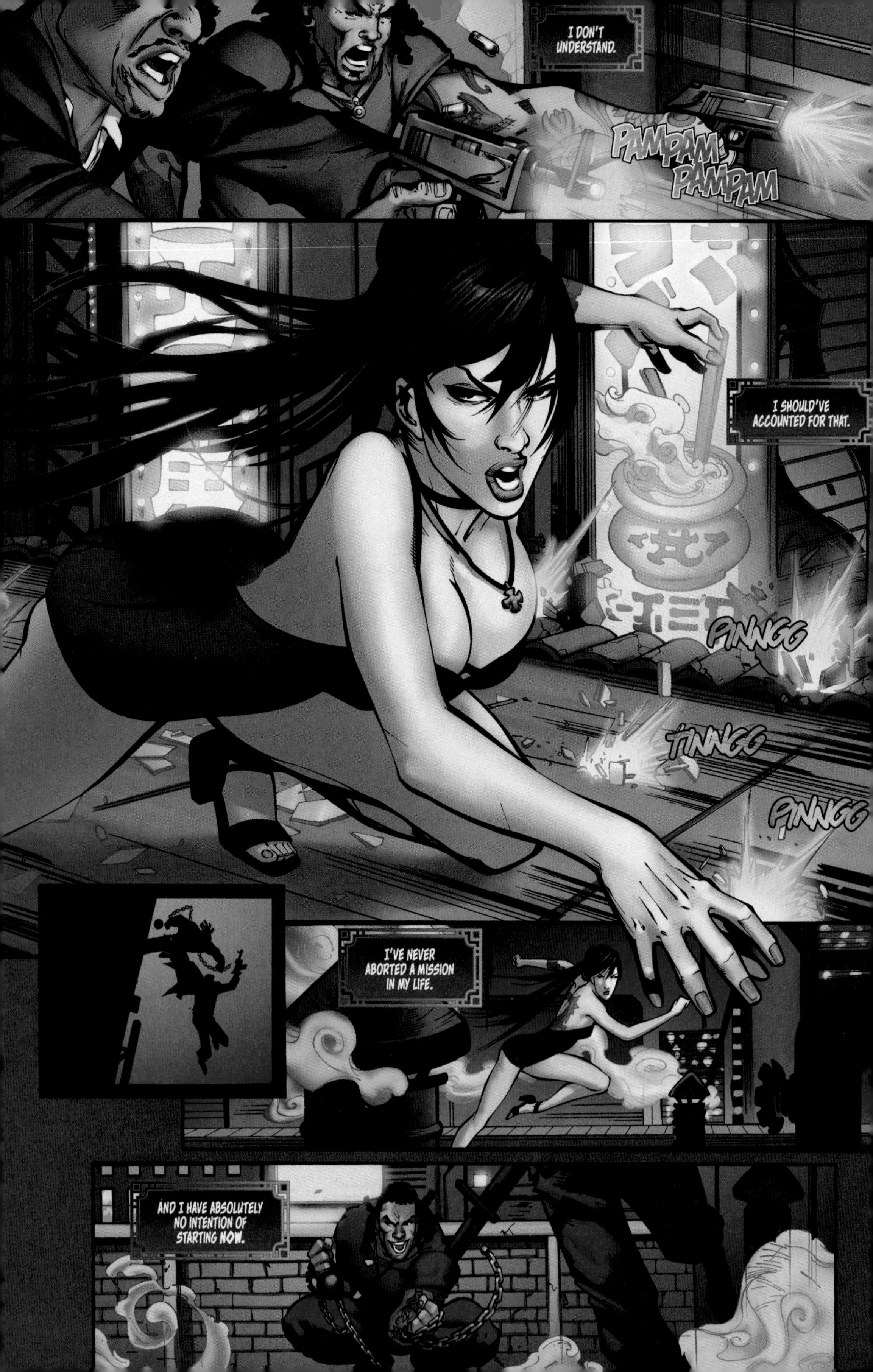
I DON'T UNDERSTAND.
PAMPAM PAMPAM
I SHOULD'VE ACCOUNTED FOR THAT.
PINNGG
TINNGG
PINNGG
I'VE NEVER ABORTED A MISSION IN MY LIFE.
AND I HAVE ABSOLUTELY NO INTENTION OF STARTING **NOW.**

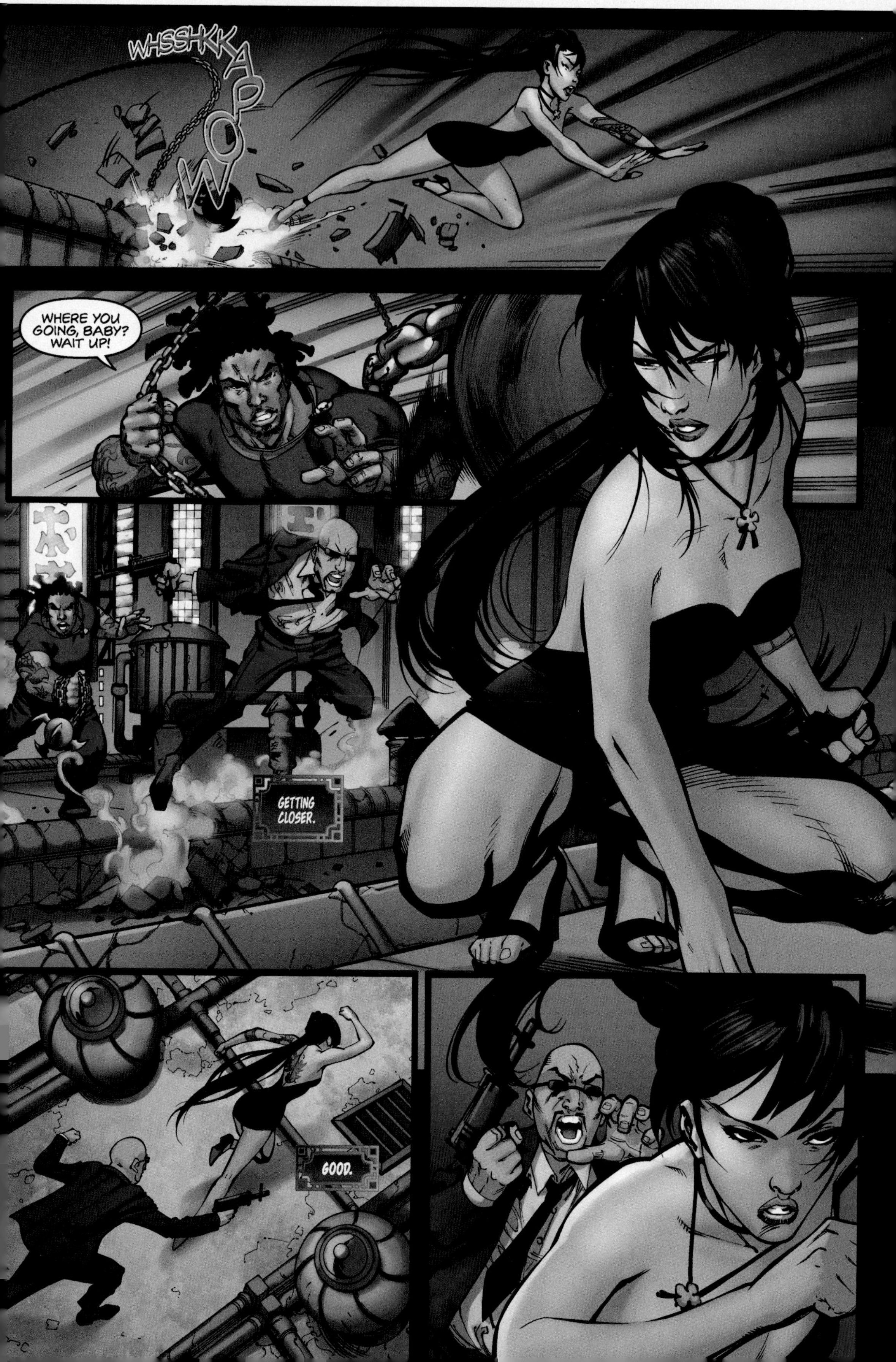
WHSSHKKAPOOW
WHERE YOU GOING, BABY? WAIT UP!
GETTING CLOSER.
GOOD.

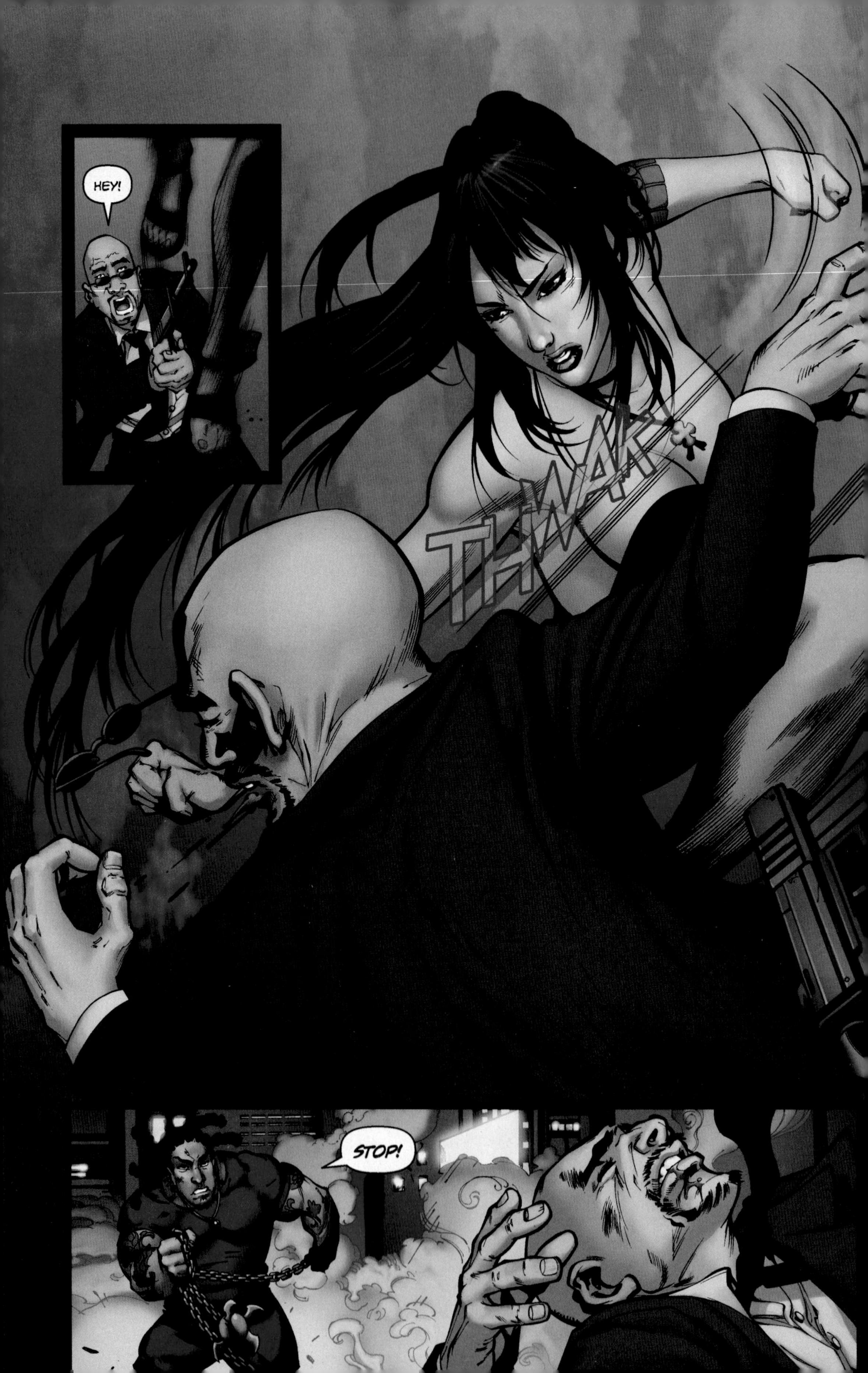
HEY!
THWAK!
STOP!

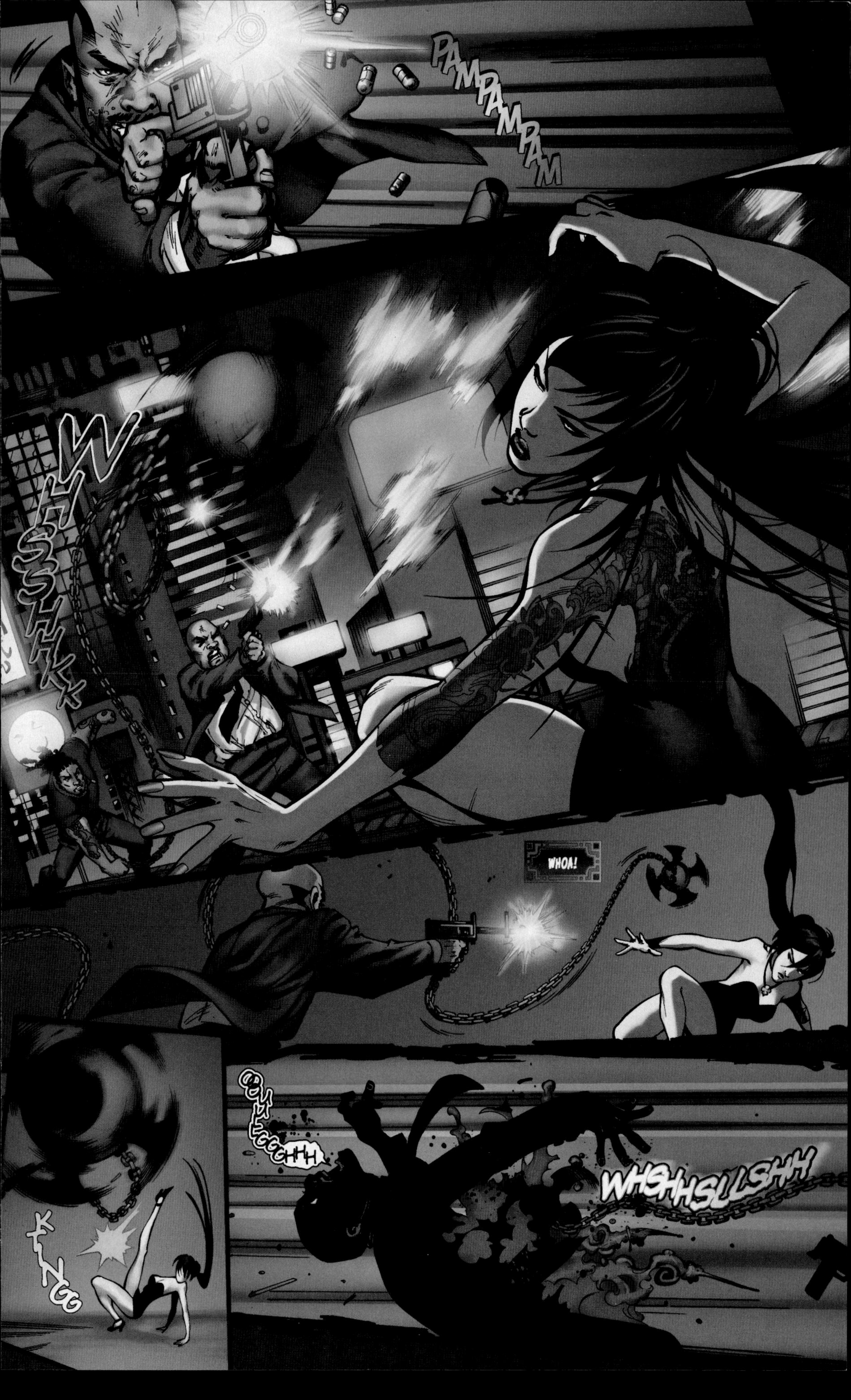
PAMPAMPAM
WHSSHHKK
WHOA!
GURLGGGHHH
WHSHHSULSHH
KLINGG

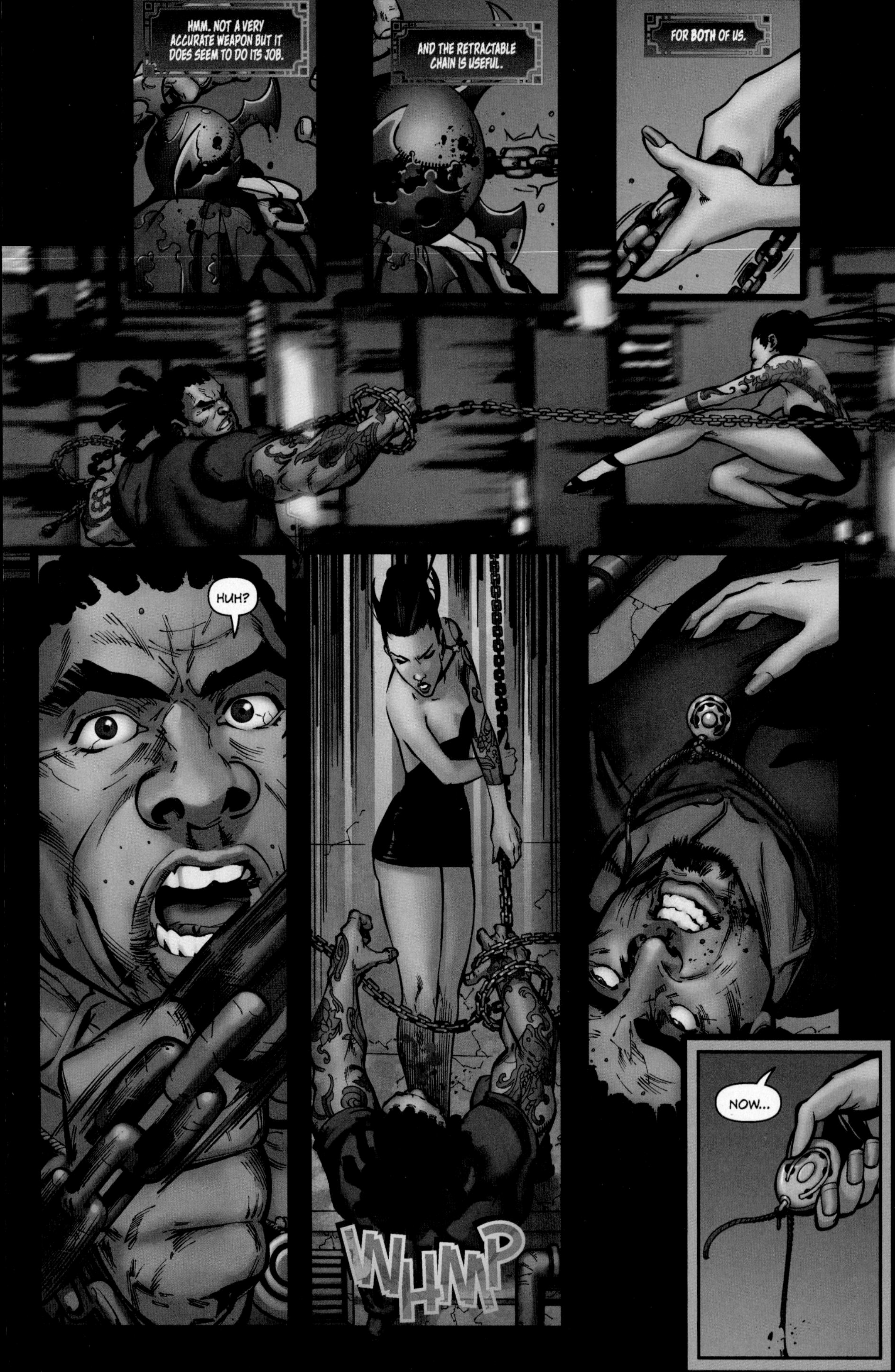
HMM. NOT A VERY ACCURATE WEAPON BUT IT DOES SEEM TO DO ITS JOB.
AND THE RETRACTABLE CHAIN IS USEFUL.
FOR BOTH OF US.
HUH?
WHMP
NOW...

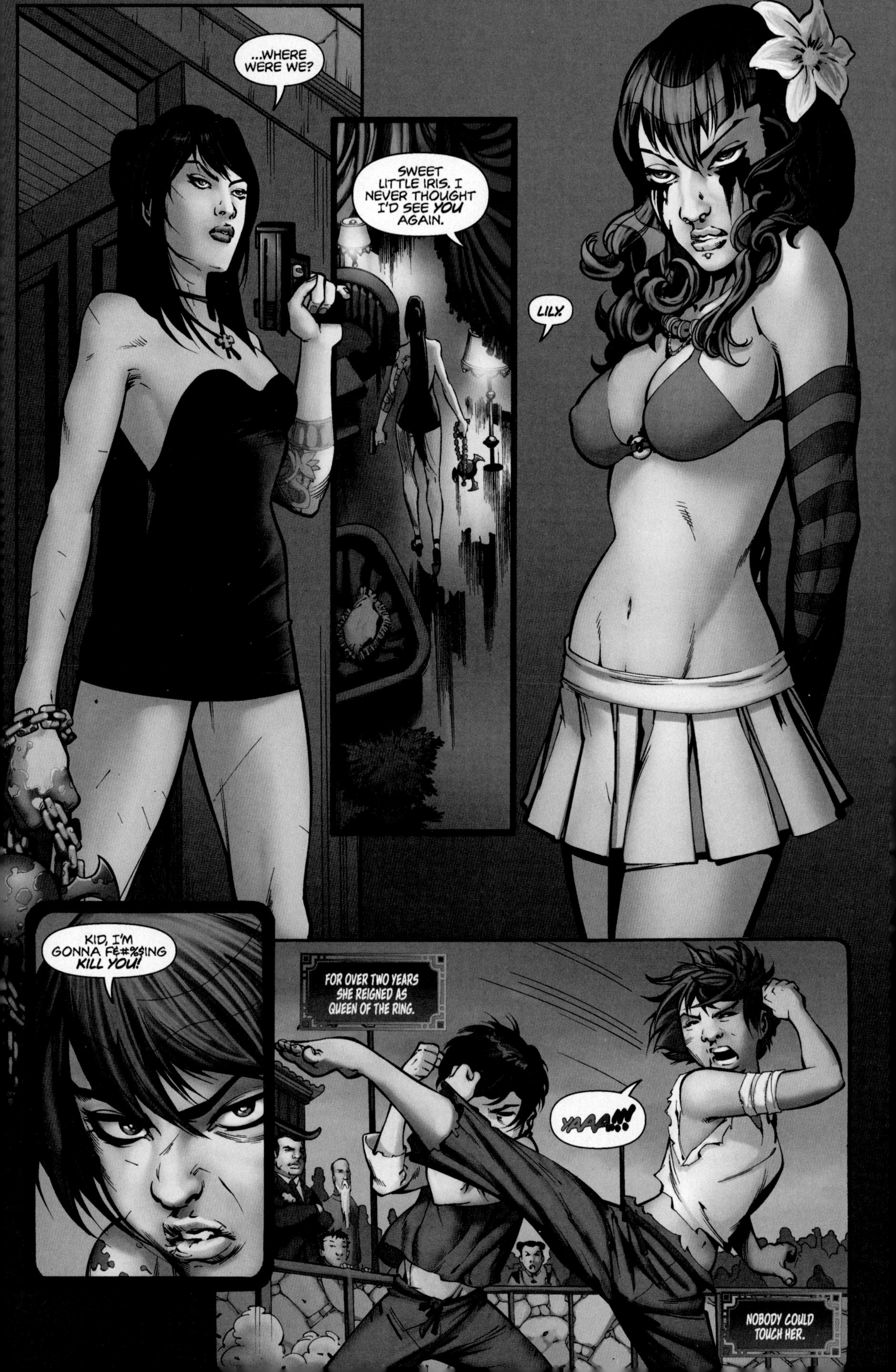
...WHERE WERE WE?
SWEET LITTLE IRIS. I NEVER THOUGHT I'D SEE YOU AGAIN.
LILY.
KID, I'M GONNA F€#%$ING KILL YOU!
FOR OVER TWO YEARS SHE REIGNED AS QUEEN OF THE RING.
YAAA!!!
NOBODY COULD TOUCH HER.

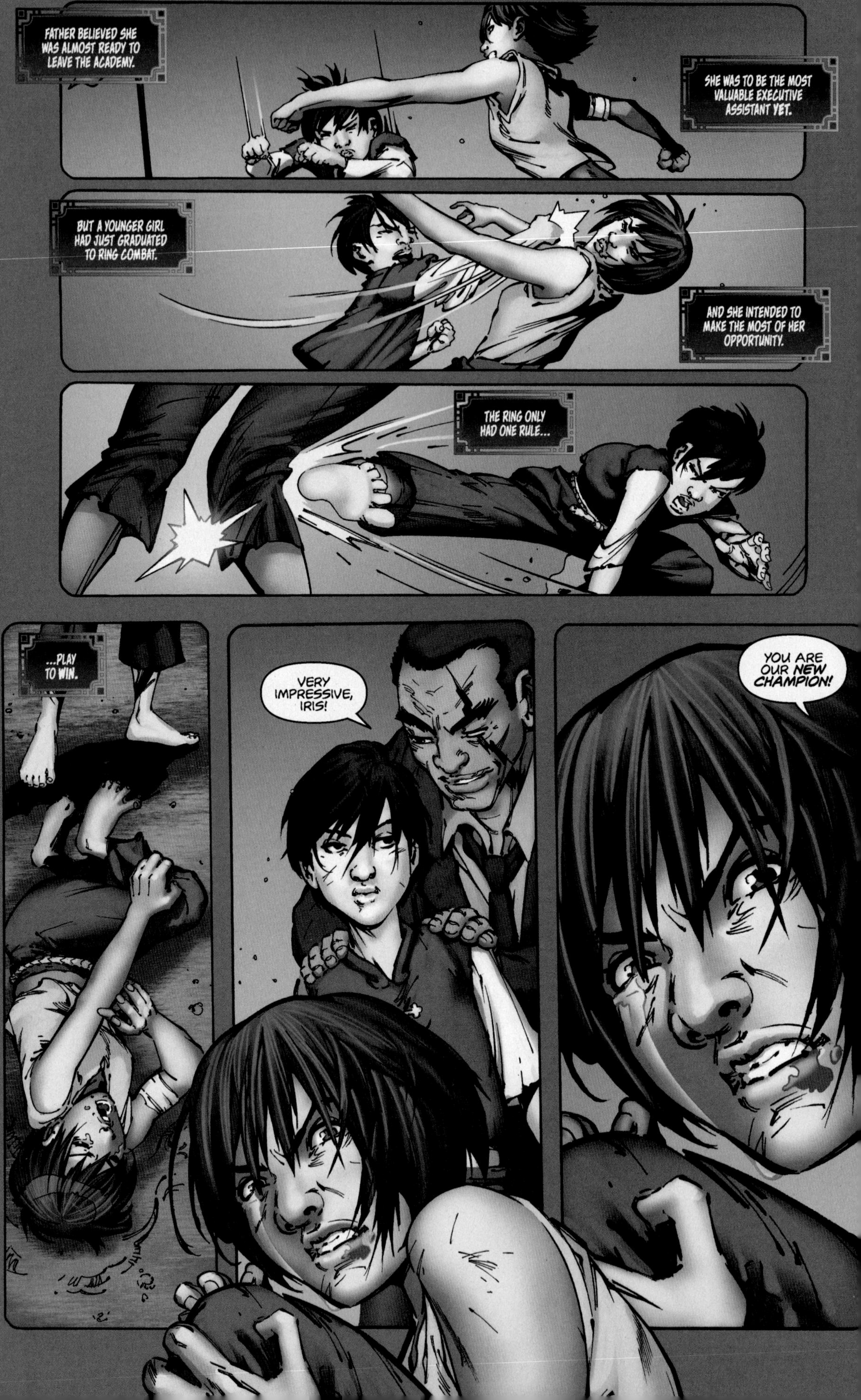
FATHER BELIEVED SHE WAS ALMOST READY TO LEAVE THE ACADEMY.
SHE WAS TO BE THE MOST VALUABLE EXECUTIVE ASSISTANT YET.
BUT A YOUNGER GIRL HAD JUST GRADUATED TO RING COMBAT.
AND SHE INTENDED TO MAKE THE MOST OF HER OPPORTUNITY.
THE RING ONLY HAD ONE RULE...
...PLAY TO WIN.
VERY IMPRESSIVE, IRIS!
YOU ARE OUR NEW CHAMPION!

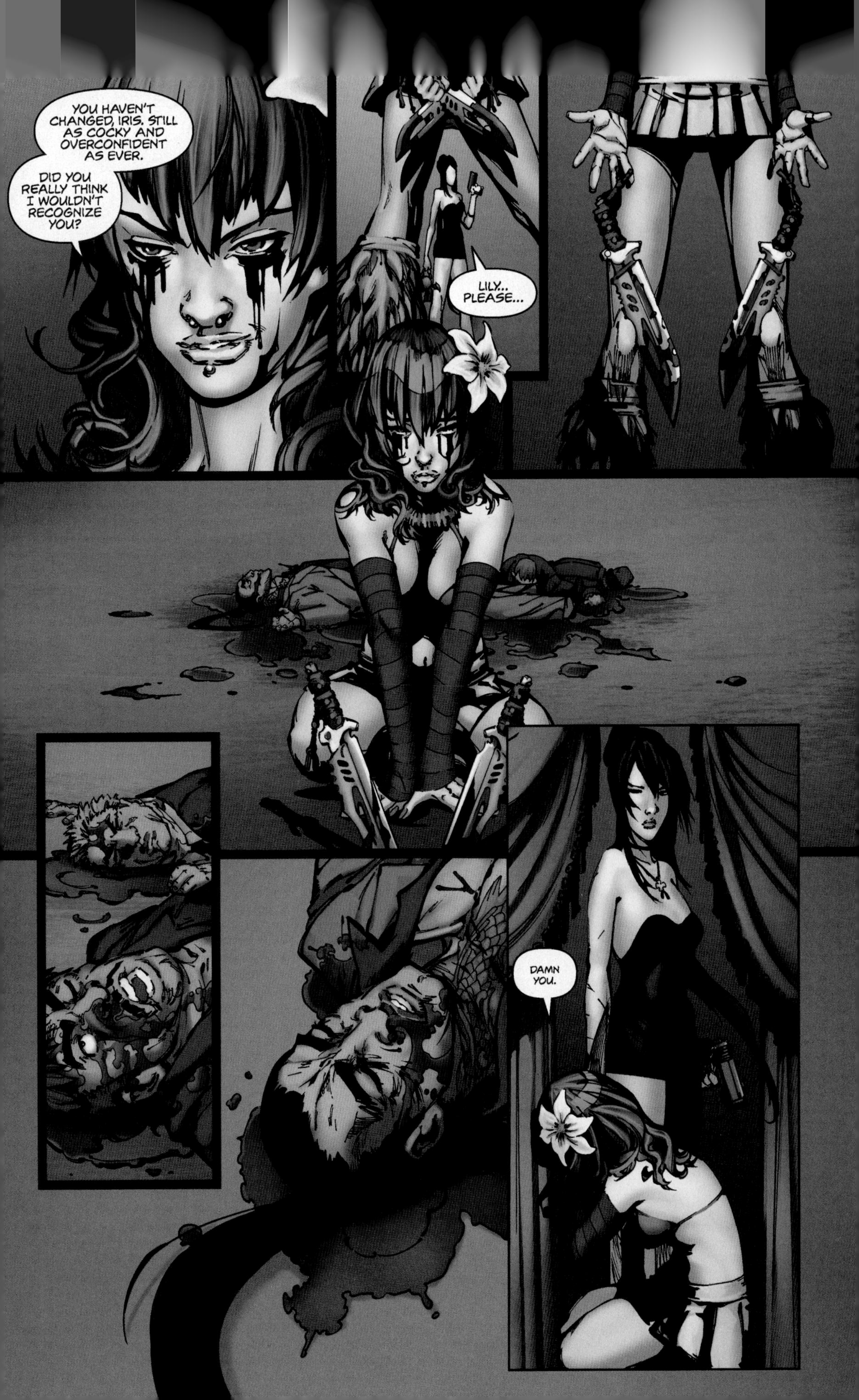
YOU HAVEN'T CHANGED, IRIS. STILL AS COCKY AND OVERCONFIDENT AS EVER.
DID YOU REALLY THINK I WOULDN'T RECOGNIZE YOU?
LILY.. PLEASE...
DAMN YOU.

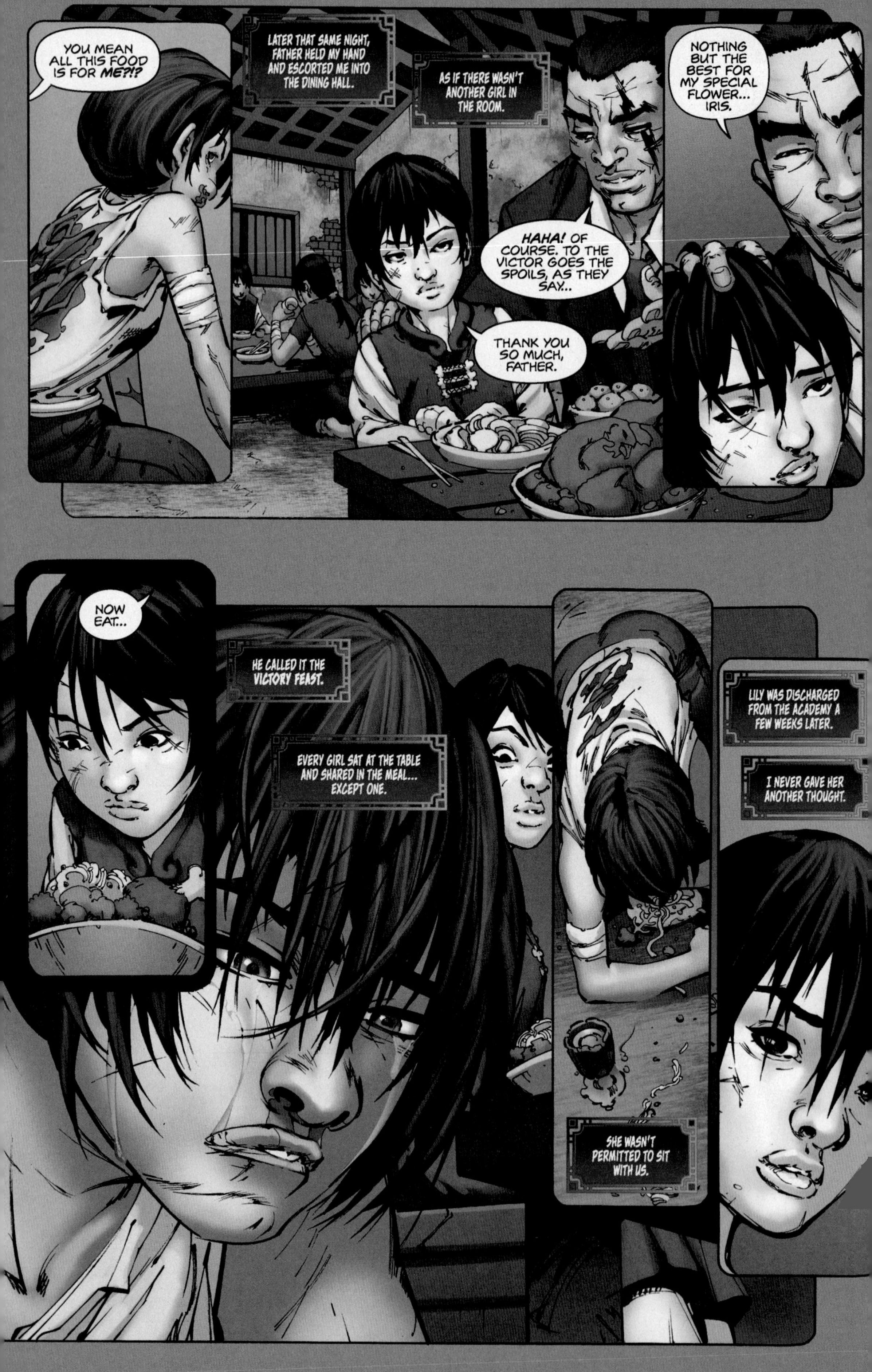
YOU MEAN ALL THIS FOOD IS FOR *ME?!?*
LATER THAT SAME NIGHT, FATHER HELD MY HAND AND ESCORTED ME INTO THE DINING HALL.
AS IF THERE WASN'T ANOTHER GIRL IN THE ROOM.
HAHA! OF COURSE. TO THE VICTOR GOES THE SPOILS, AS THEY SAY...
THANK YOU SO MUCH, FATHER.
NOTHING BUT THE BEST FOR MY SPECIAL FLOWER... IRIS.
NOW EAT...
HE CALLED IT THE *VICTORY FEAST.*
EVERY GIRL SAT AT THE TABLE AND SHARED IN THE MEAL... EXCEPT ONE.
SHE WASN'T PERMITTED TO SIT WITH US.
LILY WAS DISCHARGED FROM THE ACADEMY A FEW WEEKS LATER.
I NEVER GAVE HER ANOTHER THOUGHT.

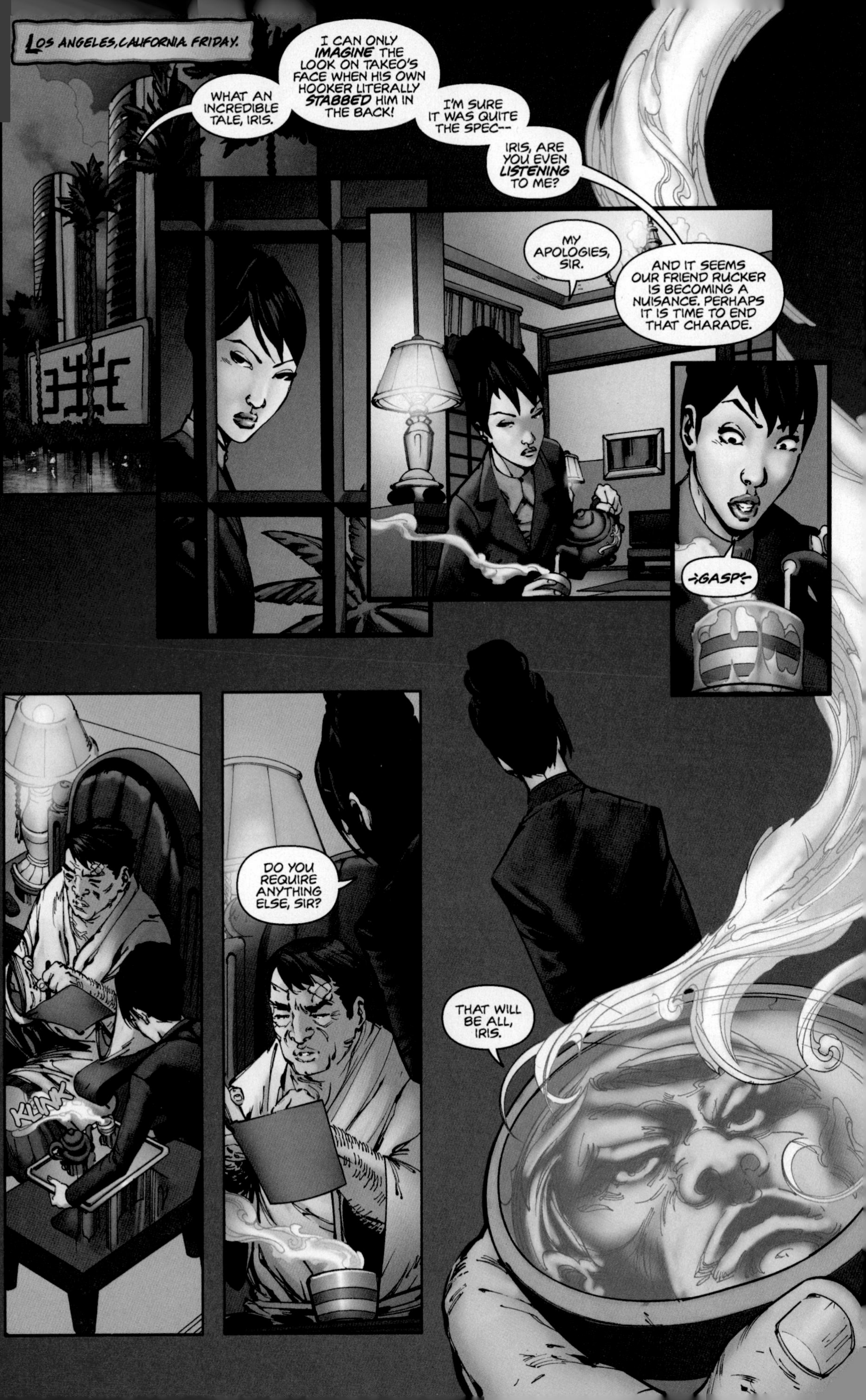

Los Angeles, California Friday.
What an incredible tale, Iris.
I can only *imagine* the look on Takeo's face when his own hooker literally *stabbed* him in the back!
I'm sure it was quite the spec--
Iris, are you even *listening* to me?
My apologies, sir.
And it seems our friend Rucker is becoming a nuisance. Perhaps it is time to end that charade.
-GASP-
KLINK
Do you require anything else, sir?
That will be all, Iris.

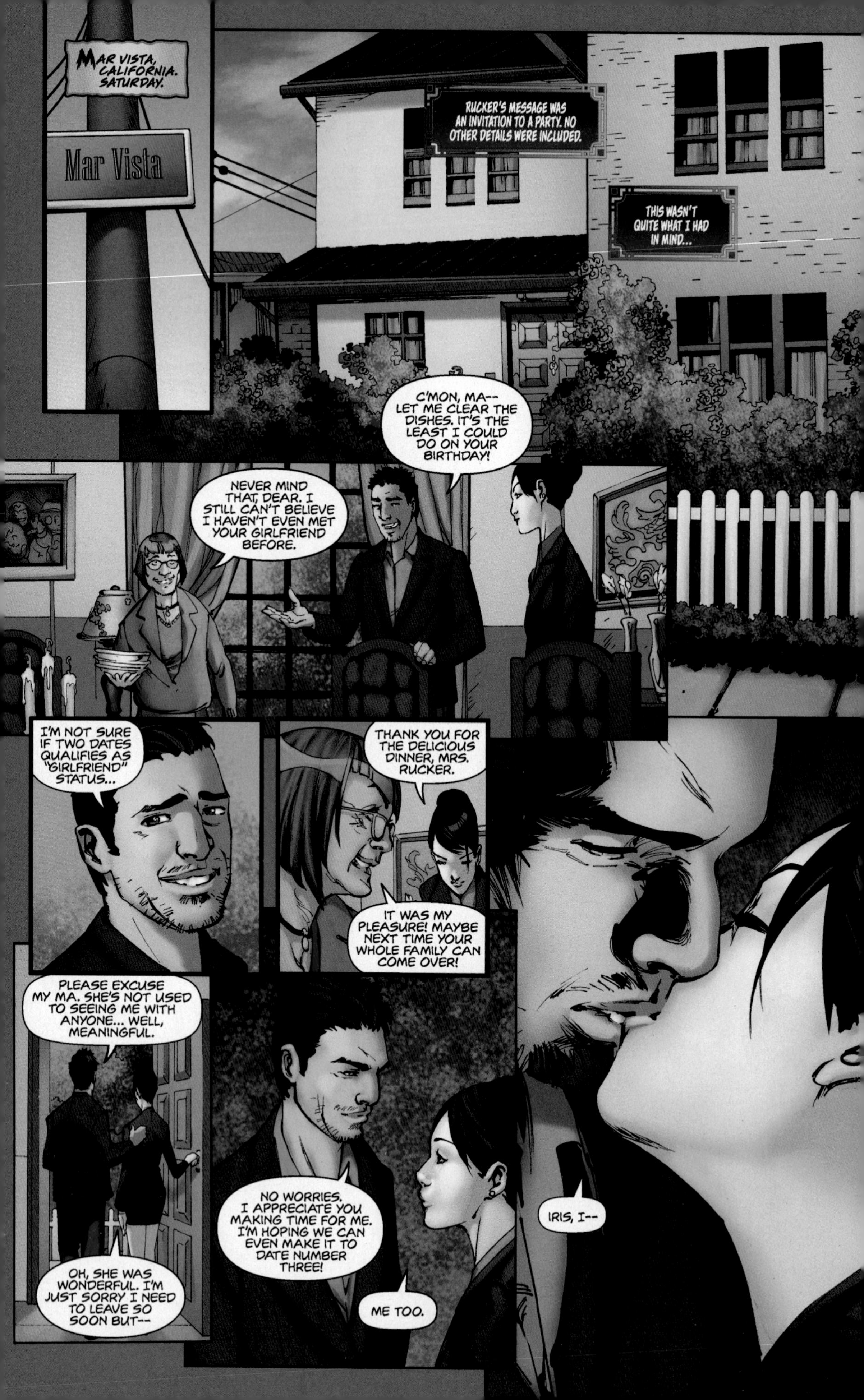
MAR VISTA, CALIFORNIA. SATURDAY.
Mar Vista
RUCKER'S MESSAGE WAS AN INVITATION TO A PARTY. NO OTHER DETAILS WERE INCLUDED.
THIS WASN'T QUITE WHAT I HAD IN MIND...
C'MON, MA-- LET ME CLEAR THE DISHES. IT'S THE LEAST I COULD DO ON YOUR BIRTHDAY!
NEVER MIND THAT, DEAR. I STILL CAN'T BELIEVE I HAVEN'T EVEN MET YOUR GIRLFRIEND BEFORE.
I'M NOT SURE IF TWO DATES QUALIFIES AS "GIRLFRIEND" STATUS...
THANK YOU FOR THE DELICIOUS DINNER, MRS. RUCKER.
IT WAS MY PLEASURE! MAYBE NEXT TIME YOUR WHOLE FAMILY CAN COME OVER!
PLEASE EXCUSE MY MA. SHE'S NOT USED TO SEEING ME WITH ANYONE... WELL, MEANINGFUL.
OH, SHE WAS WONDERFUL. I'M JUST SORRY I NEED TO LEAVE SO SOON BUT--
NO WORRIES. I APPRECIATE YOU MAKING TIME FOR ME. I'M HOPING WE CAN EVEN MAKE IT TO DATE NUMBER THREE!
ME TOO.
IRIS, I--

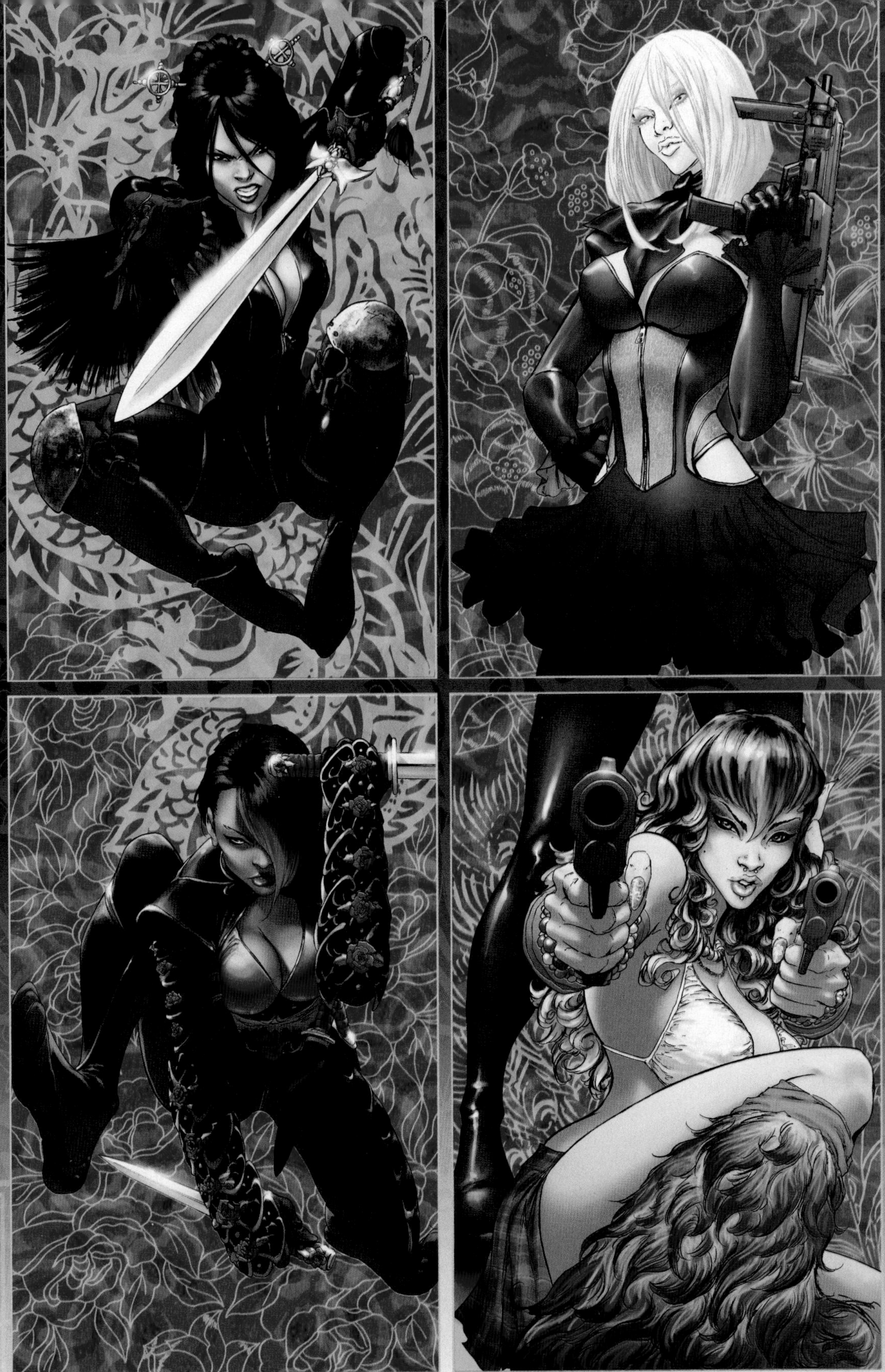

Executive Assistant: Iris #4
Covers A, B, C, D
Joe BENITEZ • Peter STEIGERWALD

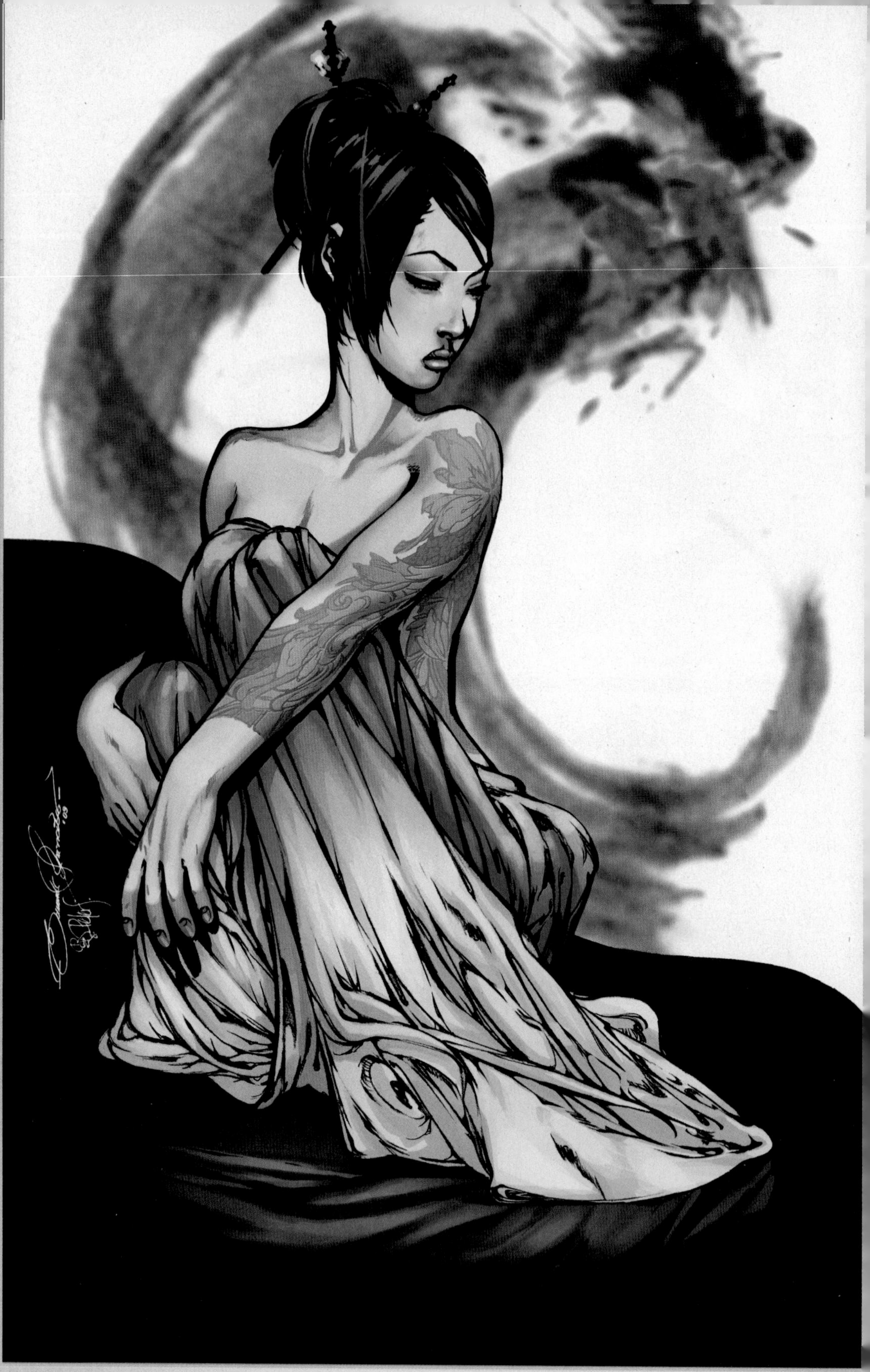

Executive Assistant: Iris #4
WonderCon Exclusive Cover E
Eduardo FRANCISCO • Peter STEIGERWALD

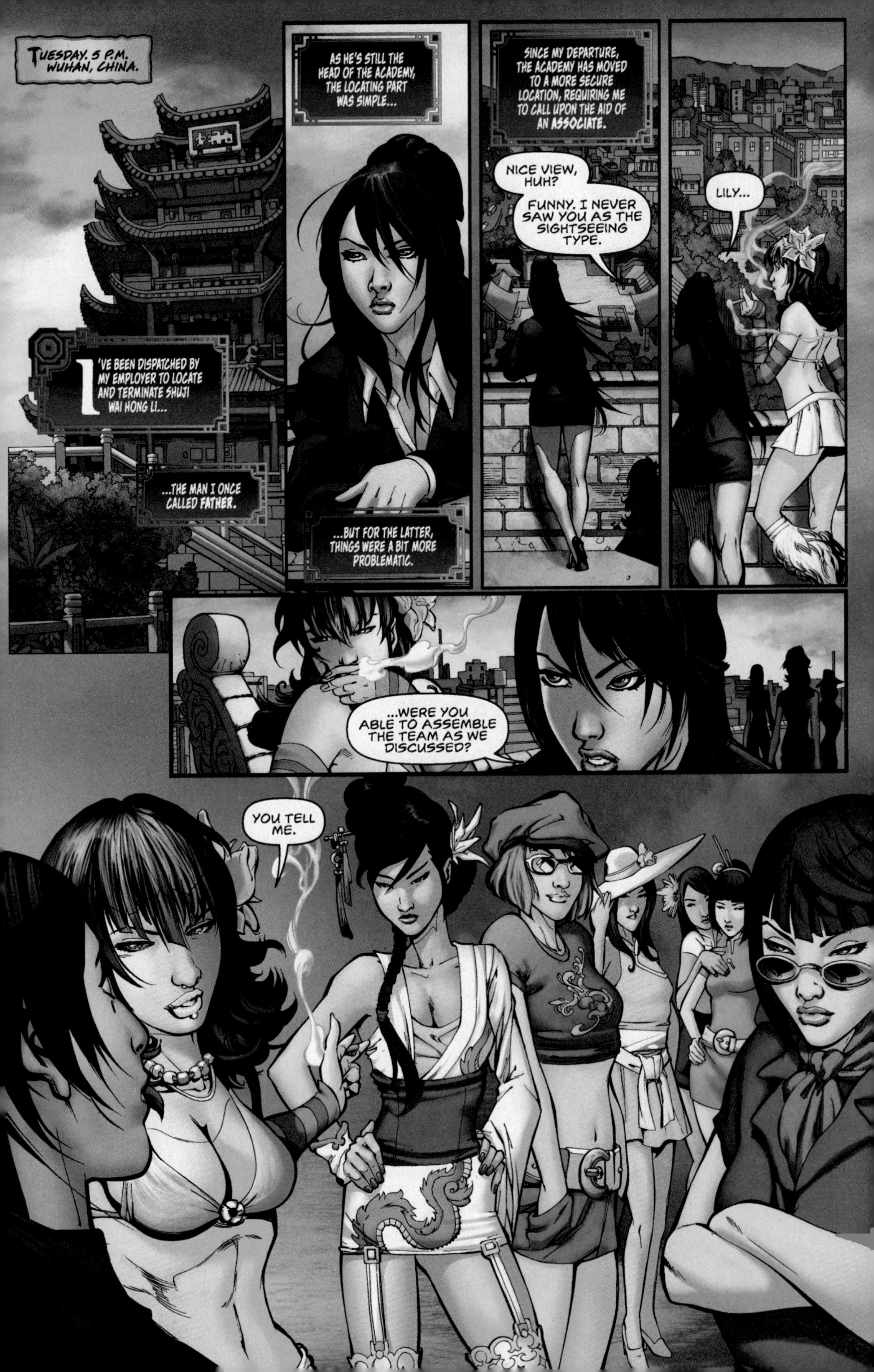
TUESDAY, 5 P.M. WUHAN, CHINA.
I'VE BEEN DISPATCHED BY MY EMPLOYER TO LOCATE AND TERMINATE SHUJI WAI HONG LI...
...THE MAN I ONCE CALLED FATHER.
AS HE'S STILL THE HEAD OF THE ACADEMY, THE LOCATING PART WAS SIMPLE...
...BUT FOR THE LATTER, THINGS WERE A BIT MORE PROBLEMATIC.
SINCE MY DEPARTURE, THE ACADEMY HAS MOVED TO A MORE SECURE LOCATION, REQUIRING ME TO CALL UPON THE AID OF AN ASSOCIATE.
NICE VIEW, HUH?
FUNNY. I NEVER SAW YOU AS THE SIGHTSEEING TYPE.
LILY...
...WERE YOU ABLE TO ASSEMBLE THE TEAM AS WE DISCUSSED?
YOU TELL ME.

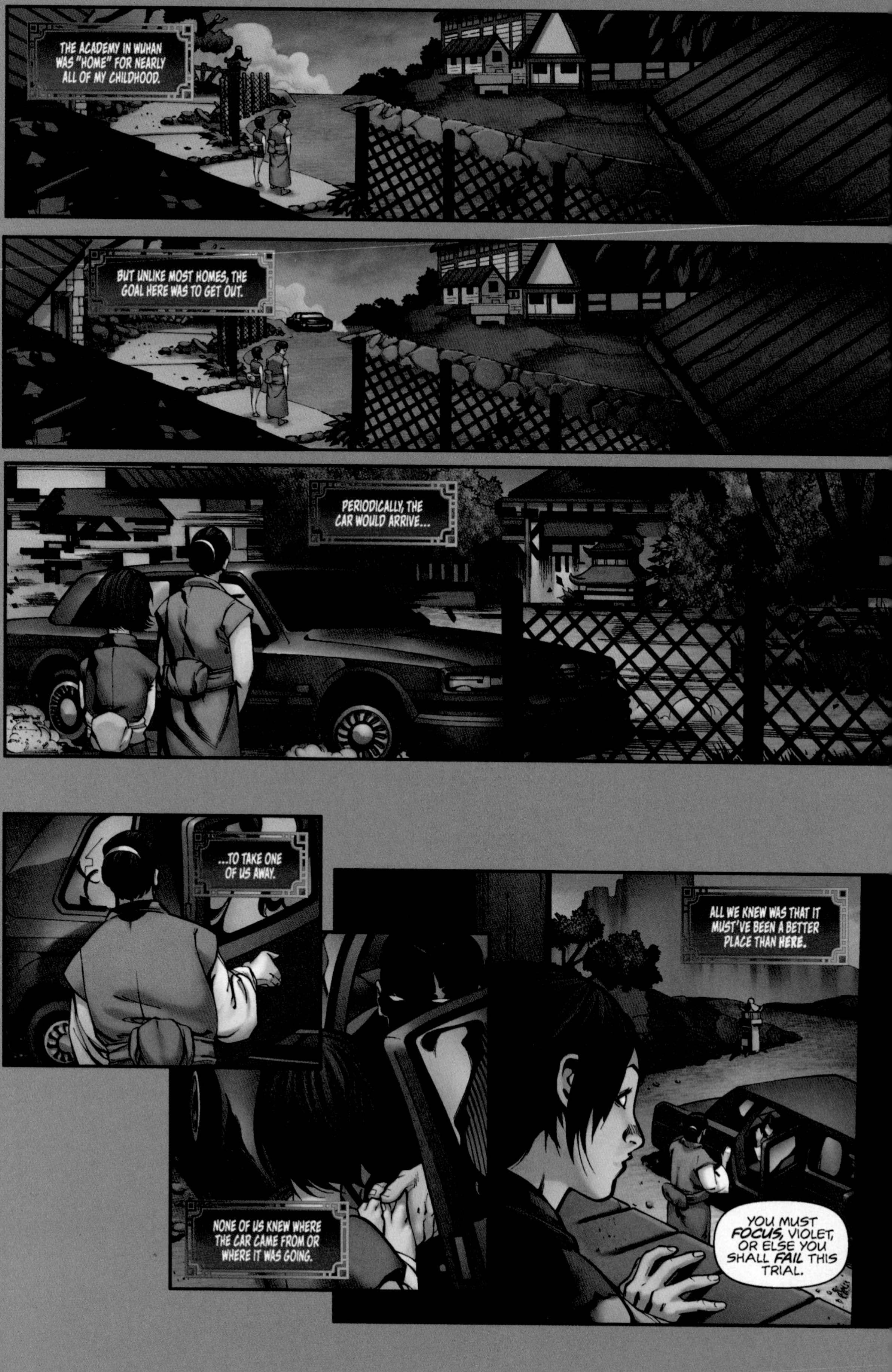
THE ACADEMY IN WUHAN WAS "HOME" FOR NEARLY ALL OF MY CHILDHOOD.
BUT UNLIKE MOST HOMES, THE GOAL HERE WAS TO GET OUT.
PERIODICALLY, THE CAR WOULD ARRIVE...
...TO TAKE ONE OF US AWAY.
NONE OF US KNEW WHERE THE CAR CAME FROM OR WHERE IT WAS GOING.
ALL WE KNEW WAS THAT IT MUST'VE BEEN A BETTER PLACE THAN HERE.
YOU MUST FOCUS, VIOLET, OR ELSE YOU SHALL FAIL THIS TRIAL.

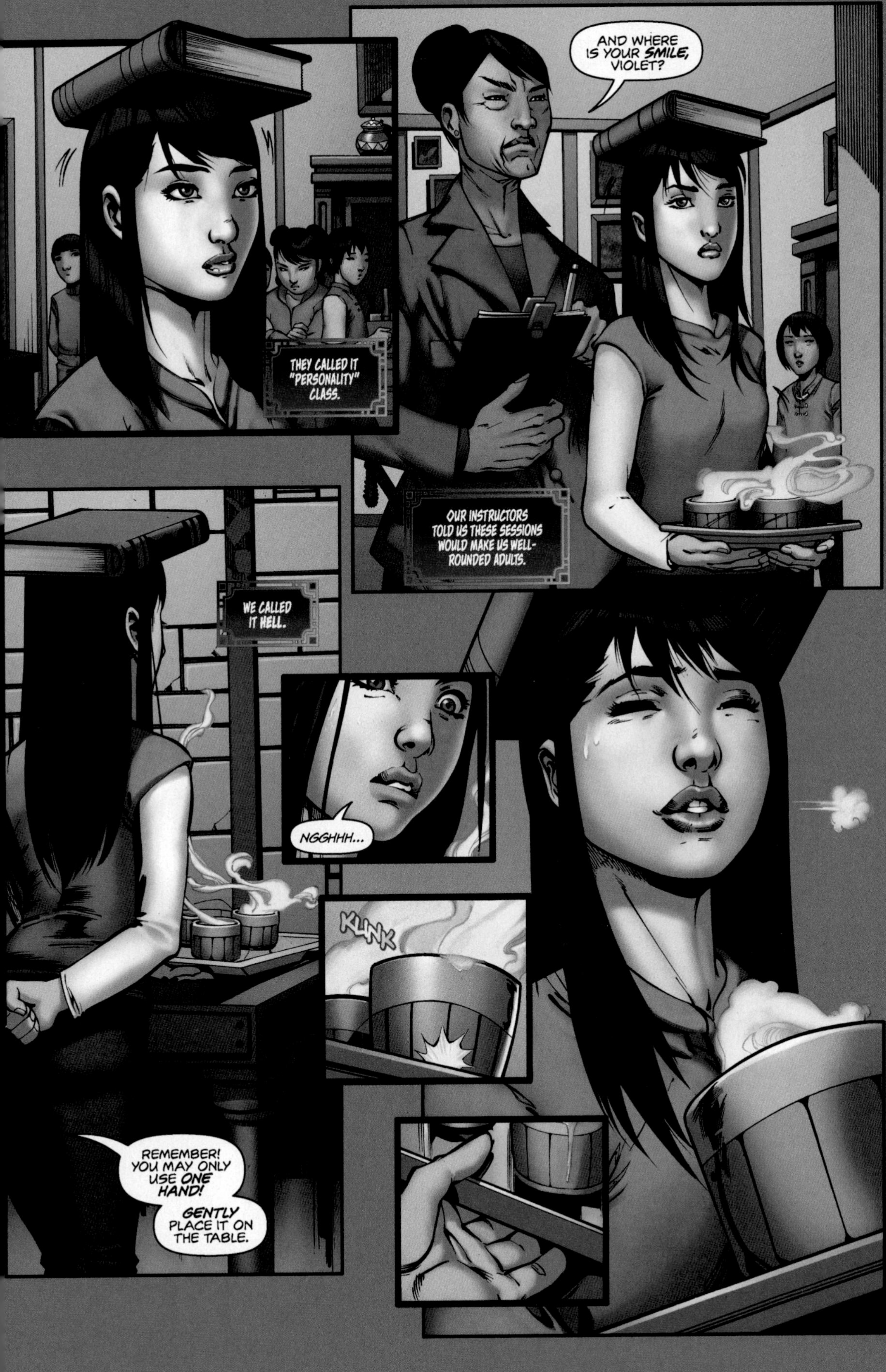
THEY CALLED IT "PERSONALITY" CLASS.
AND WHERE IS YOUR SMILE, VIOLET?
OUR INSTRUCTORS TOLD US THESE SESSIONS WOULD MAKE US WELL-ROUNDED ADULTS.
WE CALLED IT HELL.
NGGHHH...
KLINK
REMEMBER! YOU MAY ONLY USE ONE HAND!
GENTLY PLACE IT ON THE TABLE.

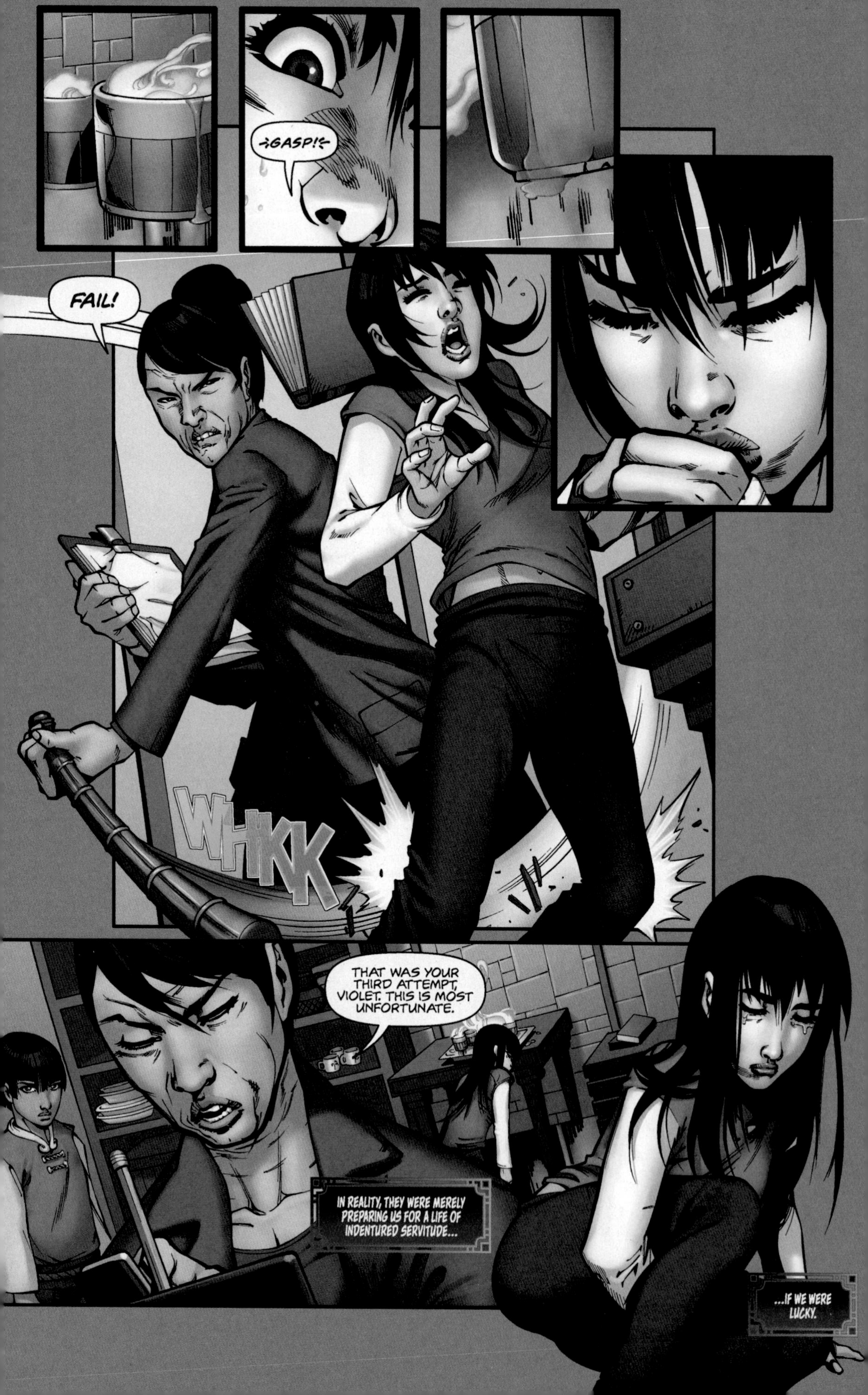

GASP!
FAIL!
WHKK
THAT WAS YOUR THIRD ATTEMPT, VIOLET. THIS IS MOST UNFORTUNATE.
IN REALITY, THEY WERE MERELY PREPARING US FOR A LIFE OF INDENTURED SERVITUDE...
...IF WE WERE LUCKY.

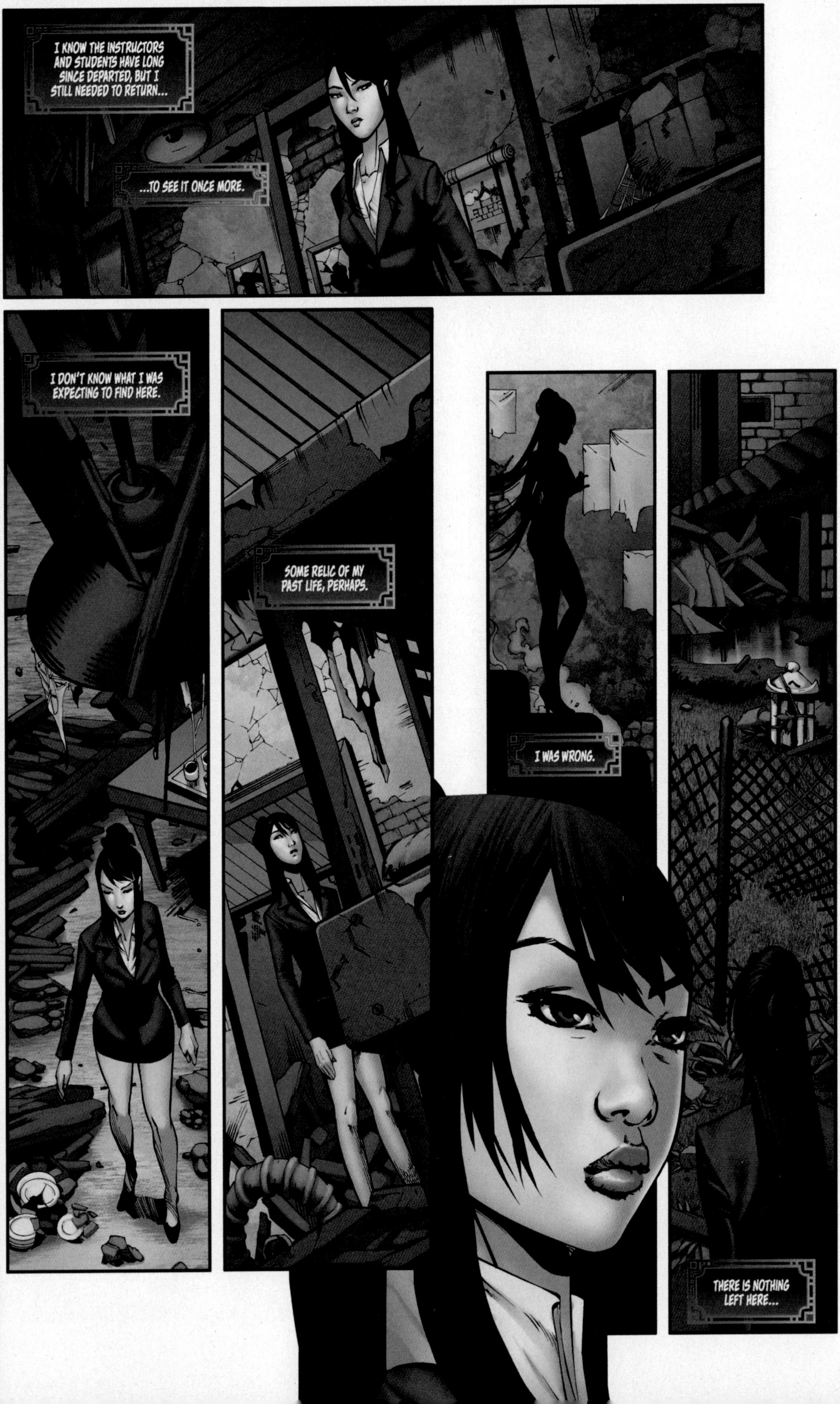
I KNOW THE INSTRUCTORS AND STUDENTS HAVE LONG SINCE DEPARTED, BUT I STILL NEEDED TO RETURN...
...TO SEE IT ONCE MORE.
I DON'T KNOW WHAT I WAS EXPECTING TO FIND HERE.
SOME RELIC OF MY PAST LIFE, PERHAPS.
I WAS WRONG.
THERE IS NOTHING LEFT HERE...

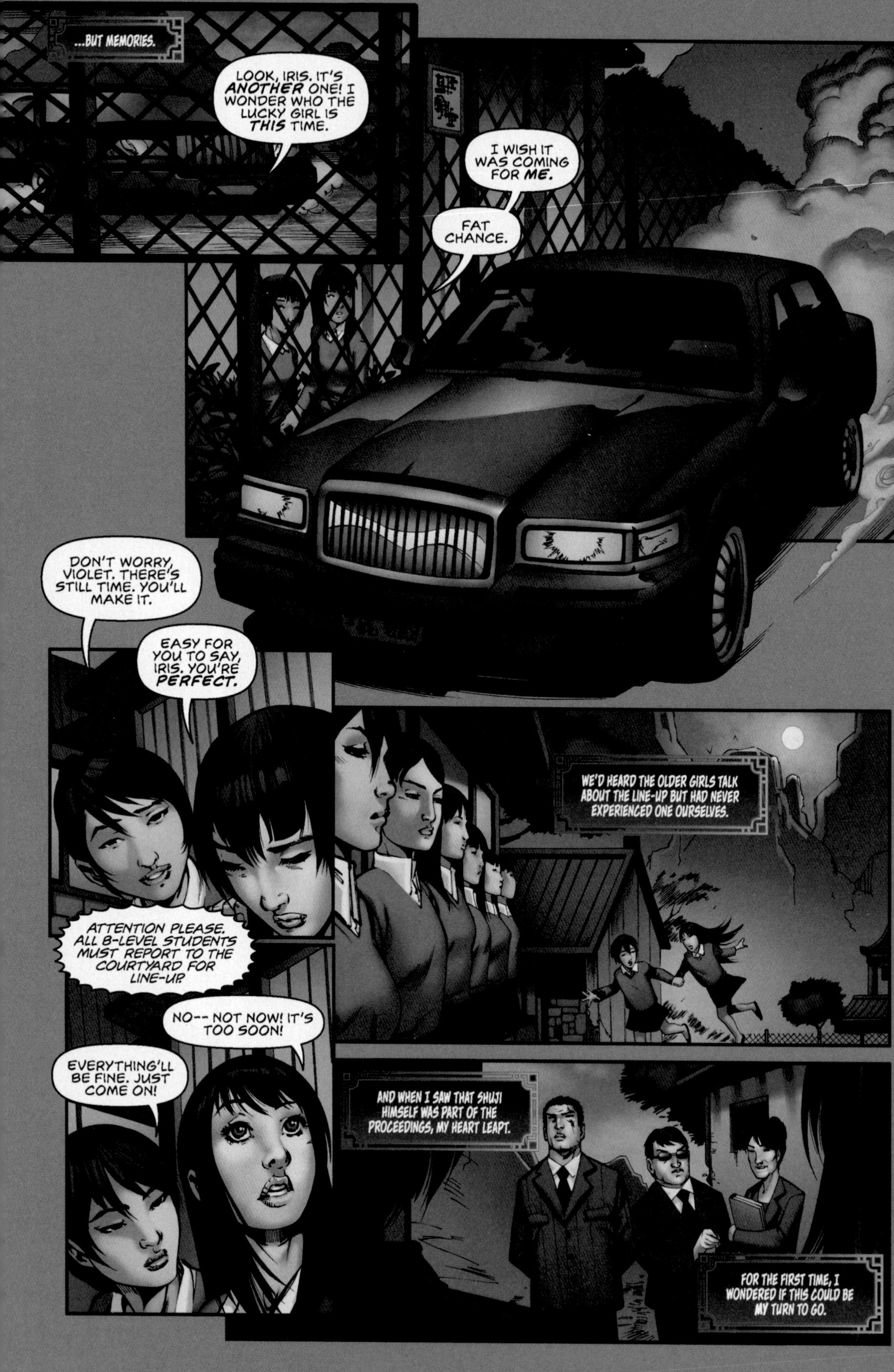

...BUT MEMORIES.
LOOK, IRIS. IT'S ANOTHER ONE! I WONDER WHO THE LUCKY GIRL IS THIS TIME.
I WISH IT WAS COMING FOR ME.
FAT CHANCE.
DON'T WORRY, VIOLET. THERE'S STILL TIME. YOU'LL MAKE IT.
EASY FOR YOU TO SAY, IRIS. YOU'RE PERFECT.
ATTENTION PLEASE. ALL B-LEVEL STUDENTS MUST REPORT TO THE COURTYARD FOR LINE-UP.
NO-- NOT NOW! IT'S TOO SOON!
EVERYTHING'LL BE FINE. JUST COME ON!
WE'D HEARD THE OLDER GIRLS TALK ABOUT THE LINE-UP BUT HAD NEVER EXPERIENCED ONE OURSELVES.
AND WHEN I SAW THAT SHUJI HIMSELF WAS PART OF THE PROCEEDINGS, MY HEART LEAPT.
FOR THE FIRST TIME, I WONDERED IF THIS COULD BE MY TURN TO GO.

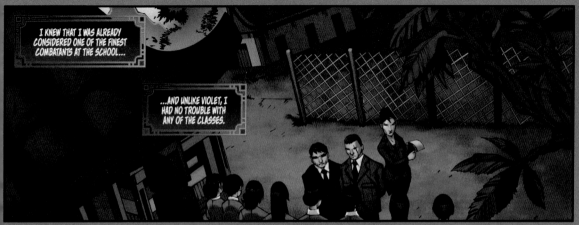

I KNEW THAT I WAS ALREADY CONSIDERED ONE OF THE FINEST COMBATANTS AT THE SCHOOL...

...AND UNLIKE VIOLET, I HAD NO TROUBLE WITH ANY OF THE CLASSES.

THIS ONE HAS BEEN WITH US SINCE SHE WAS AN INFANT. SHE'S VERY HEALTHY. VERY CLEAN. DON'T YOU AGREE, MR. TAN?

A BIT *THIN*, BUT SHE'LL DO.

VERY GOOD. MS. FONG?

NOTED, SIR. JASMINE, PLEASE EXIT THE LINE.

JASMINE WAS TWO YEARS OLDER THAN VIOLET AND MYSELF.

SHE WASN'T MUCH OF A FIGHTER, NOR DID SHE DO WELL IN THE ETIQUETTE OR PERSONALITY CLASSES.

AND THIS YOUNG LADY?

VIOLET, SIR. A FINE CANDIDATE FOR MR. TAN.

AGREED.

EXCELLENT.

NO... WAIT... I DON'T WANT TO GO ANYMORE...

VIOLET, JASMINE, PLEASE ACCOMPANY MISTER TAN TO THE EAST CAMPUS.

...PLEASE... NOT YET... I CAN IMPROVE, I PROMISE! I--

I DIDN'T SAY A WORD.

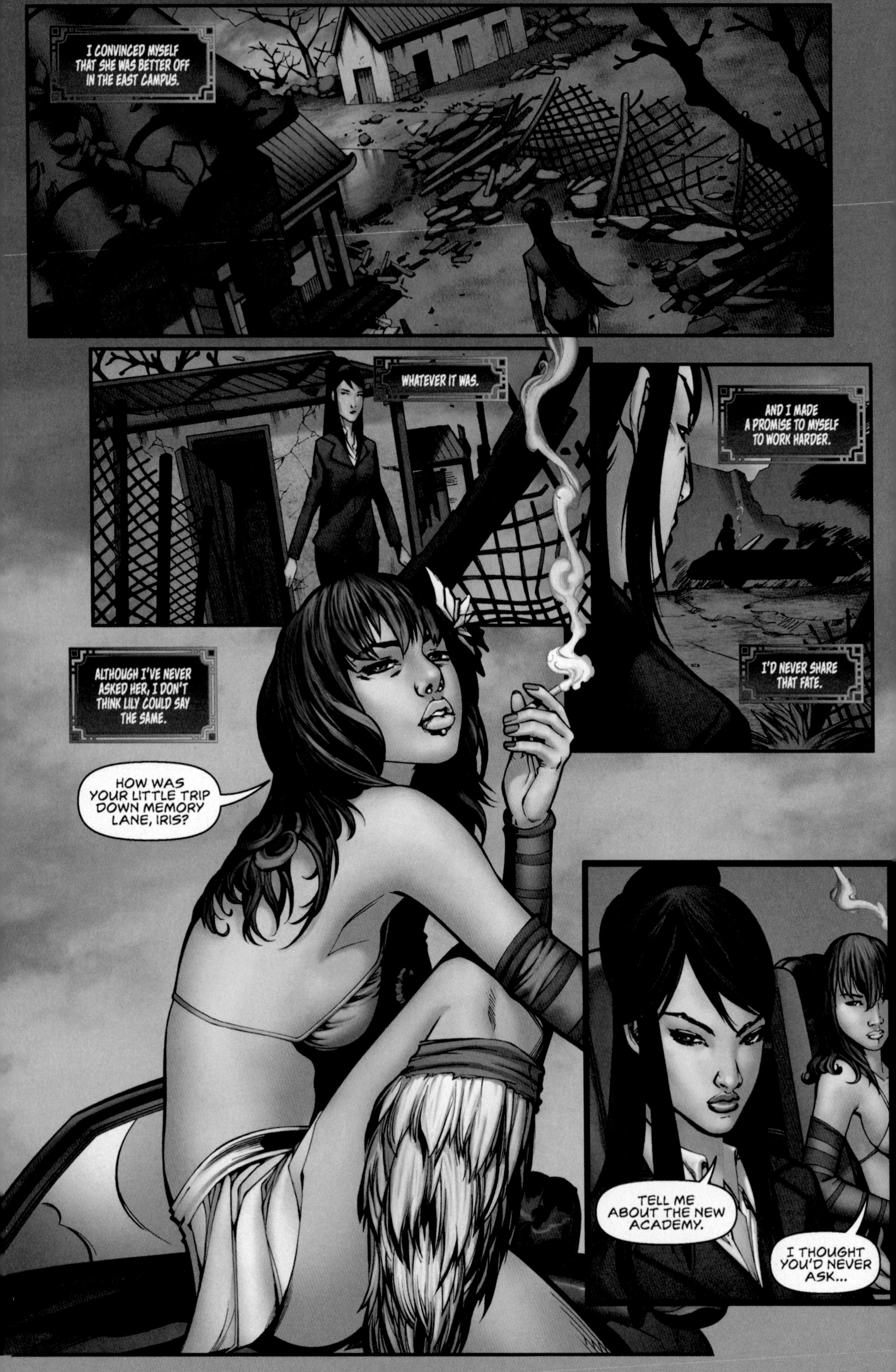
I CONVINCED MYSELF THAT SHE WAS BETTER OFF IN THE EAST CAMPUS.
WHATEVER IT WAS.
AND I MADE A PROMISE TO MYSELF TO WORK HARDER.
I'D NEVER SHARE THAT FATE.
ALTHOUGH I'VE NEVER ASKED HER, I DON'T THINK LILY COULD SAY THE SAME.
HOW WAS YOUR LITTLE TRIP DOWN MEMORY LANE, IRIS?
TELL ME ABOUT THE NEW ACADEMY.
I THOUGHT YOU'D NEVER ASK...

AS YOU KNOW, THE SCHOOL WAS SO SUCCESSFUL AT CHURNING OUT EXECUTIVE ASSISTANTS THAT THEY DECIDED TO EXPAND.
"WITH INVESTMENTS FROM THE GOVERNMENT, DEAR OLD DAD MOVED THE SCHOOL INTO A STATE FACILITY-- COMPLETE WITH MILITARY GUARDS.
"OBVIOUSLY A FRONTAL ASSAULT IS OUT OF THE QUESTION...
"...SO WHILE YOU ENTER THROUGH A LESS SECURE SPOT, I WILL PROVIDE FOR A DISTRACTION."
<HELP!!! SOMEBODY PLEASE! HELP!>*
<HALT!>
¡GASP!¡ <HELP-- I WAS ATTACKED-->
<HE-- HE'S RIGHT OVER-->
<SILENCE! YOU ARE TRESPASSING ON GOVERNMENT PROPERTY!>
*TRANSLATED FROM CHINESE MANDARIN.>

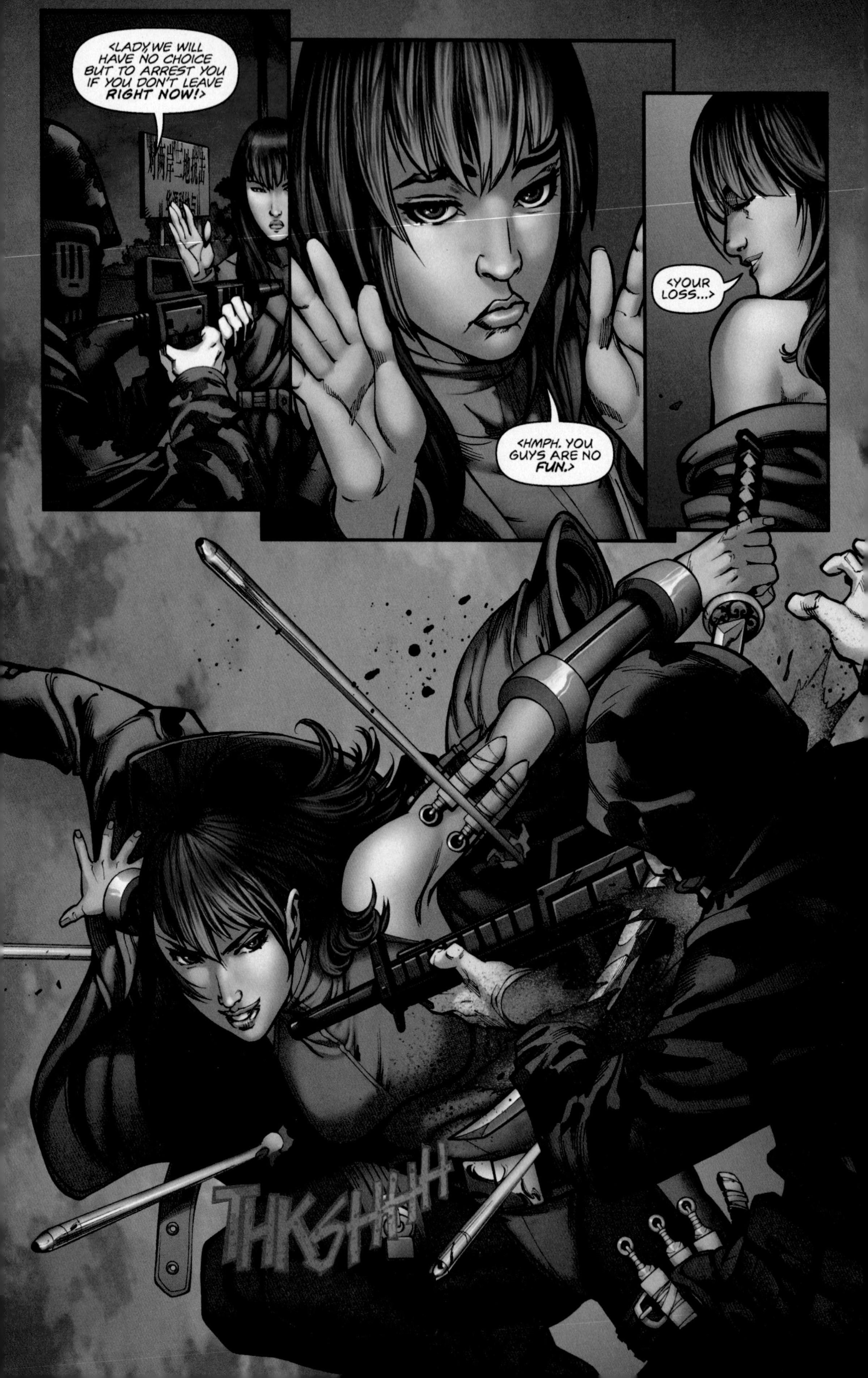
<LADY, WE WILL HAVE NO CHOICE BUT TO ARREST YOU IF YOU DON'T LEAVE RIGHT NOW!>
<HMPH. YOU GUYS ARE NO FUN.>
<YOUR LOSS...>
THKSHHH

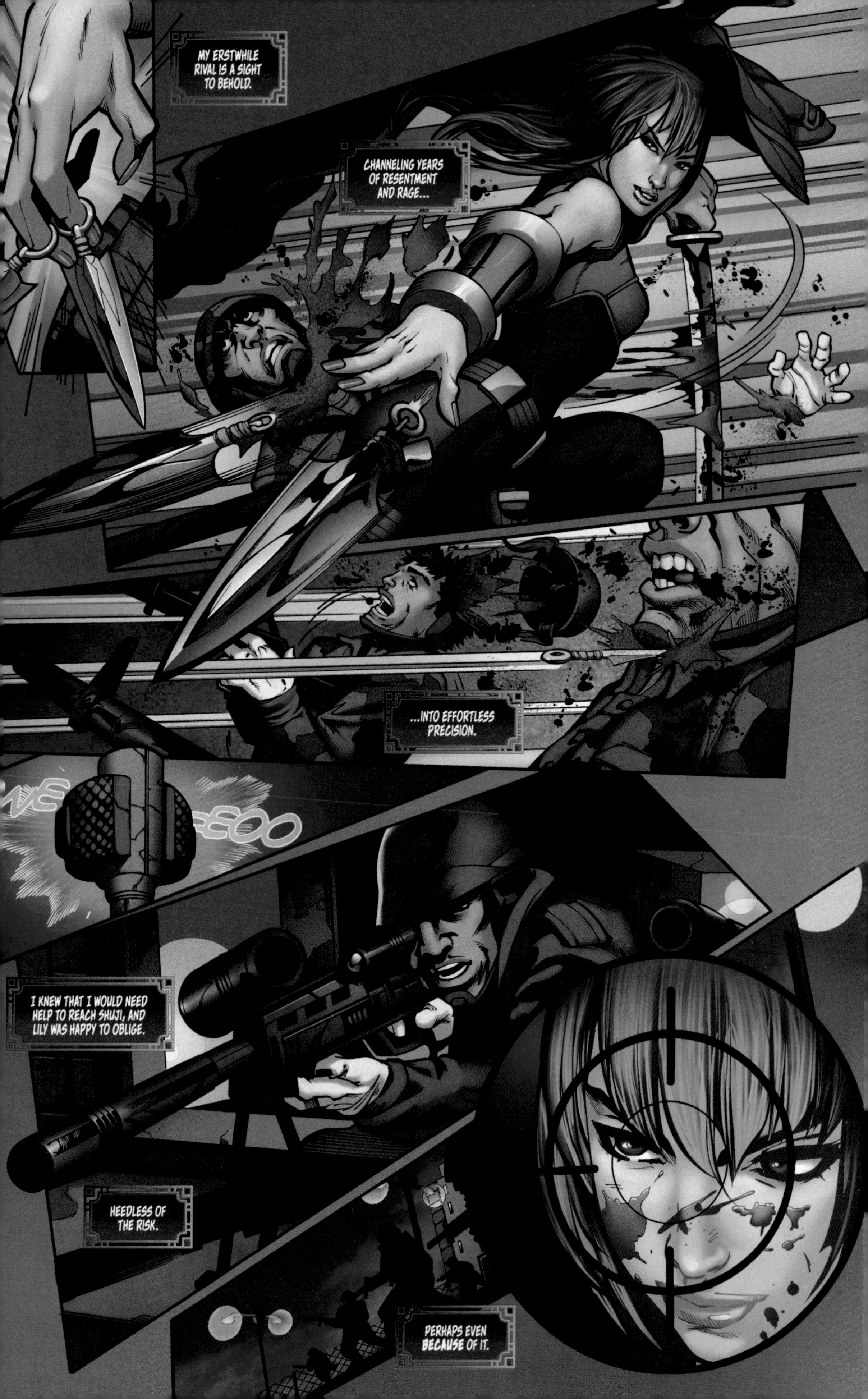
MY ERSTWHILE RIVAL IS A SIGHT TO BEHOLD.
CHANNELING YEARS OF RESENTMENT AND RAGE...
...INTO EFFORTLESS PRECISION.
I KNEW THAT I WOULD NEED HELP TO REACH SHUJI, AND LILY WAS HAPPY TO OBLIGE.
HEEDLESS OF THE RISK.
PERHAPS EVEN BECAUSE OF IT.

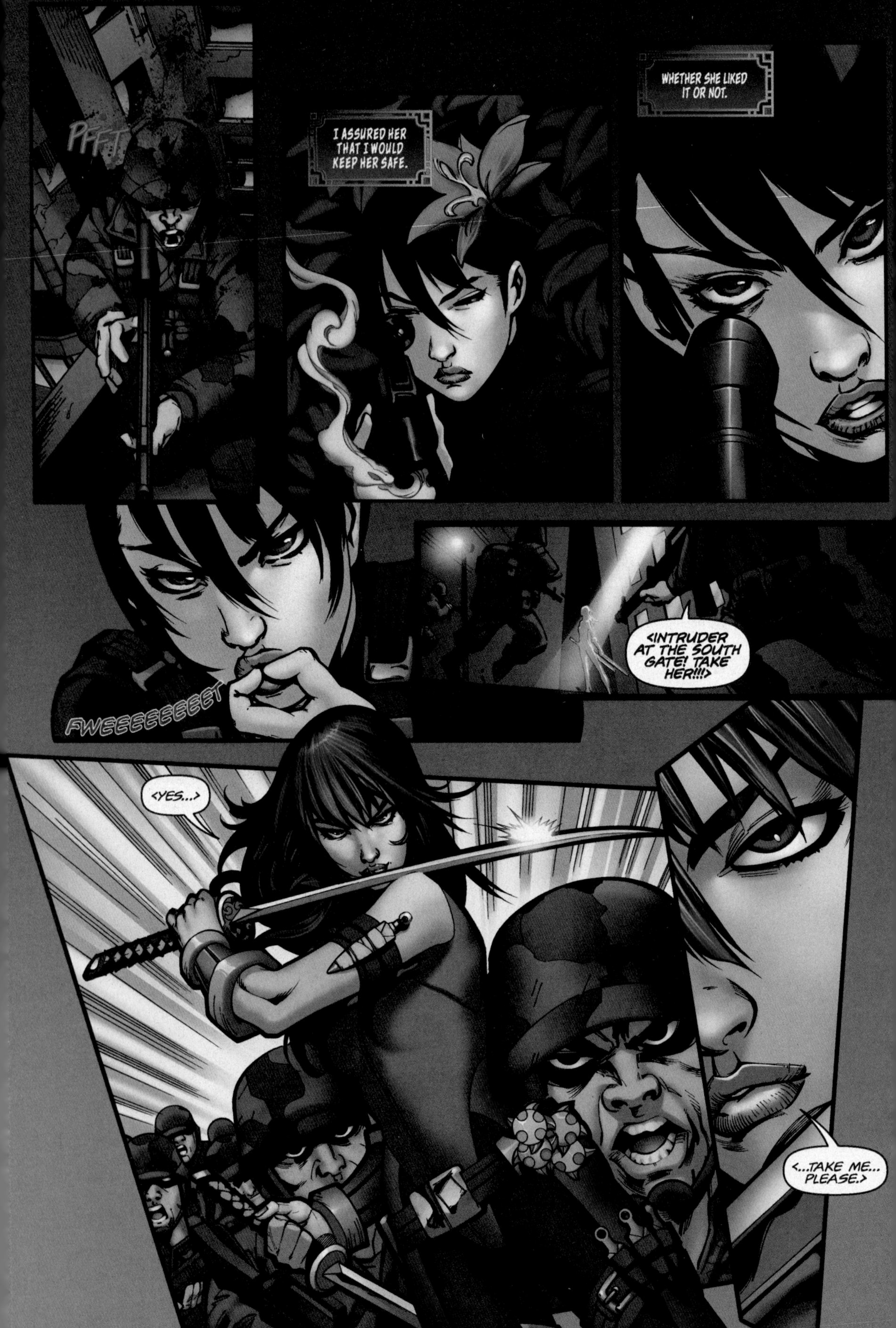
PFFT
I ASSURED HER THAT I WOULD KEEP HER SAFE.
WHETHER SHE LIKED IT OR NOT.
FWEEEEEEEEET
<INTRUDER AT THE SOUTH GATE! TAKE HER!!!>
<YES...>
<...TAKE ME... PLEASE.>

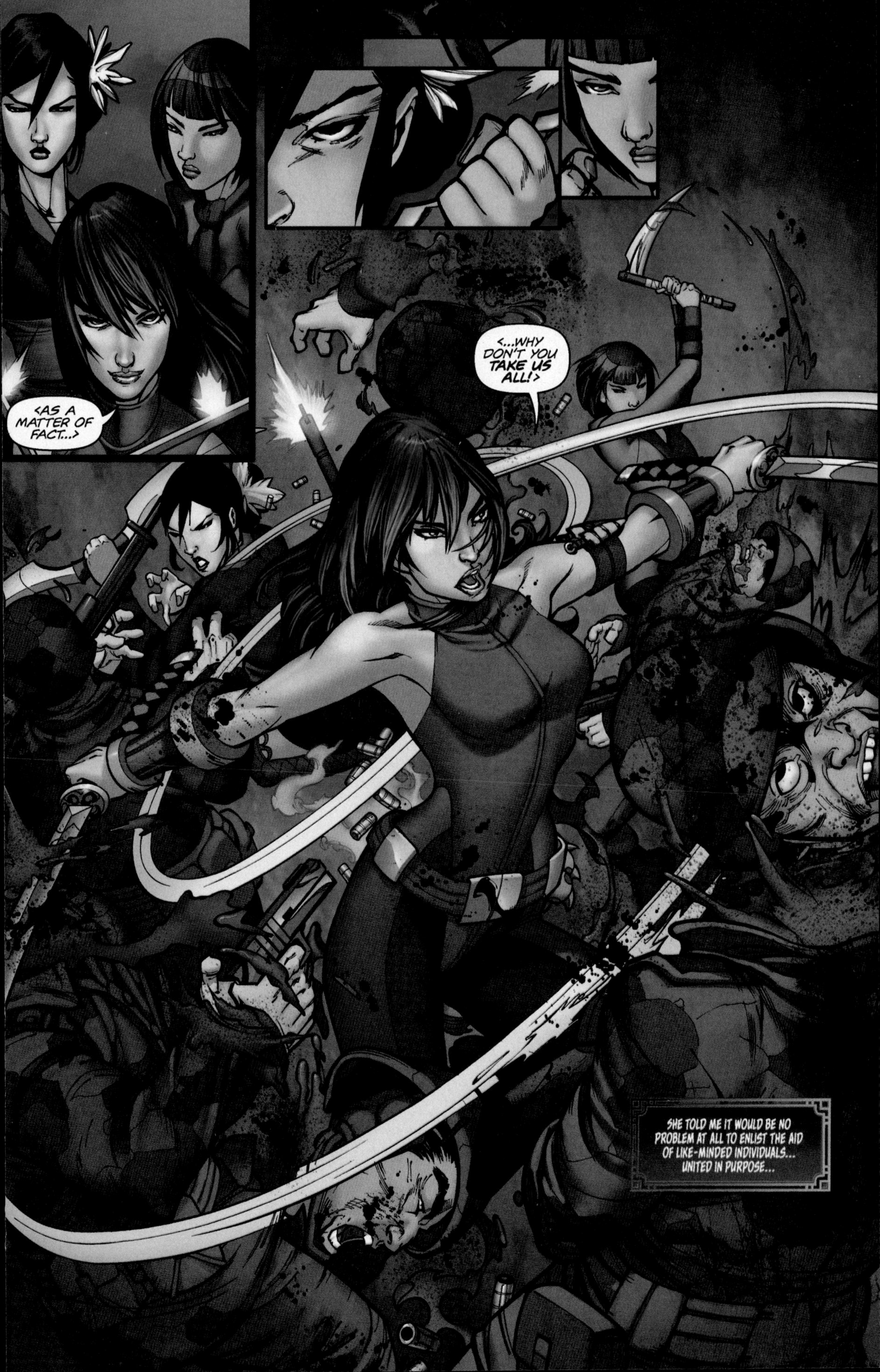
<AS A MATTER OF FACT...>
<...WHY DON'T YOU TAKE US ALL!>
SHE TOLD ME IT WOULD BE NO PROBLEM AT ALL TO ENLIST THE AID OF LIKE-MINDED INDIVIDUALS... UNITED IN PURPOSE...

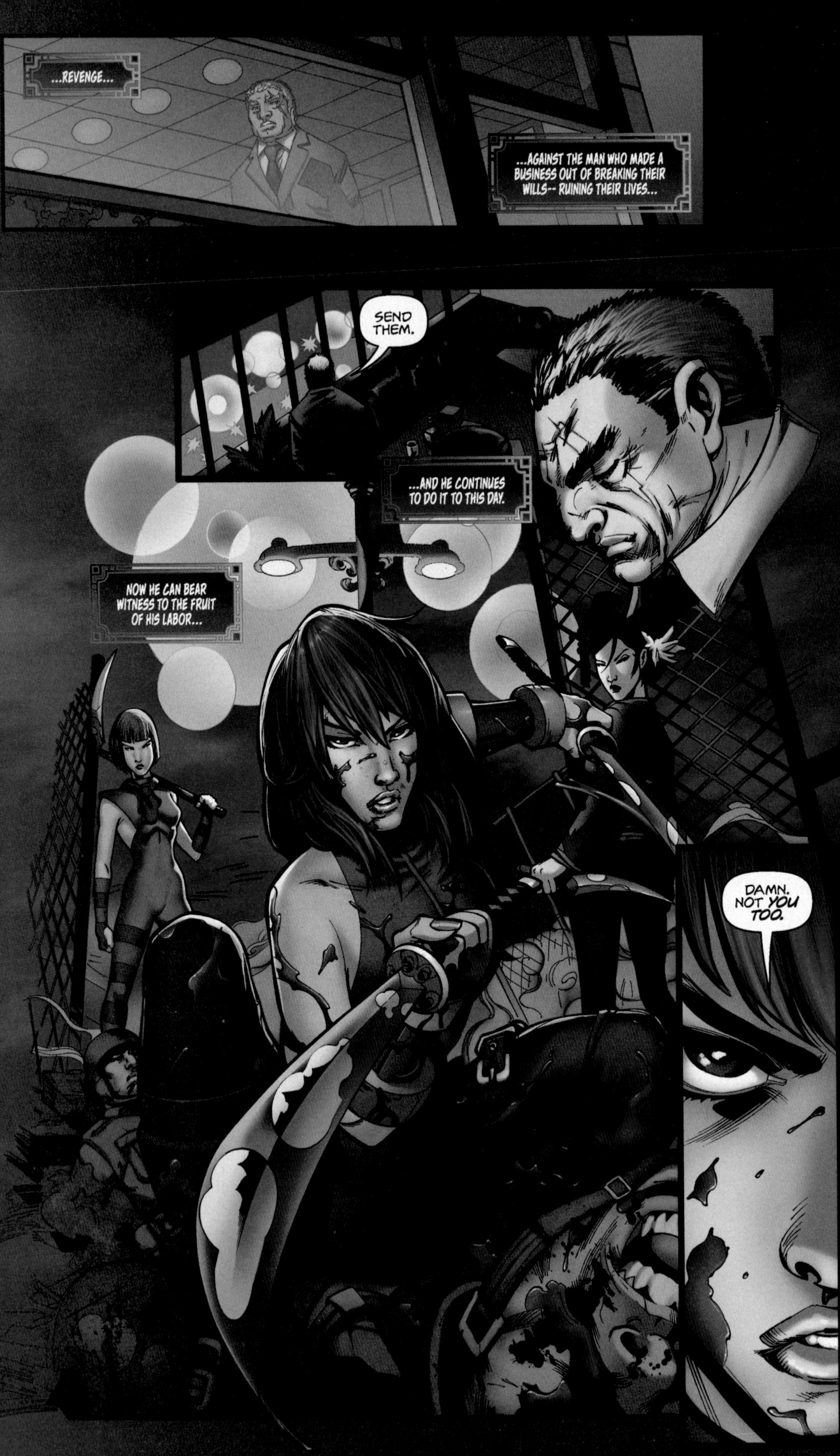
...REVENGE...
...AGAINST THE MAN WHO MADE A BUSINESS OUT OF BREAKING THEIR WILLS-- RUINING THEIR LIVES...
SEND THEM.
...AND HE CONTINUES TO DO IT TO THIS DAY.
NOW HE CAN BEAR WITNESS TO THE FRUIT OF HIS LABOR...
DAMN. NOT YOU TOO.

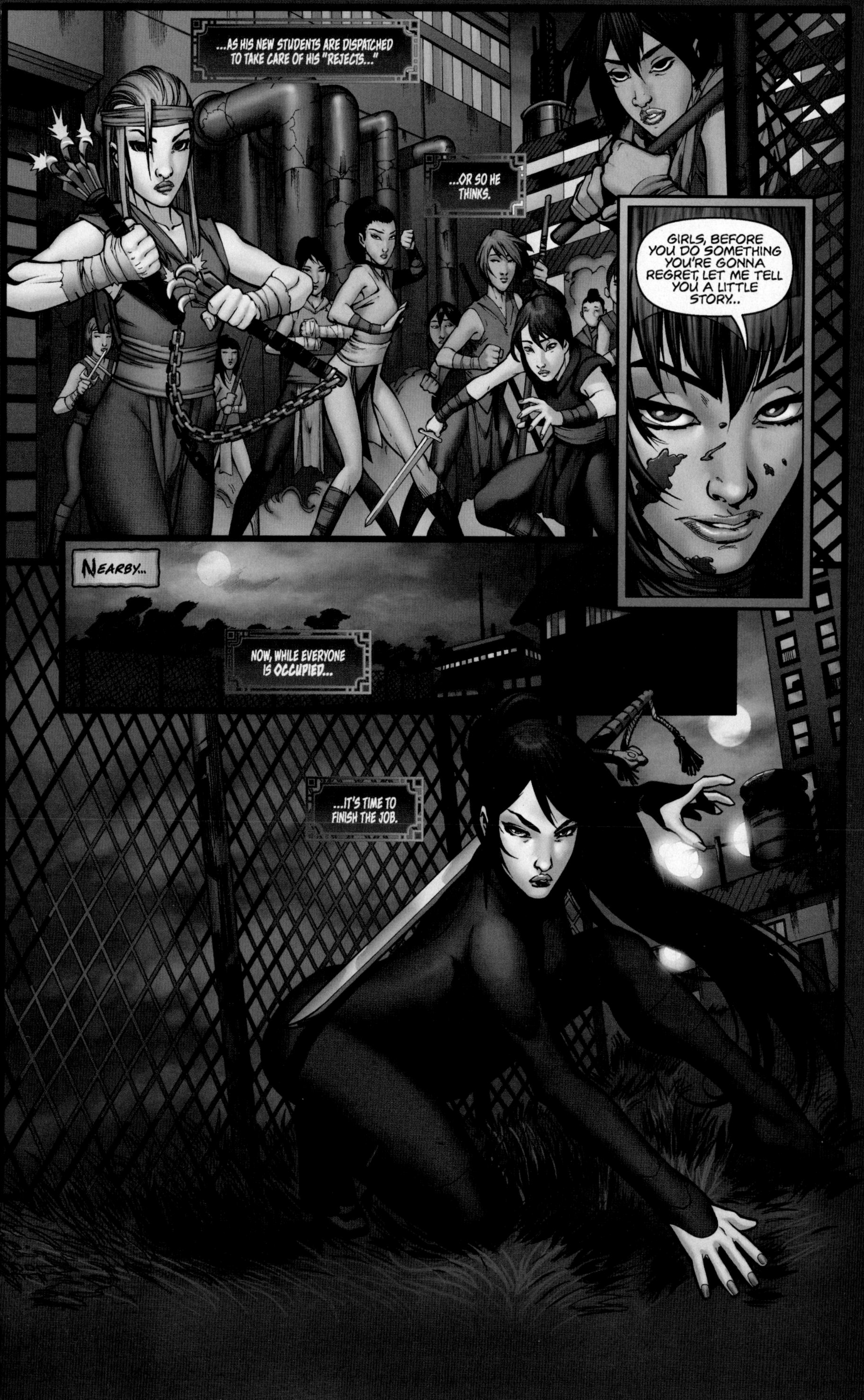
...AS HIS NEW STUDENTS ARE DISPATCHED TO TAKE CARE OF HIS "REJECTS..."
...OR SO HE THINKS.
GIRLS, BEFORE YOU DO SOMETHING YOU'RE GONNA REGRET, LET ME TELL YOU A LITTLE STORY...
NEARBY...
NOW, WHILE EVERYONE IS OCCUPIED...
...IT'S TIME TO FINISH THE JOB.

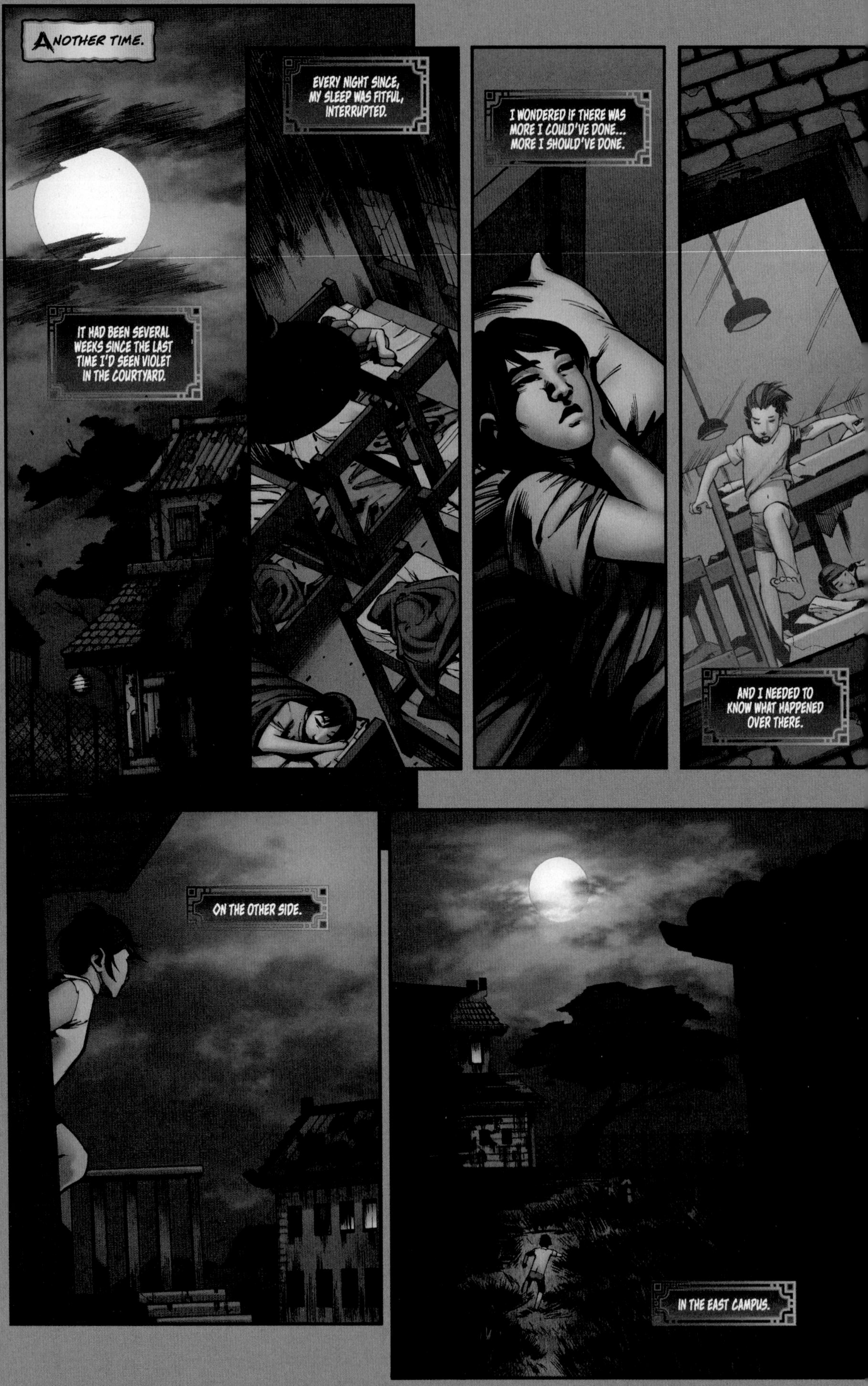
ANOTHER TIME.
IT HAD BEEN SEVERAL WEEKS SINCE THE LAST TIME I'D SEEN VIOLET IN THE COURTYARD.
EVERY NIGHT SINCE, MY SLEEP WAS FITFUL, INTERRUPTED.
I WONDERED IF THERE WAS MORE I COULD'VE DONE... MORE I SHOULD'VE DONE.
AND I NEEDED TO KNOW WHAT HAPPENED OVER THERE.
ON THE OTHER SIDE.
IN THE EAST CAMPUS.

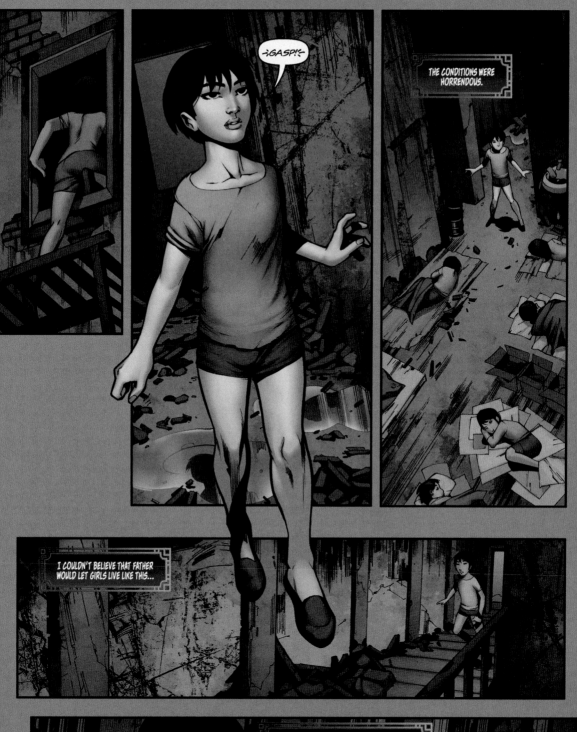

—GASP!—

THE CONDITIONS WERE HORRENDOUS.

I COULDN'T BELIEVE THAT FATHER WOULD LET GIRLS LIVE LIKE THIS...

...PERHAPS HE DIDN'T KNOW. HE COULD'VE BEEN TOO BUSY WITH OUR TRAINING TO SEE HOW THESE PEOPLE WERE TREATING HIS FORMER STUDENTS.

I DECIDED THAT I WOULD TELL HIM UPON MY RETURN, EVEN IF IT GOT ME IN TROUBLE.

WELCOME, MR. ONG. PLEASE LET ME KNOW IF ONE OF OUR FINE YOUNG LADIES SUITS YOUR FANCY.

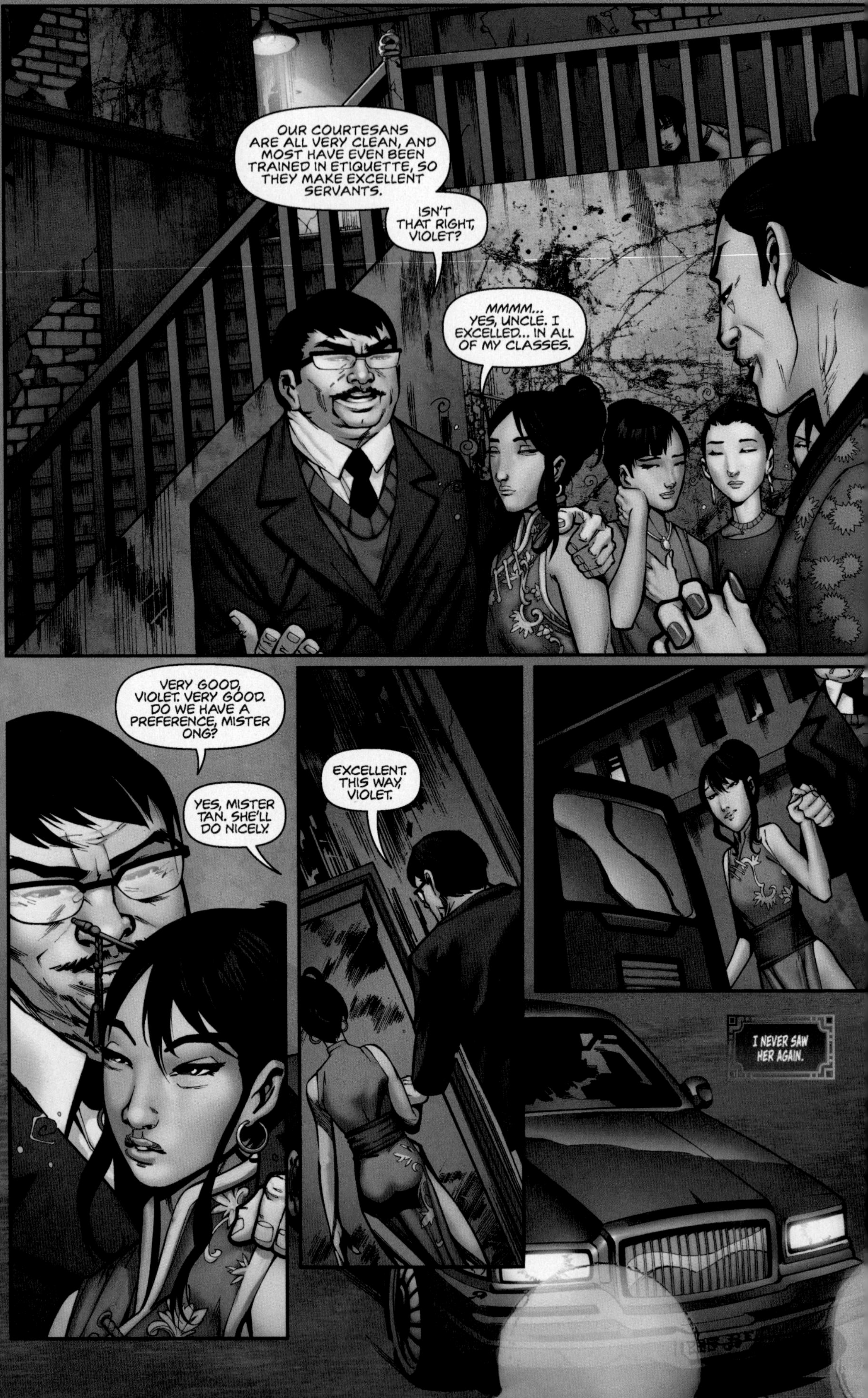
OUR COURTESANS ARE ALL VERY CLEAN, AND MOST HAVE EVEN BEEN TRAINED IN ETIQUETTE, SO THEY MAKE EXCELLENT SERVANTS.
ISN'T THAT RIGHT, VIOLET?
MMMM... YES, UNCLE. I EXCELLED... IN ALL OF MY CLASSES.
VERY GOOD, VIOLET. VERY GOOD. DO WE HAVE A PREFERENCE, MISTER ONG?
YES, MISTER TAN. SHE'LL DO NICELY.
EXCELLENT. THIS WAY, VIOLET.
I NEVER SAW HER AGAIN.

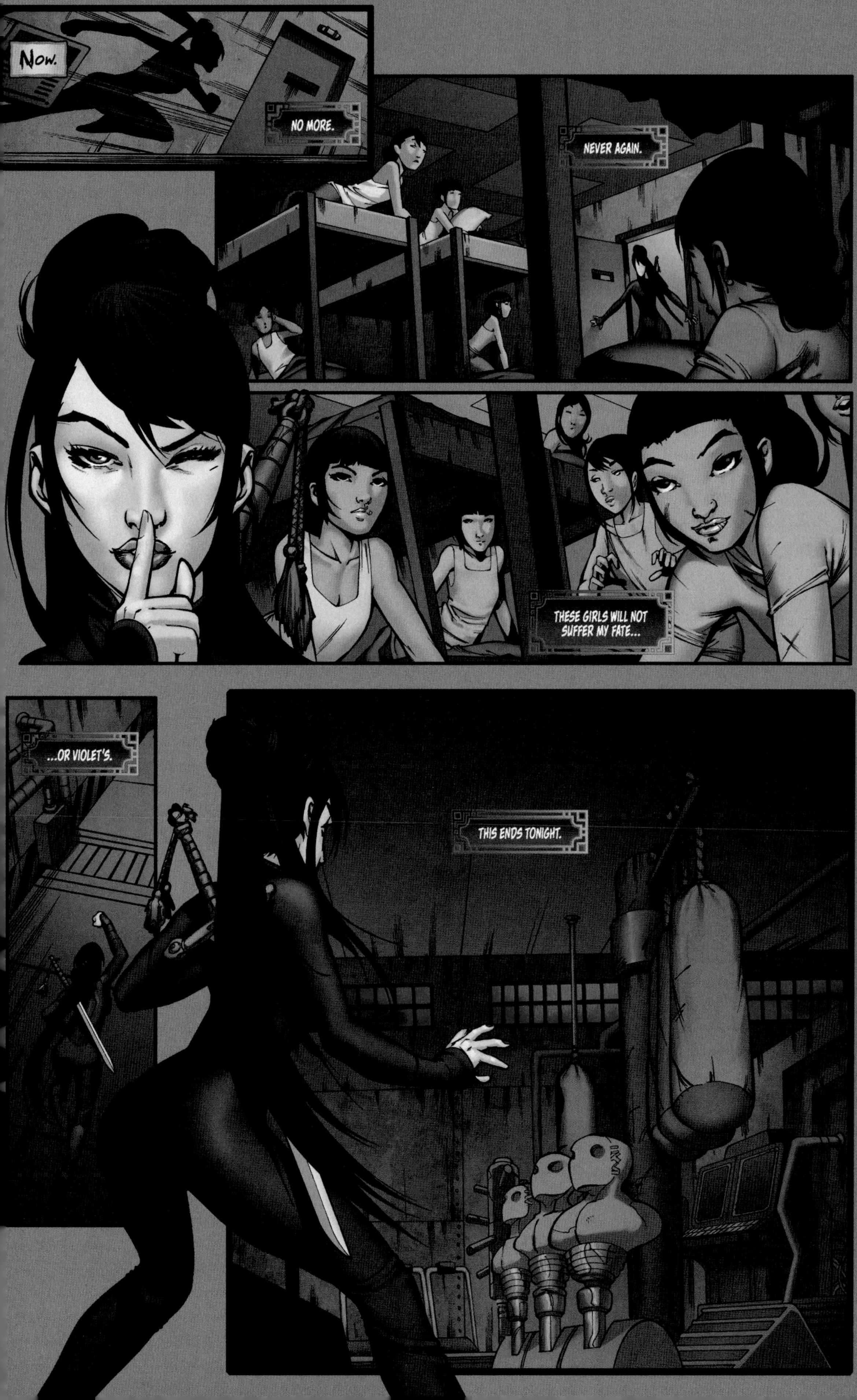
Now.
NO MORE.
NEVER AGAIN.
THESE GIRLS WILL NOT SUFFER MY FATE...
...OR VIOLET'S.
THIS ENDS TONIGHT.

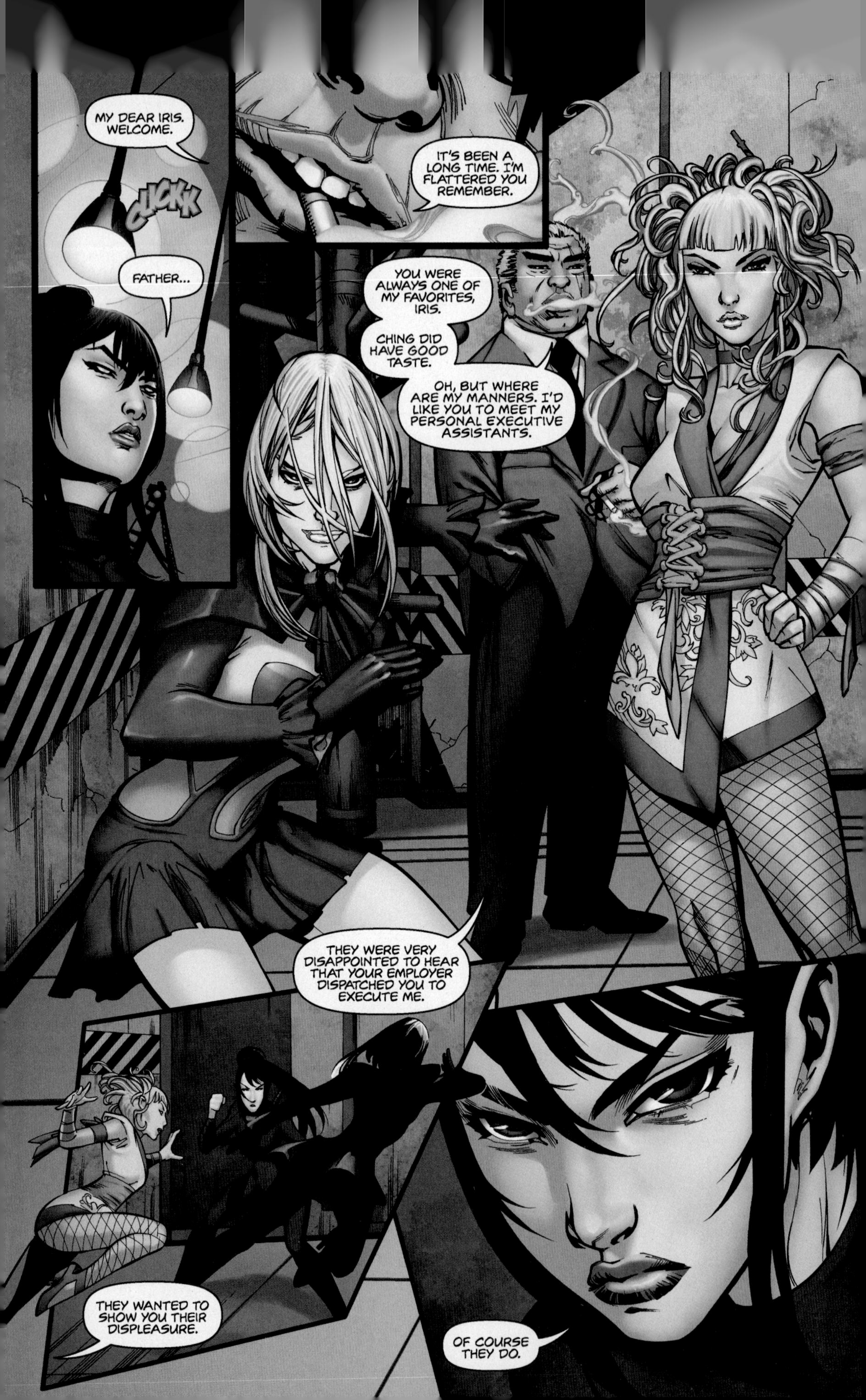
MY DEAR IRIS. WELCOME.
CLICKK
IT'S BEEN A LONG TIME. I'M FLATTERED YOU REMEMBER.
FATHER...
YOU WERE ALWAYS ONE OF MY FAVORITES, IRIS.
CHING DID HAVE GOOD TASTE.
OH, BUT WHERE ARE MY MANNERS. I'D LIKE YOU TO MEET MY PERSONAL EXECUTIVE ASSISTANTS.
THEY WERE VERY DISAPPOINTED TO HEAR THAT YOUR EMPLOYER DISPATCHED YOU TO EXECUTE ME.
THEY WANTED TO SHOW YOU THEIR DISPLEASURE.
OF COURSE THEY DO.

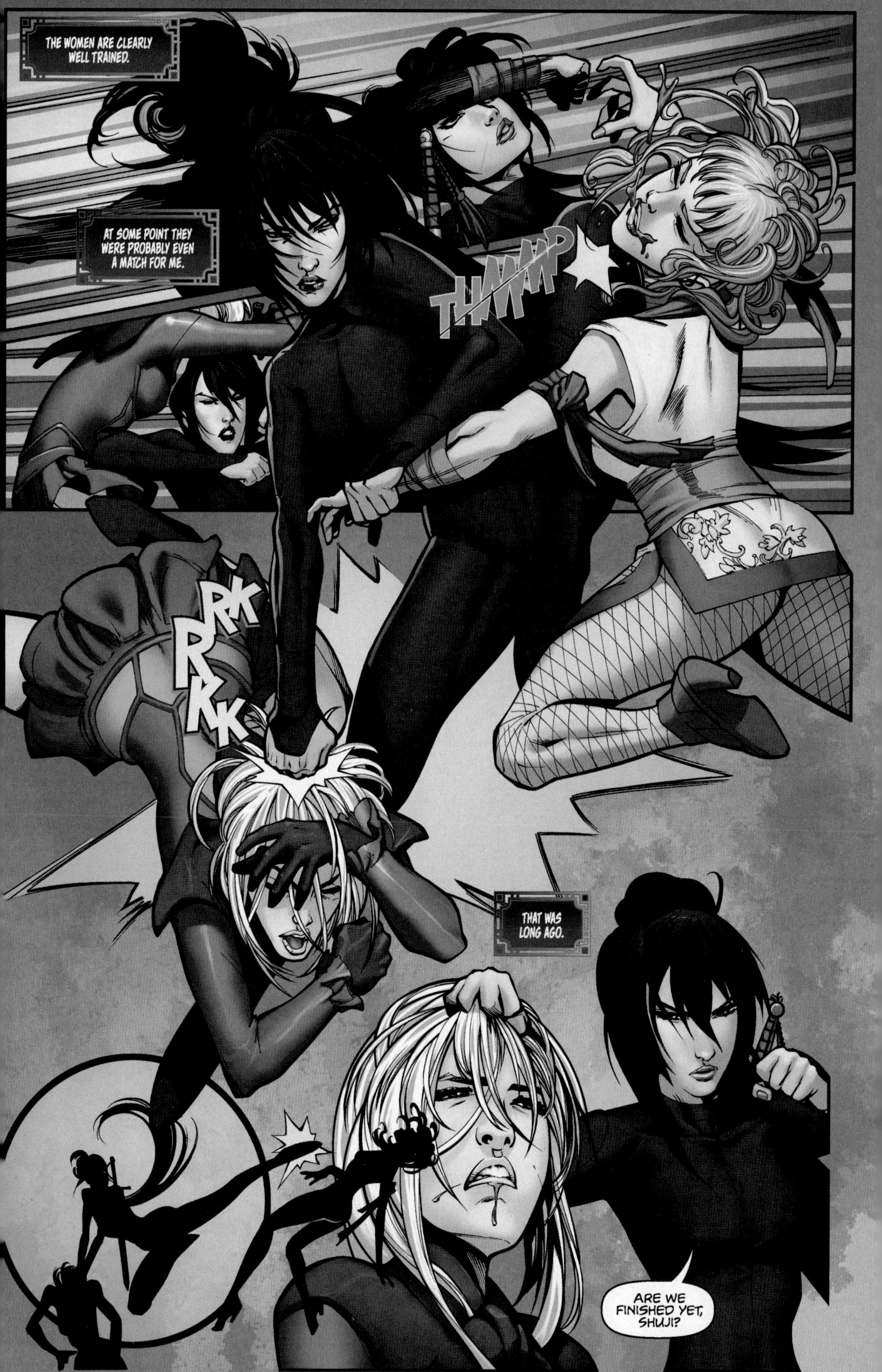
THE WOMEN ARE CLEARLY WELL TRAINED.
AT SOME POINT THEY WERE PROBABLY EVEN A MATCH FOR ME.
THWWWP
RK RKK
THAT WAS LONG AGO.
ARE WE FINISHED YET, SHUJI?

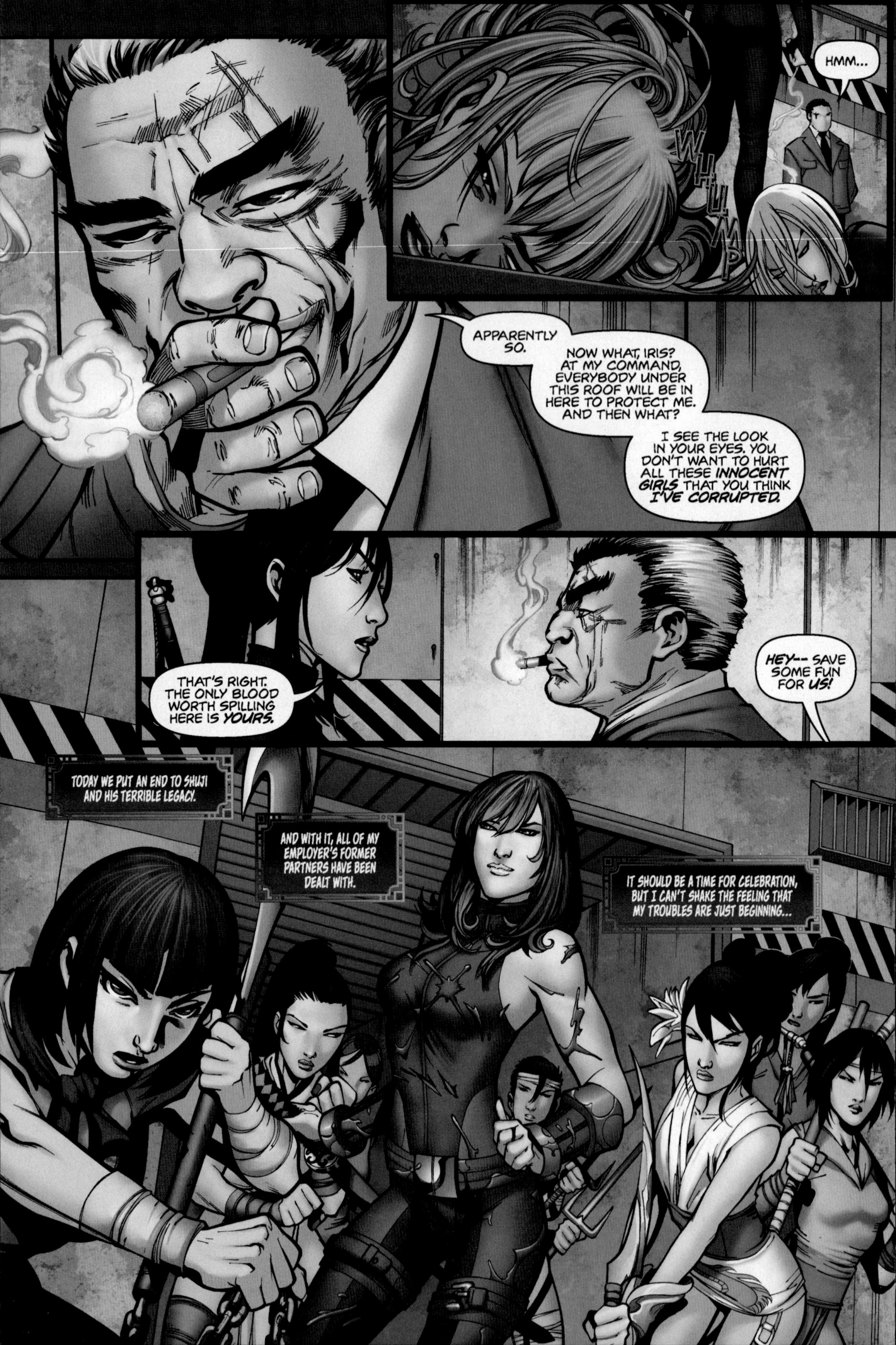
HMM...
WHUMP
APPARENTLY SO.
NOW WHAT, IRIS? AT MY COMMAND, EVERYBODY UNDER THIS ROOF WILL BE IN HERE TO PROTECT ME. AND THEN WHAT?
I SEE THE LOOK IN YOUR EYES. YOU DON'T WANT TO HURT ALL THESE INNOCENT GIRLS THAT YOU THINK I'VE CORRUPTED.
THAT'S RIGHT. THE ONLY BLOOD WORTH SPILLING HERE IS YOURS.
HEY-- SAVE SOME FUN FOR US!
TODAY WE PUT AN END TO SHUJI AND HIS TERRIBLE LEGACY.
AND WITH IT, ALL OF MY EMPLOYER'S FORMER PARTNERS HAVE BEEN DEALT WITH.
IT SHOULD BE A TIME FOR CELEBRATION, BUT I CAN'T SHAKE THE FEELING THAT MY TROUBLES ARE JUST BEGINNING...

EXECUTIVE ASSISTANT: IRIS #5
Cover A
EDUARDO FRANCISCO
JOHN STARR

EXECUTIVE ASSISTANT: IRIS #5
Cover B
JOE BENITEZ
PETER STEIGERWALD

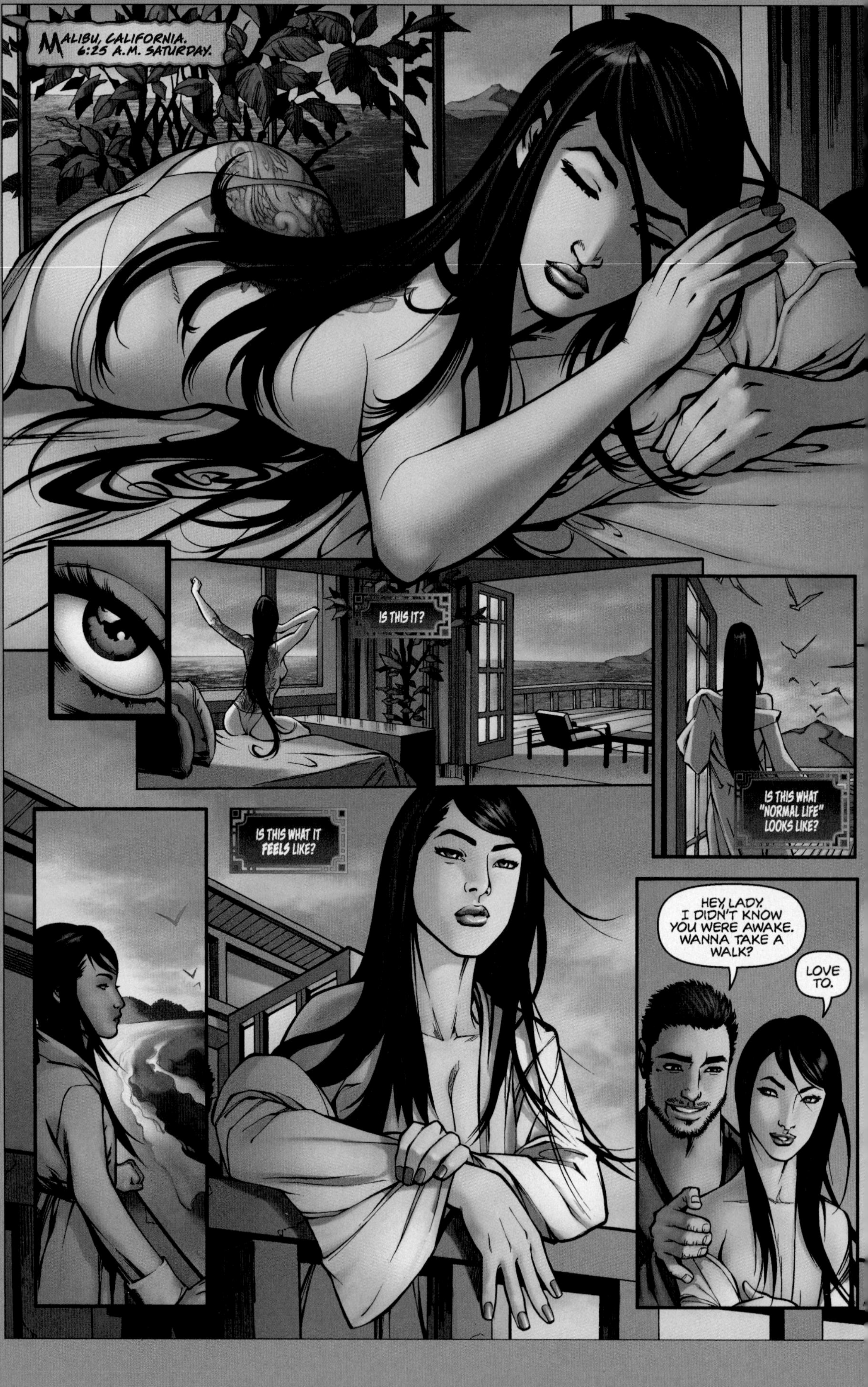
MALIBU, CALIFORNIA. 6:25 A.M. SATURDAY.
IS THIS IT?
IS THIS WHAT "NORMAL LIFE" LOOKS LIKE?
IS THIS WHAT IT FEELS LIKE?
HEY, LADY. I DIDN'T KNOW YOU WERE AWAKE. WANNA TAKE A WALK?
LOVE TO.

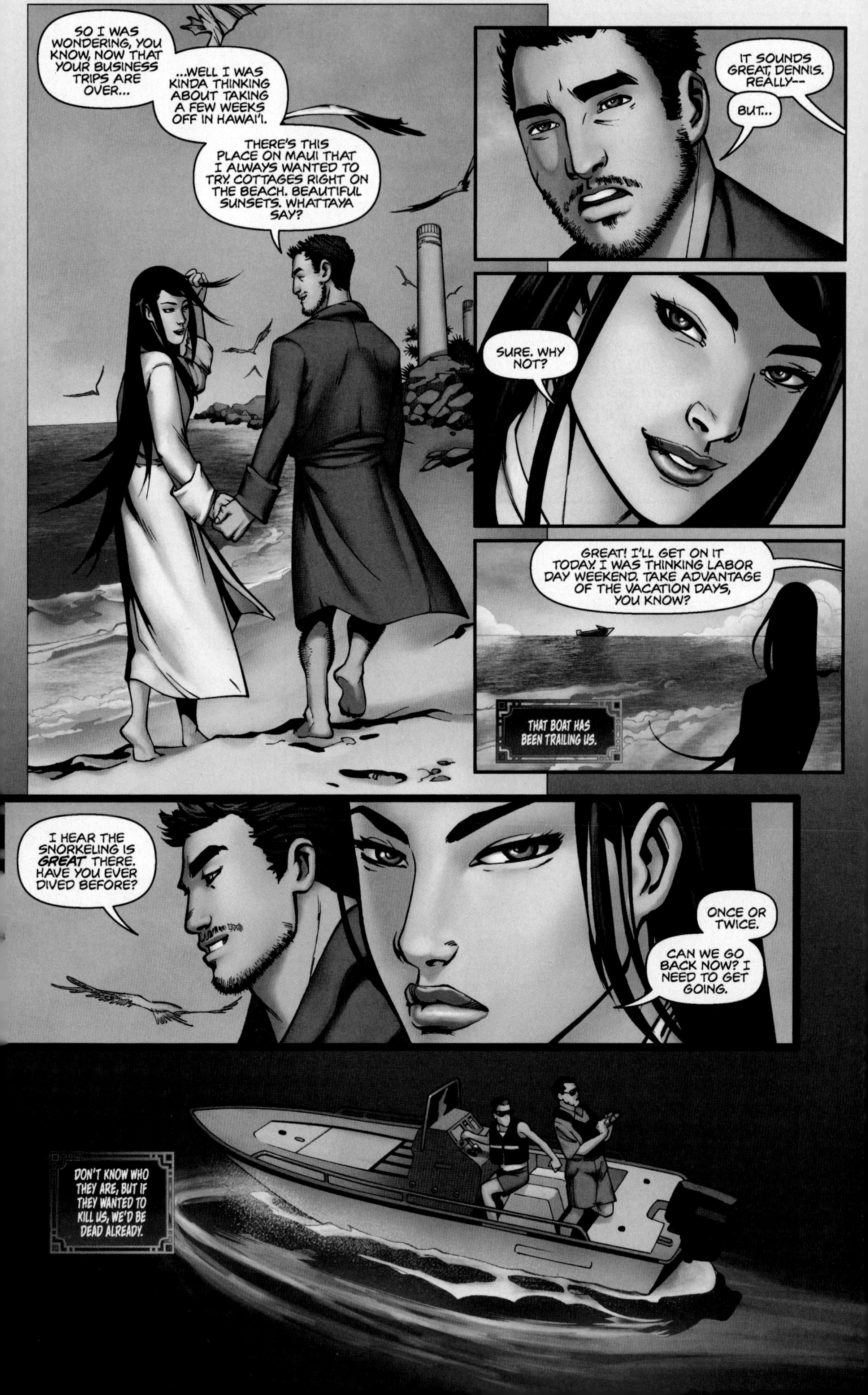
SO I WAS WONDERING, YOU KNOW, NOW THAT YOUR BUSINESS TRIPS ARE OVER...
...WELL I WAS KINDA THINKING ABOUT TAKING A FEW WEEKS OFF IN HAWAI'I.
THERE'S THIS PLACE ON MAUI THAT I ALWAYS WANTED TO TRY. COTTAGES RIGHT ON THE BEACH. BEAUTIFUL SUNSETS. WHATTAYA SAY?
IT SOUNDS GREAT, DENNIS. REALLY--
BUT...
SURE. WHY NOT?
GREAT! I'LL GET ON IT TODAY. I WAS THINKING LABOR DAY WEEKEND. TAKE ADVANTAGE OF THE VACATION DAYS, YOU KNOW?
THAT BOAT HAS BEEN TRAILING US.
I HEAR THE SNORKELING IS GREAT THERE. HAVE YOU EVER DIVED BEFORE?
ONCE OR TWICE.
CAN WE GO BACK NOW? I NEED TO GET GOING.
DON'T KNOW WHO THEY ARE, BUT IF THEY WANTED TO KILL US, WE'D BE DEAD ALREADY.

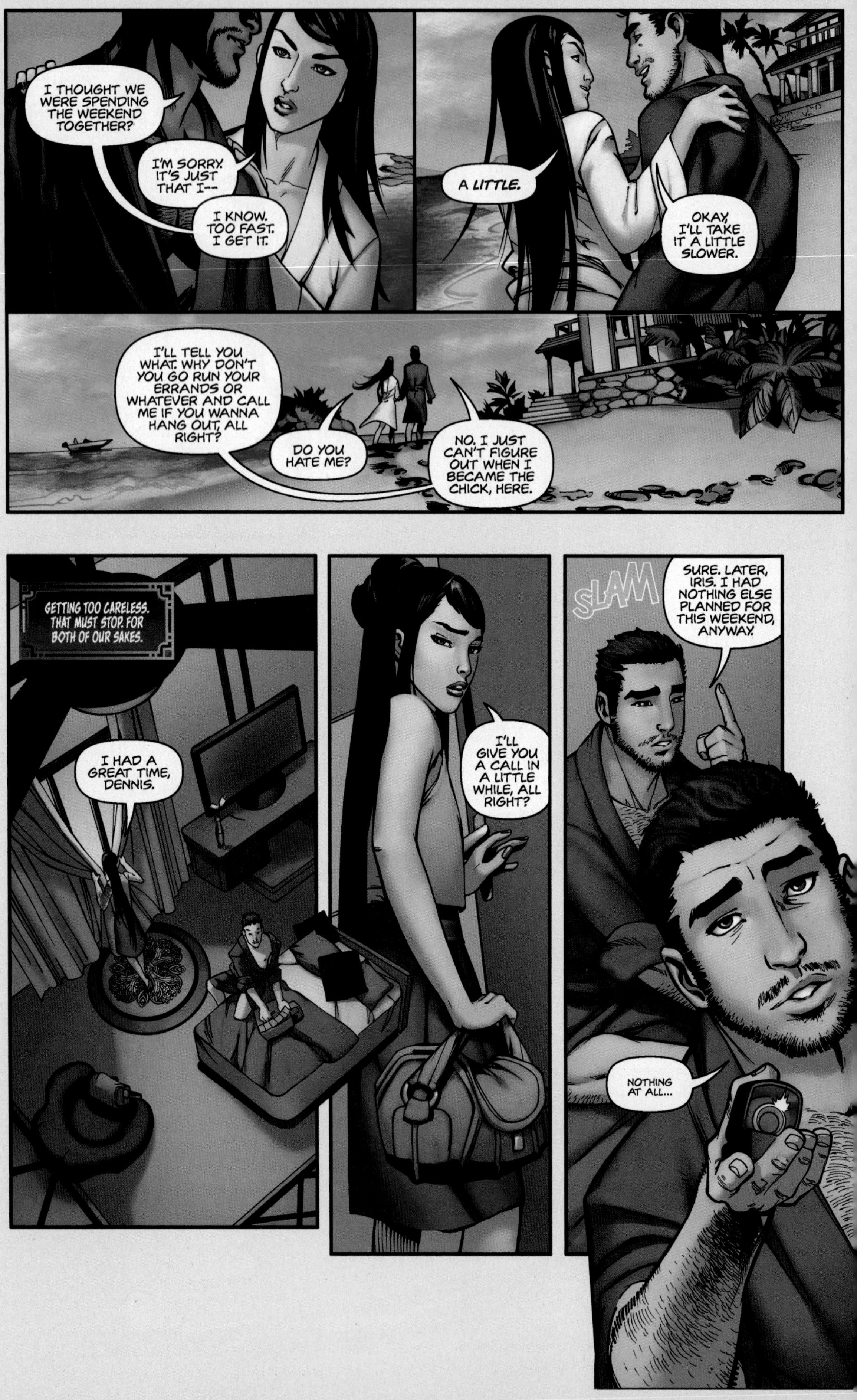
I THOUGHT WE WERE SPENDING THE WEEKEND TOGETHER?
I'M SORRY. IT'S JUST THAT I--
I KNOW. TOO FAST. I GET IT.
A LITTLE.
OKAY, I'LL TAKE IT A LITTLE SLOWER.
I'LL TELL YOU WHAT. WHY DON'T YOU GO RUN YOUR ERRANDS OR WHATEVER AND CALL ME IF YOU WANNA HANG OUT, ALL RIGHT?
DO YOU HATE ME?
NO. I JUST CAN'T FIGURE OUT WHEN I BECAME THE CHICK, HERE.
GETTING TOO CARELESS. THAT MUST STOP. FOR BOTH OF OUR SAKES.
I HAD A GREAT TIME, DENNIS.
I'LL GIVE YOU A CALL IN A LITTLE WHILE, ALL RIGHT?
SLAM
SURE. LATER, IRIS. I HAD NOTHING ELSE PLANNED FOR THIS WEEKEND, ANYWAY.
NOTHING AT ALL...

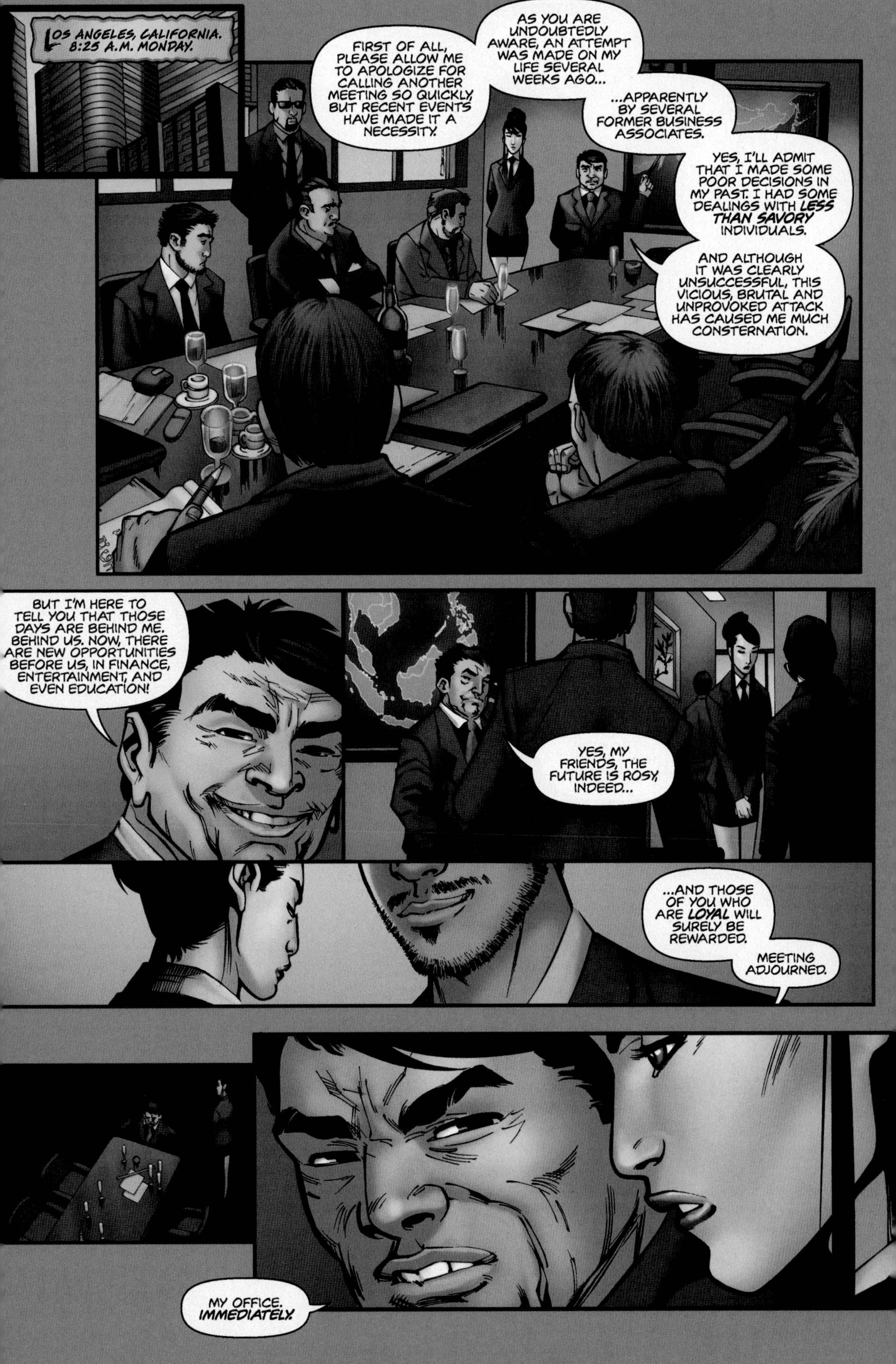
LOS ANGELES, CALIFORNIA. 8:25 A.M. MONDAY.
FIRST OF ALL, PLEASE ALLOW ME TO APOLOGIZE FOR CALLING ANOTHER MEETING SO QUICKLY, BUT RECENT EVENTS HAVE MADE IT A NECESSITY.
AS YOU ARE UNDOUBTEDLY AWARE, AN ATTEMPT WAS MADE ON MY LIFE SEVERAL WEEKS AGO...
...APPARENTLY BY SEVERAL FORMER BUSINESS ASSOCIATES.
YES, I'LL ADMIT THAT I MADE SOME POOR DECISIONS IN MY PAST. I HAD SOME DEALINGS WITH LESS THAN SAVORY INDIVIDUALS.
AND ALTHOUGH IT WAS CLEARLY UNSUCCESSFUL, THIS VICIOUS, BRUTAL AND UNPROVOKED ATTACK HAS CAUSED ME MUCH CONSTERNATION.
BUT I'M HERE TO TELL YOU THAT THOSE DAYS ARE BEHIND ME. BEHIND US. NOW, THERE ARE NEW OPPORTUNITIES BEFORE US, IN FINANCE, ENTERTAINMENT, AND EVEN EDUCATION!
YES, MY FRIENDS, THE FUTURE IS ROSY, INDEED...
...AND THOSE OF YOU WHO ARE LOYAL WILL SURELY BE REWARDED.
MEETING ADJOURNED.
MY OFFICE. IMMEDIATELY.

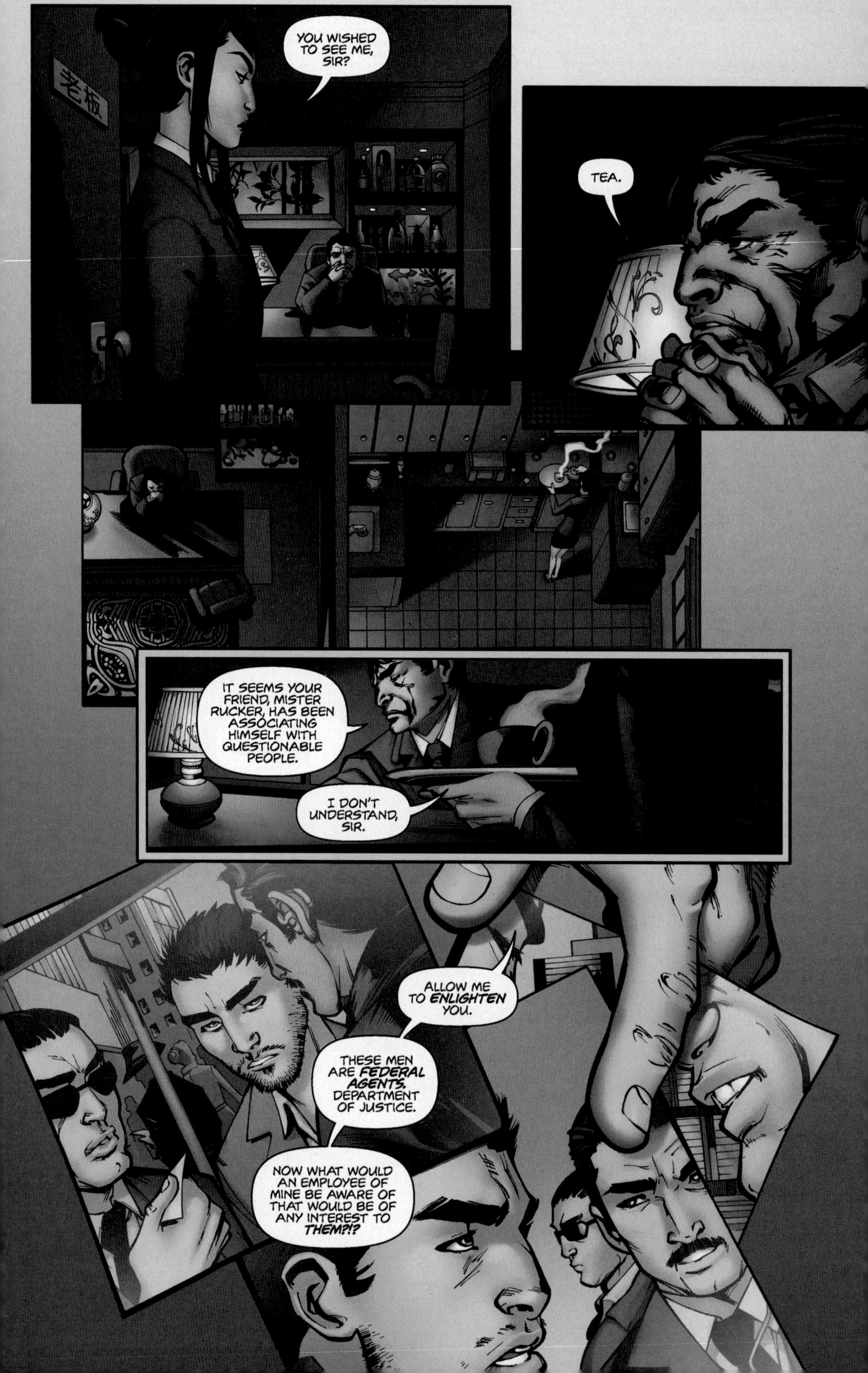

老板
YOU WISHED TO SEE ME, SIR?
TEA.
IT SEEMS YOUR FRIEND, MISTER RUCKER, HAS BEEN ASSOCIATING HIMSELF WITH QUESTIONABLE PEOPLE.
I DON'T UNDERSTAND, SIR.
ALLOW ME TO ENLIGHTEN YOU.
THESE MEN ARE FEDERAL AGENTS. DEPARTMENT OF JUSTICE.
NOW WHAT WOULD AN EMPLOYEE OF MINE BE AWARE OF THAT WOULD BE OF ANY INTEREST TO THEM?!?

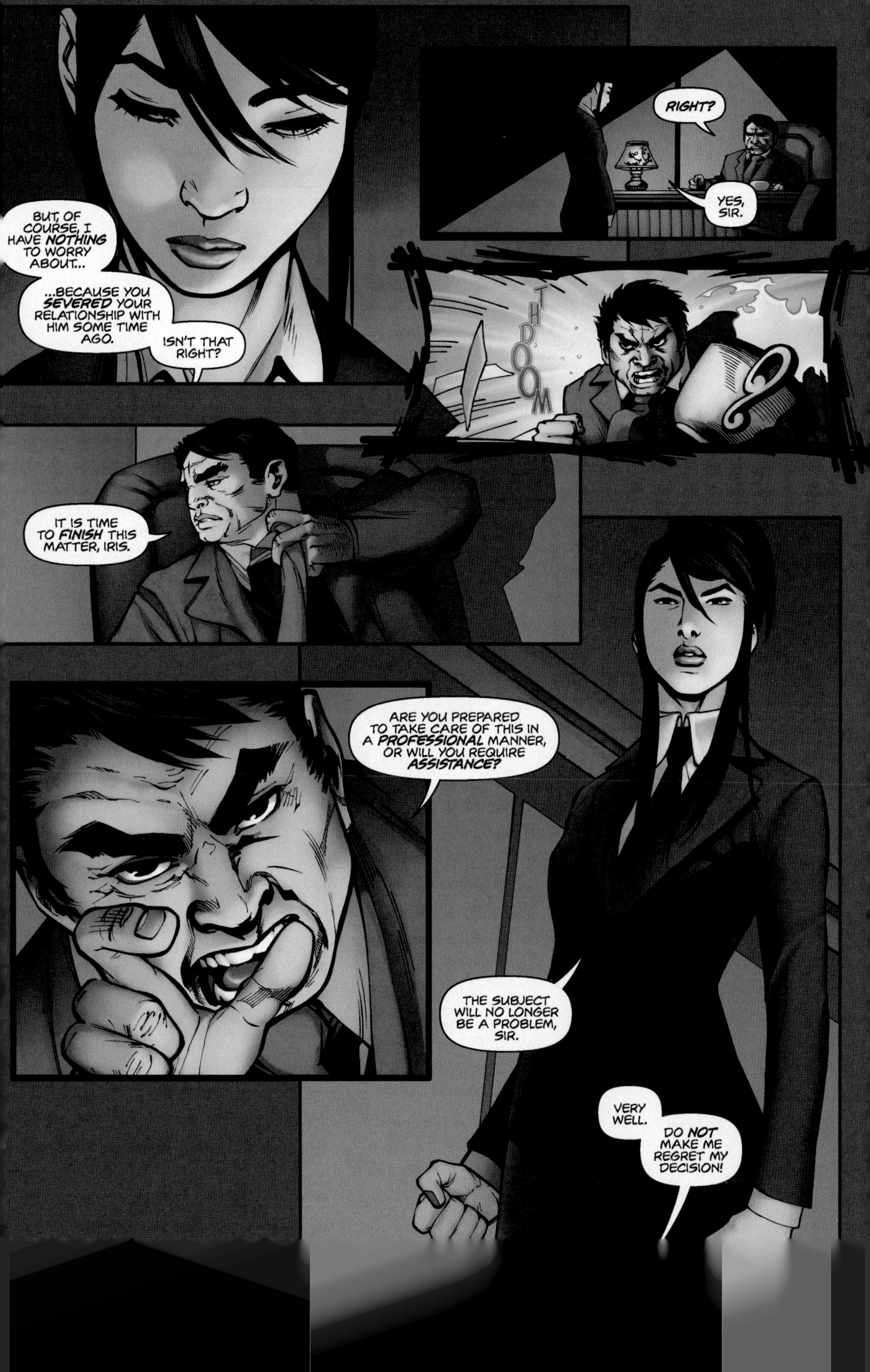

BUT, OF COURSE, I HAVE **NOTHING** TO WORRY ABOUT...
...BECAUSE YOU **SEVERED** YOUR RELATIONSHIP WITH HIM SOME TIME AGO.
ISN'T THAT RIGHT?
RIGHT?
YES, SIR.
THDOOM
IT IS TIME TO **FINISH** THIS MATTER, IRIS.
ARE YOU PREPARED TO TAKE CARE OF THIS IN A **PROFESSIONAL** MANNER, OR WILL YOU REQUIRE **ASSISTANCE?**
THE SUBJECT WILL NO LONGER BE A PROBLEM, SIR.
VERY WELL.
DO **NOT** MAKE ME REGRET MY DECISION!

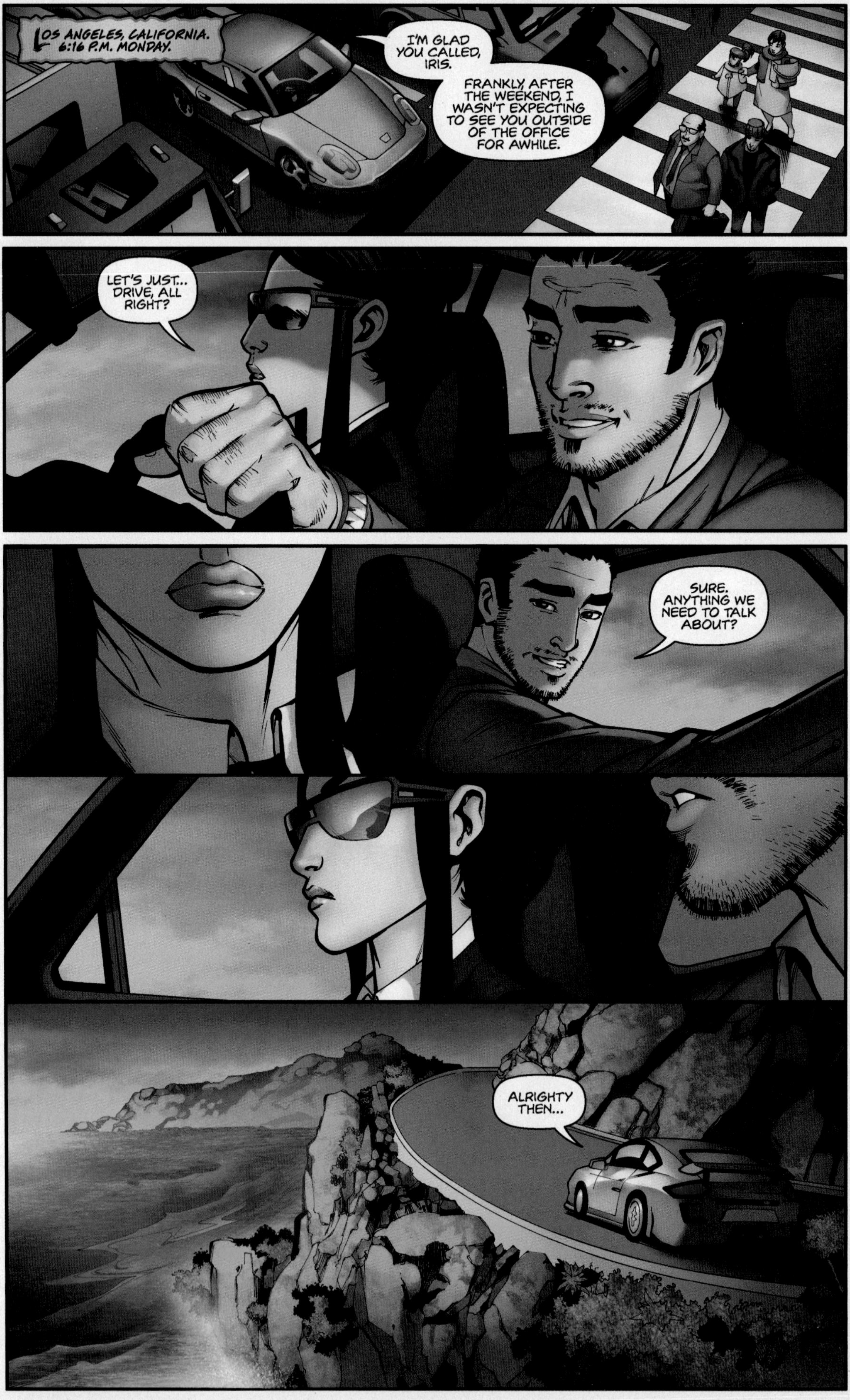

LOS ANGELES, CALIFORNIA. 6:16 P.M. MONDAY.
I'M GLAD YOU CALLED, IRIS.
FRANKLY, AFTER THE WEEKEND, I WASN'T EXPECTING TO SEE YOU OUTSIDE OF THE OFFICE FOR AWHILE.
LET'S JUST... DRIVE, ALL RIGHT?
SURE. ANYTHING WE NEED TO TALK ABOUT?
ALRIGHTY THEN...

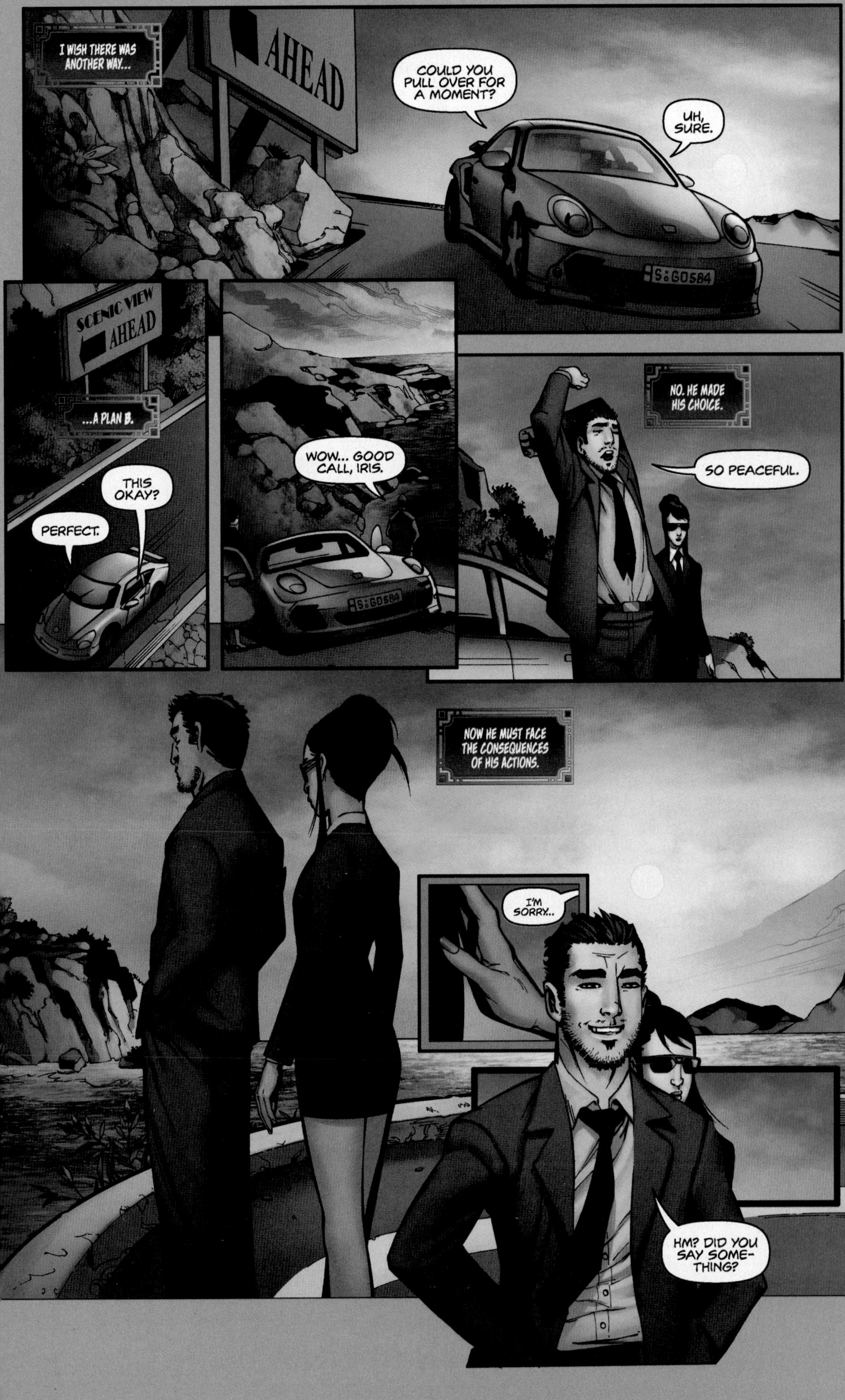
I WISH THERE WAS ANOTHER WAY...
AHEAD
COULD YOU PULL OVER FOR A MOMENT?
UH, SURE.
S:GO584
SCENIC VIEW AHEAD
...A PLAN B.
THIS OKAY?
PERFECT.
WOW... GOOD CALL, IRIS.
S:GO584
NO. HE MADE HIS CHOICE.
SO PEACEFUL.
NOW HE MUST FACE THE CONSEQUENCES OF HIS ACTIONS.
I'M SORRY...
HM? DID YOU SAY SOME-THING?

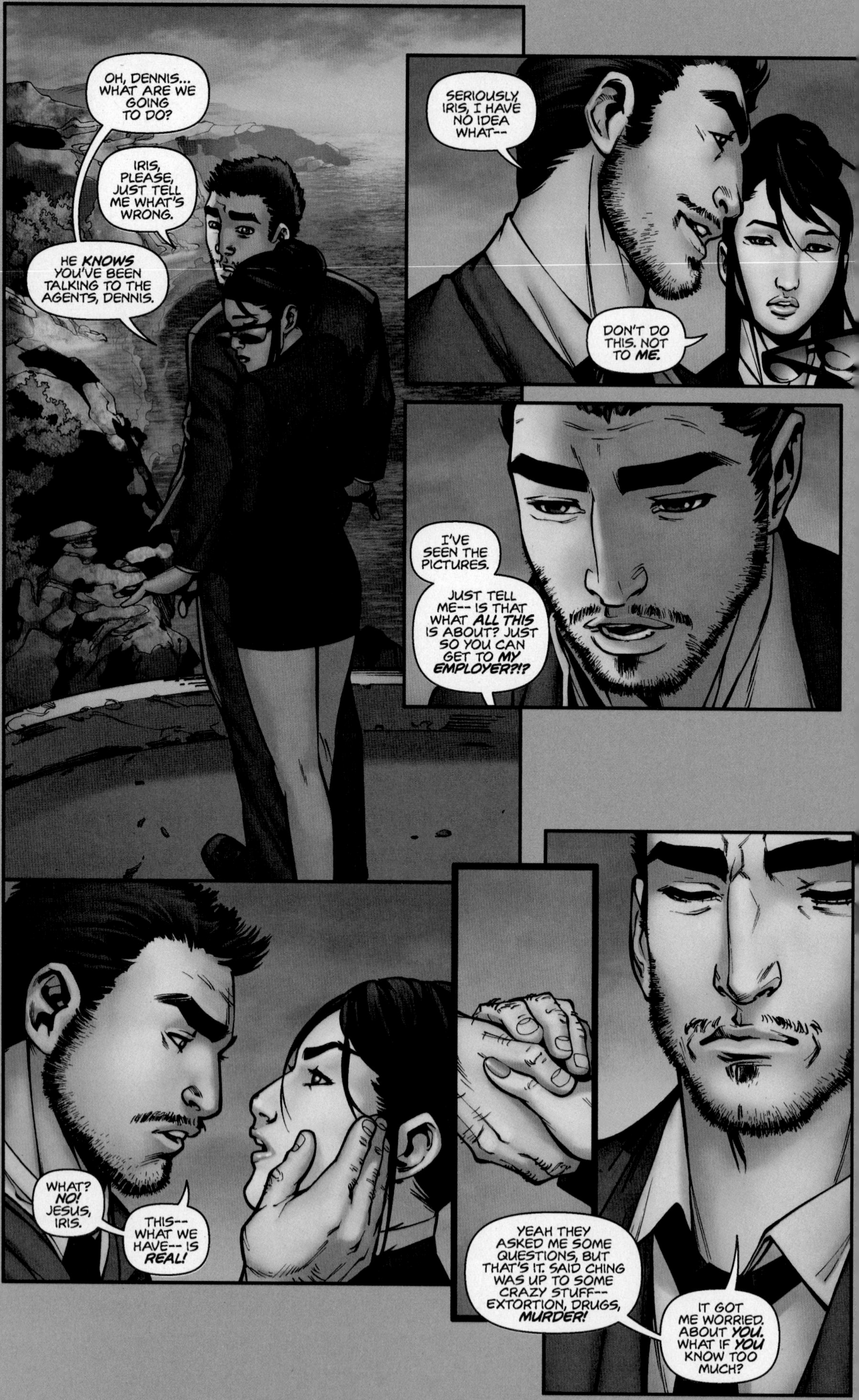

OH, DENNIS... WHAT ARE WE GOING TO DO?
IRIS, PLEASE, JUST TELL ME WHAT'S WRONG.
HE KNOWS YOU'VE BEEN TALKING TO THE AGENTS, DENNIS.
SERIOUSLY, IRIS, I HAVE NO IDEA WHAT--
DON'T DO THIS. NOT TO ME.
I'VE SEEN THE PICTURES.
JUST TELL ME-- IS THAT WHAT ALL THIS IS ABOUT? JUST SO YOU CAN GET TO MY EMPLOYER?!?
WHAT? NO! JESUS, IRIS.
THIS-- WHAT WE HAVE-- IS REAL!
YEAH THEY ASKED ME SOME QUESTIONS, BUT THAT'S IT. SAID CHING WAS UP TO SOME CRAZY STUFF-- EXTORTION, DRUGS, MURDER!
IT GOT ME WORRIED. ABOUT YOU. WHAT IF YOU KNOW TOO MUCH?

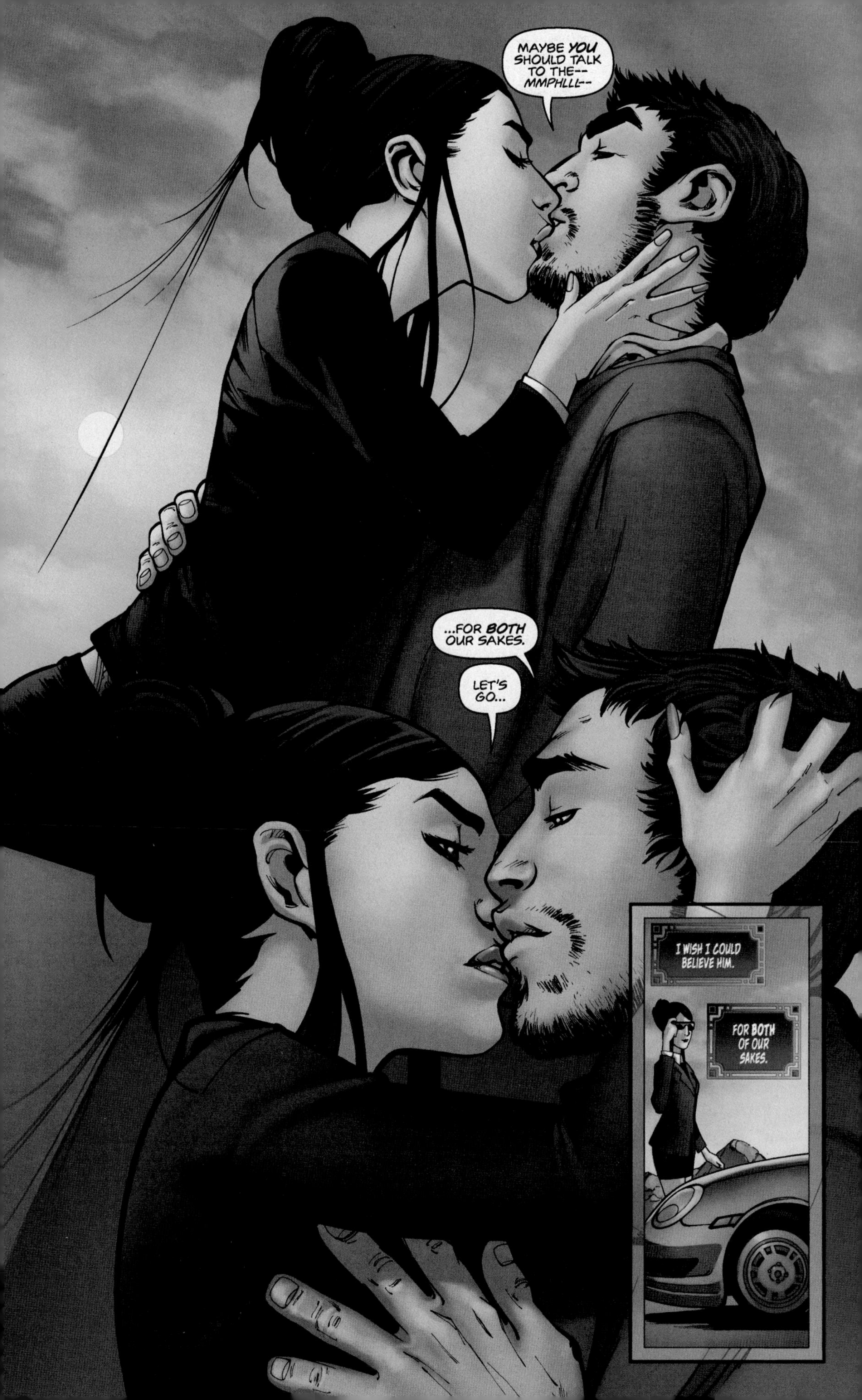
MAYBE YOU SHOULD TALK TO THE-- MMPHLLL--
...FOR BOTH OUR SAKES.
LET'S GO...
I WISH I COULD BELIEVE HIM.
FOR BOTH OF OUR SAKES.

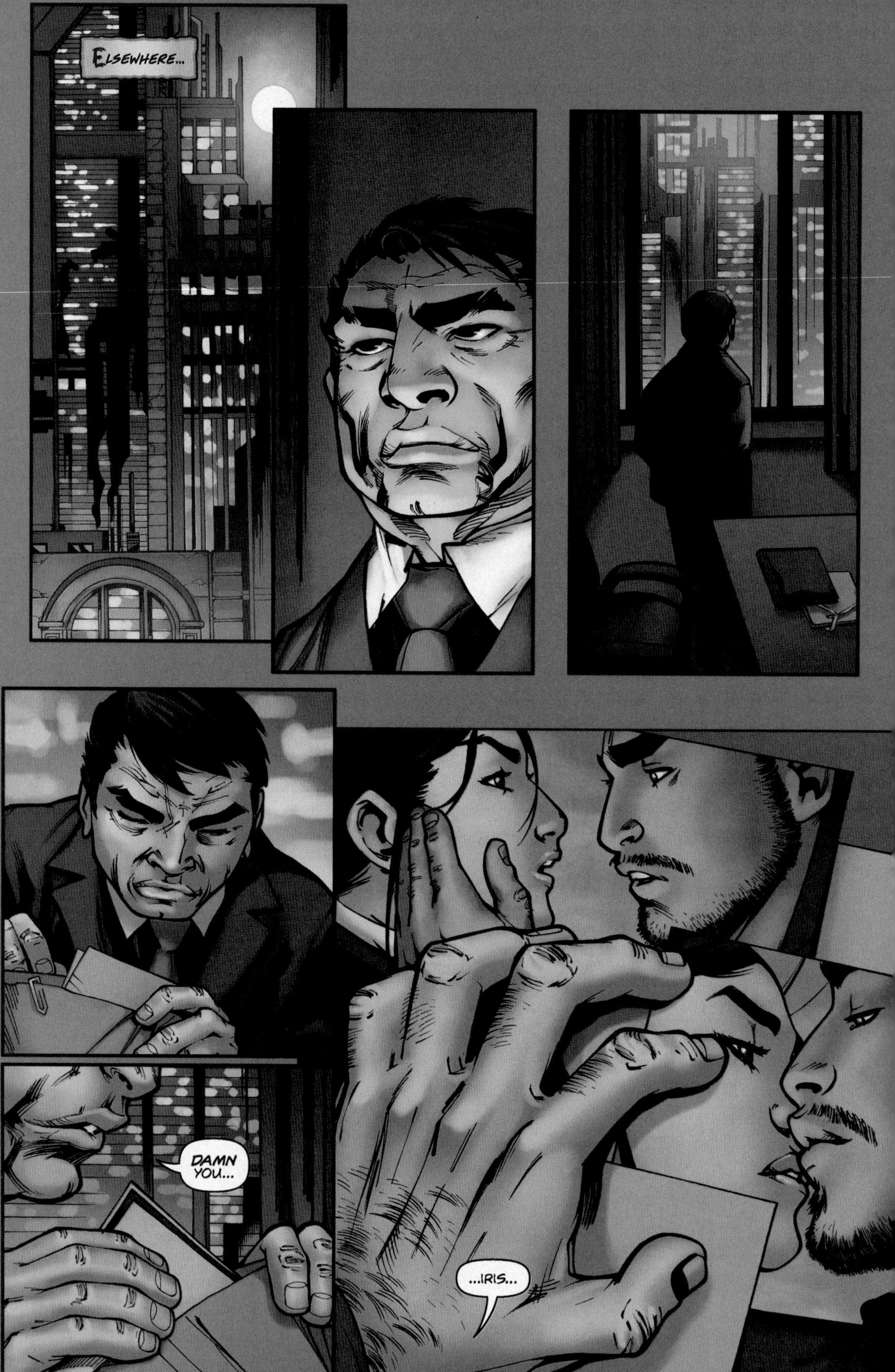
ELSEWHERE...
DAMN YOU...
...IRIS...

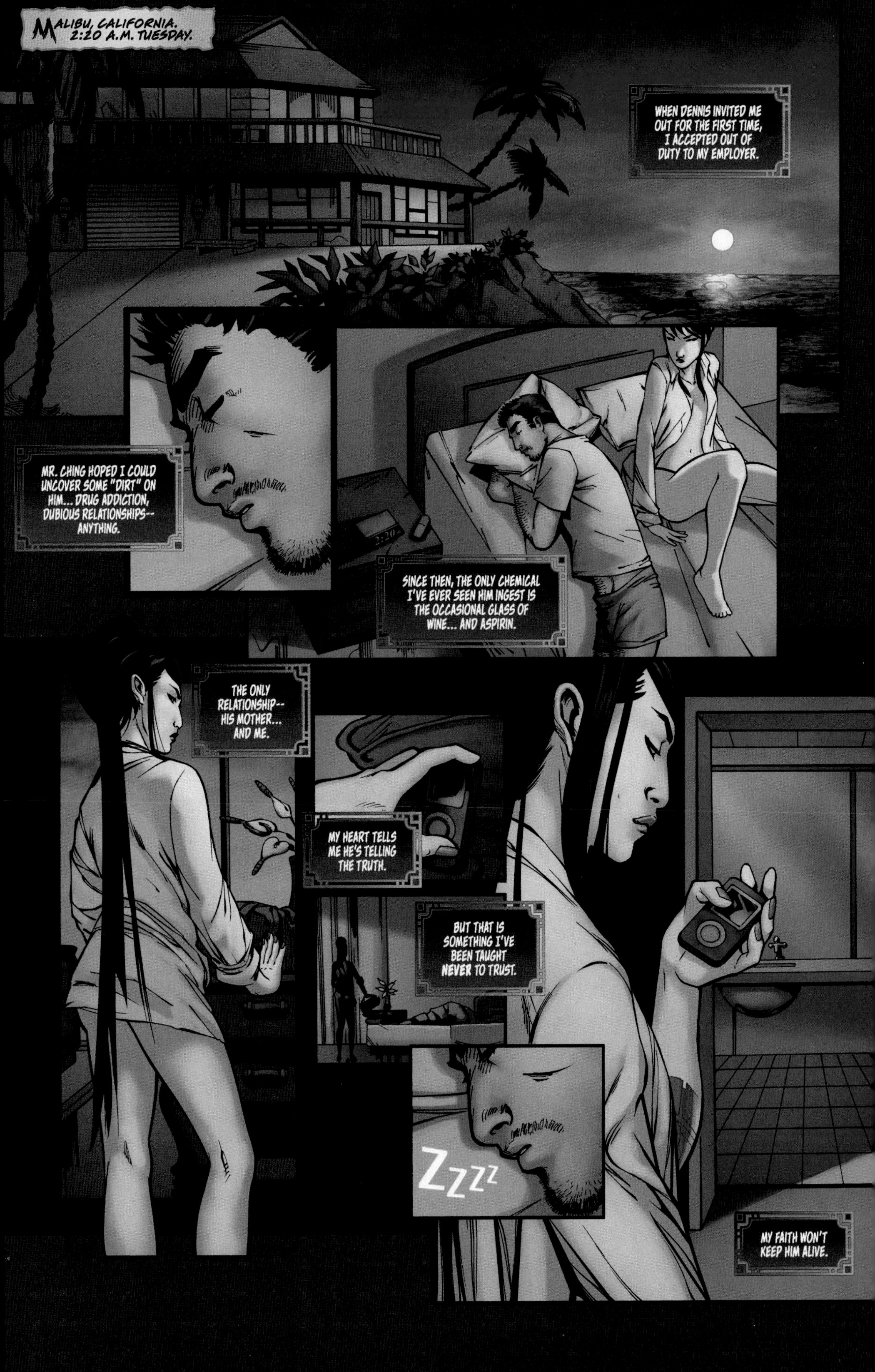
MALIBU, CALIFORNIA. 2:20 A.M. TUESDAY.
WHEN DENNIS INVITED ME OUT FOR THE FIRST TIME, I ACCEPTED OUT OF DUTY TO MY EMPLOYER.
MR. CHING HOPED I COULD UNCOVER SOME "DIRT" ON HIM... DRUG ADDICTION, DUBIOUS RELATIONSHIPS-- ANYTHING.
2:20
SINCE THEN, THE ONLY CHEMICAL I'VE EVER SEEN HIM INGEST IS THE OCCASIONAL GLASS OF WINE... AND ASPIRIN.
THE ONLY RELATIONSHIP-- HIS MOTHER... AND ME.
MY HEART TELLS ME HE'S TELLING THE TRUTH.
BUT THAT IS SOMETHING I'VE BEEN TAUGHT NEVER TO TRUST.
ZZZZ
MY FAITH WON'T KEEP HIM ALIVE.

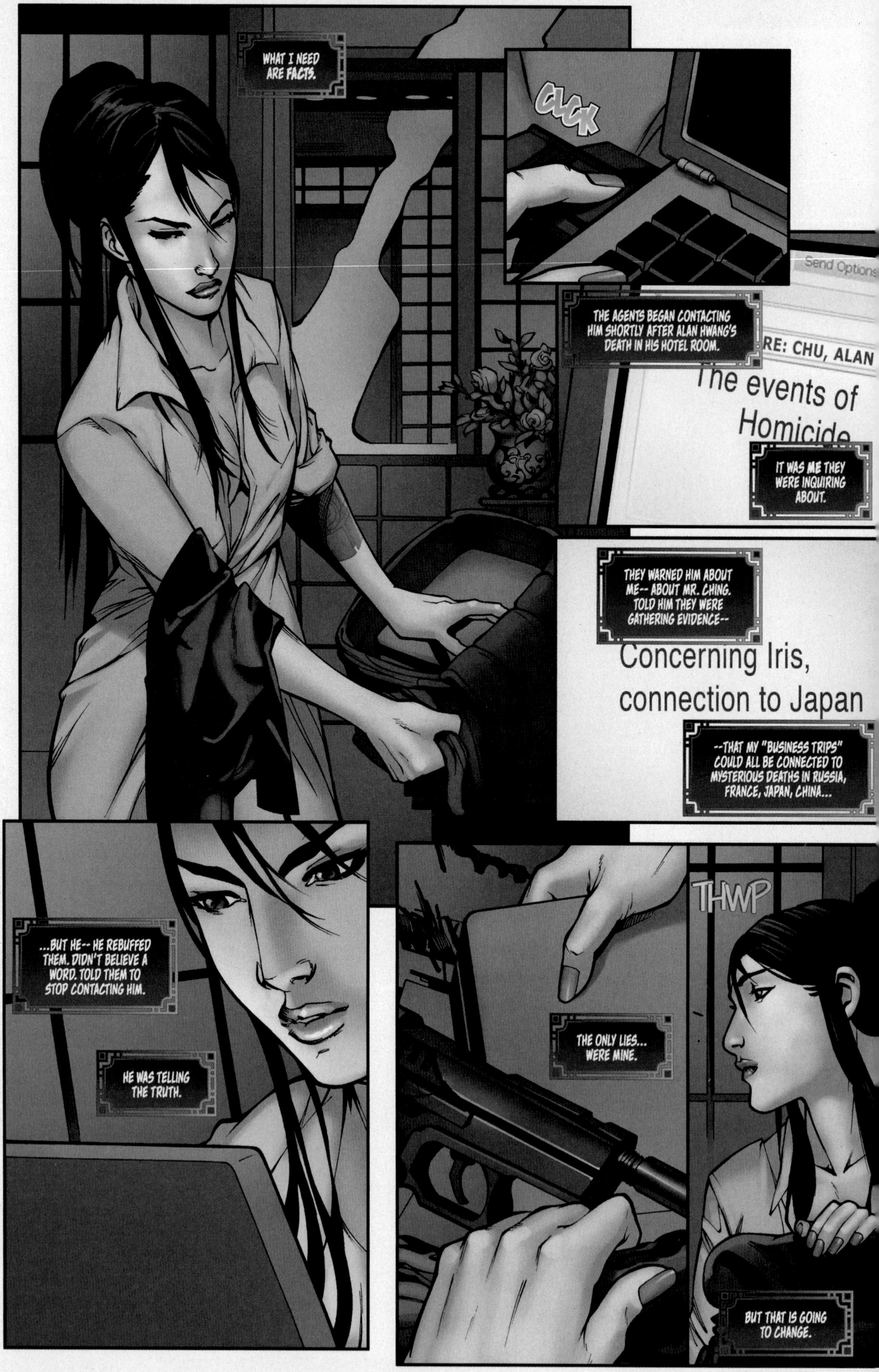
WHAT I NEED ARE FACTS.
CLICK
Send Options
THE AGENTS BEGAN CONTACTING HIM SHORTLY AFTER ALAN HWANG'S DEATH IN HIS HOTEL ROOM.
RE: CHU, ALAN
The events of Homicide
IT WAS ME THEY WERE INQUIRING ABOUT.
THEY WARNED HIM ABOUT ME-- ABOUT MR. CHING. TOLD HIM THEY WERE GATHERING EVIDENCE--
Concerning Iris, connection to Japan
--THAT MY "BUSINESS TRIPS" COULD ALL BE CONNECTED TO MYSTERIOUS DEATHS IN RUSSIA, FRANCE, JAPAN, CHINA...
...BUT HE-- HE REBUFFED THEM. DIDN'T BELIEVE A WORD. TOLD THEM TO STOP CONTACTING HIM.
HE WAS TELLING THE TRUTH.
THWP
THE ONLY LIES... WERE MINE.
BUT THAT IS GOING TO CHANGE.

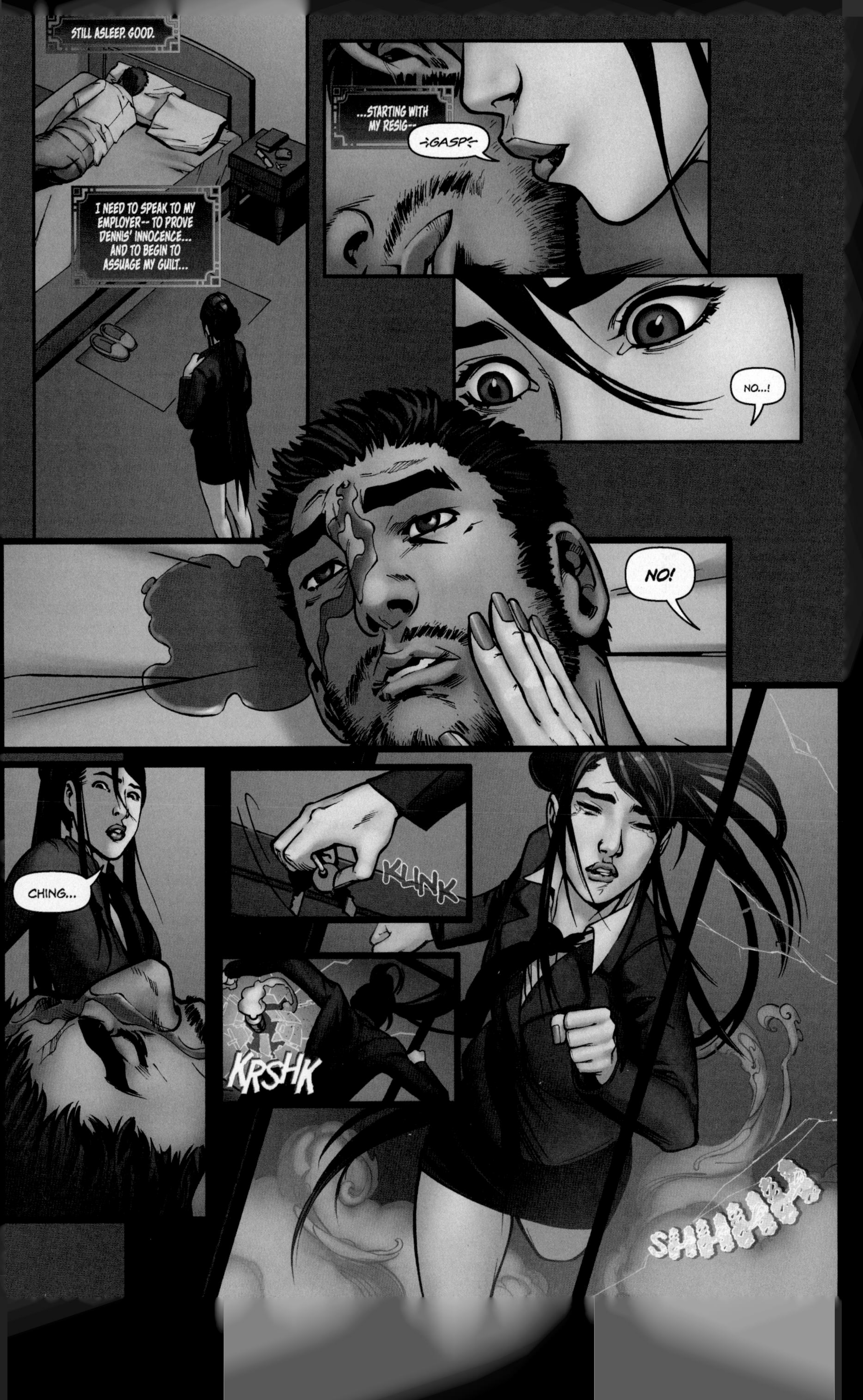
STILL ASLEEP. GOOD.
I NEED TO SPEAK TO MY EMPLOYER-- TO PROVE DENNIS' INNOCENCE... AND TO BEGIN TO ASSUAGE MY GUILT...
...STARTING WITH MY RESIG--
-GASP-
NO...!
NO!
CHING...
KLINK
KRSHK
SHHHH

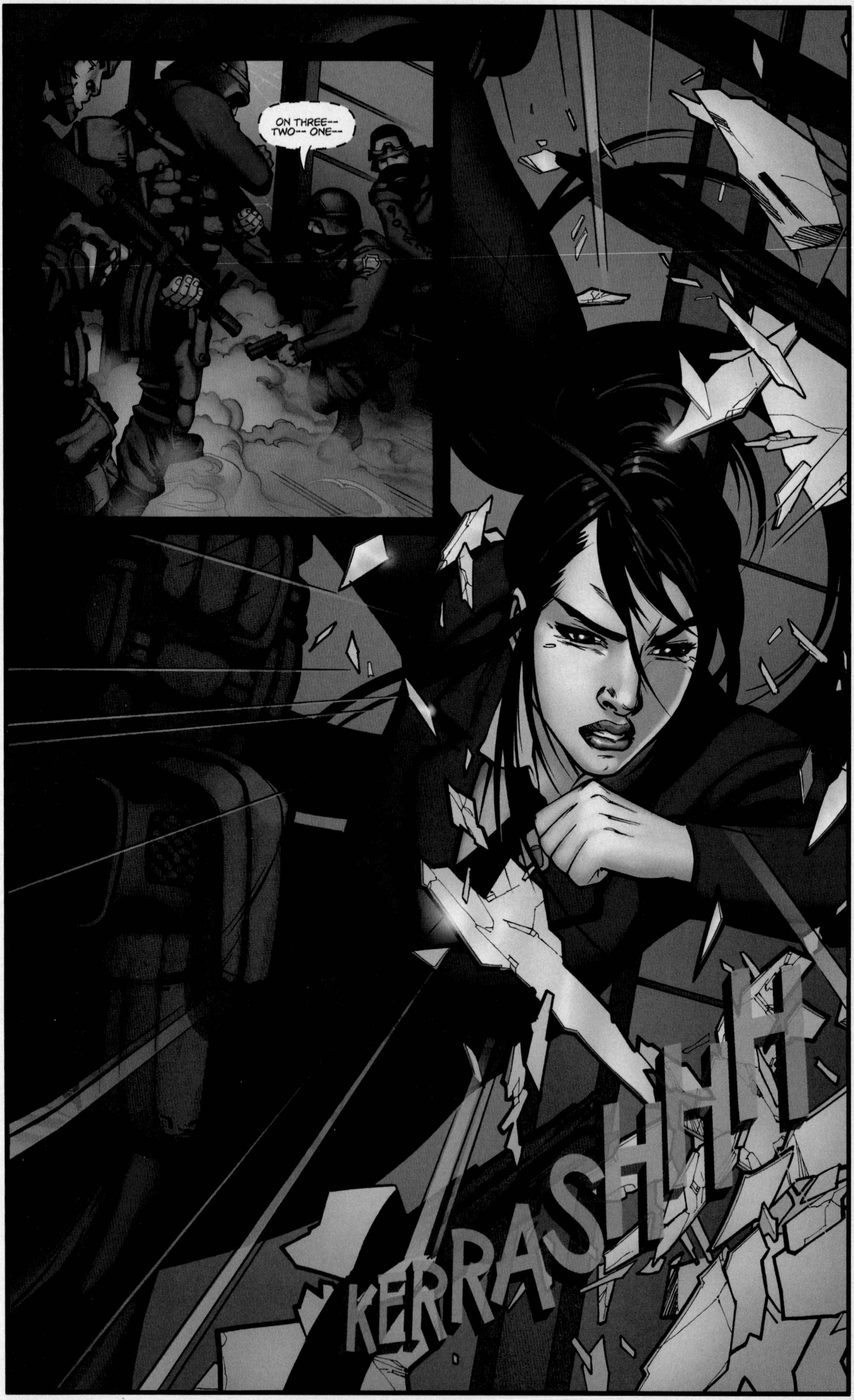
ON THREE-- TWO-- ONE--
KERRASHHH

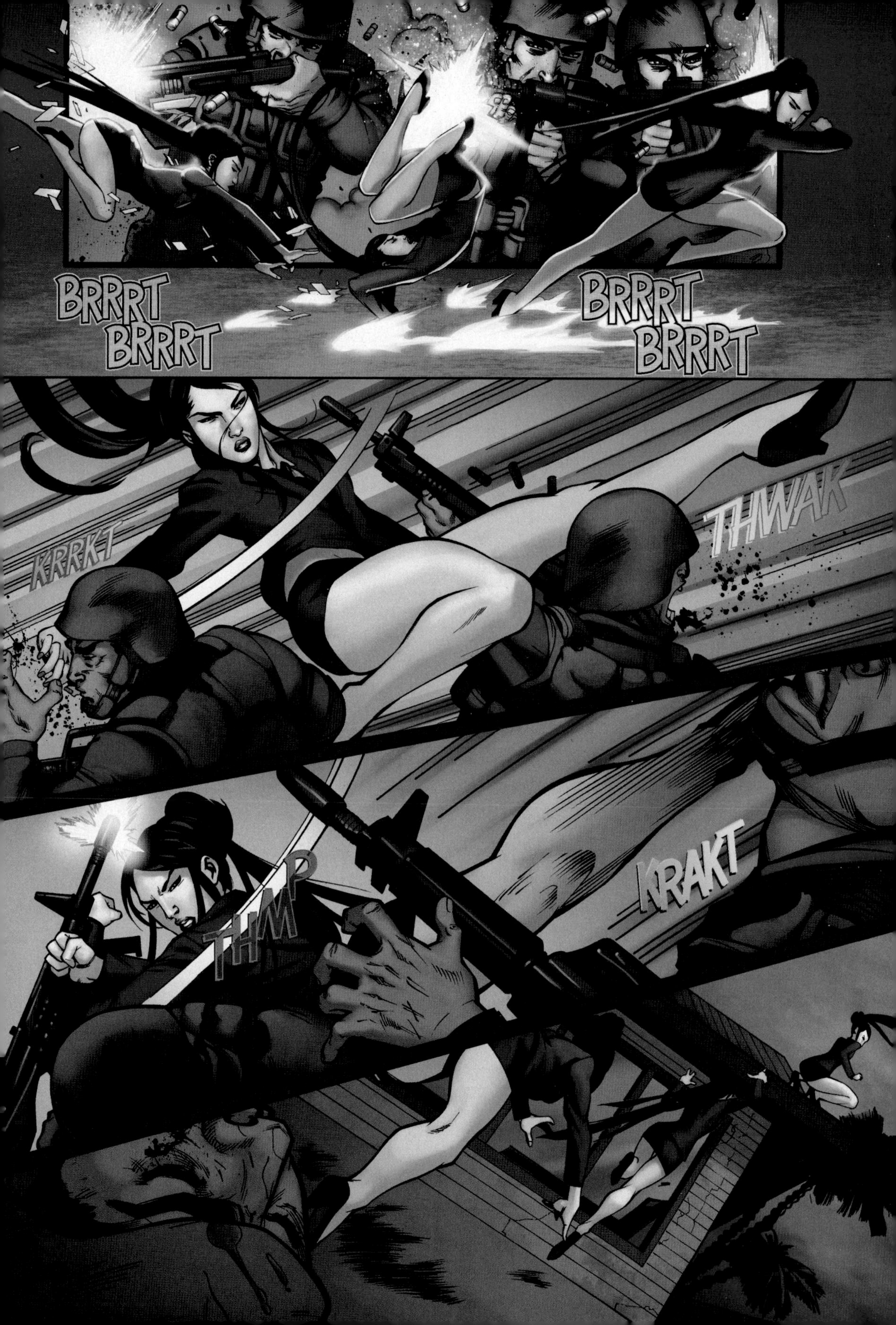
BRRRT
BRRRT
BRRRT
BRRRT
KRRKT
THWAK
THMP
KRAKT

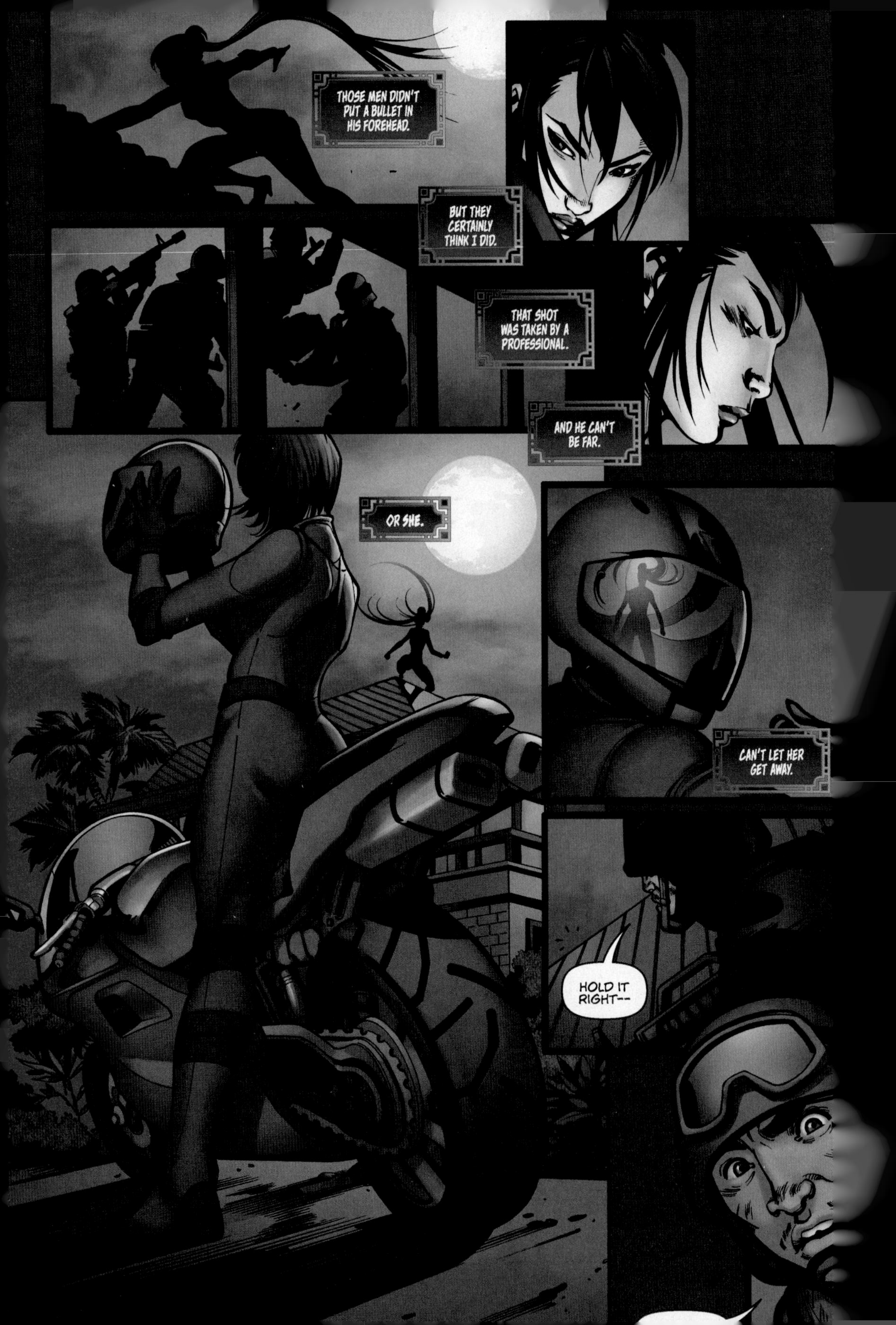
THOSE MEN DIDN'T PUT A BULLET IN HIS FOREHEAD.
BUT THEY CERTAINLY THINK I DID.
THAT SHOT WAS TAKEN BY A PROFESSIONAL.
AND HE CAN'T BE FAR.
OR SHE.
CAN'T LET HER GET AWAY.
HOLD IT RIGHT--

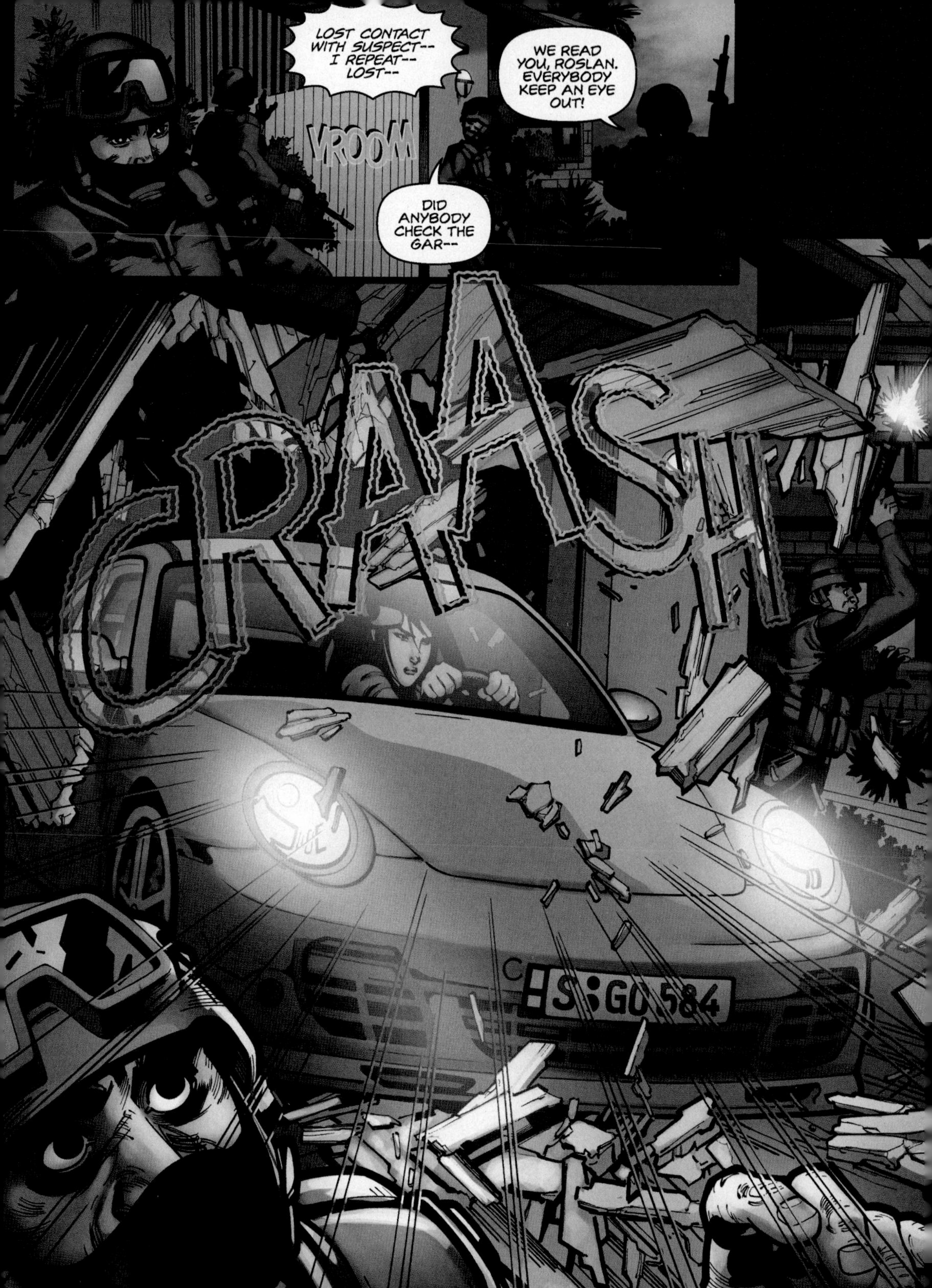
LOST CONTACT WITH SUSPECT-- I REPEAT-- LOST--
WE READ YOU, ROSLAN. EVERYBODY KEEP AN EYE OUT!
VROOM
DID ANYBODY CHECK THE GAR--
CRAASH
S GO 584

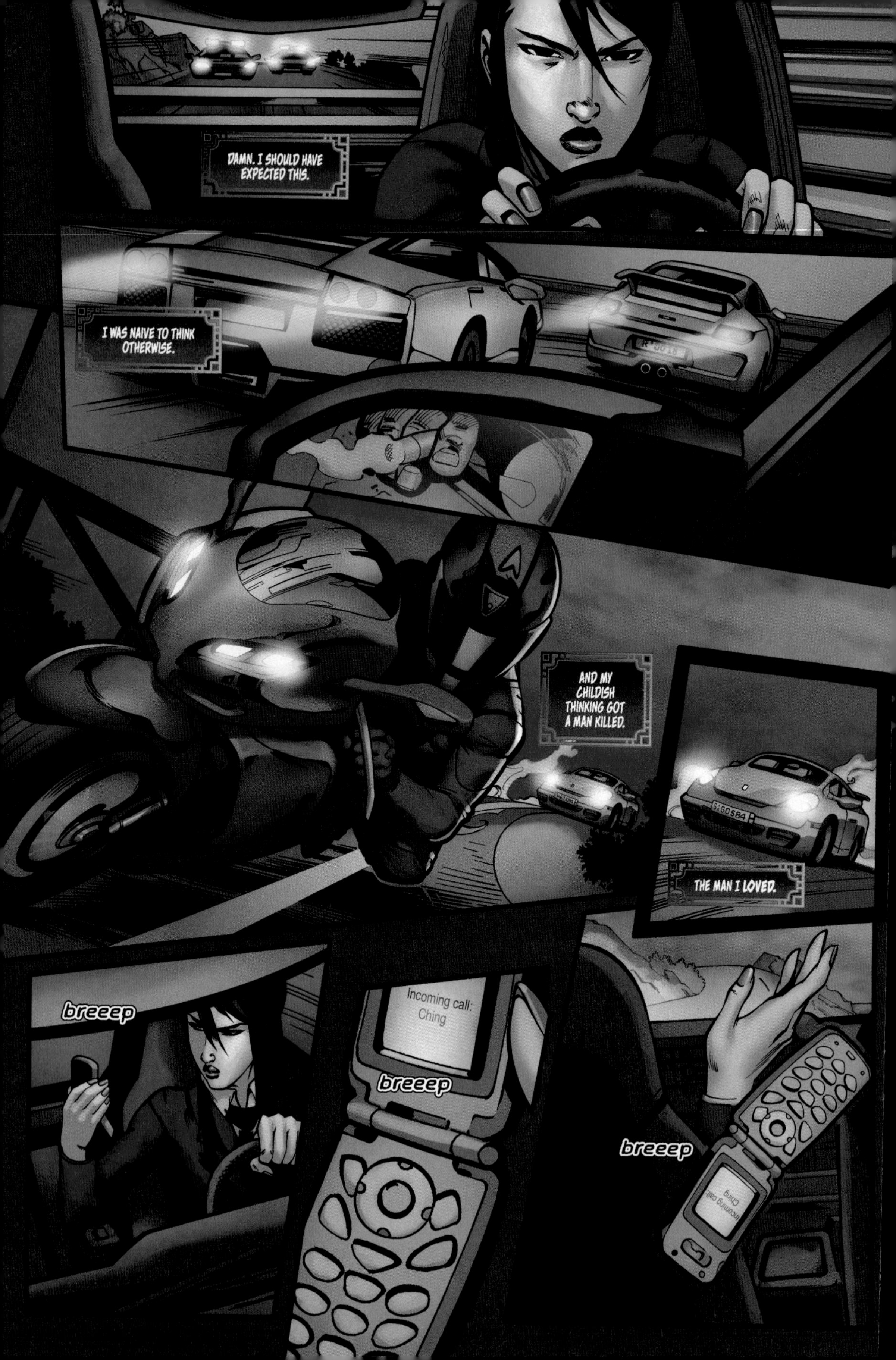
DAMN. I SHOULD HAVE EXPECTED THIS.
I WAS NAIVE TO THINK OTHERWISE.
AND MY CHILDISH THINKING GOT A MAN KILLED.
THE MAN I LOVED.
breeep
Incoming call: Ching
breeep
breeep

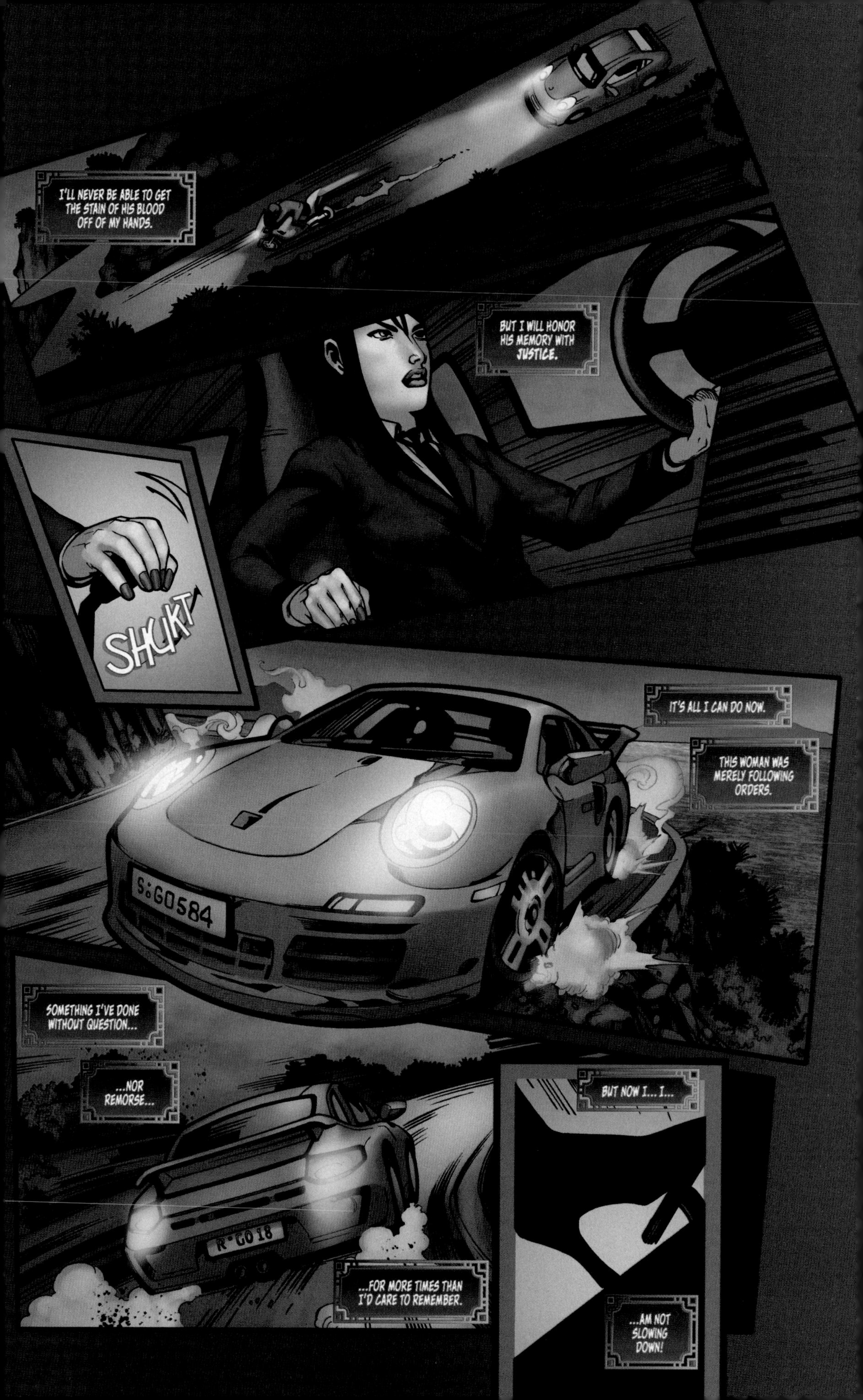
I'LL NEVER BE ABLE TO GET THE STAIN OF HIS BLOOD OFF OF MY HANDS.
BUT I WILL HONOR HIS MEMORY WITH JUSTICE.
SHUKT
IT'S ALL I CAN DO NOW.
THIS WOMAN WAS MERELY FOLLOWING ORDERS.
S·GO584
SOMETHING I'VE DONE WITHOUT QUESTION...
...NOR REMORSE...
R·GO18
...FOR MORE TIMES THAN I'D CARE TO REMEMBER.
BUT NOW I... I...
...AM NOT SLOWING DOWN!

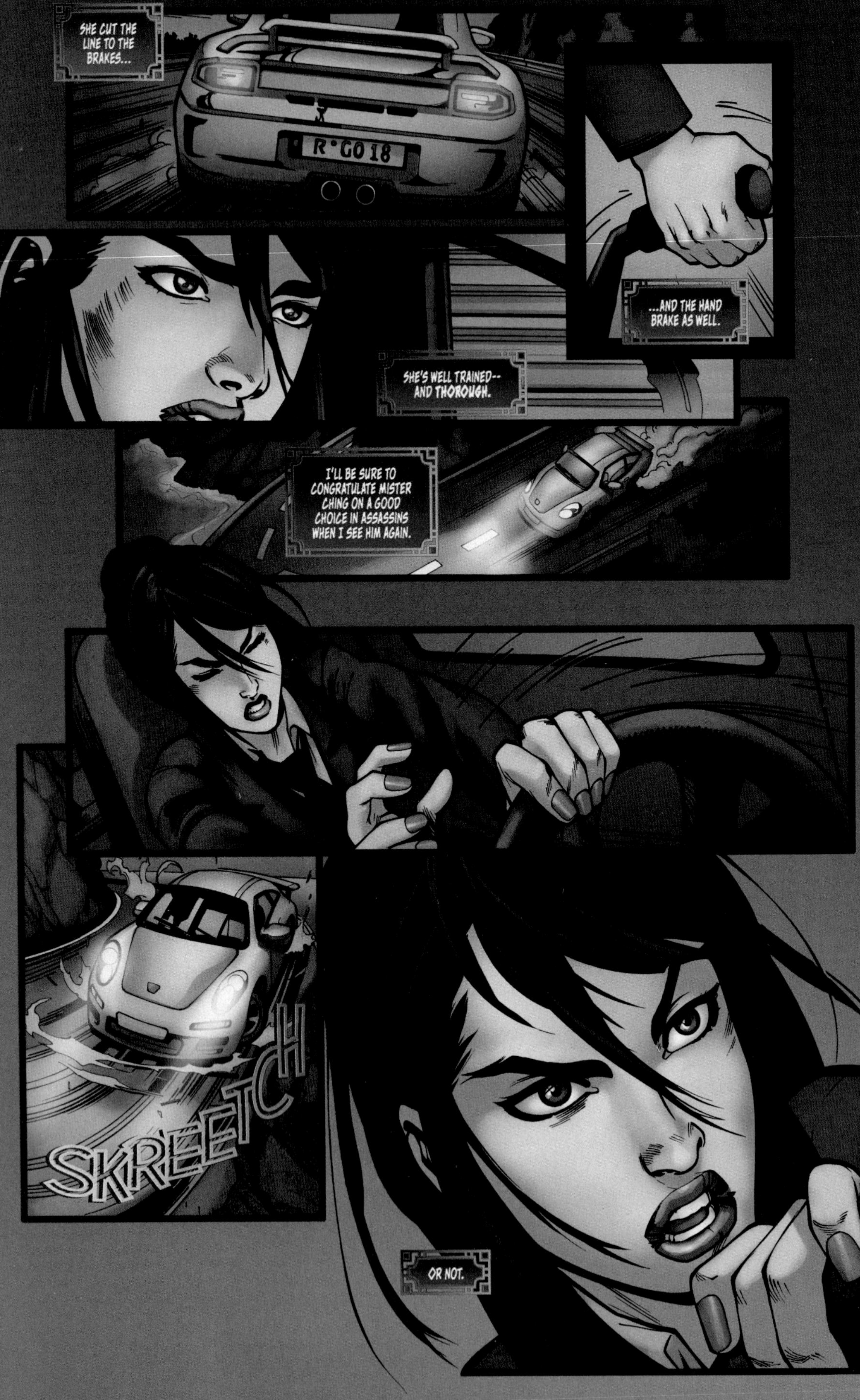
SHE CUT THE LINE TO THE BRAKES...
R°GO 18
...AND THE HAND BRAKE AS WELL.
SHE'S WELL TRAINED-- AND THOROUGH.
I'LL BE SURE TO CONGRATULATE MISTER CHING ON A GOOD CHOICE IN ASSASSINS WHEN I SEE HIM AGAIN.
SKREEETCH
OR NOT.

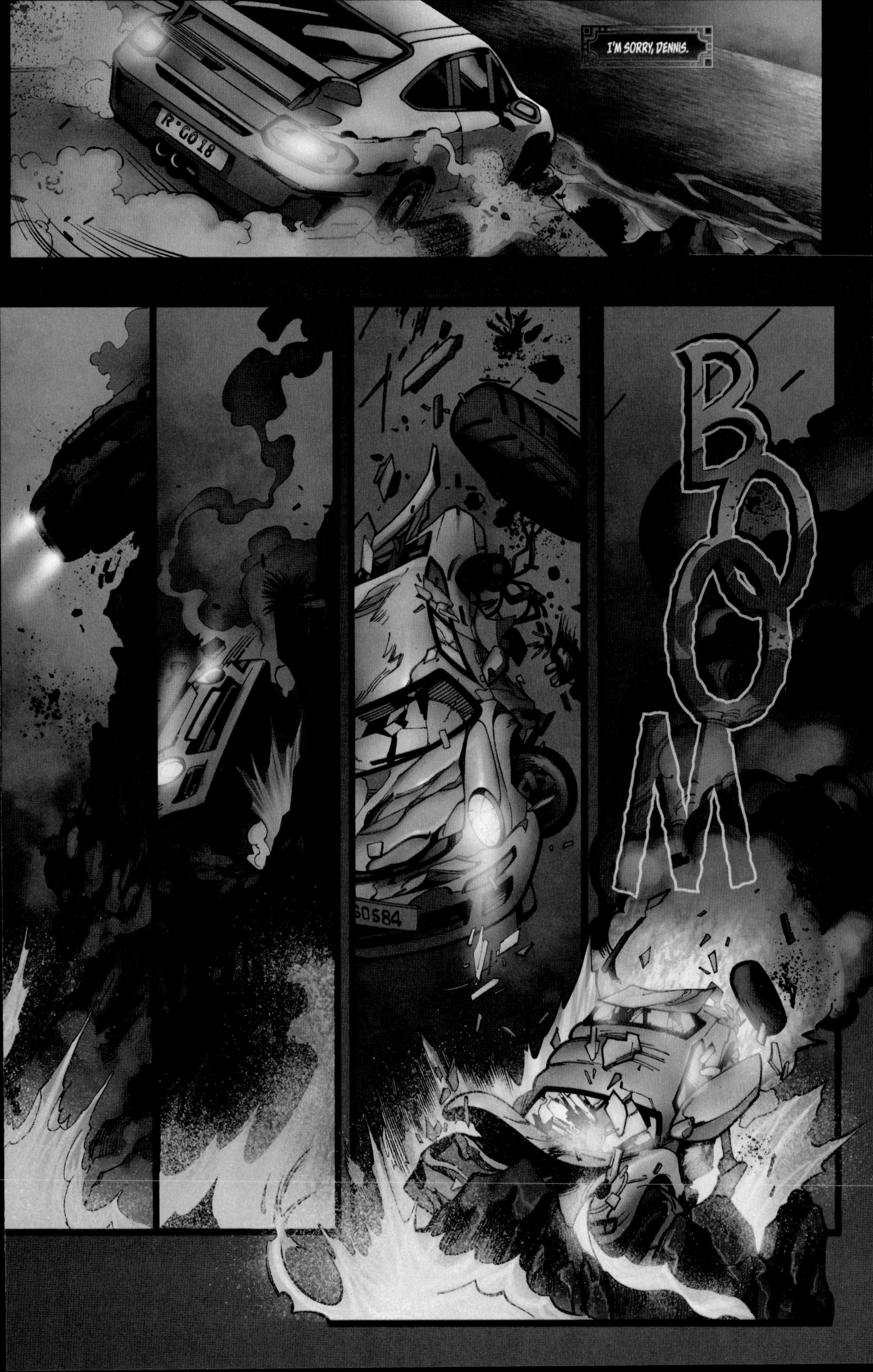
I'M SORRY, DENNIS.
BOOM

EXECUTIVE ASSISTANT: IRIS #6
Cover A
EDUARDO FRANCISCO
JOHN STARR

EXECUTIVE ASSISTANT: IRIS #6
Cover B
JOE BENITEZ
PETER STEIGERWALD

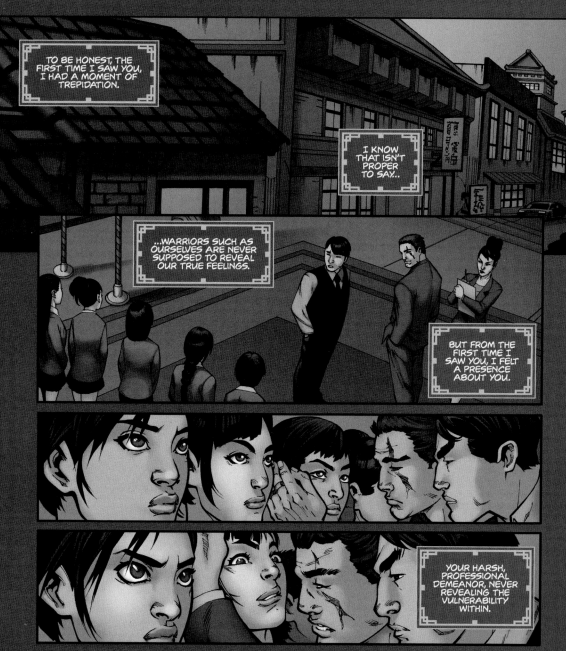

TO BE HONEST, THE FIRST TIME I SAW YOU, I HAD A MOMENT OF TREPIDATION.

I KNOW THAT ISN'T PROPER TO SAY...

...WARRIORS SUCH AS OURSELVES ARE NEVER SUPPOSED TO REVEAL OUR TRUE FEELINGS.

BUT FROM THE FIRST TIME I SAW YOU, I FELT A PRESENCE ABOUT YOU.

YOUR HARSH, PROFESSIONAL DEMEANOR, NEVER REVEALING THE VULNERABILITY WITHIN.

BUT I SAW IT.

EVEN IN THAT FIRST MOMENT, YOU REVEALED IT TO ME, BEHIND THOSE COLD EYES.

A KINDRED SPIRIT.

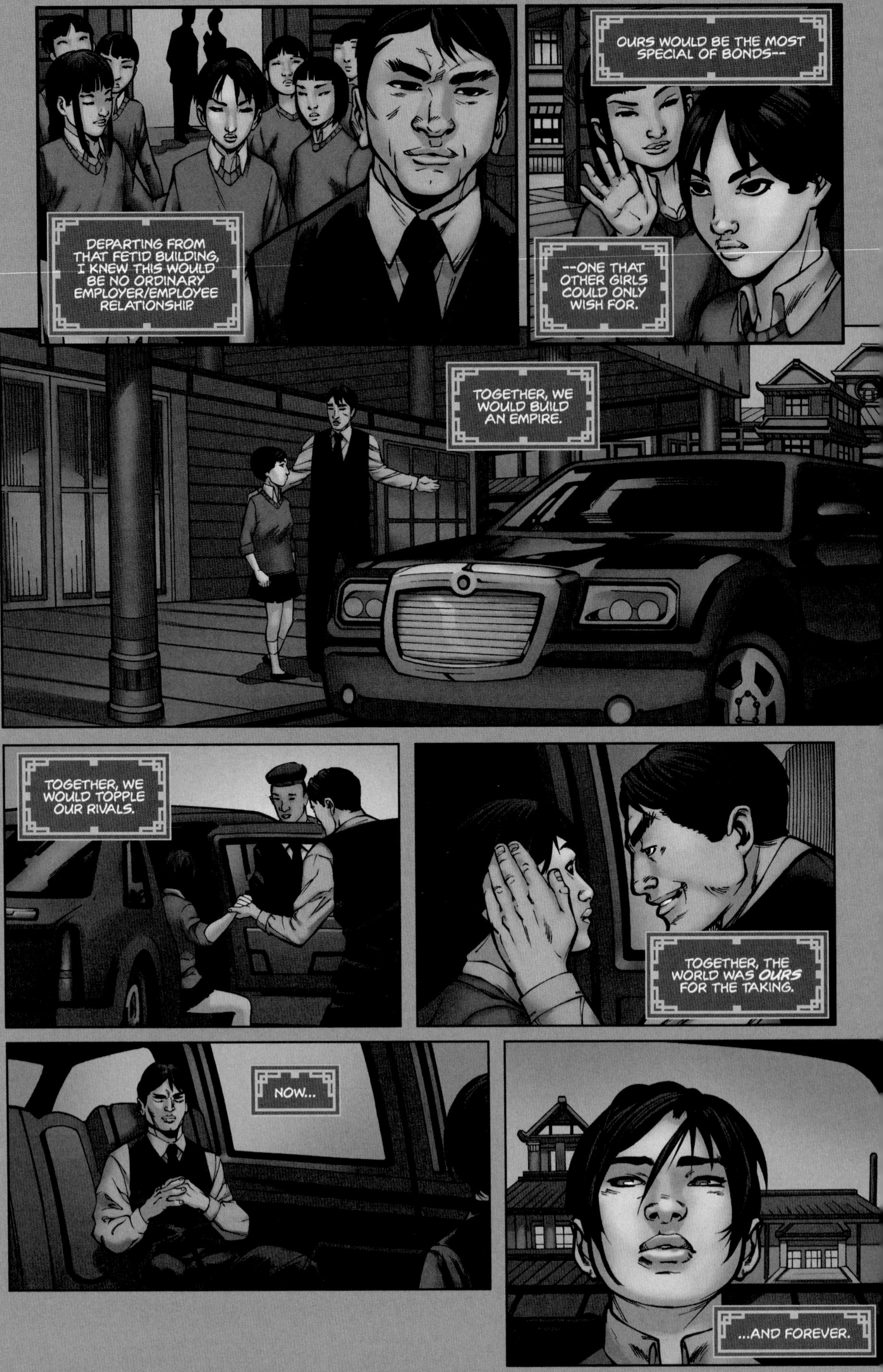
DEPARTING FROM THAT FETID BUILDING, I KNEW THIS WOULD BE NO ORDINARY EMPLOYER/EMPLOYEE RELATIONSHIP.
OURS WOULD BE THE MOST SPECIAL OF BONDS--
--ONE THAT OTHER GIRLS COULD ONLY WISH FOR.
TOGETHER, WE WOULD BUILD AN EMPIRE.
TOGETHER, WE WOULD TOPPLE OUR RIVALS.
TOGETHER, THE WORLD WAS *OURS* FOR THE TAKING.
NOW...
...AND FOREVER.

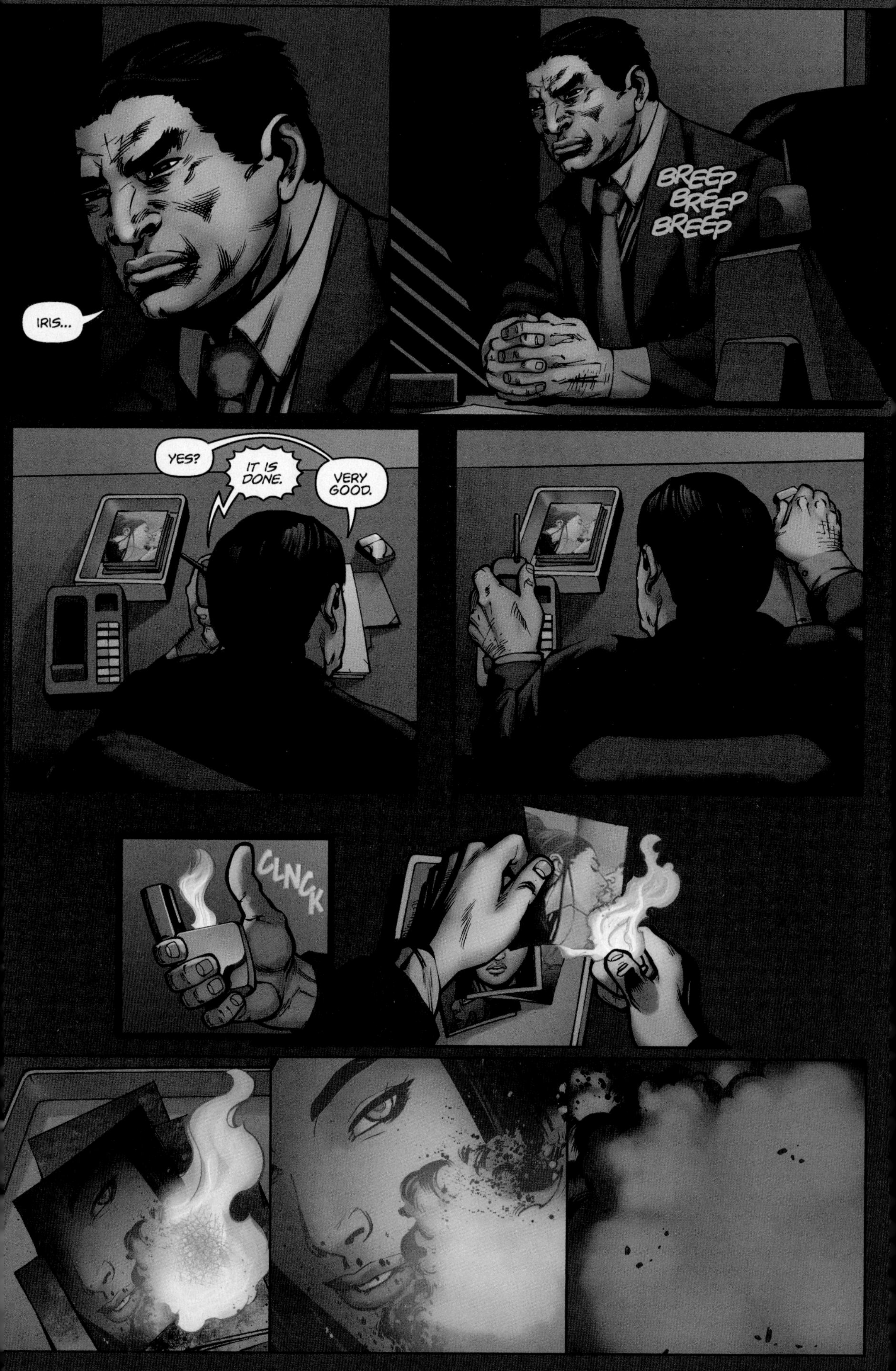
IRIS...
BREEP
BREEP
BREEP
YES?
IT IS DONE.
VERY GOOD.
CLNCK

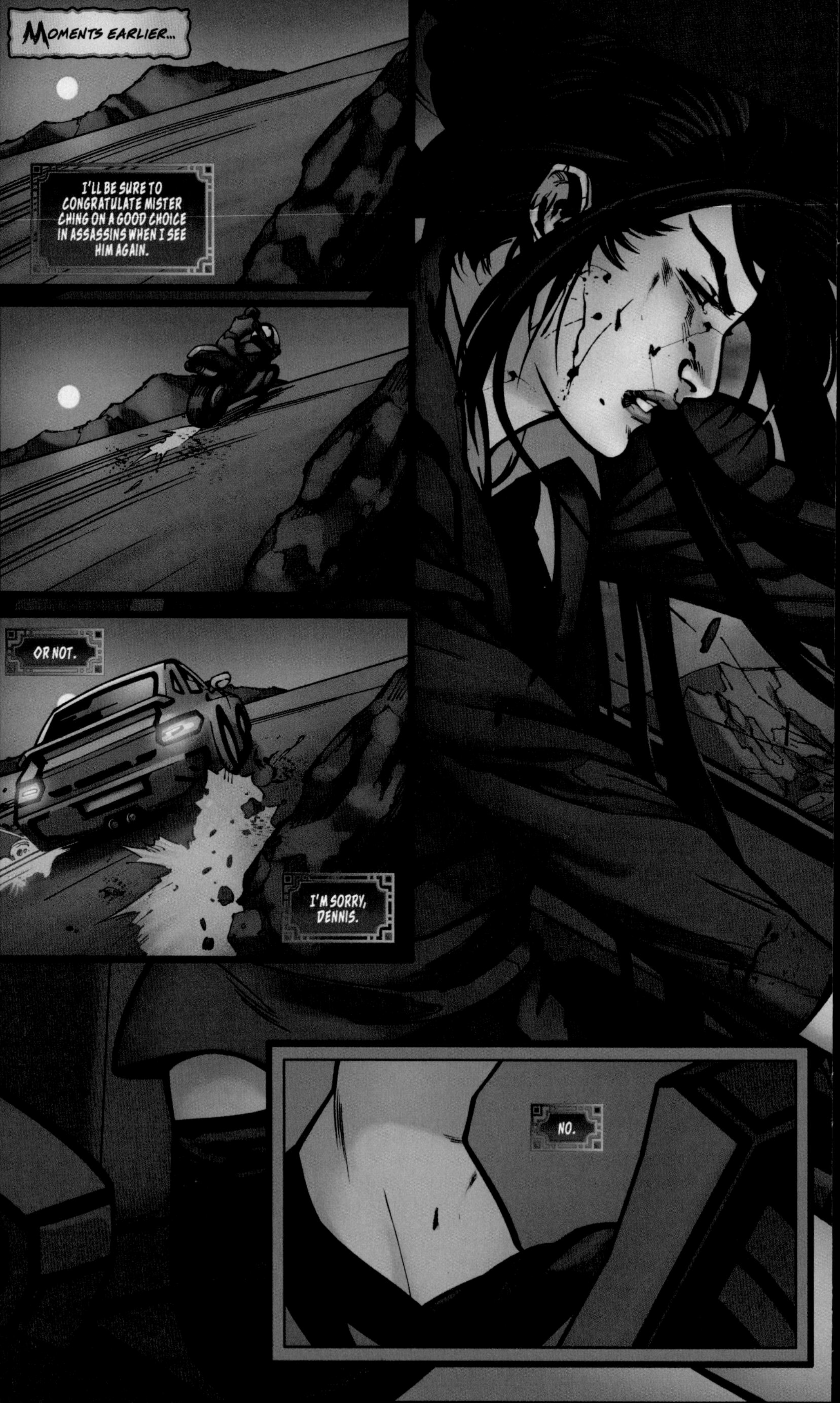
MOMENTS EARLIER...
I'LL BE SURE TO CONGRATULATE MISTER CHING ON A GOOD CHOICE IN ASSASSINS WHEN I SEE HIM AGAIN.
OR NOT.
I'M SORRY, DENNIS.
NO.

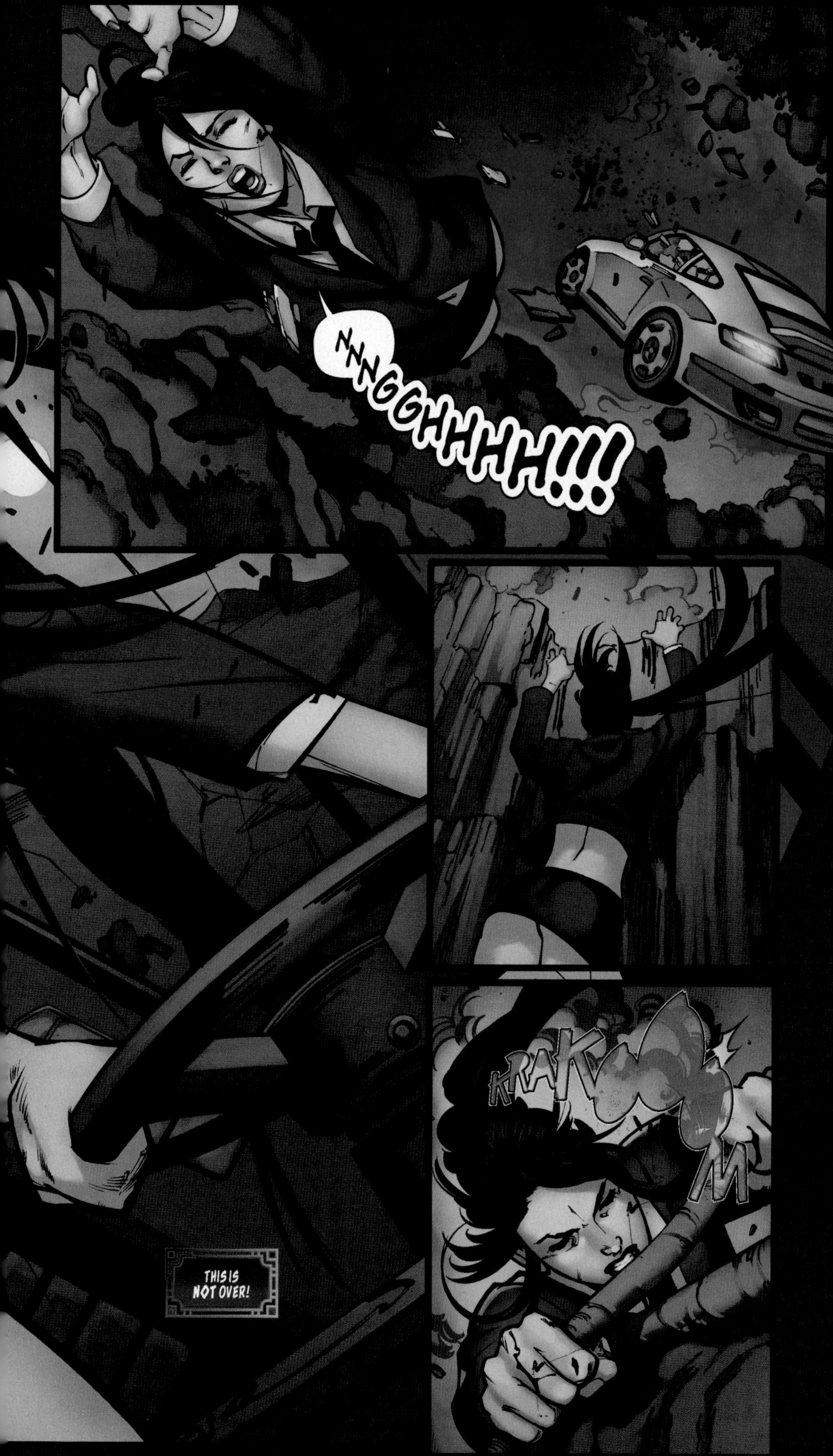
NNNGGHHHHH!!!
KRAKOOOM
THIS IS NOT OVER!

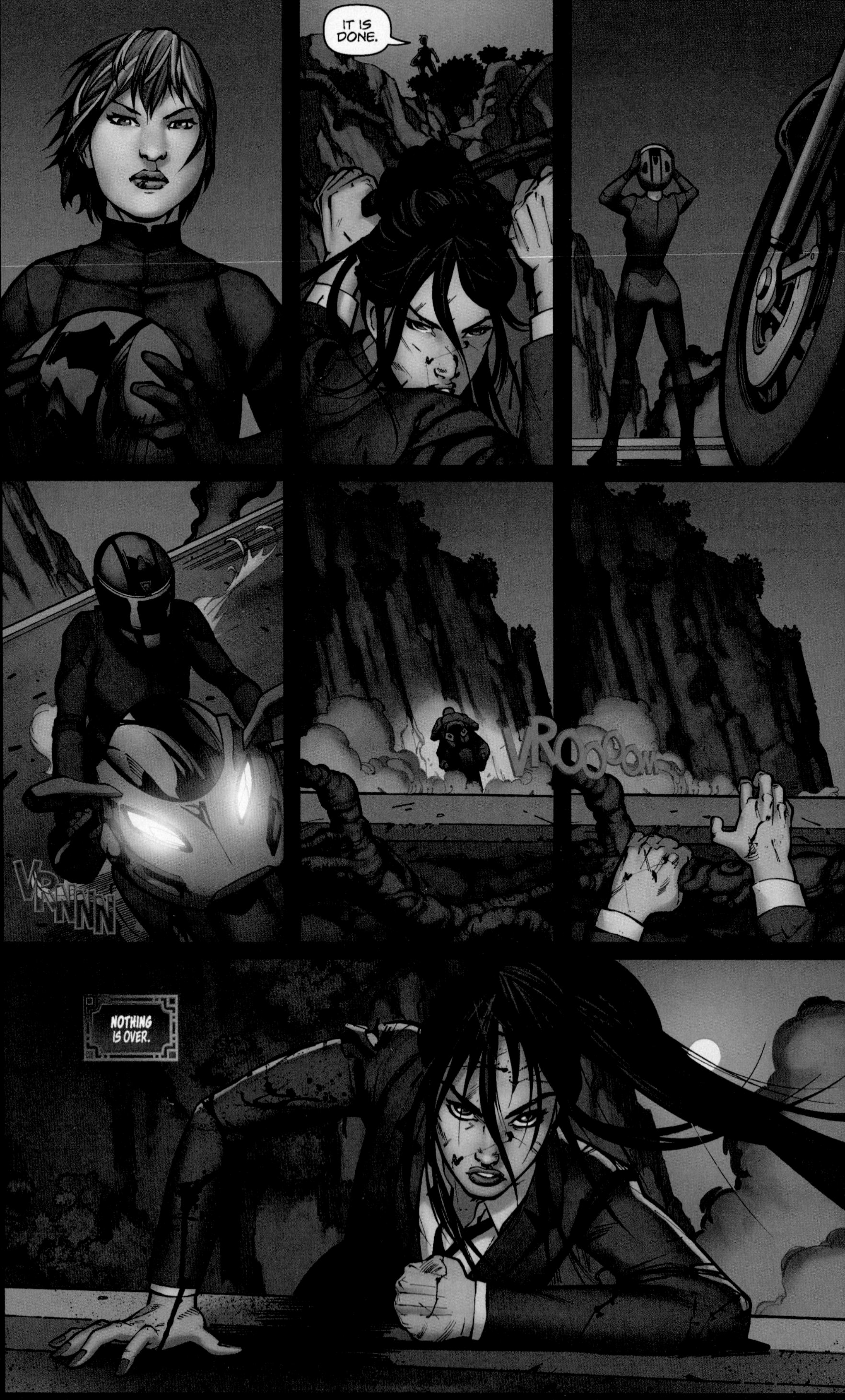
IT IS DONE.
VRNNNN
VROOOOOM
NOTHING IS OVER.

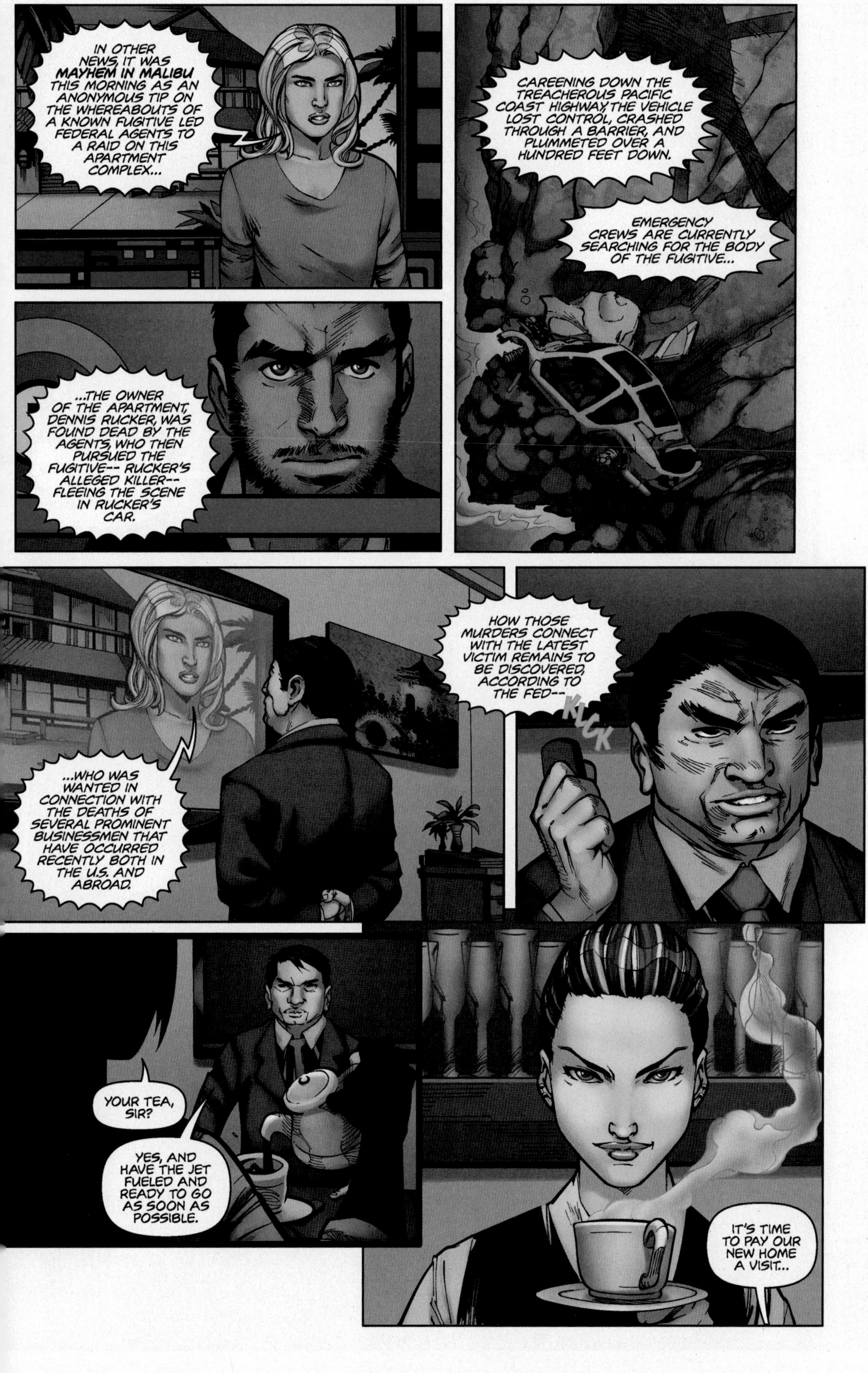
IN OTHER NEWS, IT WAS MAYHEM IN MALIBU THIS MORNING AS AN ANONYMOUS TIP ON THE WHEREABOUTS OF A KNOWN FUGITIVE LED FEDERAL AGENTS TO A RAID ON THIS APARTMENT COMPLEX...
...THE OWNER OF THE APARTMENT, DENNIS RUCKER, WAS FOUND DEAD BY THE AGENTS, WHO THEN PURSUED THE FUGITIVE-- RUCKER'S ALLEGED KILLER-- FLEEING THE SCENE IN RUCKER'S CAR.
CAREENING DOWN THE TREACHEROUS PACIFIC COAST HIGHWAY, THE VEHICLE LOST CONTROL, CRASHED THROUGH A BARRIER, AND PLUMMETED OVER A HUNDRED FEET DOWN.
EMERGENCY CREWS ARE CURRENTLY SEARCHING FOR THE BODY OF THE FUGITIVE...
...WHO WAS WANTED IN CONNECTION WITH THE DEATHS OF SEVERAL PROMINENT BUSINESSMEN THAT HAVE OCCURRED RECENTLY BOTH IN THE U.S. AND ABROAD.
HOW THOSE MURDERS CONNECT WITH THE LATEST VICTIM REMAINS TO BE DISCOVERED, ACCORDING TO THE FED--
KLICK
YOUR TEA, SIR?
YES, AND HAVE THE JET FUELED AND READY TO GO AS SOON AS POSSIBLE.
IT'S TIME TO PAY OUR NEW HOME A VISIT...

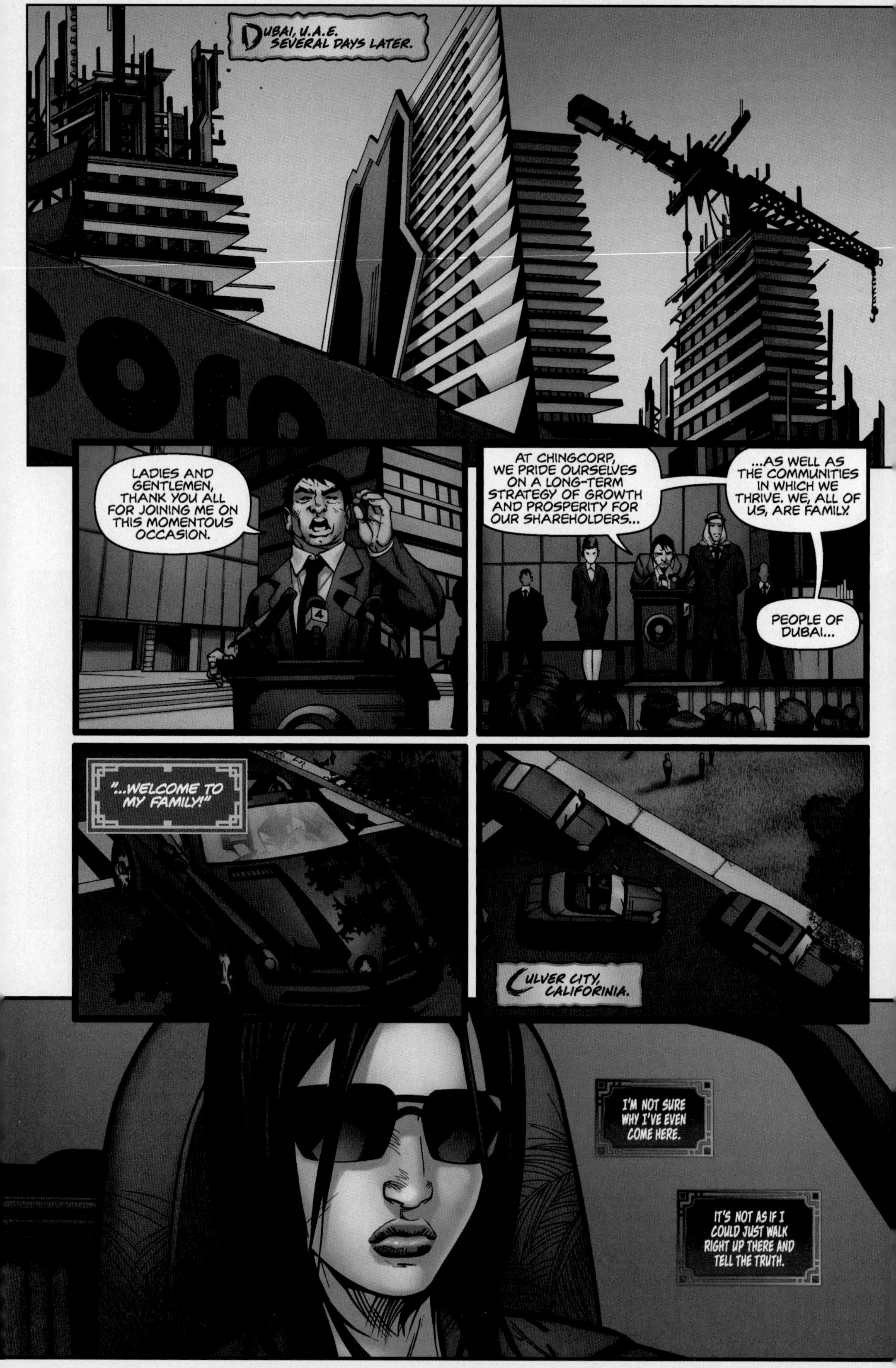
DUBAI, U.A.E. SEVERAL DAYS LATER.
LADIES AND GENTLEMEN, THANK YOU ALL FOR JOINING ME ON THIS MOMENTOUS OCCASION.
AT CHINGCORP, WE PRIDE OURSELVES ON A LONG-TERM STRATEGY OF GROWTH AND PROSPERITY FOR OUR SHAREHOLDERS...
...AS WELL AS THE COMMUNITIES IN WHICH WE THRIVE. WE, ALL OF US, ARE FAMILY.
PEOPLE OF DUBAI...
"...WELCOME TO MY FAMILY!"
CULVER CITY, CALIFORINIA.
I'M NOT SURE WHY I'VE EVEN COME HERE.
IT'S NOT AS IF I COULD JUST WALK RIGHT UP THERE AND TELL THE TRUTH.

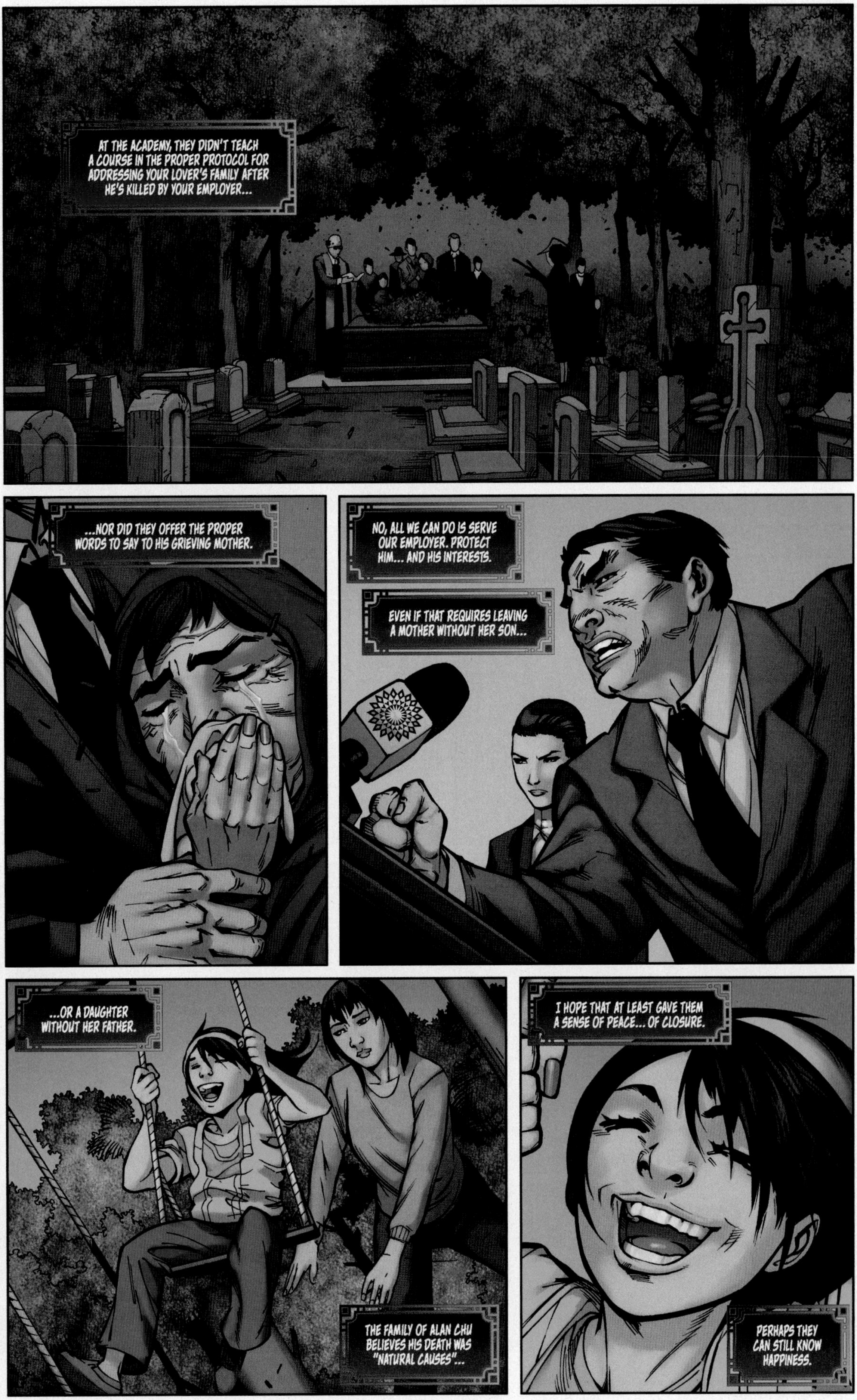
AT THE ACADEMY, THEY DIDN'T TEACH A COURSE IN THE PROPER PROTOCOL FOR ADDRESSING YOUR LOVER'S FAMILY AFTER HE'S KILLED BY YOUR EMPLOYER...
...NOR DID THEY OFFER THE PROPER WORDS TO SAY TO HIS GRIEVING MOTHER.
NO, ALL WE CAN DO IS SERVE OUR EMPLOYER. PROTECT HIM... AND HIS INTERESTS.
EVEN IF THAT REQUIRES LEAVING A MOTHER WITHOUT HER SON...
...OR A DAUGHTER WITHOUT HER FATHER.
THE FAMILY OF ALAN CHU BELIEVES HIS DEATH WAS "NATURAL CAUSES"...
I HOPE THAT AT LEAST GAVE THEM A SENSE OF PEACE... OF CLOSURE.
PERHAPS THEY CAN STILL KNOW HAPPINESS.

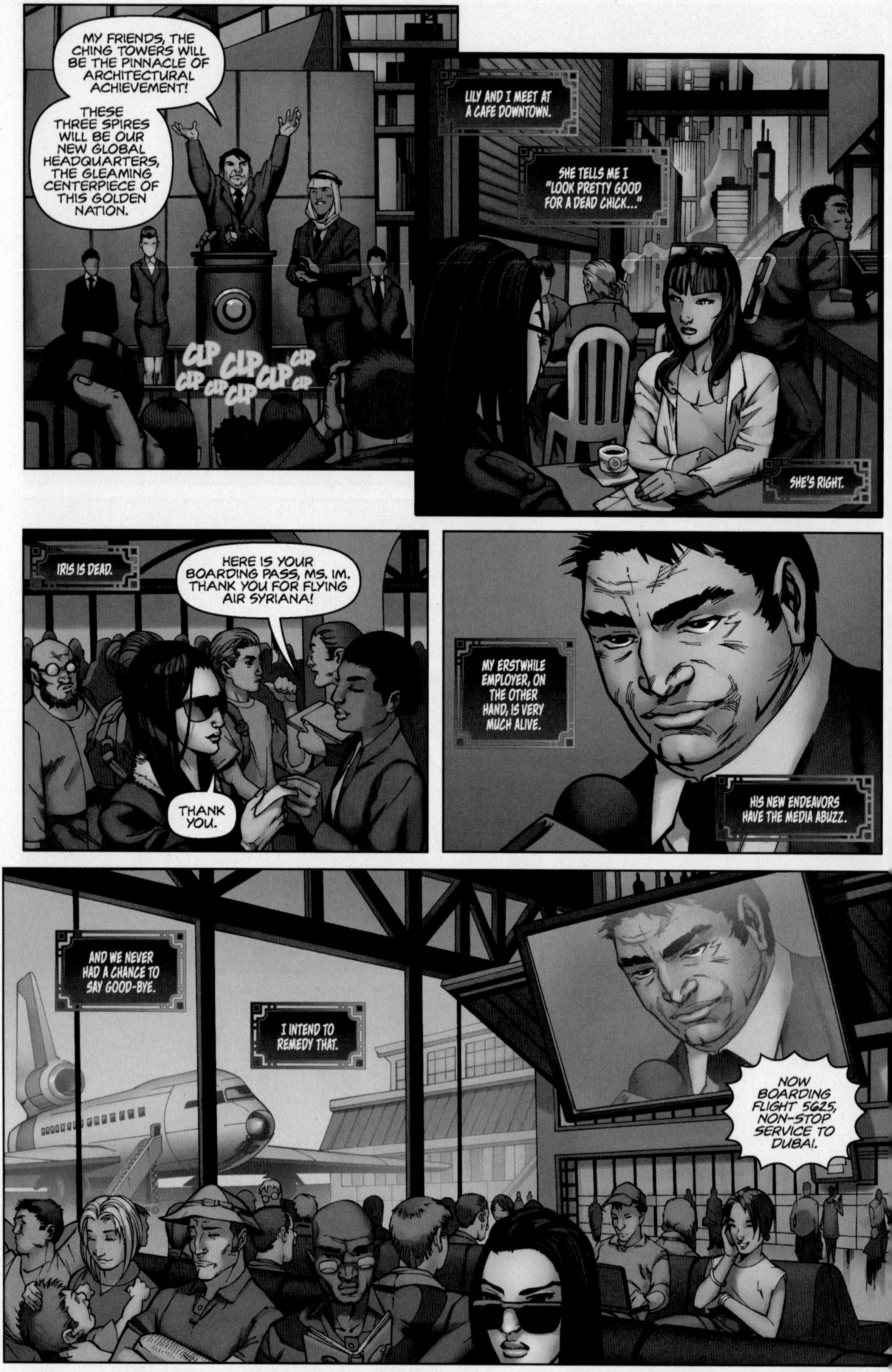
MY FRIENDS, THE CHING TOWERS WILL BE THE PINNACLE OF ARCHITECTURAL ACHIEVEMENT!
THESE THREE SPIRES WILL BE OUR NEW GLOBAL HEADQUARTERS, THE GLEAMING CENTERPIECE OF THIS GOLDEN NATION.
CLP CLP CLP CLP CLP CLP CLP CLP CLP
LILY AND I MEET AT A CAFE DOWNTOWN.
SHE TELLS ME I "LOOK PRETTY GOOD FOR A DEAD CHICK..."
SHE'S RIGHT.
IRIS IS DEAD.
HERE IS YOUR BOARDING PASS, MS. IM. THANK YOU FOR FLYING AIR SYRIANA!
THANK YOU.
MY ERSTWHILE EMPLOYER, ON THE OTHER HAND, IS VERY MUCH ALIVE.
HIS NEW ENDEAVORS HAVE THE MEDIA ABUZZ.
AND WE NEVER HAD A CHANCE TO SAY GOOD-BYE.
I INTEND TO REMEDY THAT.
NOW BOARDING FLIGHT 5625, NON-STOP SERVICE TO DUBAI.

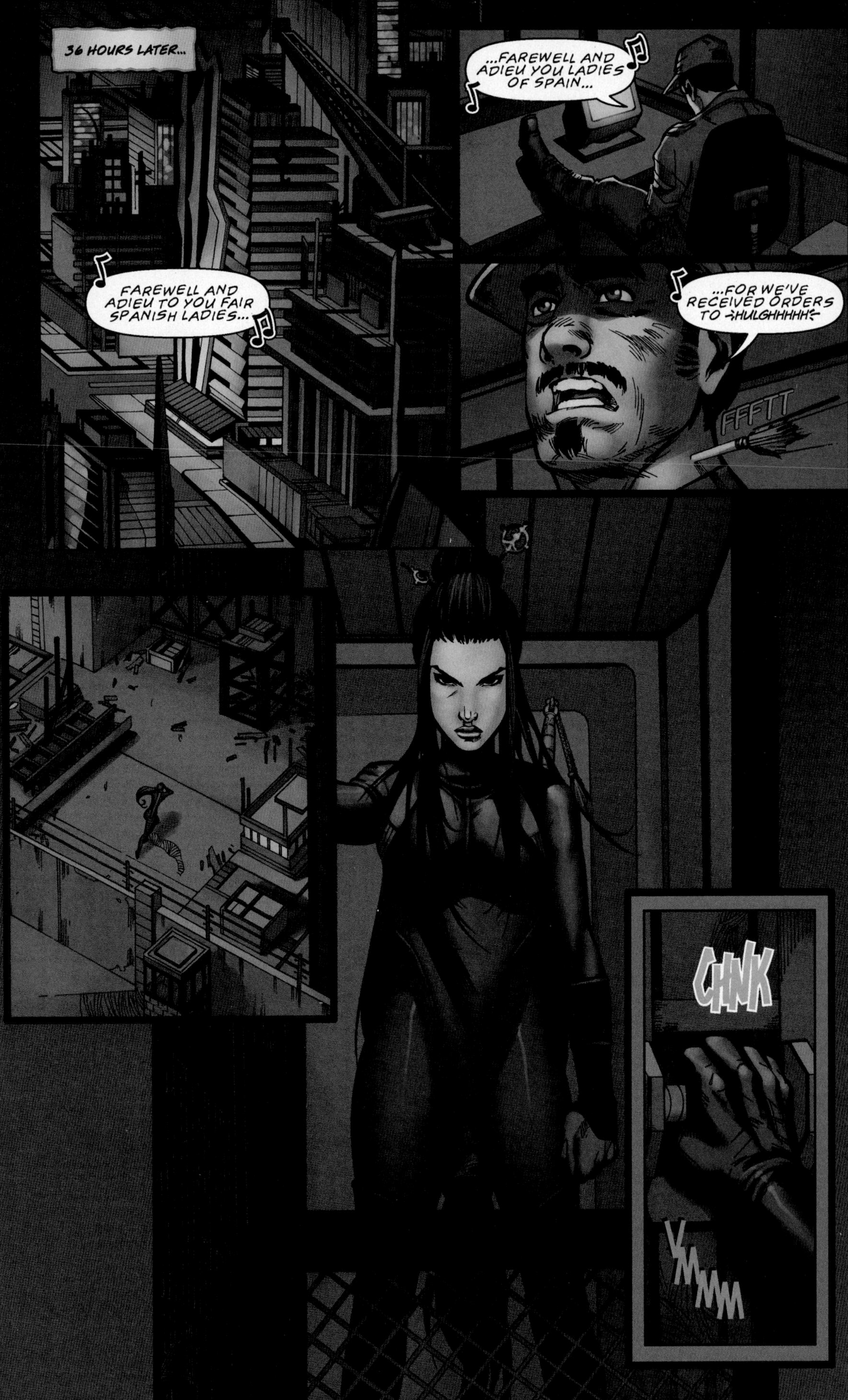
36 HOURS LATER...
FAREWELL AND ADIEU TO YOU FAIR SPANISH LADIES...
...FAREWELL AND ADIEU YOU LADIES OF SPAIN...
...FOR WE'VE RECEIVED ORDERS TO HULGHHHHH
FFFTT
CHINK
VMMMM

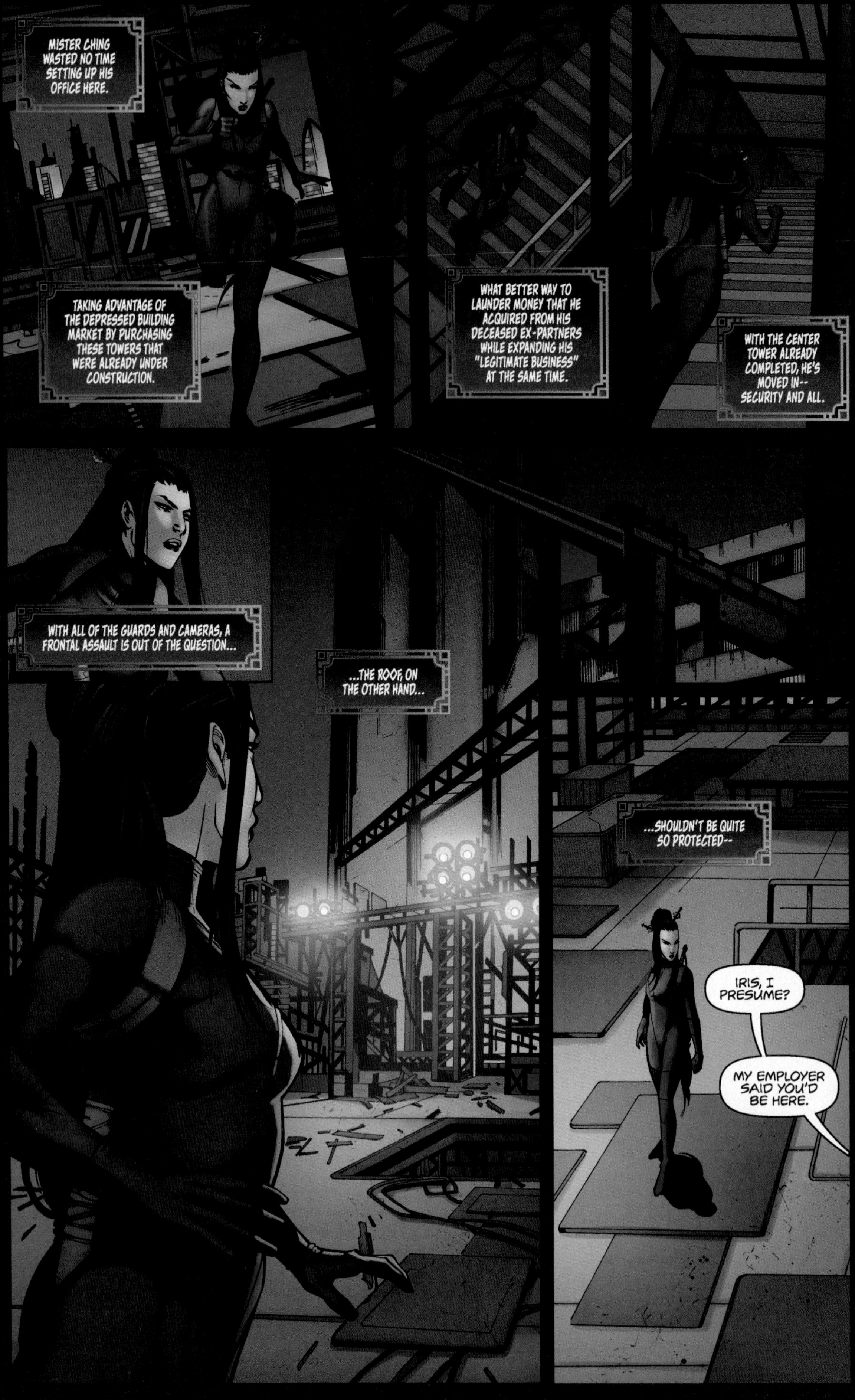
MISTER CHING WASTED NO TIME SETTING UP HIS OFFICE HERE.
TAKING ADVANTAGE OF THE DEPRESSED BUILDING MARKET BY PURCHASING THESE TOWERS THAT WERE ALREADY UNDER CONSTRUCTION.
WHAT BETTER WAY TO LAUNDER MONEY THAT HE ACQUIRED FROM HIS DECEASED EX-PARTNERS WHILE EXPANDING HIS "LEGITIMATE BUSINESS" AT THE SAME TIME.
WITH THE CENTER TOWER ALREADY COMPLETED, HE'S MOVED IN-- SECURITY AND ALL.
WITH ALL OF THE GUARDS AND CAMERAS, A FRONTAL ASSAULT IS OUT OF THE QUESTION...
...THE ROOF, ON THE OTHER HAND...
...SHOULDN'T BE QUITE SO PROTECTED--
IRIS, I PRESUME?
MY EMPLOYER SAID YOU'D BE HERE.

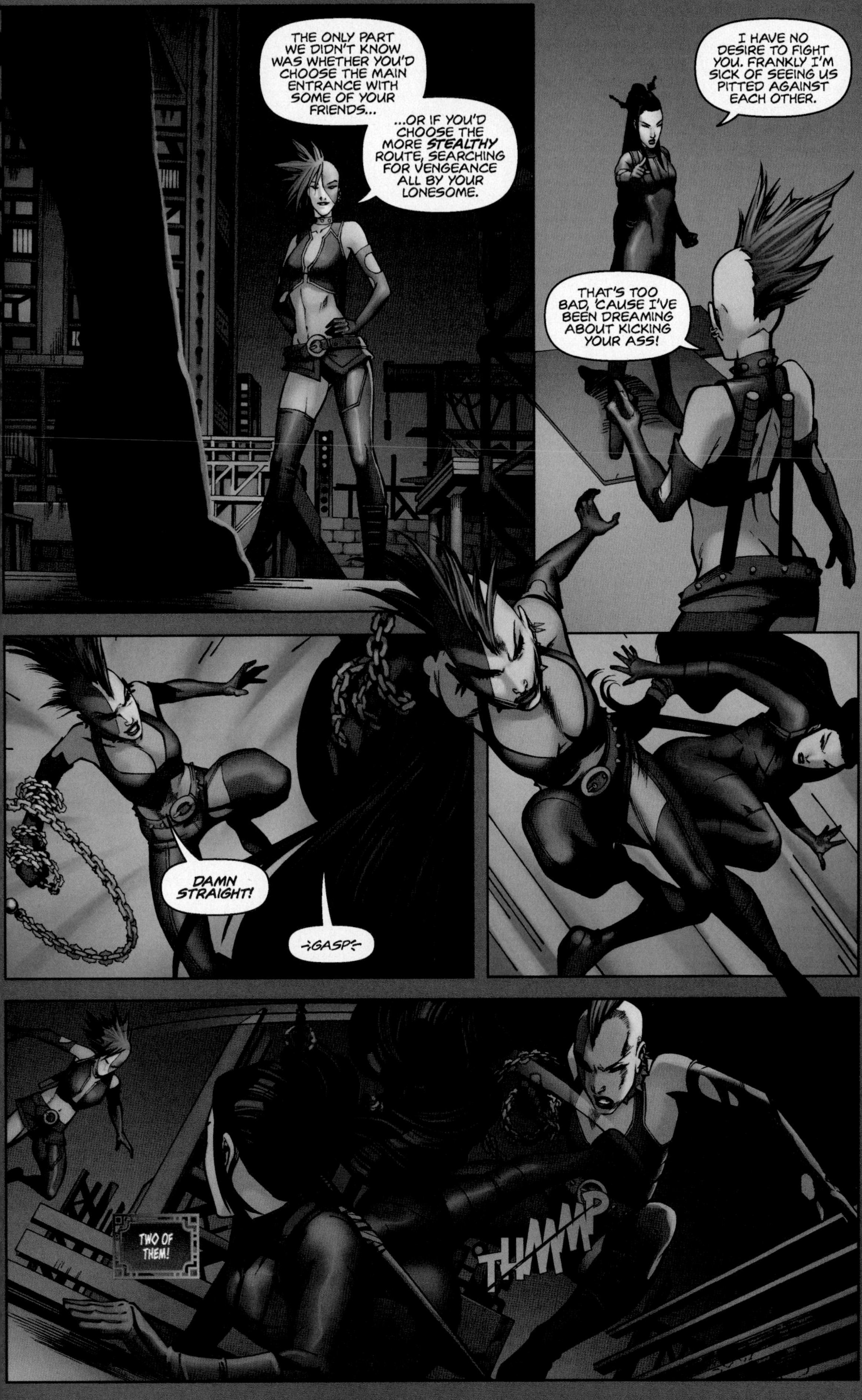

THE ONLY PART WE DIDN'T KNOW WAS WHETHER YOU'D CHOOSE THE MAIN ENTRANCE WITH SOME OF YOUR FRIENDS...
...OR IF YOU'D CHOOSE THE MORE STEALTHY ROUTE, SEARCHING FOR VENGEANCE ALL BY YOUR LONESOME.
I HAVE NO DESIRE TO FIGHT YOU. FRANKLY I'M SICK OF SEEING US PITTED AGAINST EACH OTHER.
THAT'S TOO BAD, 'CAUSE I'VE BEEN DREAMING ABOUT KICKING YOUR ASS!
DAMN STRAIGHT!
GASP
TWO OF THEM!
THWAP

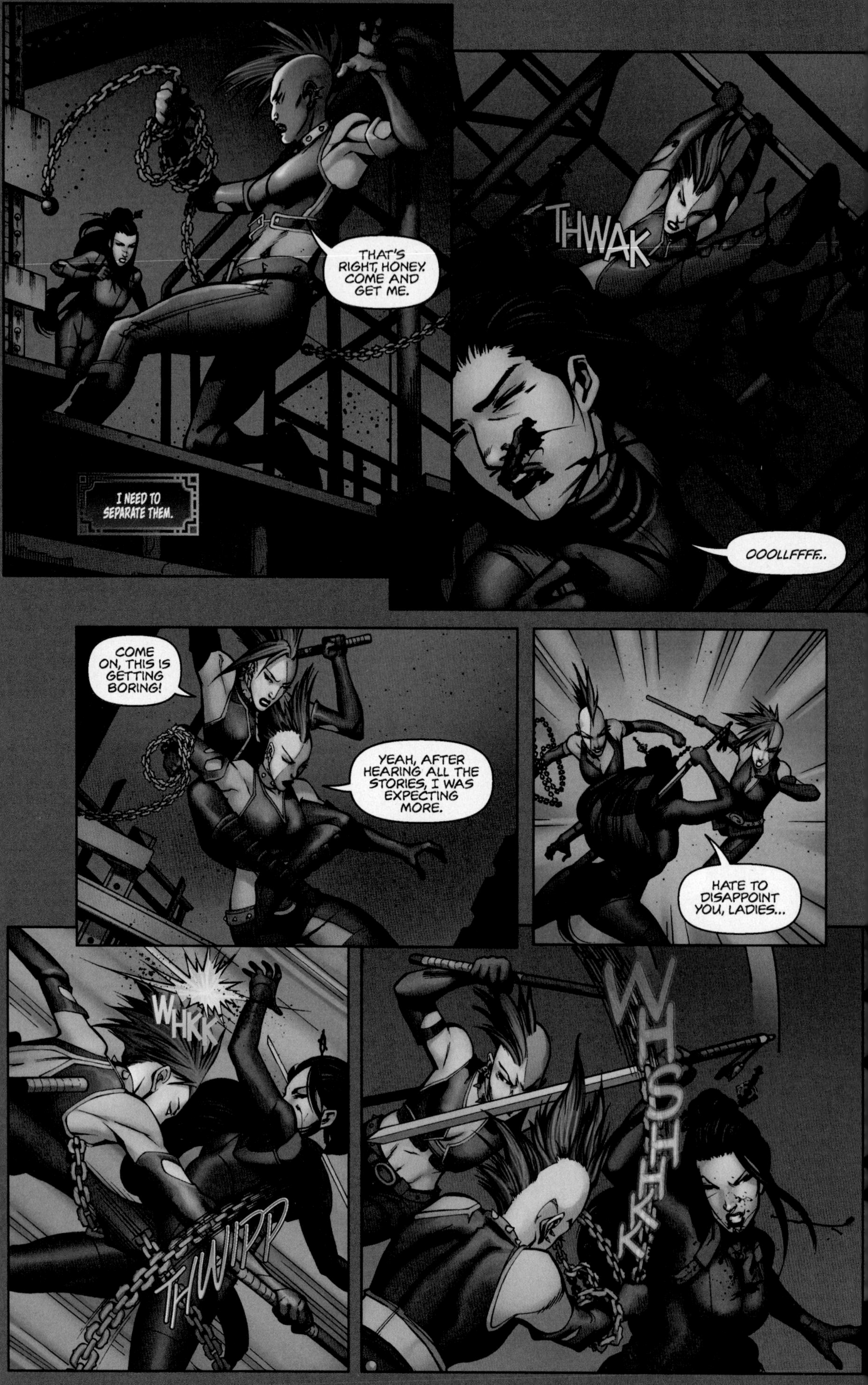
THAT'S RIGHT, HONEY. COME AND GET ME.
I NEED TO SEPARATE THEM.
THWAK
OOOLLFFFF..
COME ON, THIS IS GETTING BORING!
YEAH, AFTER HEARING ALL THE STORIES, I WAS EXPECTING MORE.
HATE TO DISAPPOINT YOU, LADIES...
WHKK
THWIPP
WHSHHKK

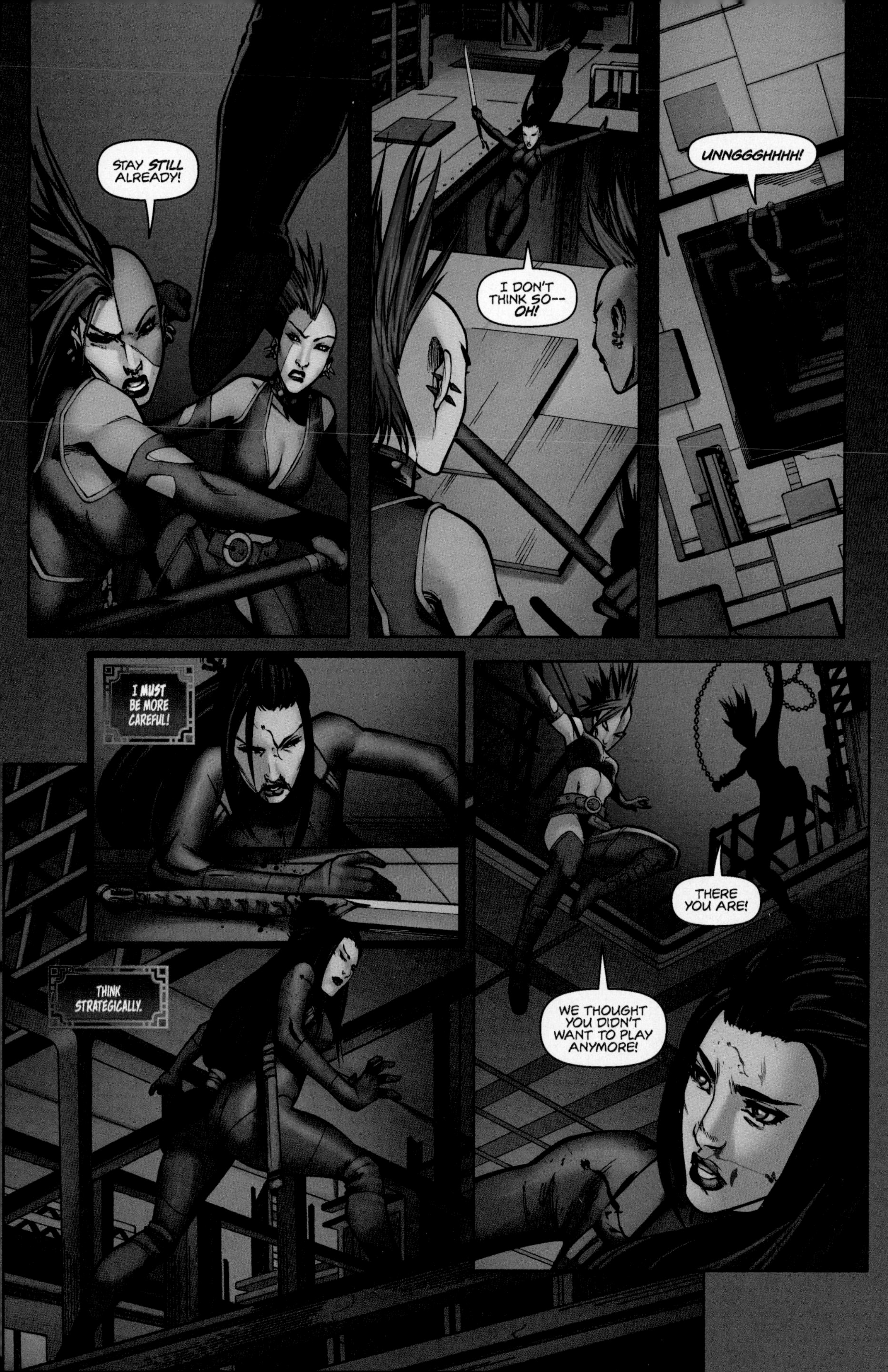
STAY STILL ALREADY!
I DON'T THINK SO-- OH!
UNNGGGHHHH!
I MUST BE MORE CAREFUL!
THINK STRATEGICALLY.
THERE YOU ARE!
WE THOUGHT YOU DIDN'T WANT TO PLAY ANYMORE!

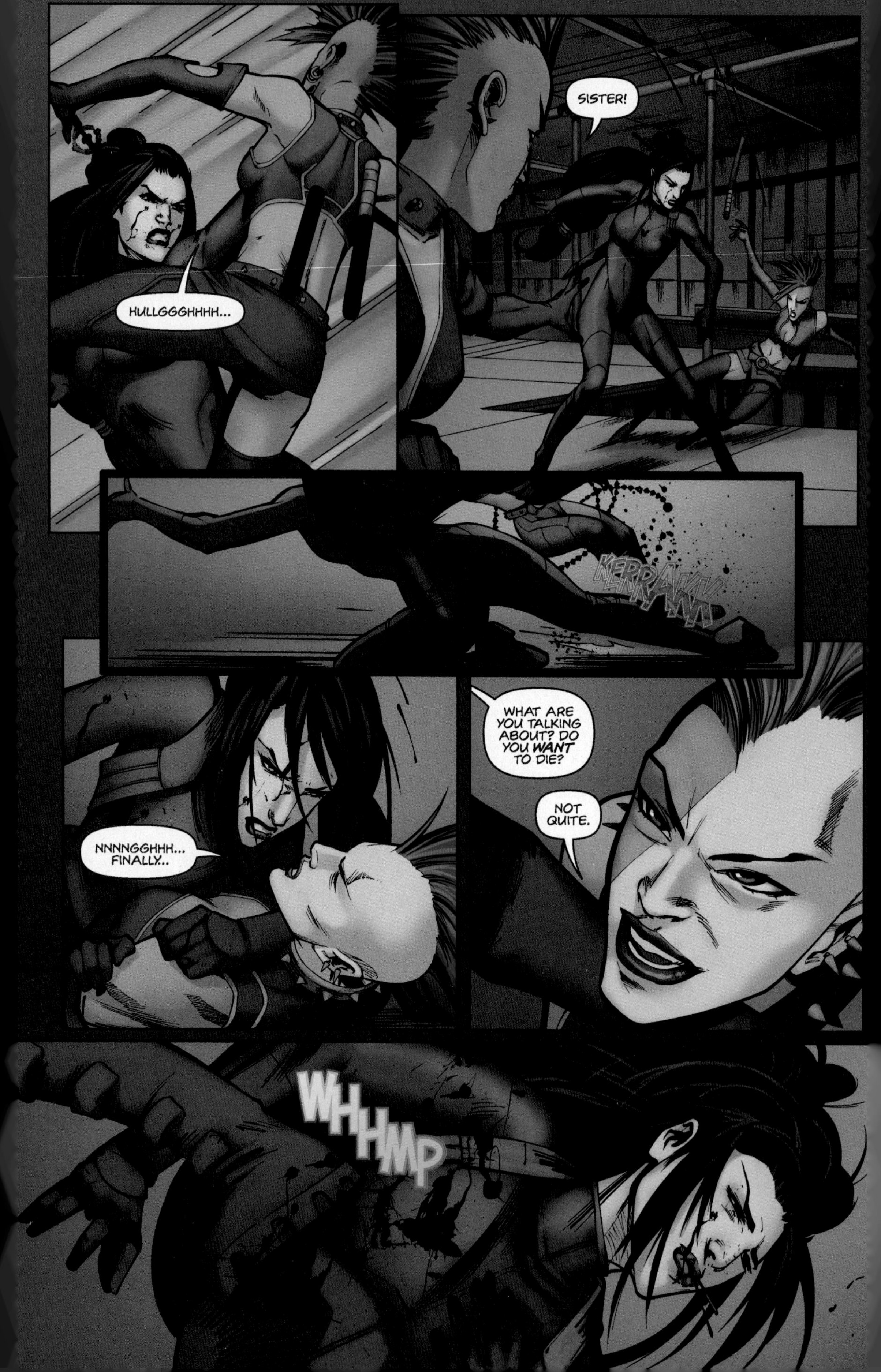
HULLGGGHHHH...
SISTER!
KERRAKKK
NNNNGGHHH... FINALLY...
WHAT ARE YOU TALKING ABOUT? DO YOU *WANT* TO DIE?
NOT QUITE.
WHHMP

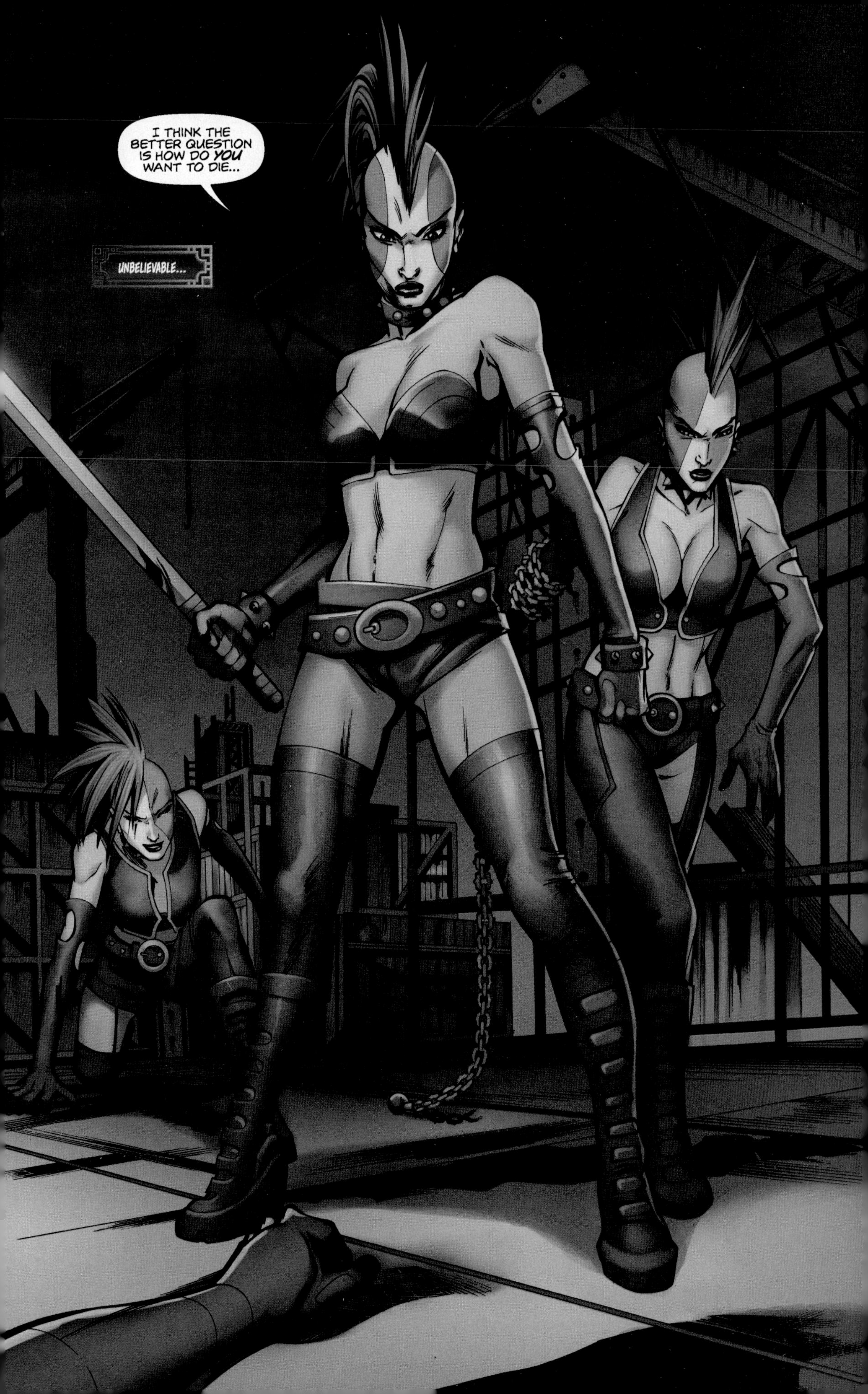
I THINK THE BETTER QUESTION IS HOW DO *YOU* WANT TO DIE...
UNBELIEVABLE...

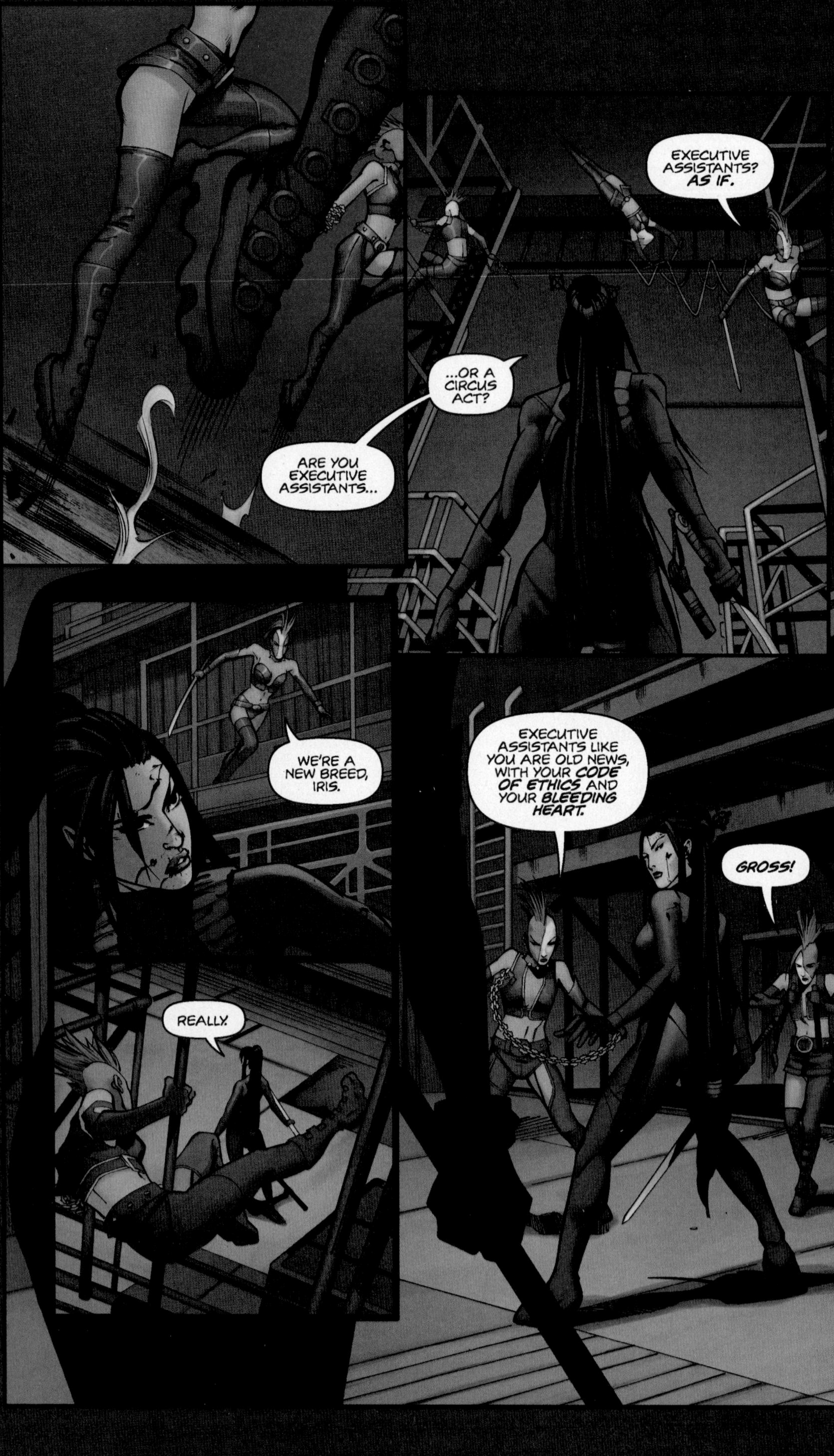
ARE YOU EXECUTIVE ASSISTANTS...
...OR A CIRCUS ACT?
EXECUTIVE ASSISTANTS? AS IF.
WE'RE A NEW BREED, IRIS.
REALLY.
EXECUTIVE ASSISTANTS LIKE YOU ARE OLD NEWS, WITH YOUR CODE OF ETHICS AND YOUR BLEEDING HEART.
GROSS!

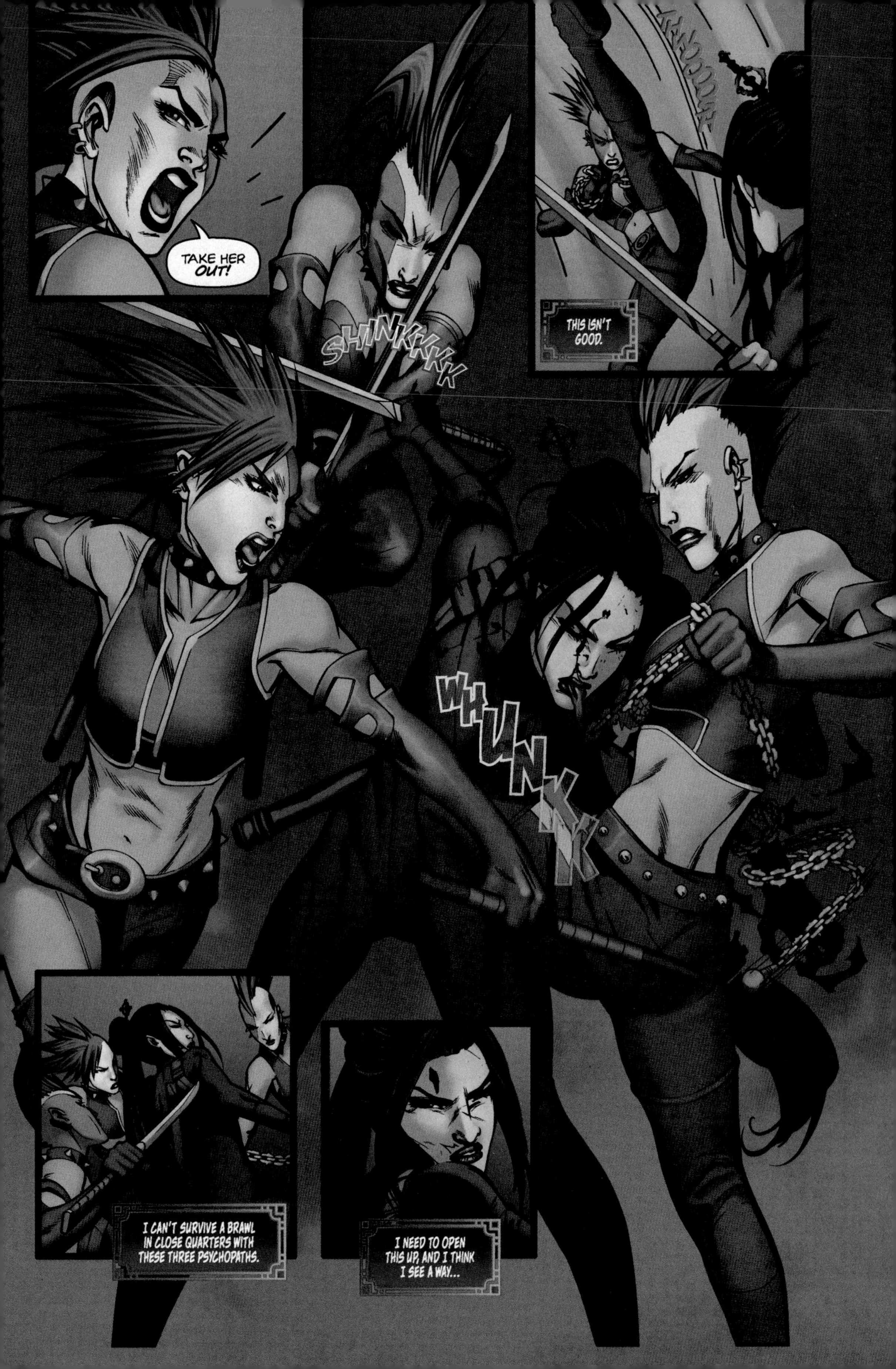
TAKE HER OUT!
SHHINKKKKK
THIS ISN'T GOOD.
WHUNKK
I CAN'T SURVIVE A BRAWL IN CLOSE QUARTERS WITH THESE THREE PSYCHOPATHS.
I NEED TO OPEN THIS UP, AND I THINK I SEE A WAY...

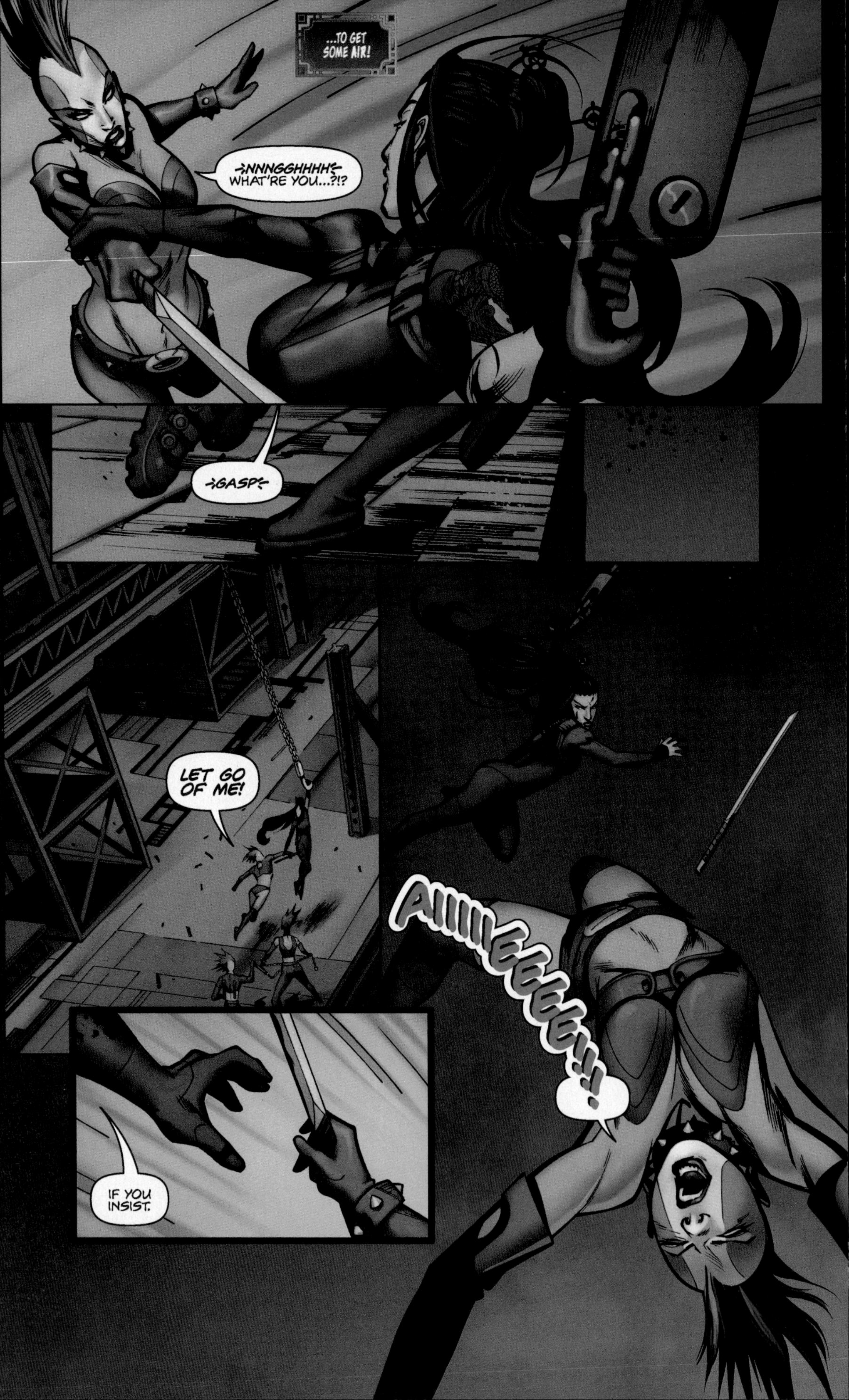
...TO GET SOME AIR!
NNNGGHHHH WHAT'RE YOU...?!?
GASP
LET GO OF ME!
IF YOU INSIST.
AIIIIIEEEEE!!!

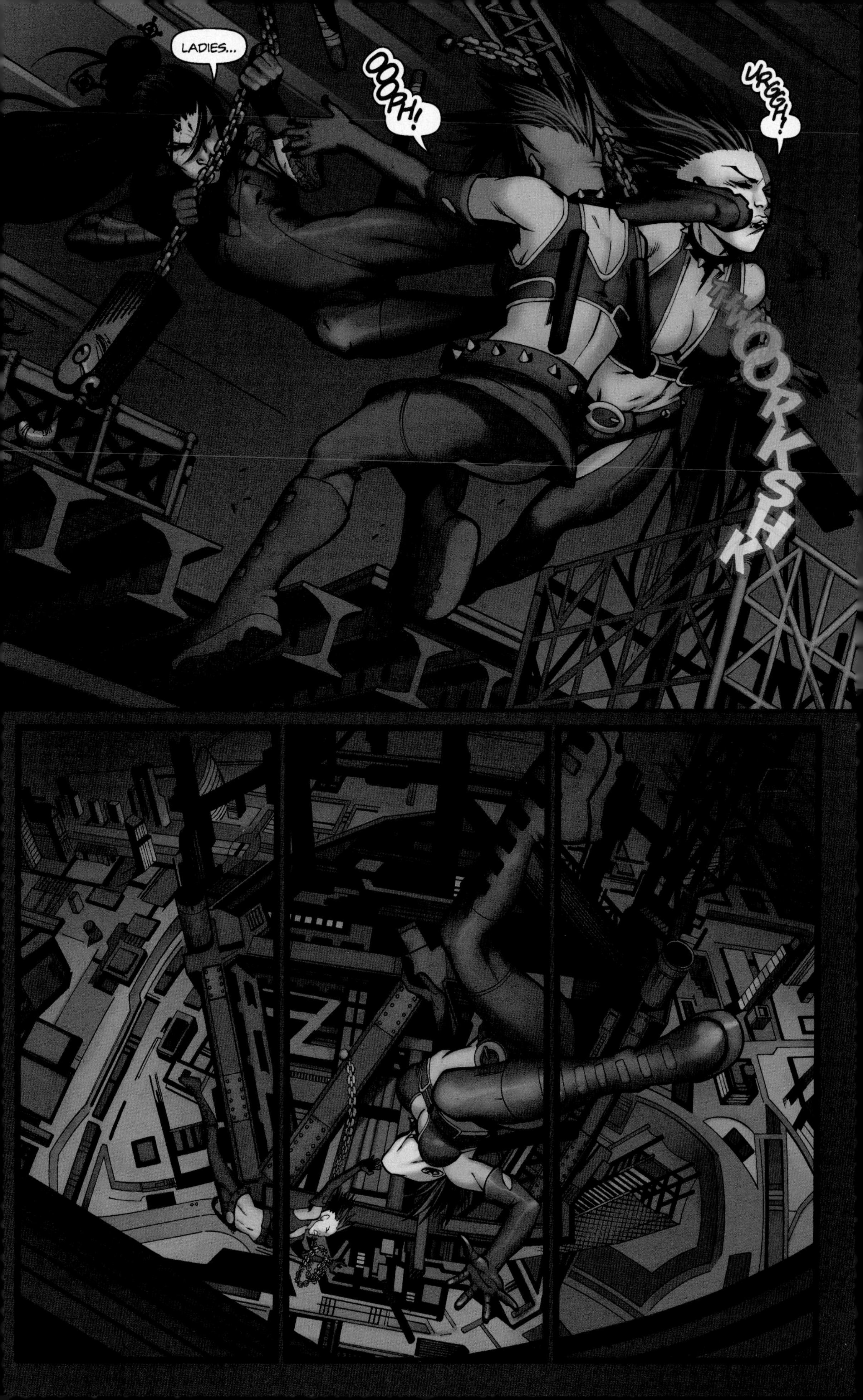

LADIES...
OOOPH!
URGGH!
THWOORKSHK

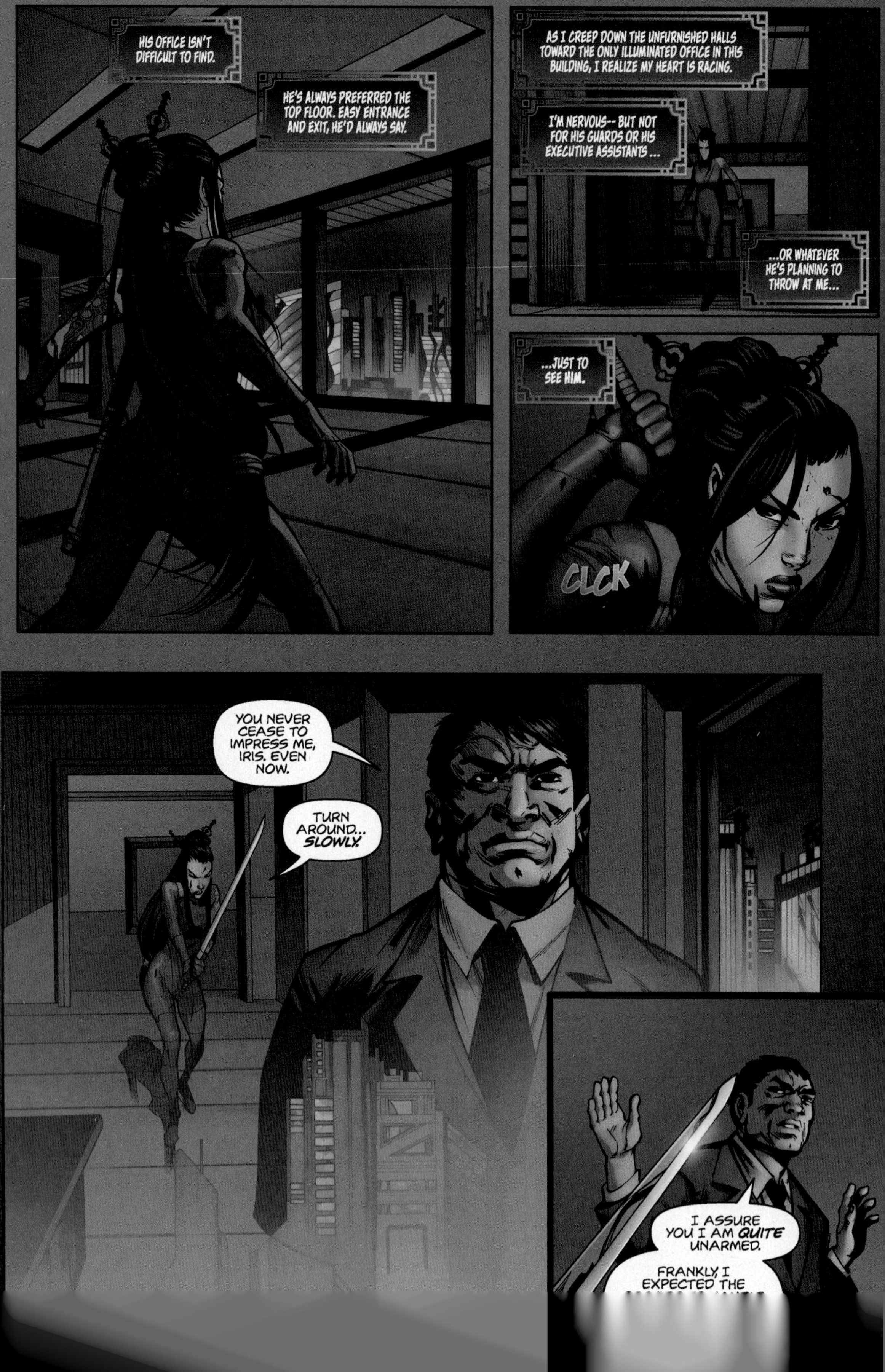
HIS OFFICE ISN'T DIFFICULT TO FIND.
HE'S ALWAYS PREFERRED THE TOP FLOOR. EASY ENTRANCE AND EXIT, HE'D ALWAYS SAY.
AS I CREEP DOWN THE UNFURNISHED HALLS TOWARD THE ONLY ILLUMINATED OFFICE IN THIS BUILDING, I REALIZE MY HEART IS RACING.
I'M NERVOUS-- BUT NOT FOR HIS GUARDS OR HIS EXECUTIVE ASSISTANTS ...
...OR WHATEVER HE'S PLANNING TO THROW AT ME...
...JUST TO SEE HIM.
CLCK
YOU NEVER CEASE TO IMPRESS ME, IRIS. EVEN NOW.
TURN AROUND... SLOWLY.
I ASSURE YOU I AM QUITE UNARMED.
FRANKLY, I EXPECTED THE

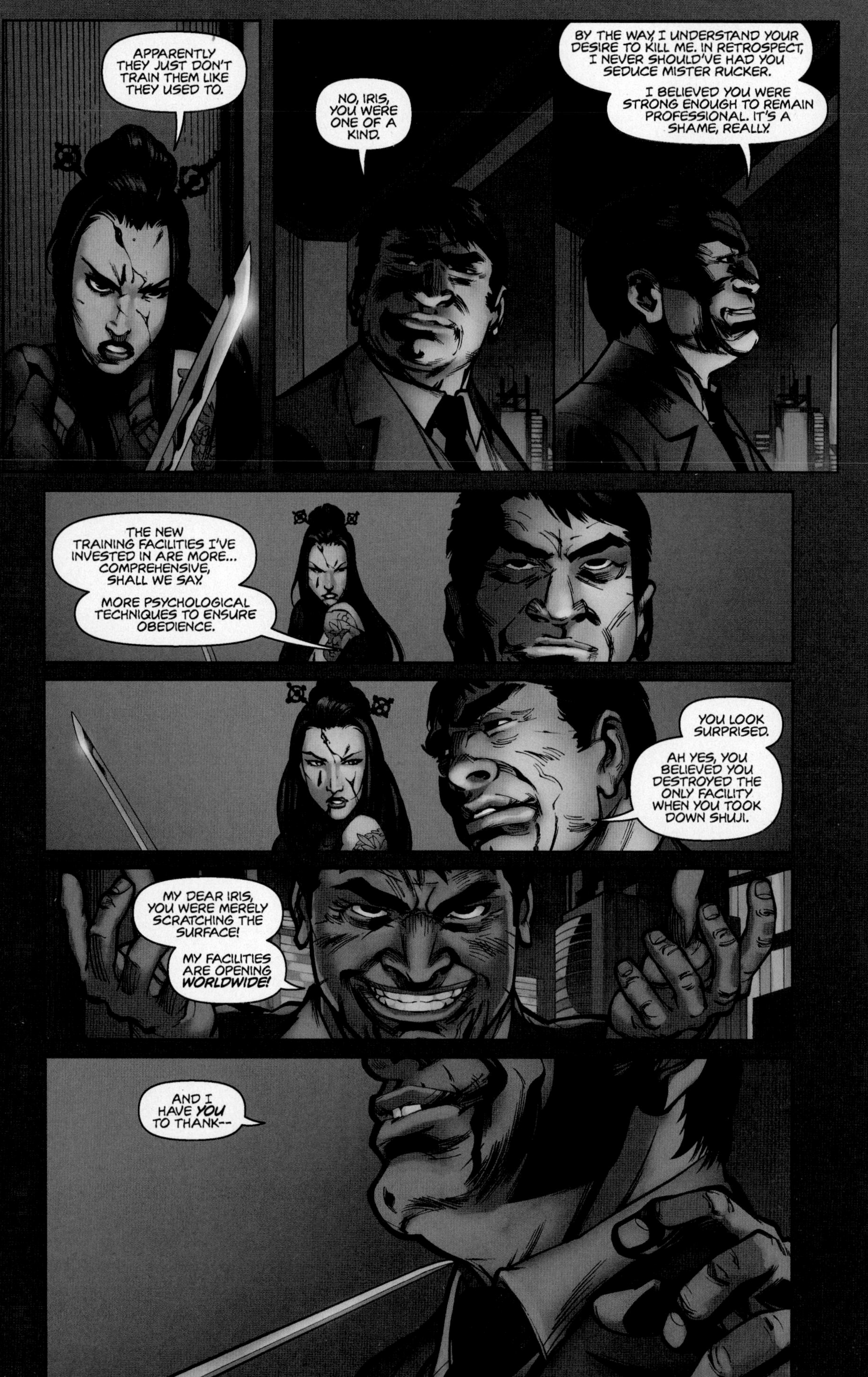
APPARENTLY THEY JUST DON'T TRAIN THEM LIKE THEY USED TO.
NO, IRIS, YOU WERE ONE OF A KIND.
BY THE WAY, I UNDERSTAND YOUR DESIRE TO KILL ME. IN RETROSPECT, I NEVER SHOULD'VE HAD YOU SEDUCE MISTER RUCKER.
I BELIEVED YOU WERE STRONG ENOUGH TO REMAIN PROFESSIONAL. IT'S A SHAME, REALLY.
THE NEW TRAINING FACILITIES I'VE INVESTED IN ARE MORE... COMPREHENSIVE, SHALL WE SAY.
MORE PSYCHOLOGICAL TECHNIQUES TO ENSURE OBEDIENCE.
YOU LOOK SURPRISED.
AH YES, YOU BELIEVED YOU DESTROYED THE ONLY FACILITY WHEN YOU TOOK DOWN SHUJI.
MY DEAR IRIS, YOU WERE MERELY SCRATCHING THE SURFACE!
MY FACILITIES ARE OPENING ***WORLDWIDE!***
AND I HAVE ***YOU*** TO THANK--

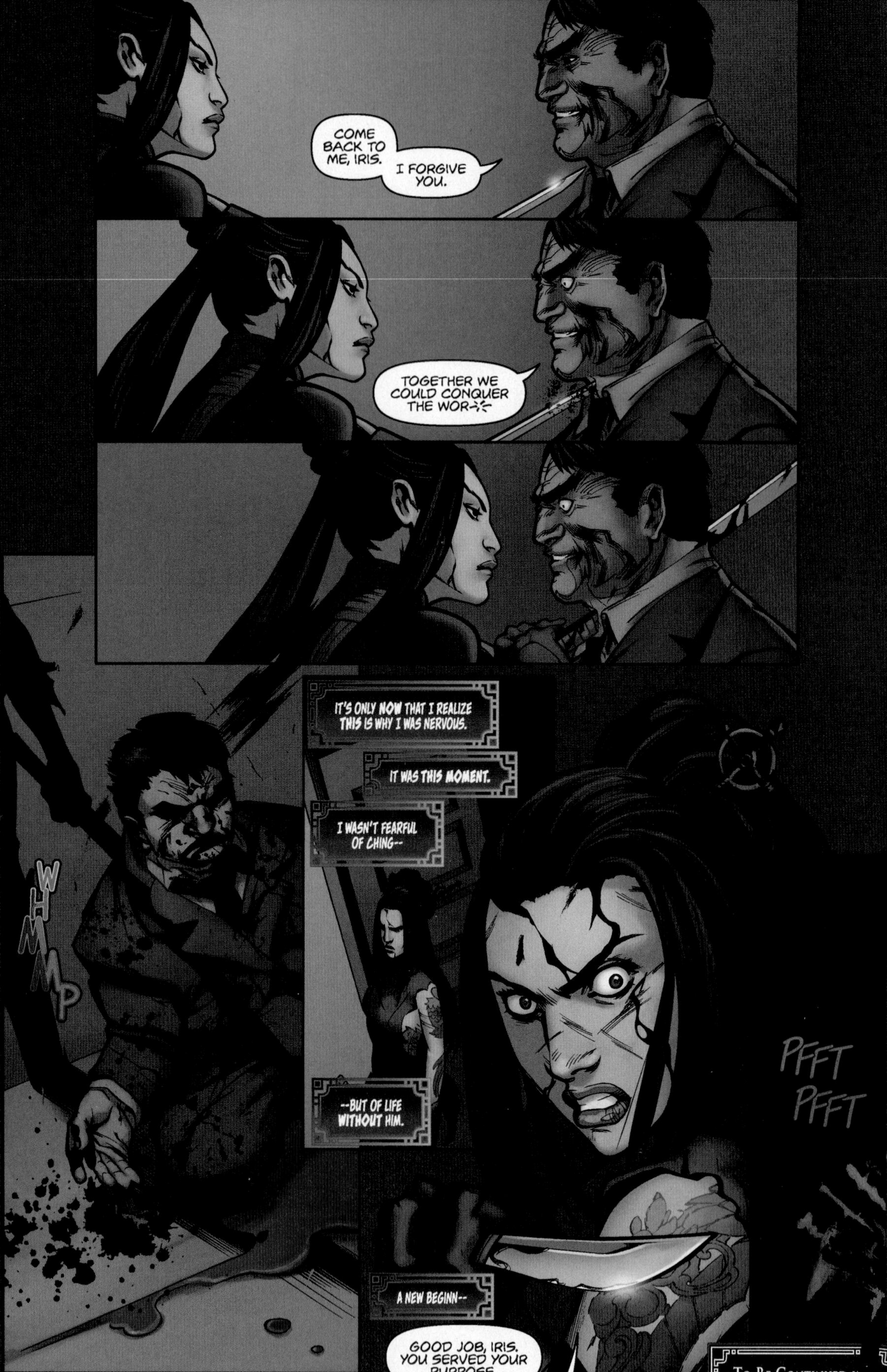
COME BACK TO ME, IRIS.
I FORGIVE YOU.
TOGETHER WE COULD CONQUER THE WOR--
IT'S ONLY NOW THAT I REALIZE THIS IS WHY I WAS NERVOUS.
IT WAS THIS MOMENT.
I WASN'T FEARFUL OF CHING--
--BUT OF LIFE WITHOUT HIM.
WHMMP
PFFT PFFT
A NEW BEGINN--
GOOD JOB, IRIS. YOU SERVED YOUR

Executive Assistant: Iris
[COVER GALLERY]

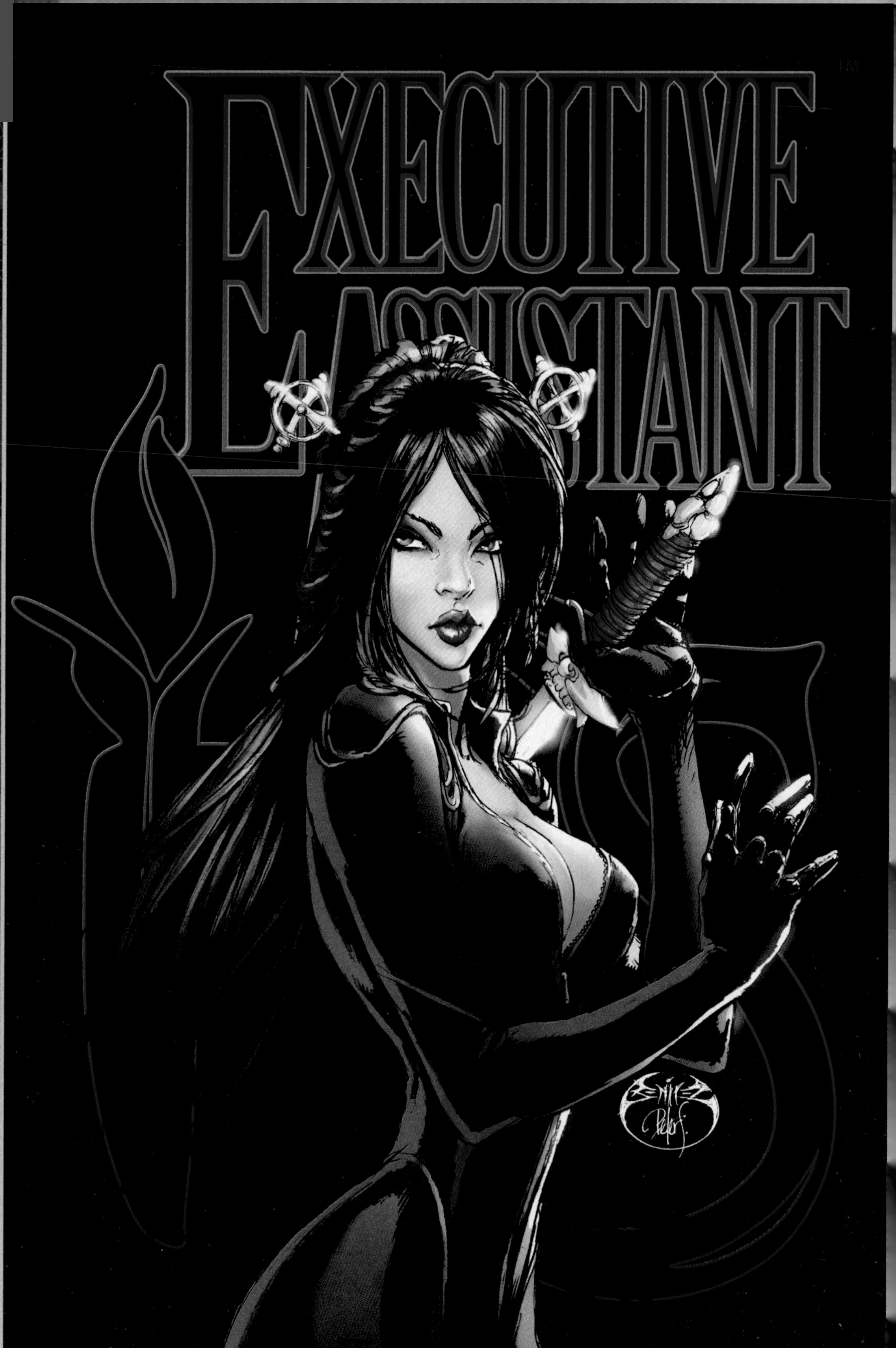
EXECUTIVE ASSISTANT
TM

EXECUTIVE ASSISTANT: IRIS #1
Convention Exclusive Cover E
JOE BENITEZ • PETER STEIGERWALD

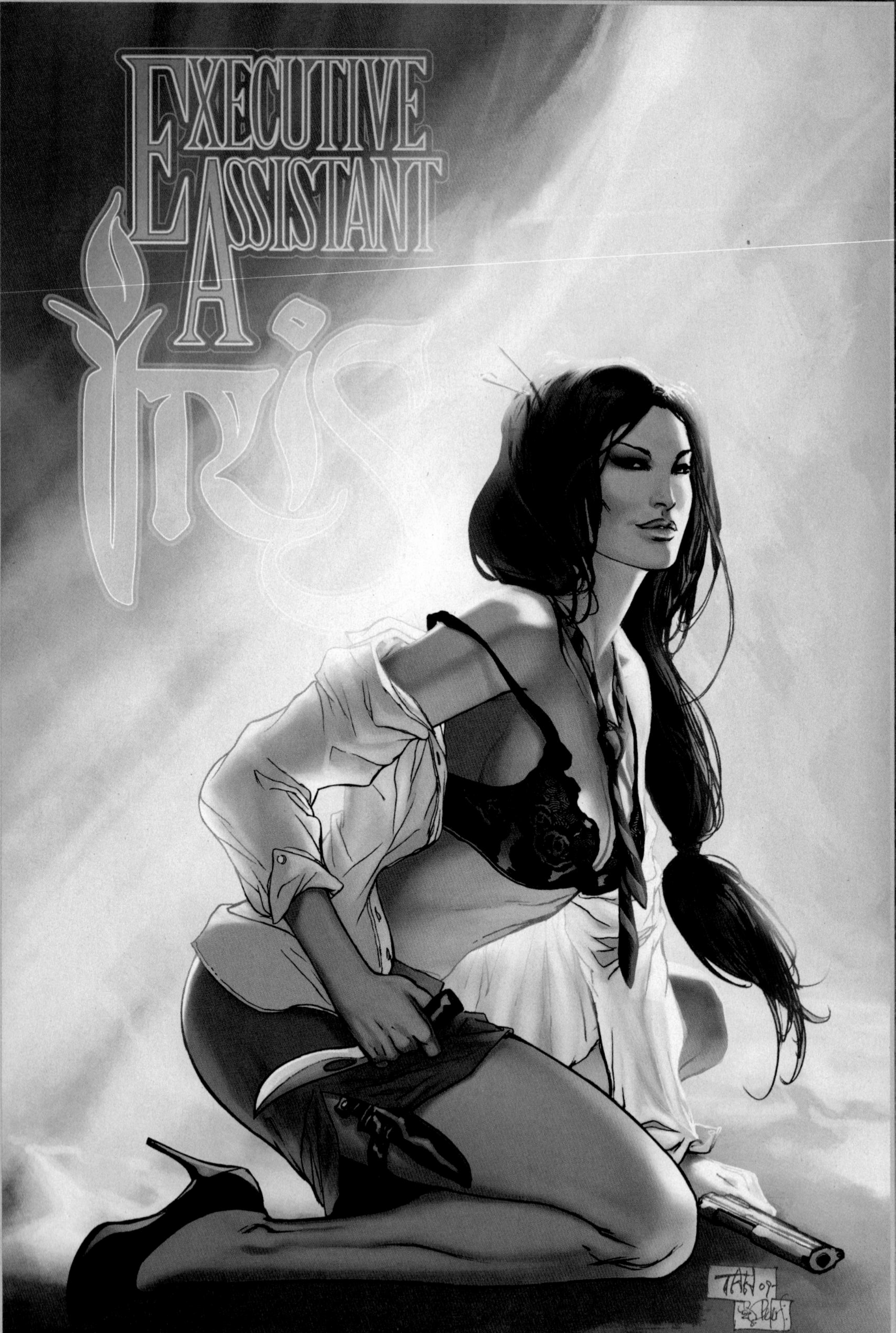
EXECUTIVE ASSISTANT
Iris
TAN 07

Executive Assistant: Iris #2

Convention Exclusive Cover D

Billy TAN • Mark ROSLAN • Peter STEIGERWALD

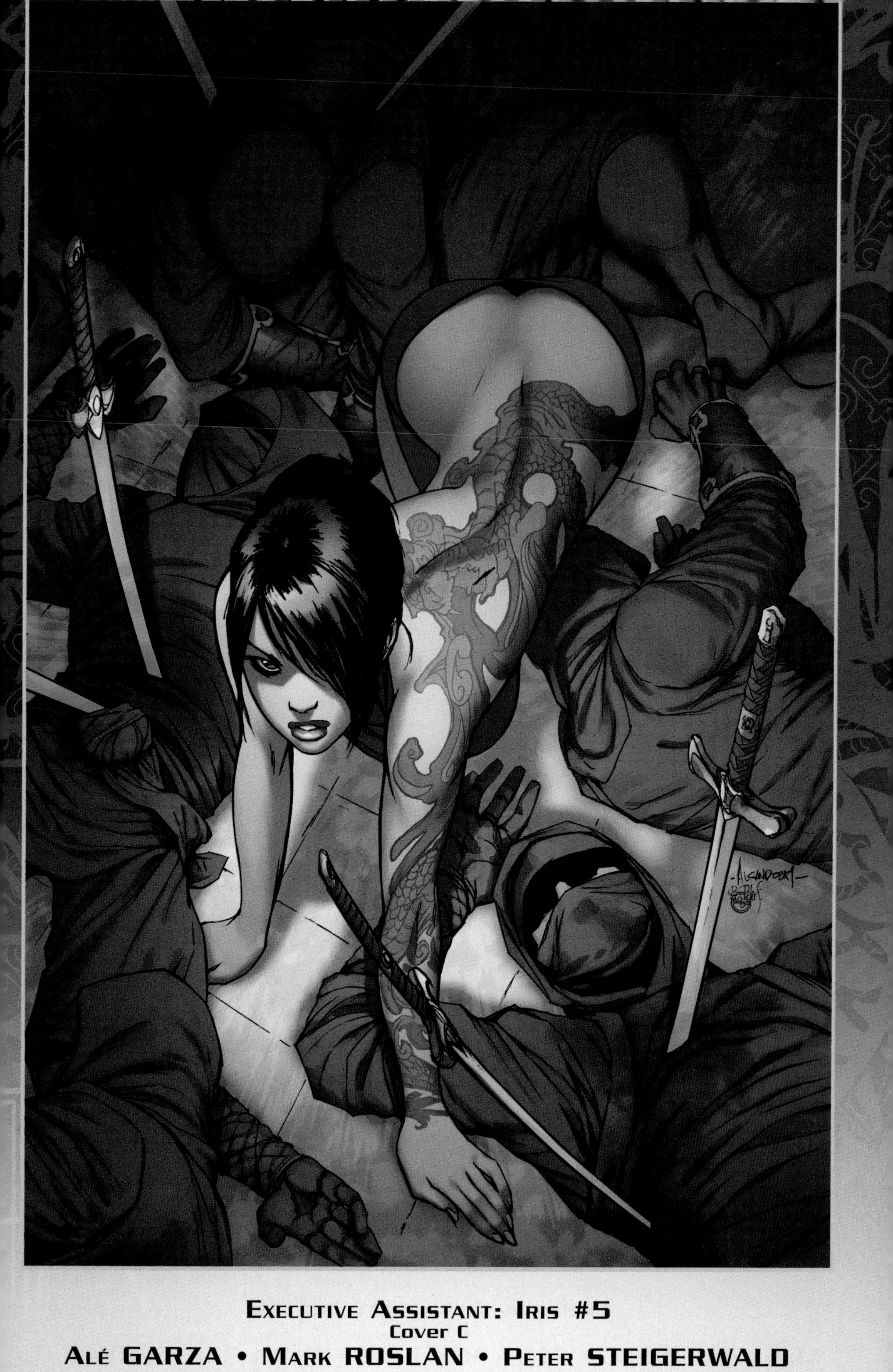

Executive Assistant: Iris #5
Cover C
Alé GARZA • Mark ROSLAN • Peter STEIGERWALD

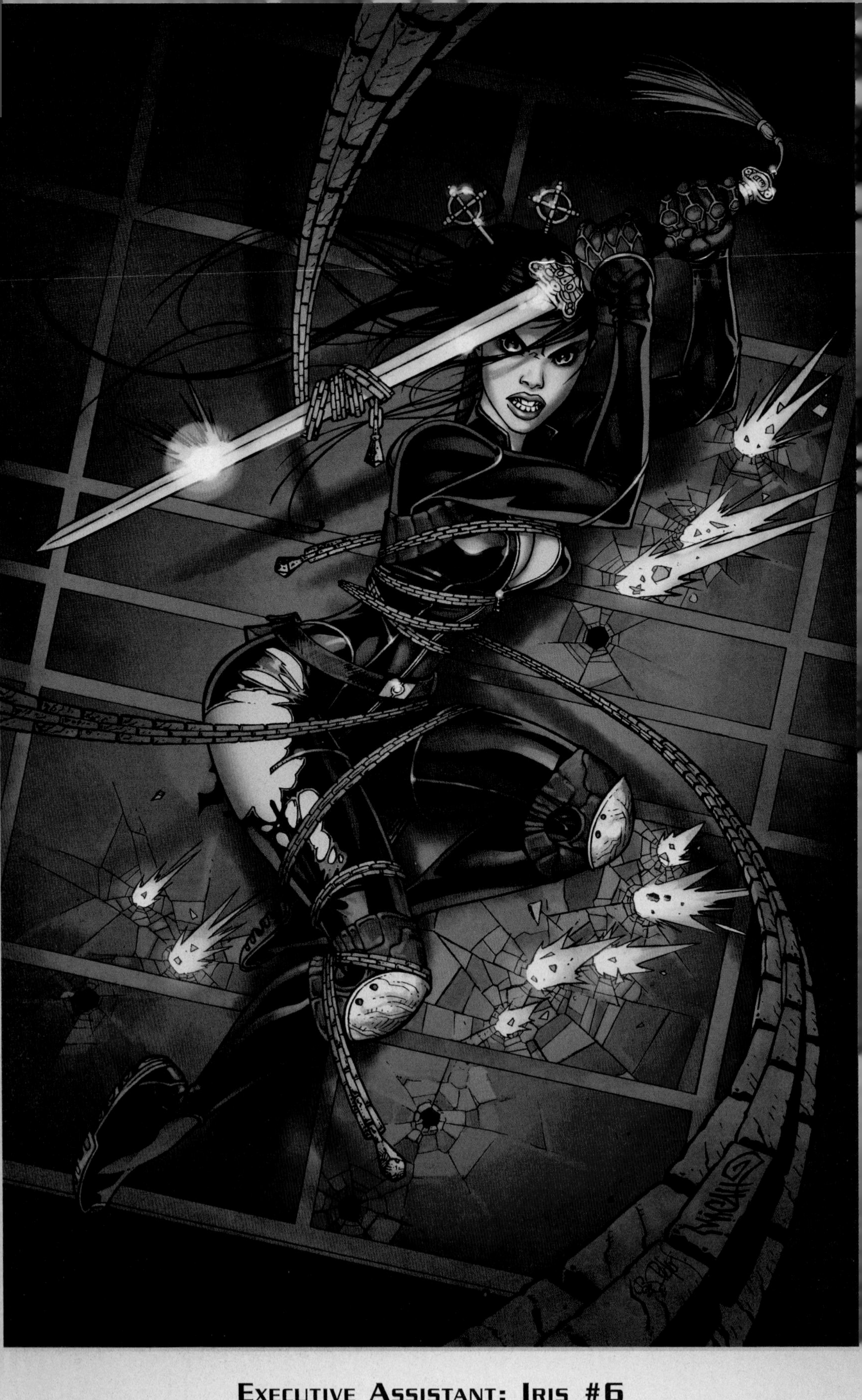

Executive Assistant: Iris #6
Cover C
Micah GUNNELL • Mark ROSLAN • Peter STEIGERWALD

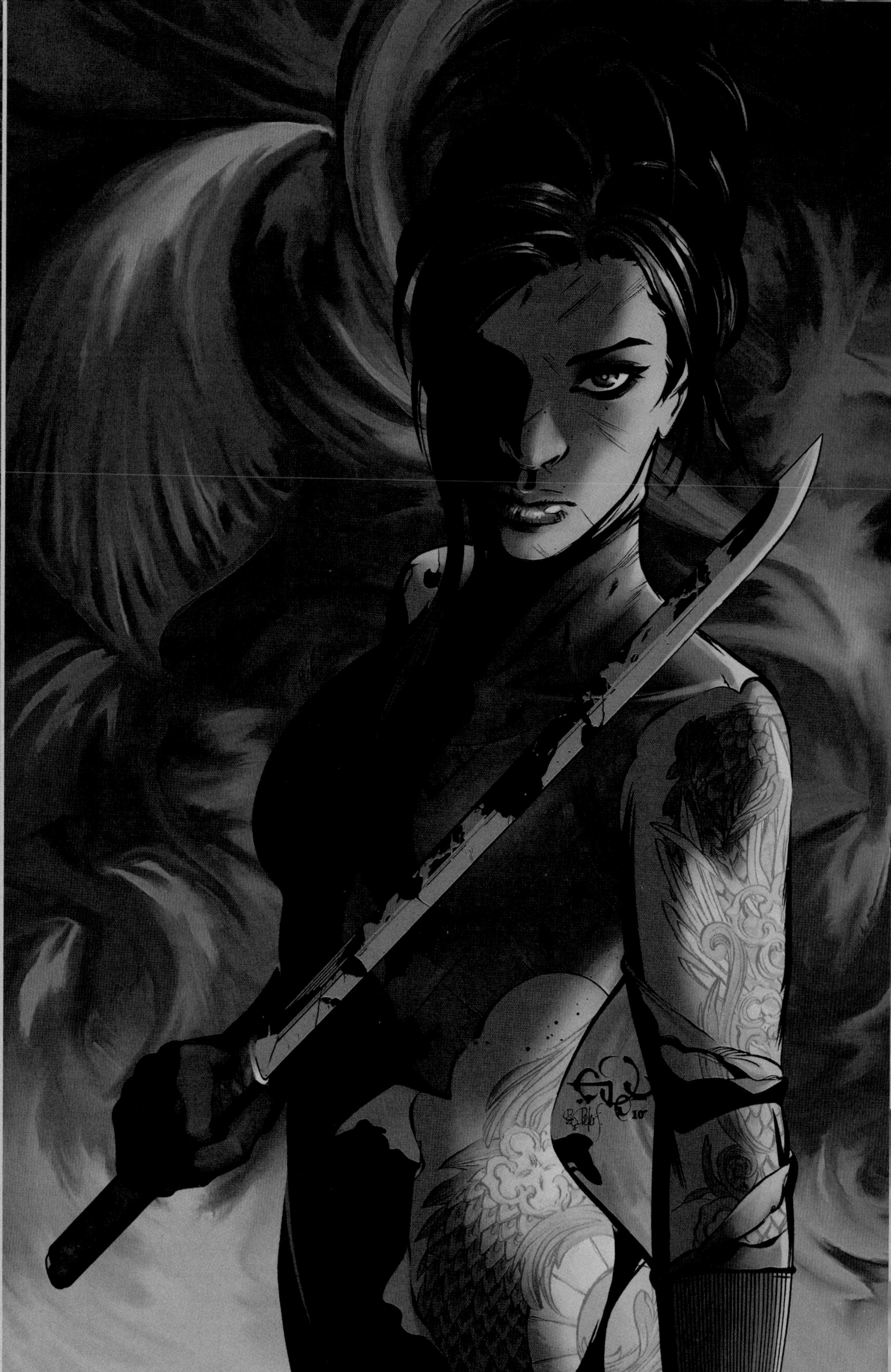

Executive Assistant: Iris #6
New York Comic-Con Exclusive Cover D
Eduardo FRANCISCO • Mark ROSLAN • Peter STEIGERWALD

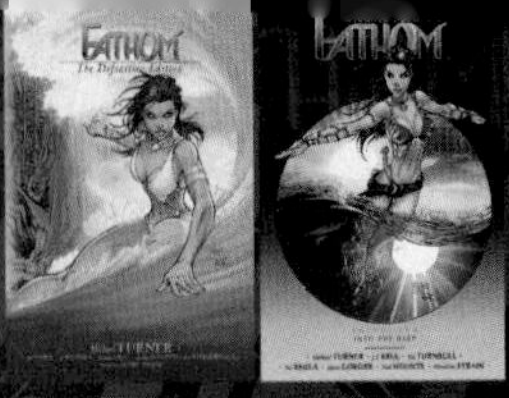

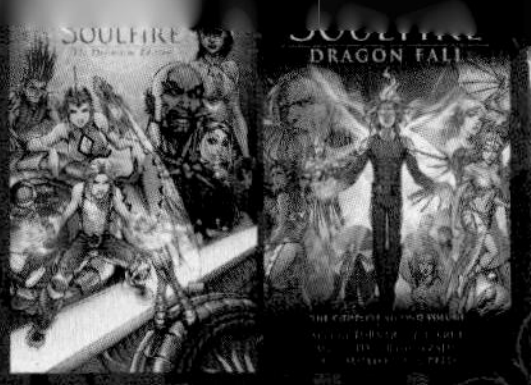

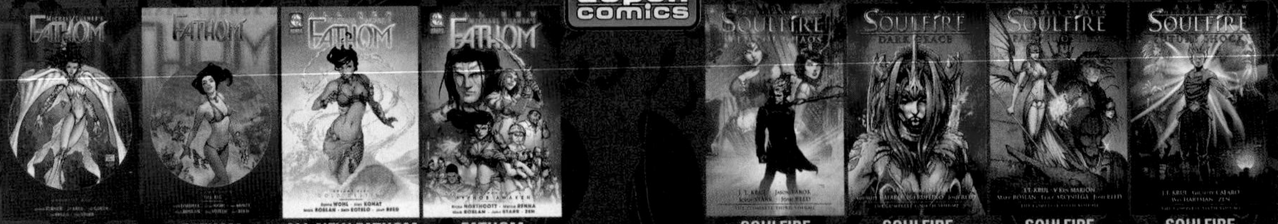

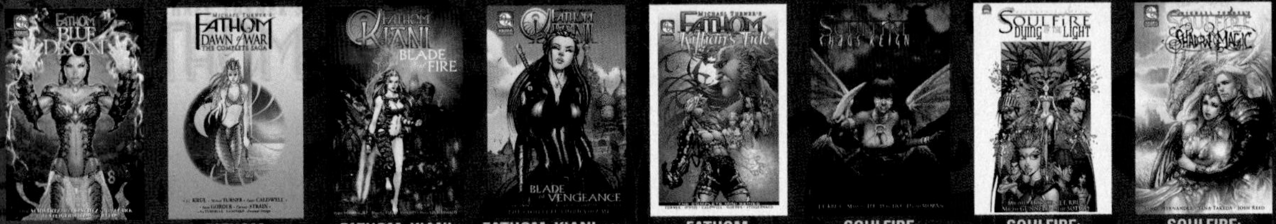

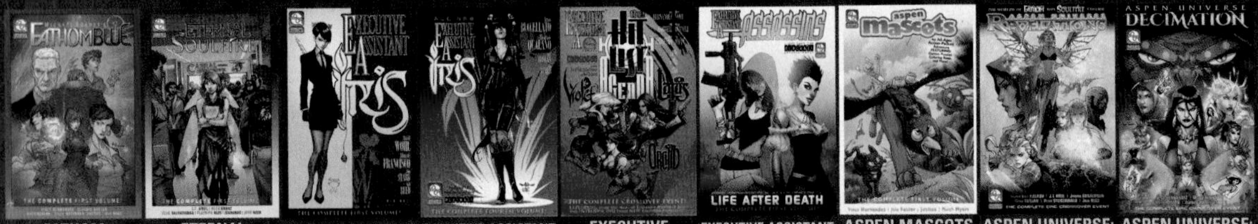

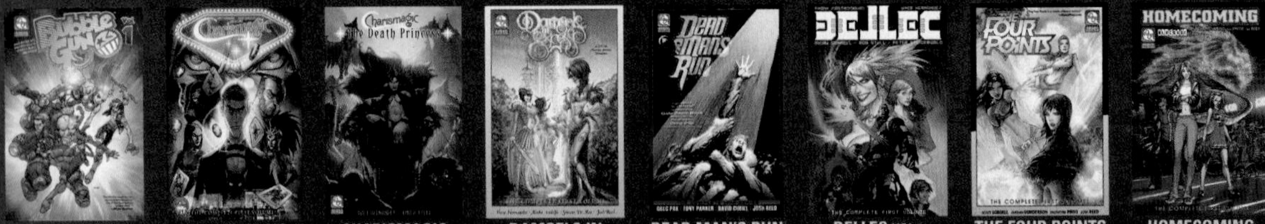

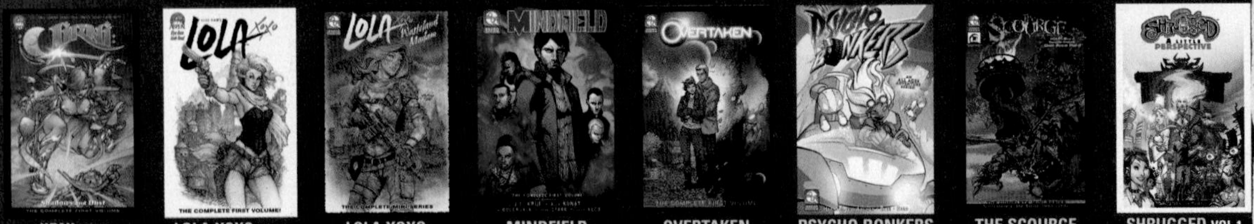

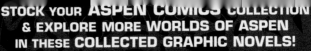

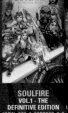

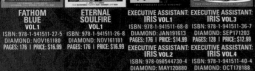